Bihar Higher Secondary Teacher

Commerce

Latest Edition
Practice Kit

10 Tests

10 Mock Test

Based On Real Exam Pattern

✓ Thoroughly Revised and Updated

✓ Detailed Analysis of all MCQs

Title : Bihar Higher Secondary Teacher Commerce
Author Name : Mr. Rohit Manglik
Published By : EduGorilla Community Pvt. Ltd.
Publishers Address : 12/651, First Floor Opp. Arvindo Park, Near Jama Masjid, Indira Nagar, Lucknow, Uttar Pradesh-226016, India

Copyright EduGorilla

ISBN : 978-93-55566-72-0

First Edition

Disclaimer EduGorilla

Compiled and created by EduGorilla Community Pvt. Ltd

ROHIT MANGLIK
CEO, EduGorilla

Editor's Note

Dear Applicants,

People say *"Success comes to those who work hard."* But I've seen people working hard for their exams day in and day out for marginal success. While others succeed in their examinations by putting in just half the work. So are they God Gifted? No! I believe that it's because they work *smart* and not just *hard*. Similarly, for your exams, you should strategize your preparation so as to increase the likelihood of success. Well with EduGorilla get ready to increase your *chances of selection* in your exam by *16x*.

EduGorilla helps you in not only working *hard* but also working in a *smart and strategic* manner. With EduGorilla's preparation package, you get a chance to make your exam preparation easy, and a fun learning path towards selection. Finding the right path to your preparations can be difficult if you don't know in which direction to head. Don't worry, we have you covered! EduGorilla will be your guide to success in your journey. With our Preparation Package, you can prepare strategically and beat the exam in just one attempt.

EduGorilla's Preparation Package includes-

- **Test Series**
- **Books**

Our preparation package is handcrafted as per the latest changes, expert opinions, and students' discretion. Thus, enabling you to get through each stage of the selection process for your exam.

Our Books are designed by the teachers and experts of the respective exam with a combined 150+ years of experience; to provide you with easy, efficient, and effective learning. Our books are smart, in the sense that not only do they give you the answers to the questions but also provide similar questions for practice.

EduGorilla's competent Test Series gives you real-time experience and confidence through which you can clear your offline or online exam in just one attempt. We currently host 93,000+ mock tests for 1,480+ competitive and academic exams.

Thus, EduGorilla misses no chance to assist you in your preparation and covers all stages of the exam, so that you don't have to look anywhere else.

We provide complete preparation packages for defense, banking, teaching, and other National & State-Level exams. Hence, it doesn't matter which exam you aspire to because you will reach your success.

ALL THE BEST !

Let EduGorilla be your Guide to Success.

Rohit Manglik,
Founder and CEO, EduGorilla

INTRODUCTION

EduGorilla focuses on guiding students to succeed in their examinations. With that in mind, our book, titled "Bihar Higher Secondary Teacher : Commerce", has been drafted through the collective efforts of our distinguished experts with 150+ years of combined experience. This book consists of questions that are created following the latest changes in the syllabus and exam pattern. We compiled the book on the basis of questions that are most likely to appear in the Bihar Higher Secondary Teacher : Commerce. Through EduGorilla's "Bihar Higher Secondary Teacher : Commerce" your chances of success will increase 16x.

EduGorilla does this through our Complete Preparation Package. This package consists of well-conceptualized and structured content in the form of questions that are tailor-made according to your needs and will help you practice for exams in a smart way by pinpointing all the necessary information. It also provides hints and solutions, along with a smart answer sheet for your self-evaluation. You can assess your shortcomings and work accordingly on areas that may require more of your attention.

EduGorilla promises to help you succeed in your examination and accomplish your dream goals. We believe in our aspirants and see them at the top of the merit list. And the first step towards the top is to start preparing with us. EduGorilla's "Bihar Higher Secondary Teacher : Commerce" includes the following attributes.

- Well-Researched Content
- Top-Notch Quality
- Detailed Answers and Analysis
- Smart Answer Sheet
- Exam Relevant Questions

Therefore, EduGorilla fortifies your preparation and makes it durable enough to help you stand tall and beat the examination.

Bihar Higher Secondary Teacher : Commerce
Scan QR code for Eligibility, Exam Pattern, Syllabus and more.

Book ID: 1325

TABLE OF CONTENTS

Mock Test 01

1. The accounting principle that states companies and owners should be accounted for separately is:
   (a) Business entity concept
   (b) Going concern concept
   (c) Monetary unit concept
   (d) Periodicity assumption

2. Compulsory winding up takes place under companies Act 2013:
   (I) If a company is unable to pay its debt.
   (II) If the company has by special resolution resolved that the company be wound up by the tribunal.
   (III) If the company has acted against the interest of the integrity or morality of India, the security of the state.
   (IV) if there is Suspension of the business for one year from the date of incorporation.
   Which of the following is/are correct?
   (a) I and II (b) II and III
   (c) I, II, and III (d) I, II, III and IV

3. Consider the following statements with reference to the Companies (Amendment) Act, 2015 :
   (I) The minimum paid-up share capital requirement has been done away with
   (II) The company cannot declare a dividend for a financial year unless the losses and depreciation carried over from past years have been set-off against the profits of the company,
   (III) thresholds will be prescribed for reporting fraud to the Central Government, or the audit committee, or the board of directors.
   (IV) Section 11 of CA 2013 has been retained.
   Which of the above statements are correct
   (a) I and II (b) II and III
   (c) I, II and III (d) II, III and IV

4. "The life expectancy of people in Kerala is more than that of Tamil Nadu." This statement is an example of:
   (a) Descriptive Hypothesis
   (b) Causal Hypothesis
   (c) Correlational Hypothesis
   (d) None of the above

5. Which one(s) of the following statements is (are) correct with respect to Decision Support System (DSS)?
   (i) DSS is used by middle level management.
   (ii) DSS applies to mostly structured problems.
   (iii) DSS relies on mathematical models for analysis.
   (iv) DSS is largely heuristics based.
   (a) (i) and (ii) are correct.
   (b) (i) and (iii) are correct.
   (c) (i), (ii) and (iii) are correct.
   (d) All the four statements are correct.

6. The black box model in marketing relates to:
   (a) Marketing planning (b) Marketing mix
   (c) Marketing control (d) Consumer behavior

7. The decision regarding demonetization is taken on the recommendation of :
   (a) Finance Ministry
   (b) Reserve Bank of India
   (c) Parliament
   (d) SBI

8. Reserve Bank of India controls the activities of which of the following banks in India:
   (i) Commercial Banks (ii) Cooperative Banks
   (iii) Foreign Banks (iv) Rural Banks
   Codes:
   (a) (i), (ii) and (iii) (b) (i), (iii) and (iv)
   (c) (ii), (iii) and (iv) (d) (i), (ii), (iii) and (iv)

9. Which of the following is not a feature of a development bank?
   (a) It is a specialized financial institution.
   (b) It provides medium and long term finance to business units.
   (c) It accepts deposits from the public.
   (d) It is essentially a development-oriented bank.

10. **Direction** : In the question given below, there are two statements marked as Assertion (A) and Reason (R). Mark your answer as per the codes provided below.
    Assertion (A) : Marginal cost and differential cost do not convey the same meaning in all the circumstances.
    Reason (R) : Differential cost increases or decreases due to change in fixed cost.
    (a) (A) is true but (R) is false.
    (b) (A) is false but (R) is true.
    (c) (A) and (R) are correct and (R) is correct explanation of (A).
    (d) Both (A) and (R) are correct, but (R) is not the correct explanation of (A).

11. Business ethics refers to
    (a) Contemporary standards or sets of values that govern the actions and behavior of an individual in the business organization.
    (b) Contemporary standards or sets of values that govern the actions and behavior of managers in the business organization.
    (c) Sets of values that govern the actions and behavior of workers in the business organization.
    (d) Rules and regulations of a business organization.

12. What is said as essence of Auditing?
    (a) Vouching (b) Verification
    (c) Valuation (d) Internal check

13. With reference to the marketing mix, consider the following statements :
    (I) It is a set of marketing tools that the firm uses to pursue its marketing objectives in the target market.
    (II) It refers to four broad levels of a marketing decision (4Ps), namely: product, price, promotion, and place.
    (III) It refers to five broad levels of marketing decision, namely: product, price, promotion, place, and people.
    (IV) In 1981, Booms and Bitner proposed a model of 7 Ps, comprising the original 4 Ps plus process, people, and physical evidence, as being more applicable for services marketing.
    Which of the following statements are correct?
    (a) I, II and III (b) I, II and IV
    (c) II, III and IV (d) I, II, III and IV

14. Indian Accounting Standards (Ind AS) is applicable to:
    (a) Individual (b) Partnership Firms

(c) Companies (d) Trust

15. With reference to working of stock exchanges in India, consider the following statements :
(I) The stock exchange is an organization that interferes between a company and an investor to raise funds for the benefit of the company as well as an investor.
(II) In India, the most prominent stock exchanges are the Bombay Stock Exchange (BSE) and National Stock Exchange (NSE).
(III) BSE is the oldest stock exchange in Asia established in 1875.
(IV) Sensex is an index for NSE.
Which of the following statements are correct?
(a) I, II and III (b) I and II
(c) II, III and IV (d) I, II, III and IV

16. **Direction** : In the question given below, there are two statements marked as Assertion (A) and Reason (R). Mark your answer as per the codes provided below.
Assertion (A) : One can be sure about the future course of action by making good plans.
Reason (R) : Planning brings certainty in the future course of actions of an organization.
(a) (R) is correct but (A) is not correct.
(b) (A) is correct but (R) is not correct.
(c) Both (A) and (R) are correct.
(d) Both (A) and (R) are not correct.

17. Read the following statements :
(i) "Working Capital is the amount of funds necessary to cover the cost of operating the enterprise."
(ii) "Circulating capital means current assets of a company that are changed in the ordinary course of business from one form to another."
(a) (i) and (ii) both are correct.
(b) (i) and (ii) both are false.
(c) (i) is correct, but (ii) is false
(d) (i) is false, but (ii) is correct.

18. With reference to the concept of accounting standards, consider the following statements :
(I) An accounting standard is a guideline for financial accounting, such as how a firm prepares and presents its business income, expenses, assets, and liabilities.
(II) Accounting standards lay down the terms and conditions of accounting policies and practices.
(III) Accounting standards do not facilitate intra-firm and inter-firm comparison.
(IV) Accounting standards relate to all aspects of an entity's finances including assets, liabilities, revenue, expenditures, and equity.
Which of the following statements are correct?
(a) I, II and III (b) I, II and IV
(c) II, III and IV (d) I, II, III and IV

19. With reference to the applicability of Ind AS, which of the following is not correct?
(a) Companies shall follow Ind AS either Voluntarily or Mandatorily.
(b) Once a company follows Ind AS, either mandatorily or voluntarily, it can't revert back to the old method of Accounting.
(c) Mandatory Applicability for the companies with a Net worth of not less than Rs. 500 crore after 1st April 2016.
(d) Mandatory Applicability from Accounting Period beginning on or after 1st April 2016 for all companies.

20. The OTC Exchange Of India (OTCEI) is an exchange meant for :
(a) Large enterprises
(b) Small companies
(c) Banks
(d) Public sector large companies

21. With reference to Inflation accounting, which of the following is not correct?
(a) Inflation accounting is a term describing a range of accounting models.
(b) It is designed to correct problems arising from historical cost accounting in the presence of high inflation and hyperinflation.
(c) Inflation accounting is used in countries experiencing high inflation or hyperinflation.
(d) Inflation accounting is a fair value accounting.

22. Which of the following is not a tier of the Nasdaq Stock Market?
(a) Capital Market (b) Global Market
(c) Global Select Market (d) National market

23. With reference to foreign portfolio investments (FPI), consider the following statements :
(I) FPIs are more volatile than loans from international financial institutions.
(II) Foreign Direct Investments are part of FPIs.
Which of the statements given above is/are correct?
(a) I only (b) II only
(c) Both I and II (d) Neither I nor II

24. With reference to SAARC, consider the following statements and select the correct statements from the given codes:
(I) The South Asian Association for Regional Cooperation (SAARC) is the regional intergovernmental organization and geopolitical union of nations in South Asia.
(II) The organization promotes the development of economic and regional integration.
(III) It launched the South Asian Free Trade Area in 2006.
(IV) Its secretariat is based in New Delhi.
(a) I, II and III
(b) I, II and IV
(c) II, III and IV
(d) All statements are correct

25. With reference to the foreign exchange market, consider the following statements :
(I) The foreign exchange market is a global decentralized market for the trading of currencies.
(II) This includes all aspects of buying, selling, and exchanging currencies at current or determined prices.
(III) The foreign exchange market works through financial institutions.
(IV) The foreign exchange market determines the relative values of different currencies.
Which of the following statements are correct?
(a) I, II and III (b) I, II and IV
(c) II, III and IV (d) I, II, III and IV

26. What is GST?

(a) Goods and Services Tax
(b) General Sales Tax
(c) General Service Tax
(d) Goods and service Tax

27. The basic conditions for determining the residential status of an individual are :
(a) He is in India in the previous year for a period of 182 days or more.
(b) He is in India for a period of 365 days or more within 4 years preceding the assessment year and periods amounting to all to 60 days or more in India in that year.
(c) He is in India in the previous year for a period of 60 days or more.
(d) Both (A) and (B)

28. Which of the following is 'true' regarding the Prudence Principle of Accounting?
(a) Taking care of the future losses
(b) Taking care of the future profits
(c) Taking care of bad debts
(d) Taking care of inventory and depreciation

29. For the purpose of extending rural banking and agro finance, the NABARD :
(a) Directly leads and monitors the rural borrowers
(b) Refinances the banks extending rural finance
(c) Refinances the rural borrowers obtaining credit from banks
(d) Directly finances the rural borrowers and gets refinance from government

30. SIDBI provides financial assistance in the following forms :
(i) Bills financing
(ii) Project financing
(iii) Re-finance assistance
(iv) Resource support to institutions
Which of the following sequence is correct?
(a) (i), (iii), (iv) and (ii) (b) (ii), (iv), (i) and (iii)
(c) (iii), (i), (iv) and (ii) (d) (iv), (i), (iii) and (ii)

31. Which among the following are important Agencies of the World Bank?
(I) The International Financial Corporation (IFC)
(II) The International Bank of Reconstruction and Development (IBRD)
(III) The International Development Association (IDA)
(IV) Small Industries Development Bank of India (SIDBI)
Which of the following statements are correct?
(a) I, II and III (b) I, II, III and IV
(c) II, III and IV (d) II and III

32. The terms refer to Total Knowledge Skills, Creative Abilities, Talents, and Aptitudes of an organization's workforce as well as Values, Attitudes, and Beliefs the individuals are valued:
(a) Human Resources
(b) Human Resource Management
(c) Human Resource Planning
(d) Human Relations

33. Which of the following is not the objective of Competition act 2002?
(a) Prohibition of abuse of dominant position
(b) Prohibition of restrictive Trade practices
(c) Prohibition of anti-competitive Agreement
(d) Regulation of combinations

34. The IIA's Practice Advisories do not contain which of the following?
(a) Approaches (b) Considerations
(c) Processes (d) Methodologies

35. In hypothesis testing, the hypothesis which is tentatively assumed to be true is called the.................hypothesis.
(a) correct hypothesis
(b) null hypothesis
(c) alternative hypothesis
(d) level of significance

36. The basic objective of export Promotion Council is to promote and develop-
(a) Particular products of country
(b) Only attractive projects of the country
(c) Only services industry products of the country
(d) Overall exports of the country

37. The ____function in human resource management is concerned with providing a work environment which is conducive to the employees and nurturing them to make them well committed and attached to the organization.
(a) Lineation (b) Development
(c) Motivation (d) Acquisition

38. Which of the following relationship is true?
(a) NBCR = BCR + I (b) NBCR = BCR - I
(c) NBCR = NPV + I (d) NBCR = NPV - I

39. Which of the following involves the process of defining expectations for employee performance, measuring, evaluation and recording actual employee performance relative the these predetermined expectations, providing the employee relevant constructive feedback.
(a) Performance appraisal
(b) Work appraisal
(c) Job appraisal
(d) None of the above

40. The stage in the product life cycle that focuses on expanding the market and creating product awareness and the trial is the:
(a) Decline stage (b) Introduction stage
(c) Growth stage (d) Maturity

41. A ________ letter of credit is a type of financial guarantee, known as a letter of credit.
(a) deferred (b) transit credit
(c) transferable (d) instalment credit

42. The IMF's ______ purpose is to ensure the stability of the international monetary system.
(a) primary (b) secondary
(c) tertiary (d) None of the above

43. In the first stage of most grievances redressal procedure, the grievance is verbally conveyed by the employee to the ______.

(a) HR representative on the arbitrator
(b) supervisor or the arbitrator
(c) officer designated by the management
(d) HR representative or the designated officer

44. The minimum number of persons required to form a private ltd. company and a public ltd company respectively are ___________.
(a) 2 and 5 (b) 5 and 7
(c) 2 and 7 (d) 7 and 2

45. Who coined the expression "Marketing Mix" ?
(a) Henry Fayol (b) James Culliton
(c) Peter Drucker (d) Abraham Maslow

46. Road blocking advertisement refers to:
(a) Advertising a product by blocking the road
(b) Creating big blocks for advertising a product
(c) Advertising a product on multiple TV channels at the same time
(d) None of the above

47. Exchange concept of marketing deals with:
(a) Exchange of products between sellers and buyers covering distribution and price aspects
(b) Mere appendage to production
(c) Achieving marketing success through product attributes
(d) Aggressively promote and push the products

48. The total area of a normal distribution between average value ± 1.96 of standard deviation is:
(a) 95% (b) 90%
(c) 99% (d) 68.34%

49. Arrange the following stages of research in a proper sequence:
(A) Report writing
(B) Budget
(C) Data collection
(D) Field work
(E) Research results
Select the correct answer from the options given below:
(a) (B), (D), (C), (E), (A) (b) (D), (A), (B), (C), (E)
(c) (D), (C), (B), (E), (A) (d) (B), (E), (D), (C), (A)

50. As the period of the moving mean increases in the time series, then:
(a) The trend curve will be closer to the original curve
(b) The trend curve ahead of the original curve will be
(c) The trend curve will be in line with the original curve
(d) The difference between the trend curve and the original curve will remain constant

51. Which of the following coefficient of correlation indicates the strongest relationship between two sets of variables?
(a) -0.98 (b) 0.90
(c) 0.00 (d) 1.20

52. Which of the following statement is true?
1. The tax rate of STCG is 10%
2. The tax rate of LTCG is 15%
3. The tax rate on casual income is 30%
4. The tax rate on dividend received from domestic company is 10%
Codes:
(a) 1 and 2 are true
(b) 2 and 4 are true
(c) 3 and 4 are true
(d) All statements are true

53. Which of the following are the types of E-filling of return?
1. E-filling through e-return intermediary.
2. E-file without digital signature.
3. E-file with digital signature.
Select the correct answer using the codes given below:
(a) Both 1 and 2 (b) Only 3
(c) Both 2 and 3 (d) All of the above

54. What is the rate of tax deduction at source from insurance commission in case of 'Person'.
(a) 2 percent (b) 5 percent
(c) 10 percent (d) 4 percent

55. Which of the following statements is/are true?
(i) Tax-shield on depreciation and interest is an important variable both for the lessor and the lessee.
(ii) Lease transactions in India are governed by the Lease Act.
(iii) A lessee should evaluate the lease options against the buying option.
(iv) As per AS - 19, financial lease is shown in the balance sheet of the lessee as an asset.
Choose the correct answer from the code given below:
(a) (i) and (iv) (b) (i), (iii) and (iv)
(c) (ii), (iii) and (iv) (d) Only (ii)

56. Which one of the following is agricultural income under Income Tax Act?
(a) Income from the land used for storing agricultural produce
(b) Dividend from a company engaged in agriculture
(c) Income from dairy farm, poultry farm, etc
(d) Income from the sale of replanted trees where denuded parts of the forest are replanted and subsequent operations in forestry are carried out

57. On fulfilling certain conditions, for an undertaking set up in special economic zones, deduction under section 10 AA of the Income Tax Act is allowed for:
(a) 5 years (b) 10 years
(c) 15 years (d) Unlimited period

58. Given is the information related to a house:
Municipal Value (M.V) Rs. 1,50,000
Fair Rent Rs. 1,80,000
Standard Rent Rs. 1,60,000
Actual Rent Rs. 20,000 pm
Municipal tax paid by owner is 20% of M.V. Unrealised rent Rs. 40,000 (conditions of rule 4 satisfied). What is the annual value of the house?
(a) Rs. 1,50,000 (b) Rs. 1,60,000
(c) Rs. 1,70,000 (d) Rs. 2,10,000

59. Trade Related Aspects of Intellectual Property Rights (TRIPs):
(a) Uruguay Round Agreements

(b) Doha Ministerial Conference
(c) Dhaka SAARC Summit
(d) World Bank Policy Research Report

60. Match the following.

List - A	List - B
(a) Type I error	(i) Small standard error
(b) Large sample	(ii) Non-parametric
(c) Multiple regressio n	(iii) False positive
(d) Chi-square test	(iv) One dependent variabl e

(a) (a) - (iv), (b) - (i), (c) - (ii), (d) - (iii)
(b) (a) - (iii), (b) - (i), (c) - (iv), (d) - (ii)
(c) (a) - (ii), (b) - (iii), (c) - (i), (d) - (iv)
(d) (a) - (iii), (b) - (iv), (c) - (i), (d) - (ii)

61. Match the following:

List - I	List - II
(a) Normal distributio n	(i) One department variabl e
(b) Chi-square test	(ii) Positively skewed
(c) Poisson distributio n	(iii) Unimodal
(d) Multiple regression	(iv) Goodness of fit test

(a) (a) - (iii), (b) - (i), (c) - (ii), (d) - (iv)
(b) (a) - (iii), (b) - (iv), (c) - (i), (d) - (ii)
(c) (a) - (ii), (b) - (iii), (c) - (iv), (d) - (i)
(d) (a) - (iii), (b) - (iv), (c) - (ii), (d) - (i)

62. **Assertion (A)** : "Price Discovery" is a function of derivatives market.
Reason (R) : 'Price Discovery' deals with the study of influence of futures price on spot price.
(a) (A) is correct, (R) is incorrect
(b) (A) is incorrect, (R) is correct
(c) Both (A) and (R) are incorrect
(d) Both (A) and (R) are correct

63. Match List I with List II:

	List I Capital Structure Preposition(s)		List II Description(s)
A.	Target Capital stru cture	I.	Expected yield on the e quity capital is equal to the p ure equity return plus a pre mium for financial risk
B.	Optimum Capital S tructure	I I.	It refers to the perceive d costs due to increased ratio o f debt in the firm.
C.	Cost of financial di stress	II I.	It is the debt ratio the fi rm strives to achieve
D.	MM preposition-II	I V.	It is the debt-equity rati o that maximises the value of t he firm.

Choose the correct answer from the options given below:
(a) A - II, B - III, C - I, D - IV
(b) A - III, B - IV, C - II, D - I
(c) A - IV, B - II, C - III, D - I
(d) A - I, B - III, C - II, D - IV

64. Arrange the following activities in the process of accounting
A. Journalising the transaction in the ledger accounts
B. Recording the business transaction in the books of entry
C. Preparation of Annual Financial statements
D. Preparation of the Trial Balance
E. Deriving meaningful inferences for business decisions
Choose the correct answer from the options given below:
(a) A, B, C, D and E (b) A, B, D, E and C
(c) D, C, E, B and A (d) B, A, D, C and E

65. Match the following theories of international trade in List-I with their propounders in List-II:

List - A	List - B
(a) Mercantilism theory	(1) Michael Po rter
(b) Theory of absolute cost advant age	(2) David Hum e
(c) National competitive advantage theory	(3) Eli Hecksch er
(d) Factor endowment theory	(4) Adam Smit h

(a) (a) - 1, (b) - 3, (c) - 4, (d) - 2
(b) (a) - 3, (b) - 2, (c) - 1, (d) - 4
(c) (a) - 2, (b) - 4, (c) - 1, (d) - 3
(d) (a) - 4, (b) - 1, (c) - 2, (d) - 3

66. Match the columns:

Group-A	Group-B
(a) Monopolis tic competitio n	(i) Sale of goods at varying prices in the foreign and domestic markets.
(b) Price rigid ity	(ii) Edward Chamberlin.
(c) Dumping	(iii) Firms working together in pric e determination.
(d) Collusion	(iv) Paul Sweezy

(a) (a)-(ii) (b)-(iii) (c)-(i) (d)-(iv)
(b) (a)-(iv) (b)-(ii) (c)-(i) (d)-(iii)
(c) (a)-(ii) (b)-(iv) (c)-(i) (d)-(iii)
(d) (a)-(iv) (b)-(i) (c)-(iii) (d)-(ii)

67. Match the following:

List - A	List - B
(a) Treasury bills	(i) Operating cycle
(b) Beta	(ii) Time value of money
(c) Capital budgeting	(iii) Risk free rate
(d) Working capital	(iv) Systematic risk

(a) (a) - (iv), (b) - (iii), (c) - (i), (d) - (ii)
(b) (a) - (iv), (b) - (i), (c) - (ii), (d) - (iii)
(c) (a) - (iii), (b) - (iv), (c) - (ii), (d) - (i)
(d) (a) - (iii), (b) - (i), (c) - (ii), (d) - (iv)

68. Match the following:

List - A	List - B
(a) Interest rate risk	(i) Unsystematic risk
(b) Financial risk	(ii) Single-factor model
(c) APM model	(iii) Systematic risk
(d) CAPM model	(iv) Multifactor model

(a) (a) - (i), (b) - (ii), (c) - (iii), (d) - (iv)
(b) (a) - (iii), (b) - (i), (c) - (iv), (d) - (ii)
(c) (a) - (iii), (b) - (iv), (c) - (ii), (d) - (i)
(d) (a) - (ii), (b) - (i), (c) - (iii), (d) - (iv)

69. Which bank took over the entire undertaking of ARDC?
(a) RBI (b) SBI
(c) NABARD (d) SEBI

70. The correct sequence in the formation of a contract is:
(a) Offer, acceptance, consideration, agreement
(b) Offer, Consideration, acceptance, agreement
(c) Agreement, consideration, offer, acceptance
(d) Offer, acceptance, agreement, consideration

71. Which of the following are true about conditions according to the Sale of Goods Act?
a) Title
b) Description
c) Quite possession
d) Encumbrances
Choose the correct answer from the following options
(a) a) and d) only (b) b) and c) only
(c) a), c) and d) only (d) a) and b) only

Ques (72-75): Directions : Please read the passage carefully and answer the questions that follow.

Ever since the Centre and the States passed the landmark legislation in 2016 adopting a single countrywide Goods and Services Tax (GST), the federal council that is tasked with overseeing all the regulatory aspects of the indirect tax has had its hands full. From recommending the rates that could apply to various products and services, to deciding on what could be tax exempted, the GST Council has had the onerous task of laying out the policy framework for administering the tax in a manner that benefits all stakeholders - the governments, the consumers and the suppliers along the value chain. Given the complexity of the legacy taxes that GST subsumed and replaced and the teething troubles of operating a new tax system, ensuring optimal outcomes has proved an abiding challenge. A significant concern relates to the loopholes that unscrupulous operators have sought to exploit, whereby revenue that ought to have accrued to the Centre and the States has leaked while allowing these elements to derive illicit profits. And the scale of some has been breath-taking. Earlier this month, the Directorate General of GST Intelligence and the Directorate General of Revenue Intelligence conducted a pan-India joint operation, which saw about 1,200 officers simultaneously conducting searches at 336 different locations. In the process they unearthed a network of exporters and their suppliers who had connived to claim fraudulent refunds of Integrated GST, with more than ₹470 crore of input tax credit availed being based on non-existent entities or suppliers with fictitious addresses. A further ₹450 crore of IGST refund is also under review.

It is against the backdrop of such cases, and the fact that frauds totalling up to a staggering ₹45,682 crore have been detected since the roll-out of the tax in July 2017, that the GST Council has decided "in principle" to recommend linking Aadhaar with registration of taxpayers. In its 37th meeting in Goa on Friday, the council also agreed to appraise the possibility of making the biometrics-based unique identifier mandatory for claiming refunds. Already the GST Network — the information technology backbone on which the whole tax system runs — has made it mandatory for new dealers registering under the composition scheme for small businesses to either authenticate their Aadhaar or submit to physical verification of their business, starting January 2020. The council too needs to follow the network's lead and move swiftly to recommend mandatory linking for refunds, especially since that has proved to be the main source of most frauds. In a becalmed economy, neither the Centre nor States can afford to forego even a rupee of revenue that is due to the public coffers.

72. Which of the following is true about GST?
I. GST applies different rates to same products.
II. The tax has become a subject of national unrest.
III. Some loopholes have been exploited to dupe government.
(a) Only I (b) Only II
(c) Only III (d) None of the above

73. According to the passage, what remedial actions are suggested to avoid fraudulent activities?
(a) Authentication of Aadhar for new registrations
(b) Biometrics-based unique identifier mandatory for claiming refunds
(c) Physical verification of their business
(d) All of the above

74. What can be concluded from the passage above?
(a) GST has some challenges in terms of administration which cannot be rectified.
(b) GST loopholes are easy to identify and it has led to a decrease in tax theft.
(c) The new tax regime has become a tiring and excruciating exercise to operate.
(d) Aadhar-Linked GST registration will help curb the malpractices and smooth operation of GST.

75. Why has the GST legislation and its successful implementation become a challenge?
(a) GST council has been very busy in day to day activities.
(b) Not all revenue has been going to the Government.
(c) Public outcry against it has made it difficult to implement.
(d) The regulatory aspects are yet to come in full force.

Ques (76-80): Direction : Read the passage and answer the questions that follow:

Over the last 15-20 years, while India has been primarily focused on "services", China started with "manufacturing" and then quickly extended its focus to "product" companies. As a result, in addition to being the manufacturing behemoth, China has also produced product brands like Lenovo, Huawei, ZTE, Xiaomi, Baidu, Alibaba, Spreadtrum, spanning hardware, software and e-commerce.

India desperately needs to create several high-value product companies to meet domestic demand and create wealth. A strong product ecosystem drives healthy manufacturing industry as well. As such, 'Make in India' shouldn't be just about "manufacturing" but also be about "making products".

Product-centric start-ups require totally different mindset and approach. They tend to take tens to hundreds of millions of dollars and five to ten years before reaching profitability. This is quite a contrast from "services" model that doesn't require lot of capital and usually make small but quick returns. But, product companies create lot more value and wealth. We must create Apple, Google, Amazon, Intel, Oracle, Lenovo, Xiaomi, and Facebooks of the world.

In my view, successful start-ups require passionate and persuasive founders, great vision, innovative technology, strong team, patient capital, good market timing and a little bit of luck. India has no dearth of entrepreneurs, innovation, talent and markets. The biggest challenge for Indian start-ups today is lack of access to risk capital especially early to pre-revenue stage. This must be addressed quickly if we want to create high-value product growth engine.

Start-ups need different kinds and levels of capital through their life cycle, from conception to profitability. At the beginning, they need seed capital typically provided by founders and the so-called angel investors, ranging from $100,000 to US$1 million.

Then, start-ups need early stage investment from venture capitalists and corporate investors, ranging from $10 million to US$100 million through multiple rounds of equity financing.

They need late-stage capital from institutional investors, private equity firms and corporate investors to support revenue ramp, profitability and IPO, ranging in hundreds of millions of dollars through a combination of equity and debt financing. My perspective comes from my own experience with cofounding Soft Machines Inc, a semiconductor company developing advanced VISCTM Microprocessor architecture and System on Chip (SoC) solutions for smart client and cloud markets.

In India, at the moment, there seems to be a lot of appetite for participating in late-stage and mezzanine rounds by global investors such as Softbank, especially in the areas of e-commerce, social media and apps. Recent investments into Flipkart, Snapdeal, housing.com, are good examples. But, I see two issues with this trend. First, these are late-stage investments, for products are already proven in the market with some revenues and customer traction. Second, most of these investments are by global investors, which means return on these investments is not going to have domino effect on other start-ups. There also seem to be good number of angel investors, incubators and start-up villages to support very early and seed-stage capital. Of course, start-ups can benefit from more organized angel investors and government-driven grants along the lines of NSF and SBR grants in the US.

76. Why has the author suggested that 'Make in India' should not focus just on manufacturing but also on 'making products'?

I. To compete with Product giant China, India also should focus on making products rather than on manufacturing.

II. To meet domestic demand and create wealth it is but imperative for India to focus on making products.

III. To fulfil the dream of becoming world economic power India should follow the path adopted by China.

(a) Only I (b) Only II
(c) Only III (d) Only I and II

77. Which of the following is the biggest challenge for Indian start-ups to create high-value product growth engine?

(a) Lack of passionate and persuasive founders
(b) Paucity of innovative technology
(c) Dearth of risk capital in the initial stage of a new company
(d) Lack of a strong and dedicated team

78. Who among the following provide financial assistance to start-ups in the early stage of a company?

I. Corporate investors
II. Venture capitalists
III. Stage governments

(a) Only I and II (b) Only II and III
(c) Only I and III (d) All I, II and III

79. Find the incorrect statement on the basis of the given passage.

(a) In the late stage of a company the start-ups get capital from corporate investors, institutional investors and private equity firms.
(b) Over the last 15-20 years the main focus of India has been on 'services'.
(c) The basic difference between the 'product making companies' and 'services' is that the former need more capital and time than the latter.
(d) Luck is not at all important for the success of start-ups.

80. What is the main aim of the writer behind writing this passage?

(a) To share his own experience as a start-up with Indian start-ups
(b) To point out the reasons for China's huge success
(c) To mention the problem Indian start-ups face as of now
(d) To show the superiority of 'manufacturing' over 'product'

// Smart Answer Sheet //

Correct Percentage of students who answered correctly.

Skipped Percentage of students who skipped.

Q.	Ans.	Correct Skipped	Q.	Ans.	Correct Skipped	Q.	Ans.	Correct Skipped
1	A	83.56% 13.21%	2	C	59.0% 39.07%	3	C	80.94% 10.69%
4	C	53.79% 37.92%	5	C	89.5% 10.02%	6	D	78.92% 17.54%
7	B	59.8% 37.63%	8	D	54.19% 35.36%	9	C	67.23% 30.95%
10	C	46.93% 33.12%	11	A	44.17% 50.62%	12	A	44.18% 44.52%
13	B	60.67% 32.01%	14	C	68.14% 31.46%	15	A	50.7% 48.56%
16	A	42.27% 51.81%	17	A	53.03% 35.6%	18	B	69.16% 30.6%
19	D	16.74% 67.08%	20	B	24.91% 71.53%	21	D	66.51% 33.21%
22	D	67.66% 30.59%	23	A	60.98% 36.19%	24	A	66.3% 30.27%
25	A	67.87% 30.83%	26	A	59.4% 35.57%	27	D	57.17% 33.24%
28	A	54.02% 37.15%	29	B	66.48% 33.46%	30	C	44.59% 38.36%
31	A	64.06% 35.23%	32	A	49.96% 32.01%	33	B	43.71% 47.1%
34	C	42.81% 42.1%	35	B	54.12% 38.34%	36	D	46.71% 41.94%
37	A	45.38% 35.24%	38	B	49.42% 37.86%	39	A	58.78% 32.02%
40	B	44.98% 36.88%	41	C	87.49% 11.21%	42	A	48.87% 33.55%
43	C	68.05% 30.85%	44	C	42.86% 39.47%	45	B	41.88% 44.67%
46	C	24.0% 68.47%	47	A	66.69% 31.42%	48	A	61.63% 31.86%
49	A	62.18%	50	B	49.57%	51	A	30.06%

		35.06%			47.71%			67.52%
52	C	44.57% 53.69%	53	D	16.34% 73.33%	54	B	59.03% 34.58%
55	B	55.11% 39.04%	56	A	54.15% 30.67%	57	C	25.09% 71.75%
58	C	13.1% 85.86%	59	B	66.0% 33.29%	60	B	77.94% 11.92%
61	D	81.98% 16.89%	62	D	76.44% 13.81%	63	B	66.67% 30.75%
64	D	57.26% 37.54%	65	C	85.76% 13.26%	66	C	89.15% 10.27%
67	C	84.07% 10.78%	68	B	78.96% 20.02%	69	C	79.29% 10.34%
70	A	87.9% 10.24%	71	D	83.31% 10.64%	72	C	62.29% 35.71%
73	D	52.75% 35.84%	74	D	45.71% 45.82%	75	B	51.31% 42.84%
76	B	88.19% 10.96%	77	C	81.27% 13.45%	78	A	87.29% 12.12%
79	D	65.62% 30.25%	80	C	82.4% 16.08%			

// Hints and Solutions //

1(A). The business entity concept states that the transactions associated with a business must be separately recorded from those of its owners or other businesses. Doing so requires the use of separate accounting records for the organization that completely exclude the assets and liabilities of any other entity or the owner.

2(C). As per the new Companies Act 2013, a company can be wound up by a tribunal in the below-mentioned circumstances:

1. When the company is unable to pay its debts.
2. If the company has by special resolution resolved that the company be wound up by the tribunal.
3. If the company has acted against the interest of the integrity or morality of India, the security of the state, or has spoiled any kind of friendly relations with foreign or neighboring countries.
4. If the company has not filed its financial statements or annual returns for the preceding five consecutive financial years.
5. If the tribunal by any means finds that it is just & equitable that the company should be wound up.
6. If the company in any way is indulged in fraudulent activities or any other unlawful business, or any person or management connected with the formation of the company is found guilty of fraud, or any kind of misconduct.

3(C). CA 2013 required all companies to file the following additional declarations with the Registrar of Companies prior to commencement of business or exercising any borrowing power:

(i) declaration by a director that minimum paid-up share capital has been paid; and

(ii) company has filed verification of registered office. The CA Amendment 2015 has removed the above requirements and deleted Section 11 of CA 2013. This reduces the filings to be made by companies in India.

4(C). A correlation is simply defined as a relationship between two variables. The whole purpose of using correlations in research is to figure out which variables are connected. The correlational Hypothesis states merely that the variables occur together in some specified manner without implying that one causes the other. For example, Level of job commitment of the officers is positively associated with their level of efficiency. Here, we do not make any claim that one variable causes the other to change. That will be possible only if we have control over all other factors that could influence our dependent variable.

5(C). DSSs include knowledge-based systems. A properly designed DSS is an interactive software-based system intended to help decision-makers compile useful information from a combination of raw data, documents, and personal knowledge, or business models to identify and solve problems and make decisions. DSS uses the summary information, exceptions, patterns, and trends using the analytical models. A decision support system helps in decision-making but does not necessarily give a decision itself. The decision-makers compile useful information from raw data, documents, personal knowledge, and/or business models to identify and solve problems and make decisions.

Characteristics of a DSS

- Support for decision-makers in semi-structured and unstructured problems.
- Support for managers at various managerial levels, ranging from the top executives to line managers.
- Support for individuals and groups. Less structured problems often require the involvement of several individuals from different departments and organization level.
- Support for interdependent or sequential decisions.
- Support for intelligence, design, choice, and implementation.
- Support for a variety of decision processes and styles.
- DSSs are adaptive over time.

6(D). The black box model in marketing relates to consumer behavior.

The black box model of consumer behavior identifies the stimuli responsible for buyer behavior. The stimuli (advertisement and other forms of promotion about the product) that are presented to the consumer by the marketer and the environment are dealt with by the buyer's black box.

7(B). The decision regarding demonetization is taken on the recommendation of Reserve Bank of India. Demonetization is the act of stripping a currency unit of its status as legal tender. Demonetization is necessary whenever there is a change in national currency. The old unit of currency must be retired and replaced with a new currency unit. The opposite of demonetization is remonetization where a form of payment is restored as legal tender. There are multiple reasons why nations demonetize their local units of currency. Some reasons include to combat inflation, to combat corruption, and to discourage a cash system. The process of demonetization involves either introducing new notes or coins of the same currency or completely replacing the old currency with new currency. In 2016, the government decided to demonetize the 500 and 1000- rupee notes, the two biggest denomination notes. These notes accounted for 86% of the country's cash supply. The government's goal was to eradicate counterfeit currency, fight tax evasion, eliminate black money gotten from money laundering and terrorist financing activities, and promote a cashless economy.

8(D). The RBI is the supreme monetary and banking authority in the country and controls the banking system in India. It is called the Reserve Bank' as it keeps the reserves of all commercial banks. Commercial banks may be defined as, any banking organization that deals with the deposits and loans of business organizations. Scheduled commercial banks (SCBs) account for a major proportion of the business of the scheduled banks. SCBs in India are categorized into five groups based on their ownership and/or their nature of operations. Scheduled commercial banks include public and private sector banks, foreign banks, regional rural banks, and cooperative banks.

9(C). The development bank is essentially a multi-purpose financial institution with a broad development outlook. A development bank may be defined as a financial institution concerned with providing all types of financial assistance (medium as well as long term) to business units, in the form of loans, underwriting, investment and guarantee operations, and promotional activities-economic development in general, and industrial development, in particular.
Following are the main characteristic features of a development bank:
1. It is a specialized financial institution.
2. It provides medium and long term finance to business units.
3. Unlike commercial banks, it does not accept deposits from the public.
4. It is not just a term-lending institution. It is a multi-purpose financial institution.
5. It is essentially a development-oriented bank. Its primary objective is to promote economic development by promoting investment and entrepreneurial activity in a developing economy. It encourages new and small entrepreneurs and seeks balanced regional growth.
6. It provides financial assistance not only to the private sector but also to the public sector undertakings.

10(C). Marginal cost represents the increase or decrease in total cost which occurs with a small change in output say, a unit of output. In Cost, Accounting variable costs represent marginal cost. Differential cost is the change (increase or decrease) in the total cost (variable as well as fixed) due to change in the level of activity, technology or production process or method of production. In other words, it can be defined as the cost of one unit of product or service which would be avoided if that unit was not produced or provided. The main point which distinguishes marginal cost and differential as that change in fixed cost when the volume of production increases or decreases by a unit of production. In the case of differential cost variable as well as a fixed cost. i.e. both costs change due to change in the level of activity, whereas under marginal costing only variable cost changes due to change in the level of activity.

11(A). Business ethics (also corporate ethics) is a form of applied ethics or professional ethics that examines ethical principles and moral or ethical problems that arise in a business environment.

- It applies to all aspects of business conduct and is relevant to the conduct of individuals and entire organizations.
- Business ethics refers to contemporary standards or sets of values that govern the actions and behavior of an individual in the business organization.
- Business ethics reflects the philosophy of business, of which one aim is to determine the fundamental purposes of a company.
- If a company's purpose is to maximize shareholder returns, then sacrificing profits to other concerns is a violation of its fiduciary responsibility.

Hence, the correct option (A).

12(A). Vouching is said as essence of Auditing.
Verification, Valuation, and Internal Checks are all parts of auditing but Vouching is the essence or backbone of auditing because when performing an audit, an auditor must have proof of all transactions. Without the proof provided by vouching, the claims provided by the auditor are just that, only claims.
In most cases, hard to detect frauds can only be discovered through the use of vouching. This means that the auditor must conduct vouching with great importance.

13(B). The 'marketing mix' (also known as the four Ps) is a foundation concept in marketing. The marketing mix has been defined as the "set of marketing tools that the firm uses to pursue its marketing objectives in the target market". Thus the marketing mix refers to four broad levels of marketing decision, namely: product, price, promotion, and place. The contemporary marketing mix, or the 4Ps, which has become the dominant framework for marketing management decisions, was first published in 1960. In services marketing, a modified and expanded marketing mix is used, typically comprising 7 Ps made up of the original 4 Ps plus process, people, physical environment. Occasionally service marketers will refer to eight Ps; comprising the 7 Ps plus performance.

14(C). Indian Accounting Standards (abbreviated as Ind-AS) were issued under the supervision and control of the Accounting Standards Board (ASB), which was constituted as a body in the year 1977. The new Ind AS was notified on February 16, 2015. Ind AS are named and numbered in the same way as the corresponding International Financial Reporting Standards (IFRS). National Advisory Committee on Accounting Standards (NACAS) has recommended these standards to the Ministry of Corporate Affairs (MCA). MCA has to spell out the accounting standards applicable to companies in India. As of date, MCA has notified 39 Ind AS. This shall be applied to the companies of the financial year 2015-16 voluntarily and from 2016-17 on a mandatory basis.

15(A). The stock exchange is an organization that interferes between company and investor to raise funds for the benefit of the company as well as an investor. India consists of 22 stock exchanges overall under government regulation. Most Prominent stock exchange is the Bombay Stock Exchange (BSE) and National Stock Exchange (NSE) as most of the trading is done in this exchange. BSE is the oldest stock exchange in Asia established in 1875 while NSE is established in the mid-1990s. The index is the benchmark of both stock exchanges for tracking market status or checking upward or downward movement of stock.

It consists of a basket of stocks of companies that are listed under exchange under the regulation of SEBI. Sensex is an index for BSE which comprises 30 constituents while Nifty is an index for NSE which comprises 50 constituents.

16(A). Planning begins with the determination of objectives. It highlights the purposes for which various activities are to be undertaken. In fact, it makes objectives more clear and specific. Planning helps in focusing the attention of employees on the objectives or goals of the enterprise. Planning compels the manager to prepare a blueprint of the courses of action to be followed for the accomplishment of objectives. Therefore, planning brings order and rationality into the organization. Planning minimizes uncertainties. There are risks of various types due to uncertainties. Planning helps in reducing uncertainties of the future as it involves anticipation of future events. Although the future cannot be predicted with cent percent accuracy planning helps management to anticipate the future and prepare for risks by necessary provisions to meet the unexpected turn of events.

17(A). Statement I:

- Working capital is the difference between the current assets .e. accounts receivable, cash, inventories of raw material and fixed goods, and its current liabilities i.e. accounts payable, short-term debt, dividend, etc.
- It is that part of the capital which helps in financing the operating activities in order to achieve short-term goals.
- In other words, " Working Capital is the amount of funds necessary to cover the cost of operating the enterprise."

Statement II:

- Circulating capital is also known as revolving capital as the money keeps on changing its form in a continuous manner.
- The money involved in circulating capital is used for core business operations and keeps on circulating from cash to current assets and back again to cash .
- It includes current assets like cash, operating expenses, finished goods inventory, raw materials, inventory in the process, and accounts receivable and one can be used to buy another.
- In other words, "Circulating capital means current assets of a company that are changed in the ordinary course of business from one form to another."

Therefore, it is clear from the above explanation that both statements are correct.

18(B). Accounting standards are the written statements consisting of rules and guidelines, issued by the accounting institutions, for the preparation of uniform and consistent financial statements and also for other disclosures affecting the different users of accounting information. Accounting standards lay down the terms and conditions of accounting policies and practices by way of codes, guidelines, and adjustments for making the interpretation of the items appearing in the financial statements easy and even their treatment in the books of account. Accounting standards relate to all aspects of an entity's finances including assets, liabilities, revenue, expenditures, and equity. Specific examples of an accounting standard include revenue recognition, asset classification, allowable methods for depreciation, what is considered depreciable, lease classifications, and outstanding share measurement.

19(D). Companies shall follow Ind AS either Voluntarily or Mandatorily. Once a company follows Ind AS, either mandatorily or voluntarily, it can't revert back to the old method of Accounting.
Mandatory applicability of IND AS to all companies from 1st April 2016, provided: It is a listed or unlisted company. Its Net worth is greater than or equal to Rs. 500 crore.

20(B). The OTC Exchange Of India (OTCEI), also known as the Over-the-Counter Exchange of India, is based in Mumbai, Maharashtra. It is India's first exchange for small companies, as well as the first screen-based nationwide stock exchange in India. OTCEI was set up to access high-technology enterprising promoters in raising finance for new product development in a cost-effective manner and to provide a transparent and efficient trading system to investors. It facilitates faster transactions, greater liquidity in the market, and transparency in transactions OTCEI is promoted by the Unit Trust of India, the Industrial Credit and Investment Corporation of India, the Industrial Development Bank of India, the Industrial Finance Corporation of India, and other institutions, and is a recognized stock exchange under the SCR Act.

21(D). Inflation accounting is a term describing a range of accounting models designed to correct problems arising from historical cost accounting in the presence of high inflation and hyperinflation. Inflation accounting is used in countries experiencing high inflation or hyperinflation. Inflation accounting is not fair value accounting. Inflation accounting, also called price level accounting, is similar to converting financial statements into another currency using an exchange rate. Under some (not all) inflation accounting models, historical costs are converted to price-level adjusted costs using general or specific price indexes.

22(D). The Nasdaq Stock Market is an American stock exchange. It is the second-largest exchange in the world by market capitalization, behind only the New York Stock Exchange. The Nasdaq Stock Market has three different market tiers: Capital Market (small cap) is an equity market for companies that have relatively small levels of market capitalization. Listing requirements for such "small cap" companies are less stringent than for other Nasdaq markets that list larger companies with significantly higher market capitalization. Global Market (mid-cap) is made up of stocks that represent the Nasdaq Global Market. The Global Market consists of 1,450 stocks that meet Nasdaq's strict financial and liquidity requirements, and corporate governance standards. Global Select Market (NASDAQ-GS large-cap) is a market capitalization-weighted index made up of US-based and international stocks that represent the Global Select Market Composite . The Global Select Market consists of 1,200 stocks that meet Nasdaq's strict financial and liquidity requirements and corporate governance standards. The Global Select Market is more exclusive than the Global Market. Every October, the Nasdaq Listing Qualifications Department reviews the Global Market Composite to determine if any of its stocks have become eligible for listing on the Global Select Market.

23(A). Foreign portfolio investment (FPI) consists of securities and other financial assets passively held by foreign investors. It does not provide the investor with direct ownership of financial assets and is relatively liquid depending on the volatility of the market. Foreign portfolio investment differs from foreign direct investment (FDI), in which a domestic company runs a foreign firm, because although FDI allows a company to maintain better control over the firm held abroad, it may face more difficulty selling the firm at a premium price in the future. FPI is also called Foreign Institutional Investments (FIIs). Because of their volatility, they are also called hot money. Loans from international financial institutions are given for a fixed tenure and hence are stable. FDI is not part of FPI but is accounted for separately.

24(A). The South Asian Association for Regional Cooperation (SAARC) is the regional intergovernmental organization and geopolitical union of nations in South Asia. Its member states include Afghanistan, Bangladesh, Bhutan, India, Nepal, the Maldives, Pakistan, and Sri Lanka. SAARC comprises 3% of the world's area, 21% of the world's population, and 3.8% of the global economy, as of 2015. SAARC was founded in Dhaka on 8th December 1985. Its secretariat is based in Kathmandu, Nepal. The organization promotes the development of economic and regional integration. It launched the South Asian Free Trade Area in 2006. SAARC maintains permanent diplomatic relations at the United Nations as an observer and has developed links with multilateral entities, including the European Union.

25(A). The foreign exchange market (forex, FX, or currency market) is a global decentralized market for the trading of currencies. This includes all aspects of buying, selling, and exchanging currencies at current or determined prices. In terms of volume of trading, it is by far the largest market in the world, followed by the Credit market. The main participants in this market are the larger international banks. Financial centers around the world function as anchors of trading between a wide range of multiple types of buyers and sellers around the clock, with the exception of weekends. The foreign exchange market does not determine the relative values of different currencies but sets the current market price of the value of one currency as demanded against another. The foreign exchange market works through financial institutions, and it operates on several levels.

26(A). Goods and Services Tax (GST) is a proposed system of indirect taxation in India merging most of the existing taxes into a single system of taxation. It was introduced The Constitution (One Hundred and First Amendment) Act 2016. GST would be a comprehensive indirect tax on the manufacture, sale, and consumption of goods and services throughout India, to replace taxes levied by the central and state governments. Goods and Services Tax would be levied and collected at each stage of sale or purchase of goods or services based on the input tax credit method.

27(D). Under the Income Tax Act, 1961 every assessee is required to pay income tax on the income earned during the previous year at the rates announced in the Annual Finance Act. According to Section 5 of the Income Tax Act, the scope of the total income of an assessee depends on his residential status. The residential status is determined on the basis of the assessee's period of residence in India during the previous year. Section 6 of the Income Tax Act, 1961 describes the rules for determining the residential status of various assesses e.g. Individual. Hindu Undivided Family, Firm, and Company. An individual is said to be a resident of India if he is in India in the previous year for a period of 182 days or more (60 days if the person is a member of the crew of an Indian ship) He is in India for a period of 365 days or more within 4 years preceding the assessment year AND periods amounting to all to 60 days or more in that year The exception is given to a member of the crew of an Indian ship because they work for moths together on duty on the seas.

28(A). The Prudence principle is the rule of becoming careful. In accounting, we can become careful about future losses. For facing the losses without tension, it is very easy to separate of profit's some part for this. Every type of loss will increase our liability. As per the prudence principle, we should make and record all estimated future losses and forget all estimated future gains. By doing this, we have to make the provisions for future losses. For example, there is a risk of defaulting some debtors. For tolerating this loss, it is good, if we make the provision for doubtful debt. This reserve will deduct our total profit. If this loss will happen, we can easily buy new stock through this provision. This provision is also called the principle of conservatism because this rule is not new. Every time, a businessman wants to play his investment on the safe side. He also wants to control every type of risk by making reserve. At that time of the making of the reserve, he should estimate the future loss correctly, otherwise, it will become a secrete reserve and it is against the principle of full disclosure.

29(B). For the purpose of extending rural banking and agro finance, the NABARD Refinances the banks extending rural finance. NABARD's refinance is available to State Co-operative Agriculture and Rural Development Banks (SCARDBs), State Co-operative Banks (SCBs), Regional Rural Banks (RRBs), Commercial Banks (CBS), and other financial institutions approved by RBI. While the ultimate beneficiaries of investment credit can be individuals, partnership concerns, companies, State-owned corporations, or co-operative societies, production credit is generally given to individuals.

30(C). (iii), (i), (iv) and (ii) sequence is correct.

1. SIDBI provides financial assistance in the following forms:
1. SIDBI refinances loans extended by the primary lending institutions to small scale industrial units and also provides resources support to them.
2. SIDBI discounts and rediscounts bills arising from the sale of machinery to or manufactured

by industrial units in the small scale sector.
3. To expand the channels for marketing the products of Small Scale Industries (SSI) sector in domestic and international markets.
4. It provides services like leasing, factoring, etc. to industrial concerns in the small-scale sector.
5. To promote employment-oriented industries especially in semi-urban areas to create more employment opportunities and thereby checking the migration of people to urban areas.
6. To initiate steps for technological up-gradation and modernization of existing units.
7. SIDBI facilitates a timely flow of credit for both term loans and working capital to SSI in collaboration with commercial banks.

Hence, the correct option (C).

31(A). The World Bank Group is a group of five international organizations responsible for providing finance and advice to counties for the purposes of economic development and eliminating poverty. Its five agencies are: The World Bank Group consists of:
i. The International Bank of Reconstruction and Development (IBRD), established in 1945, which provides debt financing on the basis of sovereign guarantees;
ii. The International Financial Corporation (IFC), established in 1956, which provides various forms of financing without sovereign guarantees, primarily to the private sector;
iii. The International Development Association (IDA), established in 1960, which provides concessional financing (interest-free loans or grants), usually with sovereign guarantees;
iv. The Multilateral Investment Guarantee Agency (MIGA), established in 1988, which provides insurance against certain types of risks, including political risk, primarily to the private sector; and,
v. The International Centre for Settlement of Investment Disputes (ICSID), established in 1966, works with governments to reduce investment risk. The term "World Bank" generally refers to the IBRD and IDA, whereas the World Bank Group is used to refer to the institutions collectively.

32(A). Human Resource refers to the total knowledge, skill, creative abilities, talent and aptitudes of an organization's workforce as well as the value, attitudes, and beliefs of the individuals involved this to a definition by Leon C. Megginson.

33(B). The Competition Act, 2002 was enacted by the Parliament of India and replaced The Monopolies and Restrictive Trade Practices Act, 1969. Two of the main features of the Competition Act, 2002 is the framework it provides for the establishment of the Competition Commission, and the tools it provides to prevent anti-competitive practices and to promote positive competition in the Indian market.

Objectives of the Competition Act, 2002: An Act, keeping in view of the economic development of the country, was laid down to provide for an establishment of a commission with the following object:
1. to provide the framework for the establishment of the Competition Commission.
2. to prevent monopolies and to promote competition in the market
3. to protect the freedom of trade for the participating individuals and entities in the market.
4. to prevent practices having an adverse effect on competition,
5. to promote and sustain competition in markets.
6. to protect the interests of consumers.
7. to regulate the operation and activities of combinations (acquisitions, mergers, and amalgamation) for matters connected therewith or incidental thereto.

34(C). Processes are part of Practice Guides, not Practice Advisories. The other three choices are part of practice advisories. Practice Advisories assist internal auditors in applying the definition of internal auditing, the Code of Ethics, and the Standards and promoting good practices. Practice Advisories address internal auditing's approach, methodologies, and consideration but not detailed processes or procedures. They include practices relating to international, country, or industry-specific issues; specific types of engagements; and legal or regulatory issues.

35(B). In hypothesis testing, the hypothesis which is tentatively assumed to be true is called the null hypothesis. A proposition that undergoes verification to determine it should be accepted or rejected in favor of an alternative proposition. Often the null hypothesis is expressed as 'There is no relationship between two quantities'. It is presumed to be true until statistical evidence nullifies it for the alternative hypothesis.

36(D). The basic objective of Export Promotion Councils is to develop and promote the exports of the nation. Each Council is in charge of the promotion of a specific group of projects, products, and services. The council helps in sponsoring the development of export-related industries.

Hence, the correct option (D).

37(A). Lineation function is a process in human resources management that is concerned with providing a conducive work environment to the employees and nurturing them to make them feel committed and attached to the organization.

38(B). BCR = PVB ÷ Initial Outlay
PVB: Present Value of Benefits
So, Net BCR (NBCR) = BCR – 1

39(A). Performance Appraisal is defined as the formal evaluation of an individual's Job Performance. It also involves giving feedback to the individual concerned and developing constructive solutions for further improvement.

40(B). In PLC, the introduction stage is a period of slow sales growth as the product is introduced in the market, profits are nonexistent because of the heavy expenses of product introduction. In this stage, promotional expenditure are at their highest ratio to sales because of the need to:
(1) inform potential consumers
(2) induce product trial and
(3) secure distribution in retail outlets

41(C). A transferable letter of credit is a type of financial guarantee, known as a letter of credit, that additionally allows the first beneficiary to transfer some or all of the credit to another party, which creates a secondary beneficiary. The party that initially accepts the transferable letter of credit from the bank is referred to as the first, or primary beneficiary.

42(A). The IMF's primary purpose is to ensure the stability of the international monetary system—the system of exchange rates and international payments that enables countries (and their citizens) to transact with each other.
Hence, the correct option (A).

43(C). Firstly, the aggrieved employee shall convey his grievance verbally in person to the officer designated by the management for this purpose. The officer has to answer within 48 hours of the presentation of the complaint.
Hence, the correct option (C).

44(C). According to Section 3 (1) (iii) of the companies Act, 1956 the minimum no. of persons required to form a private and public ltd. the company are 2 and 7.

45(B). The definition that many marketers learn as they start out in the industry is: Putting the right product in the right place, at the right price, at the right time.
Marketing Mix is one of the most fundamental concepts in marketing management. For attracting consumers and for sales promotion, every manufacturer has to concentrate on four basic elements/components. These are product, pricing, distributive channels (place), and sales promotion techniques. A fair combination of these marketing elements is called Marketing Mix.

46(C). Road blocking advertisement refers to advertising a product on multiple TV channels at the same time.
Road Blocking Advertisement is the practice of placing an advertisement on each available media within a market, to appear at exactly (or as near as possible) the same time.
Road blocking is most often used as a means of building high reach levels within a short period of time.

47(A). The exchange concept of marketing deals with the Exchange of products between sellers and buyers covering distribution and price aspects.
The central idea of marketing is the exchange of products between the seller and the buyer. Exchange covers the distribution aspect and the price mechanism of the product.
Marketing theorists consider the exchange to be the central concept without which there would be no such thing as marketing.

48(A). Standard deviation refers to how much the values are spread out from a given set of values. It is a measure of how far each observed values are from the mean.
The four commonly used confidence intervals for a normal distribution are:
68.27% of values fall within 1 standard deviation of the mean (-1s <= X <= 1s)
90% of values fall within 1.65 standard deviations of the mean (-1.65s <= X <= 1.65s)
95% of values fall within 1.96 standard deviations of the mean (-1.96s <= X <= 1.96s)
99.73% of values fall within 2.58 standard deviations of the mean (-2.58s <= X <= 2.58s)

49(A). Research is a process of systematic investigation that entails the collection of data; documentation of important information; and the analysis and interpretation of that data/information, in accordance with appropriate practices prescribed by specific business areas and academic disciplines.
The following stages of research are in proper order:
Budgeting is essential in the development of any large business project. Without a well-organized budget, projects can fall through and remain incomplete. Having a budget allows you to establish the main objectives of a project.
Fieldwork refers to the collection of primary data from consumers or business-to-business customers through surveys or observations. It is also desirable for a researcher to have sufficient knowledge of research and data collection procedures to be able to interact intelligently with a subcontractor.
Data collection is the process of gathering and measuring information on variables of interest, in an established systematic fashion that enables one to answer perceived research questions, hypothesize and evaluate results.
Research results attempt to understand the end results of particular health care practices and interventions. End results include effects that people experience and care about, such as changes in ability to function.
Thesis writing is a reliable source for narrating details about an conducted research and is often considered a true proof of all that has been done to meet the specifications of the research.

50(B). As the period of the moving mean in the time series increases, the trend curve will be further from the original curve.
The moving mean model is probably the simplest way of modeling time series.
This model simply states that the next observation is the mean of all previous observations.
Simply put, this model can be surprisingly good and it represents a good starting point.
Otherwise, the moving mean can be used to identify interesting trends in the data.
We can define a window to flatten the time series and apply the moving mean model to uncover different trends.

51(A). In psychological research, we seek to determine the relationship between two variables for forecasting purposes.
The correlation r measures the strength of the linear relationship between two quantitative variables.
Pearson $r = \frac{1}{n-1}\sum\left(\frac{x_i-\bar{x}}{S_x}\right)\left(\frac{y_i-\bar{y}}{S_y}\right)$
r is always a number between -1 and 1. So, 1.20 does not lie in this range. r > 0 indicates a positive association. r < 0 indicates a negative association. Values of r near 0 indicate a very weak linear relationship. The strength of the linear relationship increases as r moves away from 0 toward -1 or 1. The extreme values r = -1 and r = 1 occur only in the case of a perfect linear relationship.
Since -0.98 is close to -1 as compared between 0.90 and 1 therefore, -0.98 coefficients of correlation indicate the strongest relationship between two sets of variables.

52(C). Income received from winning lotteries, puzzles, card games, crosswords, gambling, betting, horse racing, etc. is known as casual income.

All these casual incomes are taxed at a flat rate of 30%.

No expenditure is allowed as a deduction from casual income and also the benefit of the basic exemption limit is not available for casual income.

The dividend received from the domestic company was exempt until 31 March 2020 (FY 19-20).

However, the Finance Act, 2020 changed the method of dividend taxation.

Henceforth, all dividend received on or after 1 April 2020 is taxable in the hands of the investor/ shareholder.

The normal rate of TDS is 10% on dividend income paid in excess of Rs 5,000 from a company or mutual fund.

However, as a COVID-19 relief measure, the government reduced the TDS rate to 7.5% for distribution from 14 May 2020 until 31 March 2021.

53(D). The process of filing Income tax returns electronically through the internet is known as e-filing.

There are three types of e-filing of return:

e-filing with Digital Signature Certificate (DSC).

There is no further action needed if filed with DSC.

The DSC used in e-filing the Income-tax return should be registered on the e-filing application.

e-filing without Digital Signature Certificate.

In this case, an ITR-V Form is generated.

The Form should be printed, signed, and submitted to CPC, Bangalore using Ordinary or Speed post only within 120 days from the date of e-filing.

There is no further action needed if ITR-V Form is submitted.

e-filing the Income-tax return through an e-Return Intermediary (ERI) with or without Digital Signature Certificate (DSC).

Therefore, all of the above are types of e-filing of return.

54(B). 5 percent is the rate of tax deduction at source from insurance commission in case of 'Person'.

Insurance can go a long way when it comes to mitigating the financial crunch caused due to medical emergencies. Therefore, it is advisable to take an insurance policy not only for oneself but for one's dependents as well. Most times people choose their insurance via agents, brokers, etc. In such cases, the insurance commission or any other remuneration/reward received by such agents, brokers, etc., are subjected to Tax Deducted at Source (TDS) as dictated under Section 194D of the Income Tax Act.

55(B). Tax-shield on depreciation and interest is an important variable both for the lessor and the lessee:

- Lessor and lessee enjoy various benefits under leasing agreement in India such as Income tax benefits, sales tax benefits, modernization through lease finance, etc.
- The lessor can claim depreciation and thereby get some concessions under the Income Tax Act.
- Sales tax will be paid by the lessor as the equipment is bought by him.
- But later on, under the financial lease, he can claim a part of the sales tax from the lessee when the equipment is transferred to the lessee.
- The lessee will be paying the sales tax on a lesser amount.
- The lessee gets certain benefits in the payment of rent, maintenance of the equipment, and other promotional expenditure incurred by him in keeping the equipment operational.
- For all these expenses, the lessee will be claiming tax benefits under the Indian Income Tax Act. Thus, the statement I is correct.

56(A). Agriculture Income earned by a taxpayer in India is exempt under Section 10(1) of the Income Tax Act, 1961. Agricultural income is defined under section 2(1A) of the Income-tax Act.

As per section 2(1A), agricultural income generally means

1. Any rent or revenue derived from land which is situated in India and is used for agricultural purposes.
2. Any income derived from such land by agriculture operations including processing of agricultural produce so as to render it fit for the market or sale of such produce.
3. Any income attributable to a farmhouse subject to satisfaction of certain conditions specified in this regard in section 2(1A).
4. Any income derived from saplings or seedlings grown in a nursery shall be deemed to be agricultural income.

57(C). Section 10AA – Special provisions in respect of newly established Units in Special Economic Zones. The benefit in respect of newly established Industrial Undertaking in SEZ is Available to all Assessees on Export of Certain Articles or things or software.

Subject to the following Conditions:

1. Begin its production, etc. on or after 01-04-2006 relevant to AY 2006-07 but before 01.04.2021.
2. Should not be formed by splitting up or reconstruction of the unit already in existence.
3. Should not be formed by transferring machinery or plant previously used. In certain conditions as specified in the Act second-hand machinery is allowed.
4. The report in Form No.56Fv.

58(C). A) Fair Value = Rs. 1,80,000

B) Municipal Value = Rs. 1,50,000

C) Higher of A and B = Rs. 1,80,000

D) Standard Rent = Rs. 1,60,000

E) Expected Rent (Lower Of C and D) = Rs. 1,60,000

F) Actual Rent = Rs. 2,40,000 (20000 × 12 Months)

GROSS ANNUAL VALUE (Higher Of E and F) = Rs. 2,40,000

NET ANNUAL VALUE = Gross Annual Value (2,40,000) - Unrealised Rent (40,000) - Municipal Tax (30,000) = Rs. 1,70,000

59(B). Trade-Related Aspects of Intellectual Property Rights (TRIPs) - Doha Ministerial Conference.

Intellectual property rights are the rights given to persons over the creations of their minds. They usually give the creator an exclusive right over the use of his/her creation for a certain period of time. The Trade-Related Aspects of Intellectual Property Rights (TRIPS) agreement requires members of the WTO to set minimum standards of legal protection, but its objective to have a "one-fits-all" protection law on Intellectual Property has been viewed with controversies regarding differences in the development level of countries.

Despite the controversy, the agreement has

extensively incorporated intellectual property rights into the global trading system for the first time in 1995, and has prevailed as the most comprehensive agreement reached by the world.

60(B). (a) - (iii), (b) - (i), (c) - (iv), (d) - (ii) is correct.
- Type I error: Type I error is also known as false positive and occurs when a researcher incorrectly rejects a true hypothesis.
- Large sample: The standard error is inversely proportional to sample size i.e. the larger the sample size, the smaller the standard error because the statistic will approach the actual value and vice-versa.
- Multiple regression: Multiple regression represents the relationship between multiple independent (predictor) variables and one dependent (criterion) variable.
- Chi-square test: The Chi-square test is a non-parametric tool designed to analyze group differences when the dependent variable is measured at a nominal level.

61(D). Normal distribution:
- A normal distribution is a probability distribution that is symmetric about the mean, showing that data near the mean are more frequent in occurrence than the data far from the mean.
- The normal distribution is an example of unimodal distribution as it has one local maximum curve (peak) which is sometimes also known as a bell curve.

Chi-square test:
- The Chi-square test is a measure of the difference between the observed and expected frequencies of the outcomes of a set of events.
- It depends on the size of the difference between actual and observed values, the degree of freedom, and the sample sizes.
- It is also known as the "Goodness of fit test" because it measures how well the observed distribution of data fits with the distribution that is expected if the variables are independent.

Poisson distribution:
- Poisson distribution is a statistical distribution that shows how many times an event is likely to occur within a specified period of time.
- Both mean and variance of the Poisson distribution are equal.
- Thus, the distribution is positively skewed and leptokurtic.

Multiple regression:
- Multiple regression is used when we want to predict the value of a variable based on a value of two or more other variables.
- The variable that needs to be predicted is known as a dependent variable (or sometimes, the outcome, target, or criterion variable).

62(D). Price discovery is the overall process, whether explicit or inferred, of setting the spot price or the proper price of an asset, security, commodity, or currency.
- The process of price discovery looks at a number of tangible and intangible factors, including supply and demand, investor risk attitudes, and the overall economic and geopolitical environment.
- Simply put, it is where a buyer and a seller agree on a price and a transaction occurs.
- The derivatives market serves as an important source of information about prices. Prices of derivative instruments such as futures and forwards can be used to determine what the market expects future spot prices to be.
- The information is accurate and reliable. Thus, the futures and forwards markets are especially helpful in the price discovery mechanism.

So, both (A) and (R) are correct

63(B). A - III, B - IV, C - II, D - I is correct.
- Target Capital structure: The target capital structure refers to the mix of debt, preferred stock, and common equity that the company is striving to attain. In other words, it is the debt ratio the firm strives to achieve.
- Optimum Capital Structure: It refers to the best mix of debt-equity financing that maximizes the company's overall market value while minimizing its cost of capital. In other words, it is the debt-equity ratio that maximizes the value of the firm.
- Cost of financial distress: The more debt a company will use to finance its operations, the more will be the chances of increased financial distressed cost. It refers to the perceived costs due to an increased ratio of debt in the firm.
- MM preposition-II: Proposition -II of MM theory states that the cost of equity is directly related and incremental to the percentage of debt in the capital structure. The expected yield on the equity capital is equal to the pure equity return plus a premium for financial risk.

64(D). Activities in the process of accounting:

Recording the business transaction in the books of entry:
- The first step in the accounting cycle is identifying transactions and recording them in the books of entry i.e. journal entry.
- Companies will have many transactions throughout the year so recordkeeping is essential for recording all types of transactions.
- Journal entries for every transaction must be created.
- The choice between accrual and cash accounting will dictate when transactions are officially recorded.

Journalising the transaction in the ledger accounts:
- Once transactions are recorded in journal entries, they must be posted in the general ledger accounts.
- The general ledger helps in the breakdown of all accounting activities by accounts.
- It allows a bookkeeper to monitor financial positions by account.

Preparation of Annual Financial Statements:
- After the adjustments are recorded as journal entries wherever necessary, the company generates its financial statements.
- For most companies, this statement will include income statements, balance sheets, and cash flow statements.
- Lastly, a company closes its books at the end of the day on a specified closing date.
- The closing statement provides a report of analysis of performance over the period.

Deriving meaningful inferences for business decisions:
- With the help of financial statements and closing statements, business owners can derive

a meaningful inference about their business activities.

- It helps to ensure accuracy, consistency, and efficient financial performance analysis.

65(C). (a) - 2, (b) - 4, (c) - 1, (d) - 3 is correct.

- Mercantilism theory: David Hume Mercantilism is an economic theory that advocates government regulation of international trade to generate wealth and strengthen national power.
- Theory of absolute cost advantage: Adam Smith Absolute advantage is when a producer can produce a good or service in greater quantity for the same cost, or the same quantity at a lower cost, than other producers.
- National competitive advantage theory: Michael Porter proposed the theory of competitive advantage in 1985.
- Factor endowment theory: Eli Heckscher A factor endowment represents how many resources a country has at its disposal to be utilized for manufacturing resources such as labor, land, money, and entrepreneurship.

66(C). (a)-(ii) (b)-(iv) (c)-(i) (d)-(iii) is correct.
Monopolistic Competition: In 1933, Edward H. Chamberlin published the Theory of Monopolistic Competition (1962).
Price Rigidity: The Kinked Demand Curve is also known as Paul M. Sweezy Model. The oligopolistic price that remains stable over a period of time is known as price rigidity.
Dumping: Dumping occurs when a country or company exports a product at a price that is lower in the foreign importing market than the price in the exporter's domestic market.
Collusion: Collusion is a non-competitive, secret, and sometimes illegal agreement between rivals which attempts to disrupt the market's equilibrium.

67(C). (a) - (iii), (b) - (iv), (c) - (ii), (d) - (i) is correct.

- Treasury bills: Treasury bills are risk-free, as individuals are backed by the highest authority in the country, and have to be paid even during the economic crisis.
- Beta: Beta is used in the capital asset pricing model which describes the relationship between systematic risk and expected return for assets.
- Capital budgeting: The time value of money is important in capital budgeting decisions because it allows small-business owners to adjust cash flows for the passage of time.
- Working capital: Working capital is also called circulating capital or revolving capital i.e. the money which circulates in various forms of current assets in a continuous manner. The amount always keeps on circulating or revolving from cash to current assets and back again to cash. Thus, it is known as the Operating cycle.

68(B). (a) - (iii), (b) - (i), (c) - (iv), (d) - (ii) is correct.

- Interest rate risk: Systematic risk, also known as market risk, is the risk that is inherent to the entire market, rather than a particular industry sector.
- Financial risk: Unsystematic risk is inherent in a specific company or industry. Unsystematic risk is caused due to internal factors so it can be avoided and controlled.
- APM model: Arbitrage Pricing Model is a Multifactor model based on the idea that ideas return can be predicted using the linear relationship between the asset's expected return and a number of macroeconomic variables that capture systematic risk.
- CAPM model: Capital Asset Pricing Model is the simplest factor model that attempts to explain the return of an individual security or portfolio.

69(C). NABARD bank took over the entire undertaking of ARDC.

- National Bank for Agriculture and Rural Development (NABARD) is an apex development financial institution under the jurisdiction of the Ministry of Finance, Government of India.
- The bank has been entrusted with "matters concerning policy, planning, and operations in the field of credit for agriculture and other economic activities in rural areas in India". NABARD is active in developing & implementing Financial Inclusion.
- NABARD was established on the recommendations of the B.Sivaramman Committee (by Act 61, 1981 of Parliament) on 12 July 1982 to implement the National Bank for Agriculture and Rural Development Act 1981.

70(A). The contract has four essential elements and is formed in the following sequence:

- An offer is made by one party to another to enter into a contract.
- The next step is acceptance of that offer by the other party involved.
- The special word "consideration" in contract law refers to something that has value in the eyes of the law. Consideration is an essential element to make a contract. must be provided for a contract to be legally binding.
- Every promise and every set of promises, forming the consideration for each other, is an agreement

Therefore, the correct sequence in the formation of a contract is offer, acceptance, consideration, agreement.

71(D). The Sale of Goods Act, 1930 herein referred to as the Act, is the law that governs the sale of goods in all parts of India. It doesn't apply to the state of Jammu & Kashmir.
Implied conditions according to the Sale of Goods Act.
(i) Seller's title to goods is valid
(ii) Goods comply with description & sample
(iii) Quality or fitness of goods for the purpose specified by Buyer
(iv) Wholesomeness of eatables

72(C). Statements I and II are incorrect as have not been stated in the passage. Statement III is correct as a case of fraud has been highlighted in the passage and is the main reason to link Aadhar with Taxpayers.

73(D). According to the passage, '...to appraise the possibility of making the biometrics-based unique identifier mandatory for claiming refunds. Already the GST Network ...has made it mandatory for new dealers registering under the composition scheme for small businesses to either authenticate their Aadhaar or submit to physical verification of their business, ...'

All the above remedial measures listed as recommendations to reduce fraudulent activities.

74(D). Option (A) is incorrect as no such issue that cannot be solved has been mentioned.
Option (B) is opposite of what has been mentioned in the passage.
Option (C) is factually incorrect.
Option (D) is correct as the author feels this step would reduce fraud.

75(B). According to the passage, 'A significant concern relates to the loopholes that unscrupulous operators have sought to exploit, whereby revenue that ought to have accrued to the Centre and the States has leaked while allowing these elements to derive illicit profits.'

76(B). According to the passage, 'India desperately needs to create several high-value product companies to meet domestic demand and create wealth. A strong product ecosystem drives healthy manufacturing industry as well. As such, 'Make in India' shouldn't be just about "manufacturing" but also be about "making products'
So, Only II is correct.

77(C). According to the passage, "The biggest challenge for Indian start-ups today is lack of access to risk capital especially early to pre-revenue stage. This must be addressed quickly if we want to create high-value product growth engine."
The biggest challenge for Indian start-ups is lack of access to risk capital especially early to pre-revenue stage.

78(A). According to the passage, " Then, start-ups need early stage investment from venture capitalists and corporate investors, ranging from $10 million to US$100 million through multiple rounds of equity financing."
Corporate investors and Venture capitalists provide financial assistance to start-ups in the early stage of a company.

79(D). According to the passage, "In my view, successful start-ups require passionate and persuasive founders, great vision, innovative technology, strong team, patient capital, good market timing and a little bit of luck."
So, 'Luck is not at all important for the success of start-ups' is not correct.

80(C). According to the passage, "The biggest challenge for Indian start-ups today is lack of access to risk capital especially early to pre-revenue stage. This must be addressed quickly if we want to create high-value product growth engine."
So, it is concluded that the aim of writer is to mention the problem Indian start-ups face as of now.

Mock Test 02

1. Select the correct code of the following statements being correct or incorrect.
   Statement (I) : The 'law of one price' states that in competitive markets free of transportation costs and barriers to trade, identical products sold in different countries must sell for the same price when their price is expressed in terms of the same currency.
   Statement (II) : An 'Efficient market' has no impediments to the free flow of goods and services, such as trade barriers.
   (a) Statement (I) is correct but (II) is incorrect.
   (b) Statement (II) is correct but (I) is incorrect
   (c) Both statements (I) and (II) are correct.
   (d) Both statements (I) and (II) are incorrect.

2. A method of sampling that ensures proportional representation of all sections of the population is termed as:
   (a) Simple Random Sampling
   (b) Stratified Sampling
   (c) Purposive Sampling
   (d) Systematic Sampling

3. Generally, the shape of the marginal physical product curve is ____________.
   (a) U-shaped (b) V-shaped
   (c) Inverse U-shaped (d) None of these

4. Which of the following introduced significant development in the sphere of foreign exchange?
   (a) Foreign Exchange Regulation Act (FERA)
   (b) Foreign Exchange Management Act (FEMA)
   (c) Export-Import Policy, 2005-06
   (d) EXIM Bank

5. Reducing the capital of a company is called ________.
   (a) Internal reconstruction
   (b) External reconstruction
   (c) Consolidation
   (d) None of these

6. The meaning of cash as per AS-3 (revised) is:
   (a) Cash in hand
   (b) Cash in bank
   (c) Cash in hand and demand deposits with the bank
   (d) None of the above

7. From the following information, calculate the cash flow from financing activities:

Particulars	31st March, 2 019 (Rs.)	31st March, 2 020 (Rs.)
Equity Share Capit al	4,00,000	5,00,000
10% Debentures	1,50,000	1,00,000
Securities Premiu m	40,000	50,000

   Additional Information: Interest paid on debentures Rs. 10,000.
   (a) 11,000 (b) 50,000
   (c) 34,000 (d) None of the above

8. When a partnership dissolves, the balance of a partner's capital account on the assets side of a balance sheet is transferred to:
   (a) On the Debit of Realization Account
   (b) On the Credit of Realization Account
   (c) On the Debit of Partner's Capital Account
   (d) On the Credit of Cash Account

9. Laws of increasing and constant returns are temporary phases of:
   (a) Law of variable proportions
   (b) Law of diminishing returns
   (c) Law of proportionality
   (d) Law of diminishing utility

10. Which of the following pricing strategies will a firm producing a large number of products follow?
    (a) Cost-plus pricing (b) Differential pricing
    (c) Product line pricing (d) Price leadership

11. Regression analysis is a measure of:
    (a) Degree and direction of relationship
    (b) Degree of association
    (c) Cause and effect relationship
    (d) None of the above

12. Match the items from List - I with the items in List - II.

List - I	List-II
a. Random sampling	i. Structured
b. Hypothesis testing	ii. Parametric test
c. Questionnaire	iii. Probability sampling
d. t-test	iv. b-error

    (a) a - iv, b - iii, c - i, d - ii (b) a - iii, b - iv, c - ii, d - i
    (c) a - iii, b - i, c - iv, d - ii (d) a - iii, b - iv, c - i, d - ii

13. Chunk sampling is known as:
    (a) Quota sampling
    (b) Convenience sampling
    (c) Judgement sampling
    (d) Cluster sampling

14. Who is the father of General Management?
    (a) Henry Fayol (b) Harold Koontz
    (c) Keith Davis (d) F. W. Taylor

15. Who propounded mega-marketing?
    (a) Mc Aurthy (b) Philip Kotler
    (c) Sheth (d) Peter F. Drucker

16. Online marketing is associated with:
    (a) Segmentation (b) Product life cycle
    (c) Distribution (d) Packing

17. Modern marketing concepts emphasize on:
    (a) Sales maximisation
    (b) Customer satisfaction
    (c) Profit maximisation
    (d) Wealth maximisation

18. Penetration pricing is:

(a) Charging high price
(b) Charging low price
(c) Charging competitive price
(d) None of the above

19. Right shares enjoy preferential rights regarding:
(a) Payment of retained earnings
(b) Payment of dividend
(c) Repayment of capital in the event of winding up of the company
(d) None of these

20. Match the items of List - I with the items of List - II.

List - I	List-II
a. Capital gearing ratio	i. Profitability
b. Fixed assets turnover	ii. Short-term solvency
c. Return on equity	iii. Activity
d. Acid test	iv. Long-term solvency

(a) a - iv, b - iii, c - i, d - ii(b) a - iv, b - iii, c - ii, d - i
(c) a - iii, b - iv, c - i, d - ii(d) a - iv, b - i, c - iii, d - ii

21. Which of the following is/are the source(s) of short-term finance?
(a) Trade credit
(b) Bank credit
(c) Short-term borrowings
(d) All of the above

22. Which of the following is the operative function of human resource management?
(a) Controlling
(b) Organising
(c) Procurement of raw material
(d) None of the above

23. Unabsorbed depreciation, which could not be set off in the same assessment year, can be carried forward:
(a) Up to 4 years
(b) Up to 8 years
(c) Up to 10 years
(d) For an indefinite period

24. A situation where any advantage given by one member of the WTO to another member is extended to all WTO members is referred to as:
(a) Trade diversion
(b) Inter regional principle
(c) Most favoured nation
(d) Least traded nation

25. According to D. Katz, morale has four dimensions
(i) job satisfaction
(ii) satisfaction with wages and promotional opportunities
(iii) identification with company
(iv) pride in the workgroup
(v) top management support
Select the correct combination.
(a) (i), (ii), (iii) and (iv) (b) (i), (ii), (iii) and (v)
(c) (i), (ii), (iv) and (v) (d) (i), (iii), (iv) and (v)

26. Consider the following statements with regard to the "Theory of Absolute Cost Advantage":
(i) Productive efficiency differed among different countries because of the diversity in natural and acquired resources possessed by them.
(ii) The difference in natural advantage manifests in varying climate, quality of land, availability of minerals, water, and other resources.
(iii) The difference in acquired resources manifests in different levels of technology and skills available.
Identify the correct code from the following :
(a) Statement (i) is correct, but (ii) and (iii) are incorrect.
(b) Statements (i) and (ii) are correct, but (iii) is incorrect.
(c) All the statements (i), (ii) and (iii) are correct.
(d) None of the statements is correct.

27. The price-setting method, which most closely corresponds to the concept of product positioning is:
(a) Cost-plus pricing
(b) Going-rate pricing
(c) Perceived value pricing
(d) Psychological pricing

28. Consider the following statements and indicate the correct alternative from the codes given below.
(i) The product management system often turns out to be costly.
(ii) When customers belong to different user groups with distinct buying preferences and practices, a market management organisation is not suitable.
(iii) Advertising department has the closest interface with the finance department of the company.
(a) (i) and (ii) are correct
(b) (ii) and (iii) are correct
(c) Only (i) is correct
(d) All are correct

29. Which of the following is correct with respect to GST in India?
I. The GST Act was passed by the Parliament in 2016.
II. GST law came into force from July 2016.
(a) Only II (b) Only I
(c) Neither I nor II (d) Both I and II

30. Marginal-costing technique is useful for:
(a) Make or buy decisions
(b) Profit planning
(c) Shut-down decisions
(d) All of the above

31. Which of the given combinations of the following factors influence the working capital requirement?
I. Market conditions
II. Production policy
III. Firm's goodwill
IV. Supply conditions
(a) I, II and III (b) II, III and IV
(c) I, III and IV (d) I, II and IV

32. **Assertion (A) :** The demand curve of FMCG products in usually relatively inelastic.
Reasoning (R) : The FMCG companies usually follow skimming pricing as a strategy to fix the price.
(a) Both (A) and (R) are incorrect
(b) Both (A) and (R) are correct
(c) (A) is incorrect and (R) is correct
(d) (A) is correct and (R) is incorrect

33. The managerial function of organising involves:
(a) Reviewing and adjusting plans in light of changing conditions
(b) Establishing programs for the accomplishment of objectives
(c) Creating the structure of functions and duties to be performed
(d) Getting things done through others

34. The leader who excels as a leader because of his superior knowledge is _______.
(a) Autocratic leader (b) Intellectual leader
(c) Liberal leader (d) Institutional leader

35. Consider the following statements. Which of the alternatives given below is correct?
(i) A firm's marketing information system is a component of its marketing research system.
(ii) The most common forms of marketing researches conducted in most of the firms are the measurement of market potential and the analysis of market share.
(iii) Survey research is seldom used for studying consumer perception and attitudes.
(iv) The concept of cognitive dissonance is relevant to study consumer's post-purchase behaviour.
(a) All the statements are true
(b) All the statements are false
(c) (i) is false and the rest are true
(d) (ii) and (iv) are true and the rest are false

36. The transfer by a company of one or more of its business divisions to another new set up company is called:
(a) Demerger (b) Merger
(c) Equity carve-out (d) Disinvestment

37. Lerner index measures which of the following?
(a) Market power (b) Price
(c) Price-marginal cost (d) None of the above

38. **Direction** : Given below are two statements, one labeled as Assertion (A) and the other labeled as Reason (R). Choose which of the following alternatives is correct?
Assertion (A): Mark-up pricing is a method of determining the price.
Reason (R): P = ATC + (m × ATC) is the expression for that.
(a) (A) is correct but (R) is not correct
(b) Both (A) and (R) are correct
(c) Both (A) and (R) are not correct
(d) (R) is correct, but (A) is not correct

39. **Direction:** Given below are two statements, one labeled as Assertion (A) and the other labeled as Reason (R). Choose which of the following alternatives is correct?
Assertion: Game theory provides an opportunity to analyze the oligopolistic firms.
Reasoning: Game theory is the study of how people behave in strategic situations.
(a) Both (A) and (R) are correct, and (R) is the correct explanation of (A)
(b) Both (A) and (R) are correct, but (R) is not the correct explanation of (A)
(c) (A) is correct, but (R) is not correct
(d) (A) is incorrect, and (R) is correct

40. As per Section ________ of the Companies Act, a certain class of companies are required to appoint an internal auditor for conducting internal audit.
(a) 138 (b) 228
(c) 356 (d) 192

41. The gains from two nations depend on:
(a) Domestic barter rates
(b) Difference in the domestic barter rates of the two countries
(c) Terms of trade
(d) Degree of absolute advantage

42. The defenders of the sustainability approach toward Corporate Social Responsibility (CSR) point out that ________
A. All economic activity exists within a biosphere that support all life
B. The success of business must be judged only against profitability
C. People have a strong ethical duty to cause no harm and only a prime facie duty to prevent harm
Choose the most appropriate answer from the options given below:
(a) A and B only (b) B, and C only
(c) A and C only (d) A only

43. A leader who serves as the head of the family and treats his followers like his family members is ______.
(a) Paternalistic leader (b) Intellectual leader
(c) Liberal leader (d) Institutional leader

44. Which of the following items is not an appropriation of profit for a limited company?
(a) Corporate tax payable
(b) Ordinary dividend payable
(c) Debenture interest payable
(d) Preference dividend payable

45. If goodwill and its full value, raised in the book of a partnership firm at the time of retirement of a partner, is to be written off, then the capital accounts of the remaining partners are debited in:
(a) Gaining ratio
(b) Old profit and loss sharing ratio
(c) New profit and loss sharing ratio
(d) Sale to strategic partner

46. Match the given lists and select the correct code for the answer.

	List - I		List - II
a.	Perfect competiti on	i.	Different prices for the sa me product
b.	Monopolistic com petition	i i.	Dominant strategy
c.	Oligopoly	ii i.	Product differentiation
d.	Discriminating m onopoly	i v.	Identical product

(a) a - (iv), b - (iii), c - (ii), d - (i)
(b) a - (i), b - (ii), c - (iii), d - (iv)
(c) a - (ii), b - (iv), c - (i), d - (iii)
(d) a - (iii), b - (i), c - (iv), d - (ii)

47. Which of the following is not the basic assumption of cardinal utility analysis?
(a) Rationality of consumer
(b) Utility cardinally measurable
(c) Diminishing marginal utility of money
(d) Hypothesis of independent utilities

48. The 'F' test cannot be used to:
(a) Test the hypothesis about a single population variance
(b) Compare more than two population means
(c) Test the hypothesis about two-population variance
(d) Study about randomised block design

49. **Direction:** In the following question, a given questions is followed by information in two statements. You have to find out the data in which statement (s) is sufficient to answer the question and mark your answer accordingly.
Statement I: Matrix organisation aims to combine the benefits of decentralisation with those of coordination.
Statement II: A divisional structure is common in organisations that have outgrown the entrepreneurial structure.
Choose the correct option from the following:
(a) Statement I is correct, Statement II is incorrect.
(b) Statement I is incorrect, Statement II is correct.
(c) Both Statement I and Statement II are correct.
(d) Both Statement I and Statement II are incorrect.

50. The degree to which the returns of the two securities change together is reflected by:
(a) Correlation (b) Leverage
(c) Covariance (d) Beta

51. Which of the following is incorrect about proactive planning?
(a) Way of thinking regarding management of future risks
(b) Anticipating future contingencies
(c) Reacting to external events
(d) Getting ready with alternative routes for unforseen situations

52. Which of the following terms includes the tasks, duties and responsibilities of a particular job?
(a) Job evaluation (b) Job enrichment
(c) Job description (d) Job enlargement

53. Under Section 87A of Income Tax Act, 1961, an individual who is resident in India and whose total income does not exceed Rs. 3,50,000 is entitled to claim rebate up to a maximum of______.
(a) Rs. 1000 (b) Rs. 4000
(c) Rs. 2500 (d) Rs. 3000

54. Match the following.

List - I	List - II
(a) Merchandis e exports	(i) Purchase of foreign goods
(b) Merchandis e imports	(ii) Sales of goods abroad
(c) Investment I ncome	(iii) Largely caused by excess of im ports over exports in merchandise
(d) Balance of P ayments Deficit s	(iv) Dividends, interest etc. receive d from abroad

(a) (a) - (i), (b) - (ii), (c) - (iii), (d) - (iv)
(b) (a) - (ii), (b) - (iii), (c) - (iv), (d) - (i)
(c) (a) - (ii), (b) - (i), (c) - (iv), (d) - (iii)
(d) (a) - (iii), (b) - (iv), (c) - (ii), (d) - (i)

55. In most countries with income taxation, corporate entities are subject to tax on their profits and, in addition, are taxed in the hands of shareholders is known as ________.
(a) Surcharges (b) Dividends
(c) Shares (d) Assets

56. Profit of the hotel business at Melbourne is taxable in the case of ______.
(a) Resident assessee
(b) Not ordinarily resident
(c) Non - resident assessee
(d) Both non - resident and not - ordinarily resident

57. Match the following:

List - A	List - B
(a) Public Corpor ation	(i) Person who has not deducted tax at source
(b) Deemed asses see	(ii) Artificial juridical person
(c) Assessee – in – default	(iii) Local authority
(d) District Board	(iv) Legal representative

(a) (a) - (iii), (b) - (ii), (c) - (i), (d) - (iv)
(b) (a) - (i), (b) - (ii), (c) - (iii), (d) - (iv)
(c) (a) - (iv), (b) - (iii), (c) - (ii), (d) - (i)
(d) (a) - (ii), (b) - (iv), (c) - (i), (d) - (iii)

58. **Direction** : Given below are two statements, one labeled as Assertion (A) and the other labeled as Reason (R). Choose which of the following alternatives is correct.
Assertion (A): Family pension is not taxable.
Reason (R): The person who receives the family pension was not an employee but despendent of the employee.
(a) Both (A) and (R) are correct
(b) (A) is correct and (R) is incorrect
(c) Both (A) and (R) are incorrect
(d) (A) is incorrect and (R) is correct

59. An individual received a salary of Rs. 2,88,000 and bonus of Rs. 32,000. He contributed 15% of the salary to RPF to which his employer contributed 14 percent. He is provided with a rent-free house in Mumbai. The interest credited to his RPF is Rs. 2,000 @ 10% per annum. His income from salary for the A.Y. 2015-16 will be:
(a) Rs. 3,68,000 (b) Rs. 3,63,200
(c) Rs. 3,73,860 (d) Rs. 3,73,760

60. In tax laws, donation to approved and notified association for scientific research is allowed as:

(a) 125% of the donation
(b) 100% of the donation
(c) 175% of the donation
(d) 150% of the donation

61. The Right to Information Act, 2005 makes the provision of _______________.
(a) Dissemination of all types of information by all Public authorities to any person.
(b) Establishment of Central, State and District Level Information Commissions as an appellate body.
(c) Transparency and accountability in Public authorities.
(d) All of the above

62. Which of the following act was created from the sections of the Indian Contract Act 1872?
(a) Indemnity and Guarantee Act
(b) Sales and Goods Act
(c) Contract Labour Act
(d) Personal Injuries Act

63. When ratios are calculated from financial statements of one year, it is termed as _______.
(a) Horizontal Analysis (b) Vertical Analysis
(c) Internal Analysis (d) Ratio Analysis

64. Non-Banking Financial Companies (NBFCs) are the Financial Intermediaries engaged primarily in the business of:
i. Accepting Deposits
ii. Lending loans and advances
iii. Leasing
iv. Hire purchasing
(a) i and ii (b) iii and iv
(c) i and iii (d) i, ii, iii and iv

Ques (65-68): Direction: Read the following passage carefully and answer the questions that follow.

The Reserve Bank of India's annual report for 2017-18 reveals that 99.3% of currency notes that were demonetised at midnight on November 8, 2016 have returned to the banking system. This is only marginally higher than its provisional estimate last year that over 99% — or Rs.15.28 lakh crore worth of the old Rs.500 and Rs.1,000 notes — out of the Rs.15.44 lakh crore that were in circulation at the time had been deposited by June 30, 2017. This makes a couple of things crystal clear. First, the hope that a large chunk of unaccounted money would not return to the system — arguably, the principal reason for the exercise — was almost wholly belied. As a result, the plan to transfer the arising surplus from the RBI to the Centre, which was not formally declared but strongly rumoured, was a non-starter. Second, given the sheer logistical difficulty in penalising all those who converted unaccounted money into legal tender, demonetisation worked as an unintended amnesty scheme. Despite the significant cost to the economy, demonetisation, to the disappointment of the Prime Minister's critics, had no political fallout. Narendra Modi succeeded in portraying the move as one that would knock out the corrupt rich — a harsh but necessary shock therapy. This was perhaps why the massive disruption caused by the overnight removal of 86% of the currency in value terms did not cause agitations.

Nevertheless, the RBI report, which points to a spurt in counterfeiting of the new Rs.500 and Rs.2,000 notes, raises the old question all over again. Was it worth the slowdown in growth, the damage to informal sector supply chains, and job losses in sectors such as construction that were the bulwark of employment creation for the unskilled? True, there have been some benefits. For instance, the number of income tax returns filed has surged a little over the trend growth rate. But surely this could have been achieved by other policy measures. Cashless modes of payment have become more common, but financial savings in the form of currency have also risen, suggesting that people still value cash. Not all policy choices work out and accepting mistakes or planning flaws helps strengthen governance processes. For example, learning from the UPA's mistakes, a cleaner auction process for natural resources has been worked out. The government must not disown its biggest reform attempt or try to sidestep parliamentary scrutiny of the outcomes of demonetisation. Instead, it could focus on fixing the problems that people still face — transactions with Rs.2,000 notes in the absence of Rs.1,000 notes are difficult as it is a departure from the currency denomination principle (every note should be twice or two and a half times its preceding denomination). Even as these issues are sorted out, the larger lesson must be heeded: sudden shocks to the economy don't always yield intended policy objectives.

65. Which among the following sums up the opinion of the author regarding the demonetization drive announced by the government?
(a) The author is very much hopeful that the demonetization drive will be able to divide the wealth among all the sections equally.
(b) The author has no opinion to give regarding demonetization since he was not staying in India at that point of time.
(c) The author is a blue eyed boy of the Prime Minister and that is why he will always praise all the moves by the government.
(d) The author feels that the move to demonetize currencies did not yield the desired results though some positive sides can be appreciated.

66. Which among the following should be the course of action of the government now that the demonetization has failed?
(a) The government should understand that there can be error in judgment on its part and it can be corrected by first accepting it.
(b) The government should cancel the whole demonetization drive and give back the currency notes to the general public.
(c) The central government should approach the Supreme Court to ensure that there is no legal issue in the future.
(d) The Government of India is of the opinion that it has done the right thing but the public could not understand the importance of it.

67. Which among the following can be considered as the takeaway from the incident described in the given passage?
(a) The economy of the country is not suffering at all and therefore anything can be done now to test the waters.
(b) The economy of India is ready to accept any change since it is now mature enough to withstand any kind of problem.
(c) The Indian government is not receptive of any international shocks since there is no mechanism in India to accept the foreign risks.
(d) The economy has its own rhythm and it should not be taken for granted that any kind of

sudden policy decision will be positive for the economy.

68. Which among the following is correct regarding the positive effects of demonetization as discussed in the passage?
I. The number of income tax returns filed post demonetization has increased since now a lot of people are going to filing of income tax returns
II. The cashless mode of transactions has become more popular post demonetization since now people are resorting to cashless modes of transactions
III. The RBI has become more proactive these days in order to prevent money laundering activities in the country.

(a) Both II and III (b) Both I and II
(c) Both I and III (d) Only II

69. Which among the followings are correct statements with regard to NBFC in India?
(A) All NBFCs should be registered with RBI.
(B) NBFCs cannot accept demand deposits.
(C) NBFCs do not form part of the payment and settlement system and cannot issue cheques drawn on itself.
(D) Deposit insurance facility of Deposit Insurance and Credit Guarantee Corporation is not available to depositors of NBFCs.
Choose the correct from the options given below:

(a) (A), (B), (C) only (b) (A), (B), (C), (D) only
(c) (A), (B), (D) only (d) (A), (D) only

70. Which of the following statement(s) is/are correct with respect to the role of RBI in the Indian economy?
I. It is the controller of money supply.
II. RBI acts as a banker to the Government of India.

(a) Neither I nor II (b) Both I and II
(c) Only II (d) Only I

71. Arrange the following initiatives taken by the Government of India to tackle the Non-performing assets in their ascending order of chronology :
(A) Corporate Debt Restructuring
(B) Compromise Settlement
(C) The Debt Recovery Tribunals (DRTs)
(D) Credit Information Bureau
(E) SARFAFSI Act
Choose the correct answer from the options given below:

(a) (C), (D) (A), (B), (E) (b) (A), (B), (E), (C), (D)
(c) (C), (D), (B), (E), (A) (d) (D), (C), (B), (E), (A)

72. Identify the principles of trade policy framework from the followings under the WTO:
(A) Reciprocity and transparent
(B) Benefactory and resilient
(C) Non-discriminatory
(D) Binding and enforceable commitments
(E) Protective and benevolent
Choose the correct answer from the options given below:

(a) (A), (B) and (C) only (b) (C), (D) and (E) only
(c) (A), (C) and (D) only (d) (B), (D) and (E) only

73. Match the items of List I with those of List II and choose the correct code of combination

	List I		List II
a.	Inability to pay interest	i)	Current ratio
b.	Liquidity crisis	ii)	Debtor turnover ratio
c.	Inefficient collection of receivable	iii)	Interest coverage ratio

(a) a-iii, b-i, c-ii (b) a-iii, b-ii, c-i
(c) a-ii, b-iii, c-i (d) a-i, b-ii, c-iii

Ques (74-77): Directions: Read the passage and answer the questions that follow:
The deadline for the completion of the resolution process under the Insolvency and Bankruptcy Code (IBC), 2016 for the first set of cases taken up has neared or even passed. The IBC provides for a time limit of 180 days (extendable by 90 days) once a case of default is brought and If no resolution plan drawn up under the supervision of a resolution professional can be agreed upon, liquidation must follow to recover whatever sums are possible. While the NCLT has considered a number of cases since its constitution, its role assumed importance when, on 13 June 2017, the Reserve Bank of India (RBI) mandated proceedings against 12 large defaulters, holding accounts with outstanding amounts of more than Rs 5,000 crore, of which at least 60% had been classified as non-performing as of 31 March 2016. These bad loans accounted for around 25% of the non-performing assets (NPAs) recognised at that time.
In most cases, the estimated value of assets on liquidation is low, and does not capture the true value of the company. Put simply, the aggregate of the individual value of a set of stripped assets tends to be much lower than the value of those assets when combined for production. So, if the IBC process and the intervention of the NCLT lead, through bidding, to an offer of a takeover by a third party which is acceptable to the creditors, the recovery against bad loans technically written off by financial creditors would be much higher. Since this was to occur in a time-bound fashion, it seemed to be a significant initiative to address the NPA problem in the banking system. The IBC was combined with legislative amendments that strengthened the powers of the RBI to order the launch of proceedings to recover the loans gone bad. These measures, it was argued, through enforced resolution or liquidation if necessary, offered a way in which the abysmal record of recovery could be corrected and the pressure on the government to bail out banks with taxpayers' money could be reduced. In the case of 11 public sector banks out of a total of 21, of the loans technically written-off between April 2014 and December 2017, recovery rates varied from nil to just above 20%, and in the case of another three, the rate ranged between 23% and 29%. The average recovery rate for all 21 banks was a pathetic 10.8%. By facilitating and accelerating the recovery effort, the IBC process was expected to raise the rate significantly.
The context in which this new strategy was launched needs recalling. Unlike the period prior to the 1990s, the NPAs that accumulated in the books of banks in recent years were not equitably distributed across different categories of borrowers, big and small, priority and non-priority. Rather, because of a change in the lending strategy during the period of the credit boom after 2003, the NPAs are now concentrated in the hands of large borrowers, primarily corporate borrowers.
The initial experience with the first phase of this multistep process involving the recognition, technical write-off and provisioning, and recovery of NPAs, is revealing for a number of reasons. First, in cases where the assets on offer were of special interest to particular bidders, the rates of recovery have been rather high. This was true of the acquisition of Bhushan Steel by Tata Steel and of Electrosteel by Vedanta. Bhushan Steel owed its financial creditors around Rs 56,000 crore, whereas the Tata Steel bid returned Rs 35,200 crore upfront to the financial creditors, besides giving them a 12.3% stake

in the company in lieu of returning the remaining debt. That was substantial relative to the estimated liquidation value of Rs 15,000 crore to Rs 20,000 crore, and far better than the average 10% recovery rate reported on aggregate write-offs in the recent past. The Tatas clearly had a special interest in the deal since its valuation of the company was far higher than that of JSW Group, the other keen bidder. The latter offered the creditors only Rs 29,700 crore.
The evidence that the assets were valuable despite the defaults emerged also from the battle between bidders who were often taken to the courts. Essar Steel, one of the largest defaulters with around Rs 44,000 crore in questionable debt, when put up for sale, elicited expressions of interest from five bidders. Interestingly, besides Tata Steel, Arcelor Mittal, Vedanta, Sumitomo, and Steel Authority of India, the interested parties include the Ruias, who are the original promoters of Essar Steel.
This effort of the defaulting promoters to regain control of the companies concerned at a discount did muddy the water. The original IBC bill did not prevent promoters from making bids for resolution at the NCLT. Some justified the Ruia bid on the grounds that extraneous factors may have led to distress for no fault of the original promoters. But, if the Committee of Creditors (CoC) has taken the firm to the NCLT, it is clearly because they saw the incumbent management as incapable of resolving the crisis faced by the firm. And, if promoters regain control, much of the debt their company owes will be forgiven, with the losses being carried by the financial and operational creditors. Recognising the travesty involved, the government was forced to amend the IBC bill to prohibit promoters from bidding under the NCLT process.

74. Why was the IBC Bill amended to stop promoters from regaining control of their companies?
I. The Committee of Creditors did not see the original management fit enough to carry on functioning.
II. The losses would be carried by the financial and operational creditors.
III. It would have led to the promoters regaining control of their companies without repaying the full amount of the loans taken.
(a) Only II (b) Only I and II
(c) Only II and III (d) All of the above

75. Which of the following is/are true as per the passage?
I. Essar Steel evoked interest even from its promoters when it was put up for sale.
II. Bhushan Steel was acquired by the JSW Group for Rs 32,500 crore.
III. The average recovery rate for the 21 banks (public plus private) was 10.8%.
(a) Only II (b) Only I and II
(c) Only II and III (d) Only I and III

76. What was the experience of the IBC process for companies which were of special interest to bidders?
I. The rate of recovery was much better than the average recovery rate.
II. Competition between bidders to take over the defaulting company.
III. The liquidation value of the assets would have been higher than the recovered value.
(a) Only II (b) Only III
(c) Only I and II (d) Only I and III

77. Why was the IBC process combined with legal powers?
I. To enable carrying out resolution or liquidation as per the need of the situation.
II. To decrease the pressure on government to bail banks out.
III. To improve the recovery rates on loans.
(a) Only II (b) Only I and III
(c) Only II and III (d) All of the above

78. Match List I with List II:

List I		List II	
(A)	Section 35 (2AA)	(I)	Payment mad e to certain ins titutions for sc ientific resear ch.
(B)	Section 35 (1) (ii a)	(I I)	Payment mad e to certain ins titutions for re search in socia l sciences.
(C)	Section 35(1) (iii)	(II I)	Payment mad e to a compan y to be used fo r scientific res earch.
(D)	Section 35(1) (ii)	(I V)	Payment mad e to Indian Ins titute of Techn ology for Scien tific Research.

Choose the correct answer from the options given below:
(a) (A) - (IV), (B) - (II), (C) - (III), (D) - (I)
(b) (A) - (IV), (B) - (III), (C) - (II), (D) - (I)
(c) (A) - (I), (B) - (II), (C) - (III), (D) - (IV)
(d) (A) - (I), (B) - (II), (C) - (IV), (D) - (III)

79. Match List I with List II:

List I		List II	
(A)	Sectio n 80 E E	(I)	Deduction in respect of rent paid
(B)	Sectio n 80 GG	(I I)	Deduction in respect of certain do nations for scientific researches
(C)	Sectio n 80 GGA	(II I)	Deduction in respect of interest on loan taken for residential house
(D)	Sectio n 80 E	(I V)	Deduction in respect of payment o f Interest on loan taken for Higher Education.

Choose the correct answer from the options given below:
(a) (A) - (II), (B) - (IV), (C) - (I), (D) - (III)
(b) (A) - (III), (B) - (I), (C) - (II), (D) - (IV)
(c) (A) - (III), (B) - (I), (C) - (IV), (D) - (II)
(d) (A) - (II), (B) - (IV), (C) - (III), (D) - (I)

80. Organizational conflict is the discord that arises when the goals, interests or values of different individuals or groups are incompatible and those individuals or groups block or thwart one another's attempts to achieve their ___________.

(a) Objective (b) Target

(c) Aim (d) Conclusion

// Smart Answer Sheet //

Correct Percentage of students who answered correctly.

Skipped Percentage of students who skipped.

Q.	Ans.	Correct	Skipped	Q.	Ans.	Correct	Skipped	Q.	Ans.	Correct	Skipped
1	C	76.27%	13.86%	2	B	66.79%	30.85%	3	C	41.36%	30.34%
4	B	63.2%	32.8%	5	A	16.1%	79.85%	6	C	21.83%	75.33%
7	B	67.84%	31.85%	8	C	58.33%	36.4%	9	B	87.7%	10.47%
10	C	27.01%	69.22%	11	C	47.95%	50.72%	12	D	53.17%	38.77%
13	B	64.69%	31.35%	14	A	45.74%	37.33%	15	B	41.98%	41.61%
16	C	83.46%	15.48%	17	B	55.29%	30.3%	18	B	44.36%	39.51%
19	A	15.82%	72.6%	20	A	67.59%	30.14%	21	D	32.35%	67.19%
22	D	62.91%	30.68%	23	D	10.13%	84.17%	24	C	54.88%	42.84%
25	A	85.55%	10.25%	26	C	61.4%	33.43%	27	C	28.21%	68.29%
28	C	27.67%	69.33%	29	C	59.08%	35.16%	30	D	43.79%	43.66%
31	D	10.88%	69.5%	32	D	55.11%	38.59%	33	C	40.28%	52.62%
34	B	81.94%	17.52%	35	D	45.65%	34.17%	36	A	53.36%	42.3%
37	A	11.6%	82.66%	38	B	40.13%	43.43%	39	A	49.29%	45.4%
40	A	41.18%	57.17%	41	C	67.63%	31.31%	42	D	62.26%	35.25%
43	A	48.76%	34.2%	44	C	85.57%	13.91%	45	B	52.24%	31.16%
46	A	66.49%	30.51%	47	C	61.83%	37.44%	48	A	66.21%	31.02%
49	A	52.56%	35.77%	50	C	67.07%	30.07%	51	C	43.11%	54.81%
52	C	78.39%	21.56%	53	C	68.06%	31.7%	54	C	49.4%	35.59%
55	A	56.29%	30.99%	56	A	41.2%	34.73%	57	D	47.4%	31.92%
58	D	40.08%	48.63%	59	C	28.61%	68.31%	60	B	55.7%	31.41%
61	D	55.03%	38.98%	62	B	57.57%	35.83%	63	D	52.96%	44.02%
64	D	53.21%	30.37%	65	D	55.76%	32.21%	66	A	46.04%	37.18%
67	D	63.58%	33.36%	68	B	47.95%	45.53%	69	B	61.17%	34.54%
70	B	45.3%	32.81%	71	A	41.84%	37.87%	72	C	51.29%	34.69%
73	A	40.45%	50.17%	74	D	44.08%	53.79%	75	D	57.59%	38.14%
76	C	62.44%	31.28%	77	D	67.2%	31.82%	78	B	58.52%	41.23%
79	B	58.35%	35.17%	80	A	51.01%	40.78%				

// Hints and Solutions //

1(C). The 'law of one price' states that in competitive markets free of transportation costs and barriers to trade, identical products sold in different countries must sell for the same price when their price is expressed in terms of the same currency.

An 'Efficient market' has no impediments to the free flow of goods and services, such as trade barriers.

Both statements are correct.

- The law of one price is an economic concept that states that the price of an identical asset or commodity will have the same price globally, regardless of location, when certain factors are considered.
- The law of one price takes into account a frictionless market, where there are no transaction costs, transportation costs, or legal restrictions, the currency exchange rates are the same, and that there is no price manipulation by buyers or sellers.
- An efficient market has no impediments to the free flow of goods and services, such as trade barriers, and prices reflect all available public information. By comparing the prices of identical products in different currencies, it would be possible to determine the "real" or PPP exchange rate that would exist if markets were efficient.

2(B). A method of sampling that ensures proportional representation of all sections of the population is termed as stratified sampling. Stratified sampling is a type of sampling method in which the total population is divided into smaller groups or strata to complete the sampling process. The strata is formed based on some common characteristics in the population data. After dividing the population into strata, the researcher randomly selects the sample proportionally.

3(C). Marginal Product Curve shows the relation between marginal product and the quantity of the variable input. This curve shows the incremental change in output at each level of a variable input. Its shape is in the form of a hump or an inverse U because of increasing marginal returns in the beginning followed by decreasing and then diminishing marginal returns.

4(B). The significant development in the sphere of foreign exchange was the introduction of the Foreign Exchange Management Act (FEMA). It was introduced to consolidate and amend the law relating to foreign exchange with the objective of facilitating external trade and payments and promoting the orderly development and maintenance of the foreign exchange market in India.

5(A). Reducing the capital of the company is called internal reconstruction. Internal reconstruction of a company is done through the reorganization of its share capital. It is a scheme of reorganization in which all interested parties in the capital structure volunteer to sacrifice.

6(C). As per AS-3 (revised), 'cash' means 'cash in hand' and demand deposits with the bank. The cash flow statement based on AS-3 (revised) represents separately cash generated and used in operating, investing, and financing activities.

7(B). Calculation of net cash flow from financing activities:

Particulars	Rs.

Cash proceeds from the issue of shares (including premium)	1,10,000
Interest paid on Debentures	(10,000)
Redemption of Debenture	(50,000)
Net cash flow from financing activities	**50,000**

- Note: Cash proceeds from the issue of shares (including premium) = Increase in equity share capital of Rs.1,00,000 from previous year to current year + Increase in securities premium of Rs.10,000 from previous year to current year.
- Net cash flow from financing activities = Cash proceeds from the issue of shares (including premium) - Interest paid on Debentures - Redemption of Debenture.

8(C). The nature of Realization account is a Nominal Account. The purpose of preparing a Realization account is to close the dissolved firm's books of accounts and determine profit or loss on the Realization of assets and payment of liabilities. It is put together by:

- Transferring all assets, except cash and bank accounts, to the account's debit side.
- Transferring all liabilities to the credit side of the account except the Partner's Loan Account and the Partners' Capital Accounts.
- Crediting the asset sale receipt to the account.
- Debiting the account for the payment of liabilities.
- Deducting the firm's dissolution expenses.
- The account balance can be either profit or loss. This balance is transferred to the Partners' Capital Accounts in their profit-sharing ratio.
- The partner's capital account on the assets side of a balance sheet is transferred to the Debit of Partner's Capital Account.

9(B). The concept of the law of diminishing returns states that if one factor of production is increased while other factors are held constant, then the output per unit of the variable factor will eventually diminish. Laws of increasing and constant returns are temporary phases of the law of diminishing returns because returns increase and remain the same temporarily, as the business expands.

10(C). A firm producing a large number of products will follow the pricing strategy known as product line pricing. Product line pricing refers to the practice of reviewing and setting prices for multiple products that a company offers in coordination with one another. This strategy aims to maximize the sales of different products by creating more complementary, rather than competing products.

11(C). Regression analysis is a measure of cause and effect relationship. In regression analysis, it's important to specify the relationship between the variables being used. The value of the dependent variable is assumed to be related to the value of the independent variables.

12(D). A probability sampling method is any method of sampling that utilizes some form of random selection. To have a random selection method, you must set up some process or procedure that assures that the different units in your population have equal probabilities of being chosen.

β (Beta) is the probability of Type II error in any hypothesis test–incorrectly failing to reject the null hypothesis.

A structured questionnaire is a document that consists of a set of standardized questions with a fixed scheme, which specifies the exact wording and order of the questions, for gathering information from respondents.

T-tests are a type of parametric method which can be used when the samples satisfy the conditions of normality, equal variance, and independence.

Hence, the correct option (D).

13(B). Convenience sampling: This method is also called chunk. Chunk means that fraction of the population being investigated neither by probability nor by judgment but on the basis of convenience. A sample is drawn from a readily available list at the convenience of the researcher.

14(A). Management is a problem-solving process of effectively achieving the organizational goal through the efficient use of scarce resources in a changing environment.

Different authors define management in different ways:

- Koontz defined management as "the process of defining and maintaining an environment in which individuals, working together in groups, efficiently accomplish selected aims".
- F.W.Taylor defined management as knowing exactly what you want men to do and then seeing that they do it in the best and cheapest way.
- "To manage is to forecast, to plan, to organize, to command, to coordinate and control" is the definition given by Henry Fayol.
- Henri Fayol, a French industrialist is considered the father of the modern theory of general and industrial management. He divided the industrial management activities into six groups and contributed fourteen principles to management.
- Fayol established the pattern upon which our modern concepts of management are built upon.

15(B). Philip Kotler propounded mega-marketing. Mega marketing refers to the marketing activities needed to manage the elements of the firm's external environment and try to control those factors. The marketing tools needed involves the additional use of public relations and power.

16(C). Online marketing is associated with the distribution of goods and services electronically. Online marketing is one of the effective strategies used to build the reputation of a company as well as increase its exposure online. This can be done using a number of internet solutions and tools.

17(B). Modern marketing concepts emphasize customer relationships. If customers are satisfied with the producer's products, then the market image of the producer will be good. This will lead to more profits and growth. Modern marketing is about customer experience at every touchpoint, building relationships with customers, adapting continuously to the new digital landscapes, and marketing across multiple channels to reach different consumers.

18(B). Penetration pricing refers to a marketing strategy used by businesses to attract customers to a new product or service. Penetration pricing is the practice of offering a low price for a new product or service during its initial offering to lure customers away from competitors.

19(A). Right shares issued to existing equity shareholders have the preferential right regarding the payment of retained earnings. A rights issue is an issue of rights to a company's existing shareholders. The benefit of rights offering to shareholders is that shares are generally offered at a discount. Retained earnings are a part of shareholder funds on which right shareholders or equity shareholders have the preferential right.

20(A). Capital gearing ratio is used to show the proportion of fixed interest-bearing capital to funds belonging to the shareholder. It is used to measure the long term solvency of the company.
Fixed asset turnover is used to measure the efficiency with which the firm uses its fixed asset to generate revenue.
Return on equity measures the profitability of the funds invested in the company. In other words, it calculates the percentage of returns generated to equity shareholders.
Acid test or quick ratio is used to measure the short term solvency of the company.

21(D). All the above options are sources of short-term finance. Here, the emphasis is on short-term financings such as trade credit, commercial paper, and other forms of instruments with a maturity structure of one year or less. Short term finance is type of business financing where it is obtained for a year or less. The sources of short term finance are: trade credit, cash advance loan and short term borrowings.

22(D). Human Resource Management (HRM) is the term used to describe formal systems devised for the management of people within an organization. The responsibilities of a human resource manager fall into three major areas: staffing, employee compensation and benefits, and defining/ designing work.

23(D). Unabsorbed Depreciation is that amount of unutilized depreciation which the assessee will not be able to claim as an expense due to lack of sufficient profit in the P&L Account. Such unabsorbed depreciation could not be set off in the same assessment year, It can be set off against any head of income and the remaining balance can be carried off for any number of periods.

24(C). A situation where any advantage given by one member of the WTO to another member is extended to all WTO members is referred to as the most favored nation.
Most-favoured-nation (MFN): treating other people equally. Under the WTO agreements, countries cannot normally discriminate between their trading partners.

25(A). According to D. Katz, morale has four dimensions are:

- Job satisfaction
- Satisfaction with wages and promotional opportunities,
- Identification with the company
- Pride in the workgroup.

26(C). The "Theory of Absolute Cost Advantage" considers the following points:

- The theory of absolute cost advantage explains that a country having an absolute cost advantage in the production of a product on account of greater efficiency should specialize in its production and export.
- It is a two-country framework with two commodities.
- It is a positive-sum game, i.e. both countries are gaining.

27(C). In the Perceived-Value Pricing method, a firm sets the price of a product by considering what product image a customer carries in his mind and how much he is willing to pay for it. In other words, pricing a product on the basis of what the customer is ready to pay for it, is called Perceived-value pricing.

28(C). The product management system often turns out to be costly. One person is appointed to manage each major product. The product-management organization does not replace the functional management organization but rather serves as another layer of management.

29(C). The Goods and Service Tax Act was passed in Parliament on 29th March 2017 and came into effect on 1st July 2017.

- GST was passed as the 101st Amendment Act.

Goods and Services Tax (GST) is an indirect tax that has replaced many indirect taxes in India such as excise duty, VAT, services tax, etc.

- It is based on the principle of destination-based consumption taxation.
- GST is applicable on 'supply' of goods or services as against the past concept on the manufacture of goods or on sale of goods or on provision of services.
- It is a dual GST with the Centre and the States simultaneously levying tax on a common base.
- GST to be levied by the Centre would be called Central GST(CGST) and that to be levied by the States would be called State GST (SGST).
- Import of goods or services would be treated as inter-state supplies and would be subject to IGST in addition to the applicable customs duties.

30(D). Marginal costing is useful in profit planning, it is helpful to determine profitability at a different level of production and sale.
Marginal costing is useful in decision making about fixation of the selling price, export decision, and make or buy decision.
Break-even analysis and P/V ratio are useful techniques of marginal costing.

31(D). Factors influencing the working capital requirement are:

- Market conditions: If the competition is intense, then the company has to spend a lot of money on running advertising campaigns and sales promotions. It will also have to keep more stock and sell on credit. So, it will require more working capital.
- Production policy: A service company usually has a short operating cycle or period. It also sells on a cash basis. So, it requires less working capital. For example, electricity and transport companies.

- Supply conditions: The working capital requirements of the company depends on the conditions of supply. If the supply of raw materials is regular, then the company can keep less inventory (stock). So, it will require less working capital. But, if the supply is irregular then the company has to hold more stock. Therefore, in such a case, it will need more working capital.

32(D). Price elasticity of demand is an indicator of the impact on the demand for a product in relation to its price change.

- Some types of consumer goods show a higher price elasticity of demand than others.
- For example, non-essential goods have a high elasticity of demand, while essential goods or consumer staples have a low elasticity of demand.
- Factors that affect the price elasticity of demand include the availability of competitive substitutes and the brand recognition of products.
- Relatively inelastic demand is one when the percentage change produced in demand is less than the percentage change in the price of a product.
- Price skimming is a product pricing strategy by which a firm charges the highest initial price that customers will pay and then lowers it over time.
- As the demand of the first customers is satisfied and competition enters the market, the firm lowers the price to attract another, a more price-sensitive segment of the population.
- This approach contrasts with the penetration pricing model, which focuses on releasing a lower-priced product to grab as much market share as possible.

33(C). Organizing is the function of management that involves developing an organizational structure and allocating human resources to ensure the accomplishment of objectives. The structure of the organization is the framework within which effort is coordinated.

34(B). The leader who excels as a leader because of his superior knowledge is intellectual leader. Intellectual Leaders are serious, focused, and goal-oriented. They think long-term about their life and enjoy developing big, complex systems. They are theoretical, logical, intelligent, and functionalistic.

35(D). The most common forms of marketing researches conducted in most of the firms are the measurement of market potential and the analysis of market share. The market potential is the entire size of the market for a product at a specific time.
The concept of cognitive dissonance is relevant to study consumer's post-purchase behaviour. The theory of "cognitive dissonance" is of great importance in consumer behaviour and marketers have lots of interest in analyzing the post-purchase behaviour of consumers experienced by them.

36(A). The transfer by a company of one or more of its business divisions to another new set up company is called demerger.
The term 'demerger' simply means one company transferring one or more of its business operations into another company. The company that transfers such business operations is known as the "demerged" company, while the company to which the business is transferred is known as the "resulting" company.

37(A). Economists use the Lerner Index to measure monopoly power, also called market power. The index is the percent markup of price over marginal cost. The Lerner Index is a positive number (L >= 0), increasing in the amount of market power.

38(B). Markup pricing refers to a pricing method in which the fixed amount or the percentage of the cost of the product is added to the product's price to get the selling price of the product. Markup pricing is more common in retailing in which a retailer sells the product to earn a profit.
P = ATC + (m × ATC) is the expression.

39(A). Oligopolistic firms are interdependent in such a way that they all need one another to do well and ensure their own success. Firms are affected not only by their own production/profit decisions but by the same actions of other firms as well.
The Game theory model is the study of how people behave in strategic situations.

40(A). As per section 138 of the Companies Act, 2013, a certain class of companies are required to appoint an internal auditor for conducting an internal audit.
This Internal audit of the company's functions and activities shall be conducted by a chartered accountant, a cost accountant, or such other professional as the Board may determine.

41(C). The gains from international trade depend upon the cost ratios of differences in comparative cost ratios in the two trading countries. The smaller the difference between the exchange rate and cost of production the smaller the gains from trade and vice versa.

42(D). The defenders of the sustainability approach toward Corporate Social Responsibility (CSR) point out that all economic activity exists within a biosphere that supports all life.

- Corporate social responsibility (CSR) is a self-regulating business model that helps a company be socially accountable—to itself, its stakeholders, and the public.
- By practicing corporate social responsibility, also called corporate citizenship, companies can be conscious of the kind of impact they are having on all aspects of society, including economic, social, and environmental.
- To engage in CSR means that, in the ordinary course of business, a company is operating in ways that enhance society and the environment, instead of contributing negatively to them.

43(A). A leader who serves as the head of the family and treats his followers like his family members is paternalistic leader. Paternalistic leadership is a managerial approach that involves a dominant authority figure who acts as a patriarch or matriarch and treats employees and partners as though they are members of a large, extended family. In exchange, the leader expects loyalty and trust from employees, as well as obedience.

44(C). Interest paid on debenture is a liability and it is fixed in nature. In the case of dividends, it is not fixed in nature to pay. Dividends are the appropriation of profits earn by the company on the other hand debenture is a long term liability of a company and its interest is expense not appropriation of profits.

45(B). If goodwill and its full value, raised in the book of a partnership firm at the time of retirement of a partner, is to be written off, then the capital accounts of the remaining partners are debited in the old profit and loss sharing ratio.

46(A). Pure or perfect competition is a theoretical market structure in which all firms sell an identical product (the product is a "commodity" or "homogeneous"). All firms are price takers (they cannot influence the market price of their products). Market share has no influence on prices.
In Monopolistic Competition, a buyer can get a specific type of product only from one producer. In other words, there is product differentiation. The firms have to incur selling expenses since there is product differentiation. The firm can improve or deteriorate the quality of its products too.
Oligopoly is a market structure in which there are a few firms producing a product. When there are few firms in the market, they may collude to set a price or output level for the market in order to maximize industry profits.
In a monopoly, there is a practice of charging different prices for an identical product is called price discrimination. According to Robinson, "Price discrimination is charging different prices for the same product or the same price for the differentiated product."s a single seller of a product called a monopolist.

47(C). The basic assumption of cardinal utility analysis is :
- Rationality of consumer
- Utility cardinally measurable
- The hypothesis of independent utilities

48(A). An F-test (Snedecor and Cochran, 1983) is used to test if the variances of two populations are equal. This test can be a two-tailed test or a one-tailed test. The two-tailed version tests against the alternative that the variances are not equal. The one-tailed version only tests in one direction, that is the variance from the first population is either greater than or less than (but not both) the second population variance. For example, if we are testing a new process, we may only be interested in knowing if the new process is less variable than the old process.

49(A). Matrix organization aims to combine the benefits of decentralization with those of coordination. It usually requires employees from distinct departments to form a group to achieve a specific target.
A functional structure is common in organizations, not divisional structures that have outgrown the entrepreneurial structure. It is appropriate for small companies having few products.

50(C). The degree to which the returns of the two securities change together is reflected by covariance. Covariance is an absolute measure of co-movement between two variables, that is, it reflects the degree to which the returns of the two securities change together.

51(C). Proactive planning involves designing a desired future and then inventing ways to create that future state. Not only is the future a preferred state, but the organization can actively control the outcome. Planners actively shape the future, rather than just trying to get ahead of events outside of their control.

52(C). The job description is a statement of information about the duties and responsibilities of a particular job. whereas job specifications are a statement of information about qualifications, special qualities, skills, and knowledge required for an employee to fit for a job.

53(C). The following are some of Section 87A of the Income Tax Act of 1961 important points:
1. The maximum deduction allowed by this clause is Rs. 2,500 or 100% of the tax liability (whichever is lower).
2. The rebate is available on the total tax amount before the 4% educational cess.
3. Under this clause, only individuals are eligible to get a rebate. Neither businesses nor the Hindu Undivided Family may apply for this rebate.
4. Senior citizens are eligible for a rebate (individuals above the age of 60 years and below 80 years)
5. Individuals who are super senior citizens (those who are over 80 years old) are not qualified for a rebate under Section 87A.
6. This rebate is only available to Indian citizens; NRIs are not allowed rebates under Section 87A.

So, Under Section 87A of the Income Tax Act, 1961, an individual who is resident in India and whose total income does not exceed Rs. 3,50,000 is entitled to claim a rebate up to a maximum of Rs 2500.

54(C). **Merchandise exports** Export merchandising is a method of offering retail goods, not services for sale in a foreign consumer market.
Merchandise imports are defined as goods that add to the stock of material resources in Australia as a result of their movement into the country.
Investment income is income that comes from interest payments, dividends, capital gains collected upon the sale of a security or other assets, and any other profit made through an investment vehicle of any kind. Generally, individuals earn most of their total net income each year through regular employment income.
A balance of payments deficit means the country imports more goods, services, and capital than they export. It must borrow from other countries to pay for its imports. In the long-term, the country becomes a net consumer, not a producer, of the world's economic output.

55(A). In most countries with income taxation, corporate entities are subject to tax on their profits and, in addition, are taxed in the hands of shareholders is known as surcharges.
A surcharge is an additional charge or tax to the tax being already levied. The separate taxation of the incomes of corporations and their shareholders follows the legal principle that corporations and shareholders are distinct entities.

56(A). Profit of the hotel business at Melbourne is taxable in the case of Resident assessee.
Foreign income from a business controlled or professional set up outside India will be taxable only in the hands of resident and ordinarily

resident and not in the hands of a resident but not ordinarily resident or a non-resident person.

57(D). The correct match is (a) - (ii), (b) - (iv), (c) - (i), (d) - (iii).

List - A	List - B
(a) Public Corporation	(i) Artificial juridical person • A **public corporation** established under a special Act of legislature and a body having a juristic personality of its own is known to be **Artificial Juridical Persons**. • Universities are an important example of this category.
(b) Deemed assessee	(ii) Legal representative • Deemed Assessee is an individual who is put in a position to pay taxes for some other person by the legal authorities. • The eldest son or any other legal heir of a deceased individual (who has expired without writing his will) is treated as a Deemed Assessee.
(c) Assessee - in - default	(iii) Person who has not deducted tax at source • Assessee-in-default is a person who has failed to fulfil his statutory obligations as per the income tax act such as not paid taxes to the government or not file his income tax return.
(d) District Board	(iv) Local authority • A local authority is an organization that is officially responsible for all the public services and facilities in a particular area. • A person legally entitled to the control or management of any local or municipal fund, or legally entitled to impose any cess, rate, duty or tax within any local area, and 'funds' used with reference to such local authority.

58(D). Pension is a retirement benefit and it is taxed as salary in the hands of an employee. Family pension is taxable under the head "Income from other sources" u/s 57(ii) a standard deduction shall be allowed to the legal heir @33.33% of such pension or Rs. 15,000, whichever is less.
The person who receives the family pension was not an employee but the dependent of the employee. People eligible for pension/family pension are the person himself, his/her spouse, children below 25 years of age, and unmarried daughter.
Therefore, statement (A) is incorrect and (R) is correct.

59(C). Computation of Income under the head "Salaries"

Particulars	Amount	Amount
i. Basic Salary		2,88,000
ii. Bonus		32,000
iii. Rent-free accommodation: 15% of (salary + bonus) as Mumbai has a population of more than 25 lakhs.		48,000
iv. Employer's contribution to RPF (14% of 2,88,000) Less: Exempt up to 12%	40,320 (34,560)	5,760
v. Interest on RPF (10%) Less: Exempt up to 9.5%	2,000 (1900)	100
Income from salary		3,73,860

Therefore, his income from salary for the A.Y. 2015-16 will be Rs. 3,73,860.

60(B). In tax laws, donation to approved and notified association for scientific research is allowed as 100% of the donation.
Section 80GGA allows deductions for donations made towards scientific research or rural development. This deduction is allowed to all assessees except those who have an income (or loss) from a business and/or a profession.
Mode of payment: Donations can be made in the form of a cheque or by a draft or in cash; however cash donations in excess of Rs 10,000 are not allowed as deductions. 100% of the amount that is donated or contributed is considered eligible for deductions.

61(D). All of the above are the provisions of the Right to Information Act, 2005.
Right to Information (RTI),2005, is an act set up by the Parliament of India that frames the procedures and rules for the right to information to the citizen. RTI is replaced by the Freedom of information act, 2002. The following are the features of the RTI Act:
- It promotes accountability and transparency in every public authority.
- It promotes effective and timely dissemination of correct information by the public authority to any individual.
- It promotes the establishment of district, state, and central level information commission as an appellate body.

62(B). Sales and Goods Act was created from the sections of the Indian Contract Act 1872.
The Indian Contract Act codifies the way we enter into a contract, execute it and the way we implement its provisions. The act is divided into total 266 sections. Important sections among those are:
- Section 1 to 75 – General Provisions
- Section 76 to 123 – Sales of Goods.
- Section 124 to 147 – Indemnity and Guarantee
- Section 148 to 181 – Bailment and Pledges
- Section 182 to 238 – Agency
- Section 239 to 266 – Partnership

In 1930 and 1932 the government separated some sections from the Indian Contract Act and created separate acts to deal with them. These acts are Sale of Goods Act, 1930 and Indian Partnership Act, 1932.

63(D). When ratios are calculated from financial statements of one year, it is termed as Ratio Analysis.
Ratio Analysis refers to the process of establishing financial ratios from a financial statement of one year to find out the financial performance of a

company. Ratio Analysis are classified into three types:
1. Profitability ratios
2. Efficiency / Operating ratios
3. Liquidity ratios

64(D). Non-Banking Financial Companies (NBFCs) are the Financial Intermediaries engaged primarily in the business of accepting Deposits, Lending loans and advances, Leasing, and Hire purchasing.
A Non-Banking Financial Company (NBFC) is a company registered under the Companies Act, 1956 engaged in the business of loans and advances, acquisition of shares/stocks/bonds/debentures/securities issued by Government or local authority or other marketable securities of a like nature, leasing, hire-purchase, insurance business, chit business but does not include any institution whose principal business is that of agriculture activity, industrial activity, purchase or sale of any goods (other than securities) or providing any services and sale/purchase/construction of the immovable property.

65(D). According to the passage, the move of the government regarding demonetization was a complete failure since the stated objective could not be met at the end of the day and actually most of the cash came back to the system. It was a total failure for the move intended to flush out black money from the country.
Among the given options, option (A) is not correct since it is not something that follows from the passage whereas the same can be said regarding options (B) and (C). Coming to option (D), it may sound true but there is no such reference in the passage that the author feels proper homework should be done by the government before launching any scheme of the magnitude of demonetization program.

66(A). Refer to, "The government must not disown its biggest reform attempt or try to sidestep parliamentary scrutiny of the outcomes of demonetisation. Instead, it could focus on fixing the problems that people still face — transactions with Rs 2,000 notes in the absence of Rs1,000 notes are difficult as it is a departure from the currency denomination principle."
It is clear that the government should not disown its mistake in implementing demonetization in the country so that it can take the corrective measures to address the issues that the public still faces in the country with the new currency notes.
Among the given options, only option A can be considered as the correct since it correctly explains the correct course of action that should be followed by the government. Other options are out of context as per the information given in the passage and hence they can be eliminated.

67(D). Refer to, "Even as these issues are sorted out, the larger lesson must be heeded: sudden shocks to the economy don't always yield intended policy objectives."
The summary of the passage is that the government may think that any sudden decision may yield intended policy objectives but it is not always true and it may also be the case that such policy decisions will affect the health of the economy more than contributing to its growth.
Among the given options, option (D) is the correct choice since it perfectly captures the essence of the passage and other options are not relevant as per the information given in the passage.

68(B). Refer to, "True, there have been some benefits. For instance, the number of income tax returns filed has surged a little over the trend growth rate. But surely this could have been achieved by other policy measures. Cashless modes of payment have become more common, but financial savings in the form of currency have also risen, suggesting that people still value cash."
Statement I is correct since people are now more into filing of income tax returns in order to be on the safe side and also to prevent any wrong impression of the income tax department towards them.
Statement II is correct since the citizens are now resorting to the cashless modes of transactions but they still value cash based transactions.
Statement III is not correct since there is no reference in the passage that the RBI has become proactive post demonetization regarding detection of money laundering activities in the country. This can be eliminated.

69(B). NBFC is defined as a company registered under the Companies Act, 2013 and also under the RBI act 1934 under section 45-IA. These type of companies provides banking services without holding any banking license.
NBFCs lend and make investments and hence their activities are akin to that of banks; however, there are a few differences as given below:
i. NBFC cannot accept demand deposits;
ii. NBFCs do not form part of the payment and settlement system and cannot issue cheques drawn on themselves;
iii. the deposit insurance facility of Deposit Insurance and Credit Guarantee Corporation is not available to depositors of NBFCs, unlike in the case of banks.

70(B). RBI is the controller of money supply.
- RBI acts as a banker to the Government of India.
- RBI full form Reserve Bank of India is the Central bank of India.
- It is also known as the Banker's Bank.
- It controls the monetary policy with respect to the national currency, the Indian Rupee.
- RBI is headquartered in Mumbai.
- Reserve Bank of India is entrusted with monetary stability, the management of currency, and the supervision of the financial as well as the payments system.
- Reserve Bank of India is the regulator of the Banking Industries in India.
- It supervises, guides, and regulates all the banks that are operating in our country.

71(A). The following initiatives are taken by the Government of India to tackle the Non-performing assets in their ascending order of chronology:
1. The Debt Recovery Tribunals (DRTs) - 1993
- To decrease the time required for settling cases.
- They are governed by the provisions of the Recovery of Debt Due to Banks and Financial Institutions Act, 1993.
- However, their number is not sufficient therefore they also suffer from time lag and cases are pending for more than 2-3 years in many areas.

2. Credit Information Bureau – 2000
- A good information system is required to prevent loans from falling into bad hands and therefore prevention of NPAs. It helps banks by maintaining and sharing data of individual defaulters and willful defaulters.

3. Compromise Settlement - 2001
- It provides a simple mechanism for recovery of NPA for the advances below Rs. 10 Crores.
- It covers lawsuits with courts and DRTs (Debt Recovery Tribunals) however willful default and fraud cases are excluded.

4. SARFAESI Act – 2002
- The Securitization and Reconstruction of Financial Assets and Enforcement of Security Interest (SARFAESI) Act, 2002 – The Act permits Banks / Financial Institutions to recover their NPAs without the involvement of the Court, through acquiring and disposing of the secured assets in NPA accounts with an outstanding amount of Rs. 1 lakh and above.

5. Corporate Debt Restructuring – 2001
- It is for reducing the burden of the debts on the company by decreasing the rates paid and increasing the time the company has to pay the obligation back.

72(C). The World Trade Organisation (WTO) is the only global international organisation dealing with the rules of trade between nations.
- At its heart are the WTO agreements, negotiated and signed by the bulk of the world's trading nations and ratified in their parliaments.
- The goal is to help producers of goods and services, exporters, and importers conduct their business.
- It officially commenced operations on 1 January 1995, pursuant to the 1994 Marrakesh Agreement, thus replacing the General Agreement on Tariffs and Trade (GATT) that had been established in 1948.

73(A). The explanation of the above ratio:

1. Current Ratio:
- The current ratio compares all of a company's current assets to its current liabilities. These are usually defined as assets that are cash or will be turned into cash in a year or less, and liabilities that will be paid in a year or less.
- The current ratio is sometimes referred to as the "working capital" ratio and helps investors understand more about a company's ability to cover its short-term debt with its current assets.
- Weaknesses of the current ratio include the difficulty of comparing the measure across industry groups, overgeneralization of the specific asset and liability balances, and the lack of trending information.
- Current Ratio= Current Assets/Current Liabilities

2. Debtor turnover ratio :
- While calculating this ratio, only the net credit sales is to be taken into consideration.
- Ideally, a company compares its debtors turnover ratio with the companies that have similar business operations and revenue and lie within the same industry.
- The formula to compute Debtors Turnover Ratio is: Debtors Turnover Ratio = Net Credit Sales/ Average Account Receivable.
    - Where Average Account Receivable includes trade debtors and bill receivables.
    - The higher the Debtors turnover ratio, the better is the credit management of the firm.

3. Interest coverage ratio:
- The interest coverage ratio is used to see how well a firm can pay the interest on outstanding debt.
- Also called the times-interest-earned ratio, this ratio is used by creditors and prospective lenders to assess the risk of lending capital to a firm.
- A higher coverage ratio is better, although the ideal ratio may vary by industry.
- The Formula for the Interest Coverage Ratio: Interest Coverage Ratio=Interest Expense/EBIT
    - Where, EBIT=Earnings before interest and taxes

Therefore, the correct match is:

List I		List II	
a.	Inability to pay interest	i)	Interest coverage ratio
b.	Liquidity crisis	ii)	Current ratio
c.	Inefficient collection of receivable	iii)	Debtor turnover ratio

74(D). Refer to: 'The original IBC bill did not prevent promoters from making bids for resolution at the NCLT. Some justified the Ruia bid on the grounds that extraneous factors may have led to distress for no fault of the original promoters. But, if the Committee of Creditors (CoC) has taken the firm to the NCLT, it is clearly because they saw the incumbent management as incapable of resolving the crisis faced by the firm. And, if promoters regain control, much of the debt their company owes will be forgiven, with the losses being carried by the financial and operational creditors.'
All of the statements are correct.

75(D). Refer to:
"Essar Steel, one of the largest defaulters with around Rs 44,000 crore in questionable debt, when put up for sale, elicited expressions of interest from five bidders.... parties include the Ruias, who are the original promoters of Essar Steel.'
I is correct.
'The acquisition of Bhushan Steel by Tata Steel and of Electrosteel by Vedanta. Bhushan Steel owed its financial creditors around Rs 56,000 crore, whereas the Tata Steel bid returned Rs 35,200 crore upfront to the financial creditors, besides giving them a 12.3% stake in the company in lieu of returning the remaining debt.'
II is incorrect.
'Between April 2014 and December 2017, recovery rates varied from nil to just above 20%, and in the case of another three, the rate ranged between 23% and 29%. The average recovery rate for all 21 banks was a pathetic 10.8%.'
III is correct.

76(C). Refer to:
'The rates of recovery have been rather high. This was true of the acquisition of Bhushan Steel by Tata Steel and of Electrosteel by Vedanta. Bhushan Steel owed its financial creditors around Rs 56,000 crore, whereas the Tata Steel bid returned Rs 35,200 crore upfront to the financial creditors, besides giving them a 12.3% stake in the company in lieu of

returning the remaining debt. That was substantial relative to the estimated liquidation value of Rs 15,000 crore to Rs 20,000 crore, and far better than the average 10% recovery rate reported on aggregate write-offs in the recent past.'
'The evidence that the assets were valuable despite the defaults emerged also from the battle between bidders who were often taken to the courts.'
I and II are correct.
III is opposite of the correct answer and is incorrect.

77(D). Refer to: 'The IBC was combined with legislative amendments that strengthened the powers of the RBI to order the launch of proceedings to recover the loans gone bad. These measures, it was argued, through enforced resolution or liquidation if necessary, offered a way in which the abysmal record of recovery could be corrected and the pressure on the government to bail out banks with taxpayers' money could be reduced. In the case of 11 public sector banks out of a ....The average recovery rate for all 21 banks was a pathetic 10.8%. By facilitating and accelerating the recovery effort, the IBC process was expected to raise the rate significantly.'
As per the fragments highlighted above, all the statements are correct.

78(D). The correct match is given below:

List I		List II	
(A)	Section 35 (2AA)	(IV)	Payment made to Indian Institute of Technology for Scientific Research.
(B)	Section 35 (1) (ii a)	(III)	Payment made to a company to be used for scientific research.
(C)	Section 35(1) (iii)	(II)	Payment made to certain institutions for research in social sciences.
(D)	Section 35(1) (ii)	(I)	Payment made to certain institutions for scientific research.

79(B). The correct match is given below:

List I		List II	
(A)	Section 80 EE	(III)	Deduction in respect of interest on loan taken for residential house
(B)	Section 80 GG	(I)	Deduction in respect of rent paid
(C)	Section 80 GGA	(II)	Deduction in respect of certain donations for scientific researches
(D)	Section 80 E	(IV)	Deduction in respect of payment of Interest on loan taken for Higher Education.

80(A). 3 Views of Conflict: Traditional View, Human Relations View, Interactionist View of Conflict. where each view treats and manages conflict uniquely and differently.

- Organizational conflict is the discord that arises when the goals, interests, or values of different individuals or groups are incompatible and those individuals or groups block or thwart one another's attempts to achieve their objective.
- Conflicts can occur because of the task, relationship, or process-related issues between personnel.
- Conflicts at the organization were perceived or viewed as only a negative object.
- But through the development of "organizational behavior" studies; conflict is now viewed differently and organizations now learned how to manage them.
- But, there is conflict over the role of conflict in groups and organizations.
- Changing Views of Organizational Conflict
- Attitude towards conflict in organizations has changed considerably in the last few decades.
- Once upon a time conflict was considered fully harmful and must be avoided for the betterment of the organization.
- With the passes of time, those views changed largely. Conflict is now an inevitable part of organizations. Its presence is positive in some aspects.
- Here explain the 3 different views on organizational conflicts. With continuous studies and researches in the field of organizational behavior and management, that thinking gradually changed.
- These views advocate the same concept that there are different types of conflicts and not all of them have to be bad and dysfunctional.

Mock Test 03

1. Identify the correct alternative from the statements given below:
Statement (I): Hygiene factors are an intrinsic part of the job carried out by an individual.
Statement (II): Theory 'Y' represents an optimistic view of human nature.
(a) Both statements are correct.
(b) Both statements are incorrect.
(c) Statement I is correct but statement II is incorrect.
(d) Statement I is incorrect but statement II is correct.

2. Investment in which of the following is most risky?
(a) Equity shares (b) Preference shares
(c) Debentures (d) Land

3. Given below are two statements:
Assertion (A): The main objective of audit shifted to ascertaining whether the accounts were true and fair rather than true and correct.
Reason (R): The emphasis of auditing was not on arithmetical accuracy but on a fair representation of the financial efforts.
(a) (A) is correct, but (R) is not correct.
(b) (A) is wrong, and (R) is correct.
(c) Both (A) and (R) are correct, but (R) is not the correct explanation of (A).
(d) Both (A) and (R) are correct, and (R) is the correct explanation of (A).

4. The people to adopt a new product first are called:
(a) early adopters (b) first users
(c) Secondary consumer (d) innovators

5. **Direction** : For the Assertion (A) and Reason (R) given below, choose the correct alternative.
Assertion (A): When two or more investment proposals are mutually exclusive, ranking the proposals on the basis of IRR, NPV and PI methods may give contradictory results.
Reason (R): The contradictory results in the ranking are due to different dimensions relating to the scale of investments, cash flow patterns and project lives.
(a) Both (A) and (R) are true
(b) (A) is true and (R) is a necessary condition, but not a sufficient condition
(c) Both (A) and (R) are false
(d) Both (A) and (R) are true and (R) explains the reason sufficiently

6. Which of the following assumptions is not covered in 'Walter's Model of dividend policy'?
(a) All financing is done through retained earnings.
(b) Firm's business risk does not change due to additional investments.
(c) The firm has an infinite life.
(d) The key variables like EPS and DPS keep on changing.

7. Which of the following emphasises the qualitative aspects of working capital management?
(a) Gross working capital
(b) Quick working capital
(c) Net working capital
(d) None of the above

8. **Direction:** Read the statements carefully and choose the correct answer.
Statements: (I): The greater is the likely level of EBIT than the financial indifference point, the stronger is the case for issuing levered financial plans to maximise the EPS.
Statements (II): The financial break-even point is found at that level of EBIT where the EPS is zero for a particular financial plan.
(a) Both statements are correct
(b) Both statements are incorrect
(c) Statement I is correct but statement II is incorrect
(d) Statement I is incorrect but statement II is correct

9. Which of the following is not a characteristic of non-programmed decisions?
(a) Problems are unique and novel
(b) There are no pre-established policies or procedures to rely on
(c) The conditions for non-programmed decisions are highly certain
(d) These are the responsibility of top management.

10. Which of the following is an example of ethical behaviour of a manager?
(a) Trading stocks on the basis of inside information.
(b) Padding expense accounts
(c) Not divulging trade secrets to competitors
(d) Being severely critical of competitors

11. Match the given lists and select the correct code for the answer.

	List - I		List - II
i.	Debit card	a.	Several storages
i i.	Credit card	b.	Online recovery of the amount
ii i.	Electronic pur se	c.	Image processing use
i v.	Cheque functi on	d.	Revolving credit

(a) i - (c), ii - (a), iii - (d), iv - (b)
(b) i - (a), ii - (b), iii - (d), iv - (c)
(c) i - (d), ii - (c), iii - (a), iv - (b)
(d) i - (d), ii - (c), iii - (b), iv - (a)

12. **Direction** : For the Assertion (A) and Reason (R) given below, choose the correct alternative.
Assertion (A): Most of the development banks in India have set up private commercial banks after the introduction of capital adequacy norms.
Reason (R): Development banks in India have not adhered to their basic objectives.

(a) (A) and (R) both are correct and (R) is the correct explanation of (A).
(b) (A) and (R) both are correct, but (R) is not a correct explanation of (A).
(c) (A) is correct, but (R) is incorrect.
(d) (R) is correct, but (A) is incorrect.

13. The optimum quantity for which an order is placed when materials are to be purchased is -
(a) purchase quantity (b) EBQ
(c) EOQ (d) purchase order

14. Which of the following stands incorrect with respect to the nature of management accounting?
(a) Management accounting mainly works as a service function
(b) It gives information regarding the future as decisions that are taken using management accounting are about the future only
(c) It provides selective information from the available data
(d) It provides management with data and decision

15. When the expected level of EBIT exceeds the indifferent point for two alternative financial plans (Equity financing and Debt financing), then the use of:
(a) Debt financing would be advantageous to increase EPS
(b) Equity financing would be advantageous to maximise EPS
(c) Debt-financing would reduce EPS
(d) Equity financing would keep the EPS constant

16. Match the given lists and select the correct code for the answer:

List - I	List - II
(i) Financial br eak-even point	(a) Rate of discount at which NPV i s zero
(ii) Cost-Volum e-Profit Analysi s	(b) Cost of capital remaining the sa me for different degrees of financia l leverage
(iii) Internal Ra te of Return	(c) Analysis to study the relationsh ip between fixed costs, variable cos ts, sales volume and profits
(iv) Net Operati ng Income App roach	(d) The minimum level of EBIT nee ded to satisfy all fixed financial cha rges

(a) (i) - (d), (ii) - (c), (iii) - (a), (iv) - (b)
(b) (i) - (a), (ii) - (b), (iii) - (c), (iv) - (d)
(c) (i) - (c), (ii) - (d), (iii) - (b), (iv) - (a)
(d) (i) - (a), (ii) - (b), (iii) - (d), (iv) - (c)

17. When a business is purchased, any amount paid in excess of total assets is called:
(a) General reserve (b) Goodwill
(c) Capital reserve (d) Capital loss

18. Which of the following is not a function of Reserve Bank of India?
(a) Creation of Credit
(b) Credit Control
(c) Monetary Policy
(d) Issue of Currency Notes

19. Which of the following is the most important retail marketing decision that a retailer has to make?
(a) Selecting the product assortment
(b) Identifying the target market
(c) Choosing the desired service level
(d) Developing an effective store atmosphere

20. Which of the following elements of the promotion mix do wholesalers primarily use?
(a) Advertising (b) Personal selling
(c) Public relations (d) Trade shows

21. Consider the following statement:
Statement 1: Formula for probable error of correlation coefficient is given by $\text{P. E.} = 0.6745\frac{1-r^2}{\sqrt{N}}$
Statement 2: Range of coefficient of correlation is 0 to 1.
(a) Only statement 1 is correct.
(b) Only statement 2 is correct.
(c) Both statements are correct.
(d) Both statements are incorrect.

22. Complete the statement with the correct option out of the following.
According to Walter, a firm should pay 100% dividend if -
(a) r > k (b) r = k
(c) r < k (d) None of the above

23. In which of the following methods of performance appraisal does the evaluator keep a written record of significant events and behaviour of difficult employees during such events?
(a) Field review method
(b) BARS method
(c) Critical incidents method
(d) Assessment centre method

24. Which of the following statements regarding HRD is incorrect?
(a) It is a reactive function.
(b) It develops all the human resources of the organisation.
(c) It focuses on autonomous workgroups.
(d) It is an integrated system.

25. Which of the following tests are not recommended for the top-level positions?
(a) Presentations
(b) Role plays
(c) Interviews
(d) Leaderless group discussions

26. The main objective of the International Monetary Fund (IMF) is to:
(a) Promote international trade
(b) Help economically backward countries
(c) Set and enforce rules for international trade
(d) Promote international liquidity

27. Which of the following theories says that "to export was good and to be encouraged but to import was bad and to be discouraged"?

(a) Comparative Cost Theory
(b) Theory of Absolute Advantage
(c) Factor Endowment Theory
(d) Mercantilist Theory

28. LIBOR term is used for:
(a) Deposit rate in European market
(b) Interest rate in Euro currency market
(c) Deposit rate applicable to interbank loans in London
(d) Interest rate in Euro bond market

29. Identify the principles of trade policy framework from the followings under the WTO:
(A) Reciprocity and transparent
(B) Benefactory and resilient
(C) Non-discriminatory
(D) Binding and enforceable commitments
(E) Protective and benevolent
Choose the correct answer from the options given below:
(a) (A), (B) and (C) (b) (C), (D) and (E)
(c) (A), (C) and (D) (d) (B), (D) and (E)

30. Adjusting Financial Statements of the company as per price indexes is a practice under:
(a) Inflation Hedging (b) Inflation Accounting
(c) Recession planning (d) Financial Hedging

31. What assumption is being made when we use the t-distribution to perform a hypothesis test?
(a) That the underlying distribution has more than one modal class.
(b) That the underlying population has a constant variance.
(c) That the underlying population has a non-symmetrical distribution.
(d) That the underlying population follows an approximately Normal distribution.

32. Money can be transferred using mobile phones through the service called:
(a) NEFT (b) ECS
(c) IMPS (d) RTGS

33. The concept of MBO originally came from -
(a) F. W. Taylor (b) A. H. Maslow
(c) Henry Fayol (d) Peter F. Drucker

34. Consider the following conditions:
(a) An individual is in India for a period of 182 days in the financial year in which he is getting his salary income.
(b) An individual is in India for a period of 60 days or more during the financial year in which he gets his salary and 365 days or more during 4 years immediately preceding to that financial year.
If one of the above conditions is satisfied, as per the provisions of Income Tax Act, 1961, he is:
(a) Resident but not ordinarily resident of India
(b) Non-resident citizen of India
(c) Resident
(d) An ordinary resident of India

35. Agricultural income is exempted from income tax under which of the following sections of Income Tax Act, 1961?
(a) 2 (1A) (b) 10 (1)
(c) 10 (2) (d) 10 (4)

36. Match the given lists and select the correct code for the answer.

List - I	List - II
(a) When the assessee is in defau lt or is deemed to be in default in making payment of tax, including the tax deducted at source	(i) Section 271 (1) (c)
(b) Failure to pay the advance tax as directed by the assessing office r	(ii) Section 273 (1)
(c) Concealment of particulars of income or furnishing of inaccurat e particulars of income	(iii) Section 201 (1)

(a) (a) - (i), (b) - (ii), (c) - (iii)
(b) (a) - (iii), (b) - (ii), (c) - (i)
(c) (a) - (iii), (b) - (i), (c) - (ii)
(d) (a) - (ii), (b) - (i), (c) - (iii)

37. The stock market theory which states that stocks are in equilibrium and impossible for investors to beat the market is classified as an:
(a) Inefficient market hypothesis
(b) Efficient market hypothesis
(c) Efficient stock hypothesis
(d) Inefficient stock hypothesis

38. The purpose of job evaluation is:
(a) Training (b) Promotion
(c) Wage fixation (d) Transfer

39. Which of the following statements is false?
(a) Nationalisation of commercial banks has achieved its objectives.
(b) Prior to nationalisation, commercial banks in India were generally concerned with profit maximisation only.
(c) Nationalisation has enhanced the efficiency of commercial banks.
(d) Bank nationalisation in India was prompted by the necessity of credit facilities reaching the rural sector and weaker sections of the society.

40. Which of the following is not a category of non-performing assets?
(a) Substandard assets (b) Doubtful debts
(c) Loss assets (d) Devaluated assets

41. As per the Indian Contract Act, an offer is complete when it has been sent by the proposer and acknowledged by the acceptor. The communication of acceptance as against the proposer is complete when:
(a) Offer comes to the knowledge of the person it is made.
(b) Acceptance comes to the knowledge of the

proposer.
(c) When the acceptor receives the offer.
(d) When acceptance is put in transmission so as to be out of his power to withdraw the same.

42. Given below are two statements.
Statement I: GST is the destination-based tax on the consumption of goods and services.
Statement II: 'I' stands for integrated in IGST.
In light of the above statements, choose the correct answer from the options given below:
(a) Only Statement I is true
(b) Only Statement II is true
(c) Both Statements are true
(d) Both Statements are false

43. Which of the following does not fall within the jurisdiction of MRTP Commission?
(a) Prevention of monopolistic trade practices
(b) Prevention of restrictive trade practices
(c) Prohibition of unfair trade practices
(d) Regulation of combinations

44. Who are the customers of cost and management accounting?
(a) Managers (b) Creditors
(c) Lenders (d) Consumers

45. The profits calculated by marginal costing and absorption costing are different because of:
(a) Depreciation on fixed assets
(b) Capital valuation
(c) Valuation of stock
(d) Closing stock

46. X Ltd. purchased land and building worth Rs. 2880000 and in lieu issued debentures of Rs. 100 each at a discount of 4%. The number of debentures issued is-
(a) 28800 (b) 30000
(c) 32000 (d) 34000

47. Which of the following is not a method of forecasting demand?
(a) Collective opinion method
(b) Total outlay method
(c) Expert opinion method
(d) Controlled opinion method

48. When marginal utility is negative, then total utility:
(a) Increases (b) Decreases
(c) Zero (d) Remains constant

49. When goods in the domestic market are sold at a high price and in the foreign market at a low price, it is a situation of:
(a) Dumping (b) Perfect competition
(c) Oligopoly (d) Duopoly

50. Probability sampling and random sampling are:
(a) Anonymous (b) Different terms
(c) Synonymous (d) None of the above

51. Match the following:

List - I	List - II
(a) Smoothed Fr equency Curve	(i) To determine and portray the n umber of proportions of cases
(b) Histogram	(ii) It is one dimensional
(c) Bar diagram	(iii) It is two dimensional
(d) Ogives	(iv) Can be drawn through various points of the polygon

(a) (a) - (i), (b) - (ii), (c) - (iii), (d) - (iv)
(b) (a) - (ii), (b) - (iii), (c) - (i), (d) - (iv)
(c) (a) - (ii), (b) - (iii), (c) - (iv), (d) - (i)
(d) (a) - (iv), (b) - (iii), (c) - (ii), (d) - (i)

52. Hypothesis testing consists of the following steps.
(i) Establish a level of significance, prior to sampling
(ii) Defining the rejection or critical regions
(iii) State the hypothesis
(iv) Determination of a suitable test statistic
Which of the following sequences is correct?
(a) (ii), (iii), (iv), (i) (b) (iii), (i), (iv), (ii)
(c) (iii), (ii), (iv), (i) (d) (iv), (iii), (ii), (i)

53. Which of the following is the process of combining the main industrial unit with all other related units?
(a) Divergent lateral combination
(b) Convergent lateral combination
(c) Horizontal combination
(d) Vertical combination

54. Which of the following represents post-purchase dissatisfaction in marketing?
(a) Caveat emptor (b) Cognitive dissonance
(c) Brand loyalty (d) None of the above

55. The risk associated with the use of fixed cost securities is called:
(a) Operating risk (b) Financial risk
(c) Business risk (d) Composite risk

56. Financial risk means:
(a) Risk of technical insolvency
(b) Magnifying the fluctuation in EBT
(c) Both (A) and (B)
(d) None of the above

57. If the sales are Rs. 6000, variable cost is Rs. 3600, and the fixed cost is Rs. 2000 then the break-even point will be -
(a) Rs. 5000 (b) Rs. 5400
(c) Rs. 6000 (d) Rs. 4000

58. Match List-I with List-II with reference to techniques of risk analysis in capital budgeting.

List-I	List-II
a. Sensitivity analysis	I. Studying Alternatives avail able
b. Simulation analysi s	ii. Monte Carlo
c. Decision Trees	iii. what-if-analysis
d. Certainty equivale nts	iv. Conventional Techniques

Choose the correct code:
(a) a-ii, b-i, c-iv, d-iii (b) a-iii, b-ii, c-i, d-iv
(c) a-iv, b-i, c-ii, d-iii (d) a-iii, b-i, c-ii, d-iv

59. Which of the following test is the non-parametric alternative to the One-way ANOVA?

(a) t-Test (b) Kruskal - Wallis test
(c) Mann Whitney Test (d) Chi Square Test

60. The correct sequence in formation of a contract is:
(a) Offer, acceptance, consideration, agreement
(b) Offer, Consideration, acceptance, agreement
(c) Agreement, consideration, offer, acceptance
(d) Offer, acceptance, agreement, consideration

61. Which is the Act which provides a legal framework for e-Governance in India?
(a) IT (amendment) Act 2008
(b) Indian Penal Code
(c) IT Act 2000
(d) None of the above

62. What is the time limit to get the information under RTI Act 2005?
(a) 15 days (b) 45 days
(c) 60 days (d) 30 days

63. What are the 3 aspects of business?
(a) Project management
(b) Knowledge management
(c) Sales management
(d) All of the above

64. In 'quid-pro-quo', quo stands for:
(a) The knowledge disclosed to the public
(b) The monopoly granted for the term of the patent
(c) The exclusive privilege of making, selling and using the invention
(d) None of the above

65. European Union (EU) organization has its own governing and decision making institutions. Which one of the following is not associated with the EU organization?
(a) The European Council
(b) The European Commission
(c) The European Legislative Council
(d) Court of Justice

66. A list of all the units of population and their description understudy is called?
(a) Frequency Distribution
(b) Sampling frame
(c) Statistic
(d) Parameter

67. **Direction:** The following are the two statements regarding elasticity of demand and its measurement.
Statement I: On every point on the straight line demand curve, the point elasticities are all equal
Statement II: On every point on the rectangular hyperbola shaped demand curve, the point elasticities are not equal
Select the correct option for those below:
(a) Both the statements are correct.
(b) Both the statements are not correct.
(c) Statement I is correct while Statement II is incorrect.
(d) Statement I is incorrect while Statement II is correct.

68. Increasing consumer awareness of a commodity or product, driving product sales and building brand credibility is:
(a) Decision (b) Location
(c) Product (d) Promotion

69. Which of the following statements is/are true with respect to Income Tax?
1. Income tax is levied on the income of individuals.
2. In India, the nature of the income tax is progressive.
3. The first income tax is generally attributed to Egypt.
4. Income tax generally is computed as the product of a tax rate times taxable income.

(a) Only 1 (b) Only 1 and 2
(c) Only 2 and 3 (d) All of the above

70. Which of the following terminology are NOT related to income tax?
1. Tax Deduction and Collection Account Number (TAN)
2. Leave Travel Allowance (LTA)
3. Dearness Allowance (DA)
4. Taxpayer Identification Number (TIN)

(a) Only 1 (b) Only 2
(c) Only 2 and 3 (d) Only 4

Ques (71-74): Direction : Read the passage carefully and select the best answer to each question out of the given five alternatives.

The Reserve Bank of India's Monetary Policy Committee (MPC) on Wednesday left policy rates unchanged at record low levels as it was still unsure about the sustainability of economic recovery due to the second wave of Covid-19 infections.

The central bank, however, announced a bond-buying calendar that will ensure that borrowers reap the benefits of a low-interest rate regime.

The repo rate, the main policy rate (it is the rate at which the RBI lends money to commercial banks), has been retained at 4 percent because the MPC wants to ensure that "the prospects of sustained recovery are well secured". "The renewed jump in Covid-19 infections in certain parts of the country and the associated localized lockdowns could dampen the demand for contact-intensive services, restrain growth impulses, and prolong the return to normalcy. In such an environment, continued policy support remains necessary," the MPC stated.

India recently became the second country after the US to report daily fresh infections of over 100,000.

In Wednesday's statement, the MPC retained its assessment of FY22 GDP growth of 10.5 percent. It also raised its projection for consumer price inflation a bit to 5.2 percent for the first half of the current fiscal year.

The RBI announced a government securities acquisition programme (GSAP), essentially a calendar of its bond-buying programme, starting with Rs 1 lakh crore of securities purchases in the first quarter of the current fiscal year.

This new GSAP programme will run along with the RBI's regular open market operations and other liquidity management facilities, RBI Governor Shaktikanta Das reiterated in a post-policy announcement interaction. Earlier, the central bank had committed that it would purchase not less than Rs 3 lakh crore of bond purchases in FY22.

Meanwhile, the rupee lost 1.5 percent Wednesday, its biggest single-day fall in 20 months, as the RBI laid out plans for the government bond-buying programme.

Government bond yields have been rising sharply since the Centre announced a big borrowing programme for the current fiscal. That, along with the rise in sovereign bond yields in the rest of the world, and inflation fears, meant that the yield on the 10-year benchmark government bond, an average of 5.93 percent between April 2020 and January 2021, had risen to a high of 6.25 percent in March.

Bond yields and prices move in opposite directions — when there is demand for bonds such as due to extra buying from RBI, bond prices go up while yields come down.

Government security yields represent the risk-free rate in the economy and act as a base for all other interest rates. Thus, between February and March-end, yields on AAA corporate bonds (the highest rated) increased by as much as 31 basis points, despite the RBI not increasing rates or withdrawing liquidity.

Corporate bond issuance in February at Rs 45,685 crore moderated from its peak of Rs 88,130 crore recorded in December 2020. In effect, the rising bond yields weakened the central bank's easy monetary stance and it had to do something about it.

The RBI's bond purchase calendar will give confidence to bond market participants that a huge supply of government borrowings will not drive up yields too much. It also supports the easy monetary policy stance at a time when the second wave adds to uncertainty about economic growth and inflation. "The evolving CPI inflation trajectory is likely to be subjected to both upside and downside pressures," said the MPC. It said that the bumper food grain production and imports should keep a lid on food prices but warned about high international commodity prices, increased logistics costs, and heightened inflation expectations of households as risk factors.

The central bank also extended measures to improve credit flow to the economy, some of which were introduced last year to fight the pandemic. It extended its long-term repo operations (lending money to banks), extended refinance facilities for NABARD and SIDBI to help MSMEs, and made it easier for banks to continue lending to sectors such as agriculture and MSMEs via NBFCs.

71. Find the relation between the statements given below:
Statement I: The RBI's bond purchase calendar will give confidence to bond market participants.
Statement II: Bond-buying calendar will ensure that borrowers reap the benefits of a low interest rate regime.
(a) Statement (I) is the cause and Statement (II) is the effect.
(b) Statement (II) is the cause and Statement (I) is the effect.
(c) Both the Statement (I) and Statement (II) are independent causes.
(d) Both the statements (I) and (II) are effects of independent causes.

72. What is the rate of GDP growth that is predicted for FY22?
(a) 5.93% (b) 31%
(c) 5.2% (d) 10.5%

73. Why did the central bank extend the refinance facilities for the SIDBI?
(a) To help the agricultural sectors
(b) To help the MSMEs
(c) It would help to control the inflation of the economy
(d) To increase the demand of corporate bonds

74. What is the rate of the consumer price inflation for the first half of the current fiscal year?
(a) 1.49% (b) 4.5%
(c) 5.2% (d) 5.6%

75. Which two of the following statements are true?
(a) The sum of the deviations from mean (ignoring algebraic signs) is greater than the sum of the deviations from median (ignoring algebraic signs).
(b) Standard deviation is independent of change of origin and change of scale.
(c) In a symmetrical distribution, mean deviation equals 4/5 of standard deviation.
(d) In a symmetrical and bell shaped distribution quartile deviation is 1/3 of standard deviation.
Choose the correct answer from the options given below:
(a) (b) and (d) (b) (a) and (c)
(c) (c) and (d) (d) (a) and (b)

76. The meaning of the acronym HRM is:
(a) Human Relations Management
(b) Humanistic Resource Management
(c) Human Resource Management
(d) Human Resourceful Management

Ques (77-80): Direction: Read the passage carefully and select the best answer to each question out of the given four alternatives.

A tax is an amount of money that governments require to be paid to support the government. Taxes have been around for a long time. In fact, there is a very old saying that in this world nothing is certain but death and taxes. Many centuries ago people were already paying taxes. Six-thousand-year-old clay tablets were found, in what is now modern day Iraq, containing the earliest known tax records.

The early Greeks paid taxes like those that are still enforced today, taxes on what people owned and sold. Roman taxes are mentioned in the Bible, and the fall of the Roman Empire is said to be in part due to the huge burden of taxes Romans imposed on the people. In ancient times, the Chinese civilization had a form of taxation that required that one-tenth of each person's land and what was earned from it belonged to the government. Where there were taxes there always seemed to be the question of whether the taxes were fair. During the Middle Ages, there were many taxes. Every adult had to pay a poll tax , a tax just for being there, and existing as a person. There were also property taxes , even if one did not own property, and part of every person's work or what they grew must go to the Church.

Nobles revolted against King John in 1215 because he asked for payment of new taxes, made current taxes greater, and tried to tax people to pay for a war effort. King John's leadership was not trusted by the people who felt they had no obligation to pay to support this war.

During the Colonial Period settlers went to new lands and these lands became new sources of taxes. Taxes were especially needed to pay for wars. In 1779, the first income tax , a tax on employment income, was used by Great Britain to pay for wars against Napoleon.

The American Revolution was in part caused by what the colonists in America considered unfair taxation. The colonists had to pay taxes to England but were not represented in the English government. Their battle cry was, 'No taxation without representation.'

When the United States was first established there were few taxes. There was not much need as times were peaceful and there was little need to pay for an army. The government was also small and had no great need for extra money.

However, as the country grew there was a greater need for taxes. Citizens who earned a certain amount of money were taxed to pay for the Civil War. This was the first federal income tax. It lasted until the 1870's when it was withdrawn, but new federal taxes , taxes imposed by the national government, went into effect again in 1894.

Today some of our taxes go for protecting our country, helping those in need, keeping us healthy, paying off debts our country owes, and taking care of those who have fought in our wars. Without taxes, governments could not exist. But as history shows us, it is always important for each one of us to make sure that taxes are just, fair and necessary.

77. Which of the following defines taxes?
(a) Extra costs of things
(b) Part of what people owe
(c) Money people don't want to pay
(d) Money that goes to support the government

78. How long have taxes been in existence?
(a) 2000 years (b) 6000 years
(c) 5000 years (d) 4000 years

79. Which of the following tells why the nobles revolted against King John?
(a) He took their land
(b) He made them pay taxes they hated
(c) He didn't give them enough freedom
(d) He wouldn't fight in any wars

80. Which of the following was the battle cry of the American Revolution?
(a) Down with Britain
(b) No tea for me
(c) No taxation without representation
(d) One if by land, two if by sea

// Smart Answer Sheet //

Correct Percentage of students who answered correctly.
Skipped Percentage of students who skipped.

Q.	Ans.	Correct	Skipped	Q.	Ans.	Correct	Skipped	Q.	Ans.	Correct	Skipped
1	D	57.52%	34.05%	2	A	79.07%	11.32%	3	A	54.78%	33.41%
4	D	86.49%	10.95%	5	B	44.3%	39.41%	6	D	55.86%	33.39%
7	C	83.45%	13.34%	8	A	60.15%	35.29%	9	C	84.44%	12.14%
10	C	85.28%	10.95%	11	C	56.32%	42.63%	12	C	68.37%	30.2%
13	C	77.03%	10.82%	14	D	78.64%	20.8%	15	A	80.84%	17.02%
16	A	64.79%	34.37%	17	B	85.69%	13.58%	18	A	12.0%	71.23%
19	B	86.47%	11.37%	20	B	84.9%	13.48%	21	D	30.51%	67.97%
22	C	47.73%	39.54%	23	C	60.04%	31.48%	24	C	87.07%	12.01%
25	B	78.61%	16.23%	26	A	76.53%	21.33%	27	D	86.43%	11.88%
28	C	88.28%	11.44%	29	C	60.2%	32.46%	30	B	46.57%	53.36%
31	D	58.7%	30.29%	32	C	48.46%	38.91%	33	D	88.8%	11.19%
34	C	76.19%	14.14%	35	B	69.21%	30.14%	36	B	58.4%	31.81%
37	B	79.61%	19.39%	38	C	87.74%	10.98%	39	A	22.99%	74.29%
40	D	43.62%	54.31%	41	D	43.8%	38.23%	42	C	63.8%	31.08%
43	D	59.47%	36.94%	44	A	84.5%	13.01%	45	C	55.78%	36.9%
46	B	59.42%	40.11%	47	B	58.29%	32.65%	48	B	87.39%	10.6%
49	A	31.18%	67.94%	50	C	89.0%	10.77%	51	D	28.14%	71.57%
52	B	11.15%	86.59%	53	D	16.33%	82.78%	54	B	82.65%	17.21%
55	B	40.9%	39.21%	56	B	77.64%	16.48%	57	A	46.53%	52.74%
58	B	54.86%	35.27%	59	B	64.91%	34.81%	60	A	46.31%	52.51%
61	C	21.09%	77.85%	62	D	62.11%	37.45%	63	D	86.94%	12.23%
64	B	29.63%	68.49%	65	C	55.98%	32.12%	66	B	63.12%	31.2%
67	B	63.28%	35.5%	68	D	54.37%	35.44%	69	D	62.18%	32.66%
70	D	68.03%	31.28%	71	A	55.77%	35.81%	72	D	48.65%	39.08%
73	B	43.13%	40.43%	74	C	79.96%	12.99%	75	B	66.48%	33.4%
76	C	60.15%	34.3%	77	D	44.36%	35.19%	78	B	69.99%	30.01%
79	B	65.92%	31.81%	80	C	64.78%	33.11%				

// Hints and Solutions //

1(D). Theory Y represents an optimistic and positive view of human nature. Herzberg used the term 'hygiene' to describe factors that cause dissatisfaction in the workplace, are extrinsic and are linked to compensation, job security, organisational politics, working conditions, quality of leadership and relationships between supervisors and subordinates.

2(A). Investment in Equity shares is the most risky. The higher the volatility of a stock, or any asset, the higher its risk. Unit trusts that invest only in equities are higher risk than those that invest in other assets. Their prices move further and the chance of loss is higher.

3(A). In India, the companies Act made audit of company accounts compulsory with the increase in the size of the companies and the volume of transactions. The main objective of audit shifted to ascertaining whether the accounts were true and fair rather than true and correct. So, the emphasis was not on arithmetical accuracy but on a fair representation of the financial efforts.

4(D). The process of adoption over time is typically illustrated as a classical normal distribution or "bell curve". The people to adopt a new product first are called innovators.

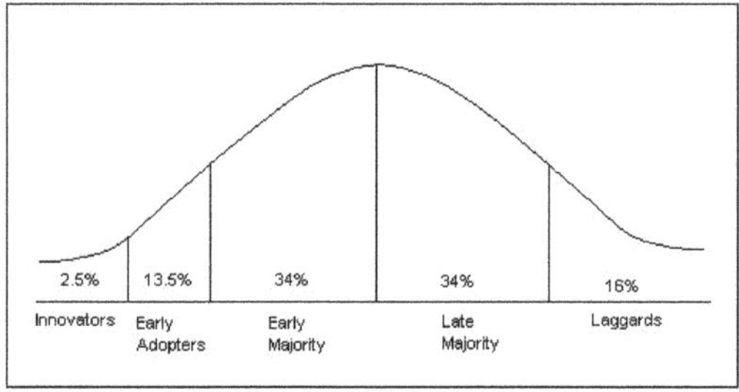

5(B). Mutually exclusive projects are projects in which acceptance of one project excludes the others from consideration. In such a case, the best project is accepted. NPV and IRR conflict, which can sometimes arise in case of mutually exclusive projects, becomes critical. The conflict either arises due to the relative size of the project or due to the different cash flow distribution of the projects.

6(D). Walter's model is based on the following assumptions:
1. The firm finances all investment through retained earnings (debt or new equity is not issued).
2. The firm's internal rate of return (r) and its cost of capital (k) is constant.
3. All earnings are either distributed as dividend or reinvested internally immediately.
4. Initial earnings and dividends never change.
5. The firm has a very long or infinite life.

7(C). Net working capital = Excess of current assets over current liabilities
Net working capital emphasises the qualitative aspects of working capital management, which indicate the firm's ability to meet its operating expenses and short term liabilities.

8(A). The financial break-even point is the level of EBIT where the EPS is zero for a particular given financial plan. Indifference point is the point where the EPS will be the same for the given financial plans irrespective of the debt-equity mix. If the expected level of EBIT exceeds the indifference point, then it would be beneficial to use the fixed charge source of funds to increase the EPS i.e. use of levered funds.

9(C). Non-programmed decisions are used for new, unique, unstructured and badly defined problems which are non-recurring in nature. The top-level of management makes these decisions. There is no pre-established policy to take non-programmed decisions. Therefore, in non-programmed decisions, conditions are highly uncertain because they deal with unusual problems. In this, situations are poorly structured and decisions being made are non-routine and complex.

10(C). A manager's ethical behaviour is required to lead the organization towards success and for the benefit of stakeholders such as employees, investors, creditors, etc., not dividing trade secrets to competitors is one of the ethical behaviours of managers. Keeping trade secrets securely and maintaining secrecy about business practices is an essential element to the success of an organization

11(C). Correct match:

	List - I		List - II
i.	Debit card	d.	Revolving credit
i i.	Credit card	c.	Image processing use
ii i.	Electronic pur se	a.	Several storages
i v.	Cheque functi on	b.	Online recovery of the amount

12(C). The assertion is true that most of the development banks in India have set up private commercial banks after the introduction of capital adequacy norms, but the reason is not true because development banks in India have adhered to their basic objectives.

13(C). The Economic Order Quantity (EOQ) is the number of units that a company should add to inventory with each order to minimise the total costs of inventory. The optimum quantity for which an order is placed when materials are to be purchased is known as Economic Order Quantity (EOQ).

14(D). It provides management with data and decision stands incorrect with respect to the nature of management accounting.
Management accounting is a specialized branch of accounting that helps management in decision-making by supplying relevant accounting information.
This is an accounting branch that records various financial and statistical data and presents this data in form of reports to the internal management for better decision making. This is a form of the service function.

15(A). When the expected level of EBIT exceeds the indifferent point for two alternative financial plans (Equity financing and Debt financing), then the use of debt financing (fixed cost source of the fund) would be advantageous to increase EPS and financial leverage would be favourable. The higher the degree of financial leverage, the more volatile the EPS. Since interest is a fixed expense, leverage magnifies returns and EPS.

16(A). Correct match:

List - I	List - II
(i) Financial b reak-even poi nt	(d) The minimum level of EBIT n eeded to satisfy all fixed financia l charges
(ii) Cost-Volu me-Profit Anal ysis	(c) Analysis to study the relation ship between fixed costs, variabl e costs, sales volume and profits
(iii) Internal R ate of Return	(a) Rate of discount at which NP V is zero
(iv) Net Opera ting Income A pproach	(b) Cost of capital remaining the same for different degrees of fin ancial leverage

17(B). When a business is purchased, any amount paid in excess of the total assets is called goodwill. The goodwill amounts to the excess of the "purchase consideration" (the money paid to purchase the asset or business) over the total value of the assets and liabilities. It is classified as an intangible asset on the balance sheet since it can neither be seen nor touched.

18(A). The functions of RBI includes:
- Credit control: RBI controls the credit created by commercial banks in India, using quantitative and qualitative methods.
- Monetary Policy: Under the Reserve Bank of India, Act,1934 RBI is entrusted with the responsibility of conducting monetary policy.
- Issue of Currency Notes: The Reserve Bank is the nation's sole note issuing authority.

Commercial banks perform the function of credit creation in an economy. Therefore, the money that is created by commercial banks is known as credit money. This is achieved by the commercial banks in the form of purchasing securities and providing loans.
Thus, Creation of credit is not a function of Reserve Bank of India.

19(B). Identifying the target market is the most important retail marketing decision that a retailer has to make. The target market indicates the market where the retailer can sell maximum products, where demand for customers is high and desired profits can be earned.

20(B). Personal selling is the element of promotion mix which wholesalers primarily use. Businesses use personal selling by using a sales force to sell its products, after meeting face to face with customers.

21(D). The probable error of a correlation coefficient can be obtained by applying the following formula:

$$\text{P. E.}\, r = 0.6745\frac{1-r^2}{\sqrt{N}}$$

r = coefficient of correlation

N = number of observations

The correlation coefficient is a statistical measure that calculates the strength of the relationship between the relative movements of two variables. The values range between −1 and 1. A calculated number greater than 1 or less than −1 means that there was an error in the correlation measurement. A correlation of −1 shows a perfect negative correlation, while a correlation of 1.0 shows a perfect positive correlation. A correlation of 0.0 shows no relationship between the movement of the two variables.

22(C). Walter's Model shows the clear relationship between the return on investments or internal rate of return (r) and the cost of capital (K). If r < K, the firm should pay all its earnings to the shareholders in the form of dividends because they have better investment opportunities than a firm.

23(C). The critical incident method of performance appraisal involves identifying and describing specific events (or incidents) where the employee did something really well or something that needs improvement. Thus, in the critical incident method of performance appraisal, the evaluator keeps a written record of significant events and how difficult employees behaved during such events.

24(C). HRD does not focus on autonomous workgroups. HRD focuses on all the human resources of the organisation i.e. individual staff members.

25(B). Role-plays are not recommended for top-level positions. Interviews, presentations and group discussions are mandatorily required for top-level positions.

26(A). The main objective of the International Monetary Fund (IMF) is to promote international trade.

The International Monetary Fund (IMF) is an organisation set up to promote international cooperation and trade, to facilitate the expansion and balanced growth of international trade, to promote exchange stability and to assist in the establishment of a multilateral system of payments.

27(D). The Mercantilist Theory holds that "exports were good and had to be encouraged but imports were bad and had to be discouraged". His policy was to export to the countries he controlled and not to import.

28(C). LIBOR is the London Interbank Offered Rate. It is the average rate of estimated rates by each leading bank in London.

It is the global reference rate for unsecured short-term borrowing in the interbank market. It acts as a benchmark for short-term interest rates. It is used for the pricing of interest rate swaps, currency rate swaps as well as mortgages.

29(C). **World Trade Organisation (WTO):**

- The World Trade Organisation (WTO) is the only global international organisation dealing with the rules of trade between nations.
- At its heart are the WTO agreements, negotiated and signed by the bulk of the world's trading nations and ratified in their parliaments.

Reciprocity: It involves reducing the potential for free riding caused by the MFN rule. It makes it possible to obtain trade liberalisation in exchange for something.

Non-discriminatory: The W.T.O.'s main clause is non-discrimination. This provision grants all members MFN (Most Favoured Nation) status, which mandates that goods made in the other Member Country must be treated equally.

Binding and enforceable commitments: A list of agreements includes the tariff pledges made by WTO members during a multilateral trade negotiation and upon membership.

30(B). Price level Accounting or inflation accounting refers to the adjustment of financial statements of the company as per price indexes cause the historical figures and book values of the statements are no longer of any significance.

31(D). The common assumptions made when doing a t-test include those regarding the scale of measurement, random sampling, normality of data distribution, adequacy of sample size and equality of variance in standard deviation.

32(C). Money can be transferred using mobile phones through the service called IMPS.

Immediate Payment Service is an instant payment inter-bank electronic funds transfer system in India. IMPS offers an inter-bank electronic fund transfer service through mobile phones. The service is available 24×7 throughout the year including bank holidays.

33(D). The concept of MBO originally came from Peter F. Drucker in 1954. Management by Objectives is a personnel management technique where managers and employees work together to set, record and monitor goals for a specific period of time. Organisational goals and planning flow top-down through the organisation and are translated into personal goals for organisational members.

34(C). Residential status's conditions: A person is in India for 182 days or more in that financial year or is in India for 60 days or more during that financial year and has been in India for 365 days or more during 4 previous years immediately preceding the relevant financial year. If an individual satisfies any one of the above conditions, he is treated as a resident of India.

35(B). As per Section 10 (1), agricultural income earned by the taxpayer in India is exempted from tax. Agricultural income is defined under Section 2 (1A) of the Income Tax Act.

36(B). As we know that,

When the assessee is in default or is deemed to be in default in making payment of tax, including the tax deducted at source s ection 201 (1). Penalty u/s

221is payable when an assessee is in default or is deemed to be in default in making the payment of tax and fails to pay the tax.

Failure to pay the advance tax as directed by the assessing officer section 273 (1). Officer, in the course of any proceedings in connection with the regular assessment for any assessment year, is satisfied that any assessee has furnished under clause (a) of sub- section (1) of section 209A a statement of the advance tax payable by him.

The false verification must be held to be indictable on its own terms. section 271 (1) (c), on the contrary, enables the officer to levy penalty only if he is satisfied, in the course of any proceedings, that the assessee has concealed particulars of his income.

37(B). The stock market theory which states that stocks are in equilibrium and impossible for investors to beat the market is classified as an efficient market hypothesis. The efficient-market hypothesis is a hypothesis in financial economics that states that asset prices reflect all available information. A direct implication is that it is impossible to "beat the market" consistently on a risk-adjusted basis since market prices should only react to new information.

38(C). Job evaluation is a systematic way of determining the worth of a job in relation to other jobs to establish the pay structure. The purpose of job evaluation is wage fixation.

39(A). Nationalisation of commercial banks has achieved its objectives is false because the nationalisation of commercial banks has not achieved its objectives yet.

The major objectives of nationalisation were: Increase in efficiency, better management, better service condition, check of undesirable activities, utilisation of savings for productive purposes, to meet the legitimate credit needs of private sector industry and trade, to foster the growth of the new and progressive entrepreneurs, to reduce the regional and sectoral imbalance in banking, etc. It has not achieved some of its objectives, i.e. deterioration in customer service, political interference, social banking inadequate, the window dressing of balance sheet and large scale irregularities.

40(D). Devaluated assets is not a category of non-performing assets.

Debt is classified as NPA when payment due is not paid within 90 days. NPAs are classified into 3 categories:

- Loss assets
- doubtful debts
- Substandard assets

41(D). Section 4 of the Indian Contract Act 1872 states that "The communication of a proposal is complete when it comes to the knowledge of the person to whom it is made. The communication of an acceptance is complete-as against the proposer, when it is put in a course of transmission to him so as to be out of the power of the acceptor; as against the acceptor when it comes to the knowledge of the proposer.

42(C). **Statement I:** GST is the destination-based tax on the consumption of goods and services. GST is a destination-based tax and levied at a single point at the time of consumption of goods or services by the ultimate consumer. GST will be levied on all goods and services except on goods outside the scope of GST, exempted goods & services, and transactions below the threshold limit.

Statement II: 'I' stands for integrated in IGST. Integrated goods and services tax (IGST) would mean the tax levied under the IGST Act on the supply of any goods and/or services in the course of inter-state trade or commerce. Integrated GST shall also apply to the import of goods and services into India.

Thus, both statements are correct.

43(D). Regulation of combination falls under the Competition Act, not under the MRTP Act.

Regulation of combination: Prohibits the formation of combinations that are likely to have an appreciable adverse effect on competition in the relevant market in India and further declares that such combinations should be deemed void.

44(A). Managers are the customers of cost and management accounting because the information is used by managers in making decisions.

45(C). The profits calculated by marginal costing and absorption costing are different because of over and under absorbed overheads and differences in stock valuation. In marginal costing, work in progress and finished stocks are valued at marginal cost, but in absorption costing, they are valued at total production cost. So, profit will differ as different amounts of fixed overheads are considered in two accounts.

46(B). Debentures Value = Rs. 100 .

4% of 100 = Rs. 4 Discount. Debentures are issued at Price of Rs. 96

Number of Debentures issued $= \frac{2880000}{96} = 30000$

Hence, the correct option is (B)

47(B). The total outlay method is not a method of forecasting demand.

The total outlay method is the major method of measuring the price elasticity of demand. It is also generally known as the total expenditure method. In this method, elasticity is measured by comparing the total expenditure of the consumer during the change in the price of commodities.

Methods of forecasting demand are:

- Survey of buyer's intentions
- Collective opinion
- Trend projection
- Executive judgment method
- Controlled experiments
- Expert's opinions

48(B). Total utility is the total satisfaction received from consuming a given total quantity of a good or service, while the marginal utility is the satisfaction gained from consuming another quantity of a good or service. Negative marginal utility is when the consumption of an additional item decreases the total utility.

49(A). Dumping in economics is a kind of predatory pricing, especially in the context of international trade. It occurs when manufacturers export a product to another country at a price below the price charged in its home market or below its cost of production. Therefore, when goods in the domestic market are sold at a high price and in the foreign market at a low price, it is a situation of dumping.

50(C). The probability sampling method is any method of sampling that utilises some form of random selection. In order to have a random selection method, you must set up some process or procedure that assures that the different units in your population have equal probabilities of being chosen. That's why both are synonymous.

51(D). Smooth frequency curve can be drawn through various points of the polygon.
The histogram is two dimensional. Bar diagram is one dimensional. Ogives determine and portray the number of proportions of cases.

52(B). Hypothesis testing consists of the following steps are:
(iii) State the hypothesis
(i) Establish a level of significance, prior to sampling
(iv) Determination of a suitable test statistic
(ii) Defining the rejection or critical regions

53(D). In the case of vertical combination, several independent businesses operating in successive stages in the same industry come together. It is also known as sequence combination, process combination or industry combination.
Hence, the correct option (D).

54(B). Cognitive dissonance is buyer discomfort caused by post-purchase conflict resulting from dissatisfaction.

55(B). The risk associated with the use of fixed cost securities is called financial risk. Financial risk is the possibility of losing money on an investment or business venture. Some more common and distinct financial risks include credit risk, liquidity risk, and operational risk. Financial risk is a type of danger that can result in the loss of capital to interested parties.

56(B). Financial risk is the risk associated with the company having debts and arises when the company is not able to meet its debt obligations. It is related to the debt obligations of the company. Earnings available before interest and tax are used to pay interest on the debts taken, it gives earning before tax. More debts mean more financial risk is associated.

57(A). $\frac{P}{V}$ ratio $= \frac{Contribution}{Sales} \times 100$
Contribution = Sales – Variable cost
$6000 - 3600 = 2400$
$= \frac{2400}{6000} \times 100 = 40\%$
BEP $= \frac{Fixed\ cost}{PV\ ratio}$
$= \frac{2000}{0.4}$
= Rs. 5000

58(B). Risk analysis deals with identifying risks and potential threats to a company's operations and processes and analyzing them to measure their severity of impact and likelihood of occurrence.
Sensitivity analysis: It is the first step to risk analysis. Basically, it is a "What if" analysis testing which variables are important to project outcomes. It applies to all projects with quantified benefits and costs.
Simulation analysis: Monte Carlo simulations are used to model the probability of different outcomes in a process that cannot easily be predicted due to the intervention of random variables.
Decision Trees: This way, they can gauge the different possibilities and prepare for the worst of them, and expect the best.
Certainty equivalents: A number of techniques to handle risk are used by managers in practice. certainty equivalents and paybacks are conventional techniques.

59(B). The Kruskal - Wallis test is the nonparametric equivalent of the one - way ANOVA and essentially tests whether the medians of three or more independent groups are significantly different.

60(A). **The Indian Contract Act, 1872:**
The Indian Contract Act, 1872 defines the term Contract under its section 2(h) as "An agreement enforceable by law". This Act is based upon the principles of English Common Law.
All agreements are contracts if they are made by the free consent of parties that are involved in the contract, for a lawful consideration with a lawful object, and are not hereby expressed to be void.
The contract has four essential elements and is formed in the following sequence:
An offer is made by one party to another to enter into a contract.
The next step is acceptance of that offer by the other party involved.
The special word "consideration" in contract law refers to something that has value in the eyes of the law. Consideration is an essential element to make a contract. must be provided for a contract to be legally binding.
Every promise and every set of promises, forming the consideration for each other, is an agreement.
Therefore, the correct sequence in the formation of a contract is offer, acceptance, consideration, agreement.

61(C). The act that provides the legal framework for e-Governance in India is the IT Act 2000.
With the advent of the Internet and the growing penetration of the Internet in India, the government has commenced shifting its functions to the Internet. India aims to regulate all digital activity through the Information Technology Act 2000. The Act contains detailed provisions regarding electronic governance.

62(D). The Time limit to get the information under RTI Act 2005 is 30 days.
Right to information act refers to an Act which provides for setting out the practical regime of right to information for citizens to secure access to information under the control of public authorities, in order to promote transparency and accountability in the working of every public authority, the constitution of a Central Information Commission and State Information Commissions and for matters connected therewith or incidental thereto.
Section 7(1) of the RTI Act, 2005 obliges PIO to provide information within 30 days (in normal case)/48 hours (in case the information sought pertains to the life and liberty of a person) of the receipt of the request for information.

63(D). 4 aspects of business that affect the growth of a startup:

- Project management
- Knowledge management
- Sales management
- Customer support

64(B). Quid pro quo', quo stands for the monopoly granted for the term of the patent.
"Quid pro quo" means "this for that." It is a phrase used to indicate that something is given in exchange for something else.
In the case of patents, the exchange is that one discloses to the patent office, and therefore to the public, the great invention that they have made or are working on.
In return, the government will give you a limited monopoly on your invention, for about 20 years, to keep competitors at bay.
In other words, the government is dangling this benefit to get one to share their invention ideas with the world.
They hope that this will increase the development of new technologies because ideas are being shared.

65(C). The European Legislative Council is not associated with the EU organization.
The European Union adopts legislation through a variety of legislative procedures. The procedure used for a given legislative proposal depends on the policy area in question.
Most legislation needs to be proposed by the European Commission and approved by the Council of the European Union and European Parliament to become law. Therefore, there is no such body as the European legislative council.

66(B). A list of all the units of population and their description understudy is called a sampling frame.
A sampling frame is the source material or device from which a sample is drawn. It is a list of all those within a population who can be sampled and may include individuals, households, or institutions.

67(B). **Statement I:** On every point on the straight-line demand curve, the point elasticities are all equal.
Statement II: On every point on the rectangular hyperbola shaped demand curve, the point elasticities are not equal.
Elasticity and demand slope: The slope of a straight-line demand curve, one with a constant slope, has constantly changing elasticity. It includes all five elasticity alternatives--perfectly elastic, relatively elastic, unit elastic, relatively inelastic, and perfectly inelastic. No two points on a straight-line demand curve have the same elasticity.
Rectangular hyperbola is a curve under which all rectangular areas are equal. When the elasticity of demand is equal to unity (ed = 1) at all points of the demand curve, then the demand curve is a rectangular hyperbola.

68(D). Increasing consumer awareness of a commodity or product, driving product sales and building brand credibility is Promotion. Promotions refer to the entire set of activities, which communicate the product, brand or service to the user.
There are five primary methods of Promotion:
- Direct selling
- Advertising
- Public relations
- Personal selling
- Sales promotion

69(D). An income tax is a tax imposed on individuals or entities (taxpayers) that varies with respective income or profits (taxable income).
Income tax generally is computed as the product of a tax rate times taxable income. Taxation rates may vary by type or characteristics of the taxpayer.
In India, the nature of the income tax is progressive. The tax rate may increase as taxable income increases (referred to as graduated or progressive rates).
The first income tax is generally attributed to Egypt. In the early days of the Roman Republic, public taxes consisted of modest assessments on owned wealth and property. The tax rate under normal circumstances was 1% and sometimes would climb as high as 3% in situations such as war.
Retirement oriented taxes, such as Social Security or national insurance, also are a type of income tax, though not generally referred to as such.

70(D). Taxpayer Identification Number is a number issued to individuals and organizations to track tax obligations and payments they make to the Internal Revenue Service (IRS). TIN is issued by the federal government. TAN is to be obtained by all persons who are responsible for deducting tax at source (TDS) or who are required to collect tax at source (TCS). Leave Travel Allowance (LTA) is an exemption for allowance/assistance received by the employee from his employer for travelling on leave. Dearness Allowance is paid by the government to its employees as well as a pensioner to offset the impact of inflation.

71(A). According to the passage, "The RBI's bond purchase calendar will give confidence to bond market participants that huge supply of government borrowings will not drive up yields too much."......"The central bank, however, announced a bond-buying calendar which will ensure that borrowers reap the benefits of a low-interest rate regime."
The RBI's bond purchase calendar will give confidence to bond market participants because it will ensure that borrowers reap the benefits of a low-interest rate regime.
So, statement (I) is the cause, and statement (II) is the effect.

72(D). The rate of GDP growth that is predicted for FY22 is 10.5%.
According to the passage, "In Wednesday's statement, the MPC retained its assessment of FY22 GDP growth of 10.5 percent."

73(B). The central bank extends the refinance facilities for the SIDBI to help the MSMEs.
According to the passage, "The central bank also extended measures to improve credit flow to the economy, some of which were introduced last year to fight the pandemic. It extended its long-term repo operations (lending money to banks), extended refinance facilities for NABARD and SIDBI to help MSMEs."

74(C). The rate of consumer price inflation is 5.2% for the first half of the current fiscal year.
According to the passage, "It also raised its projection for consumer price inflation a bit to 5.2 percent for the first half of the current fiscal year."

75(B). Method of Mean Deviation does not give accurate

results. The reason is that the mean deviation gives the best results when deviations are taken from the median. But the median is not a satisfactory measure when the degree of variability in a series is very high. And if we compute mean deviation from mean that is also not desirable because the sum of the deviations from the mean (ignoring signs) is greater than the sum of the deviations from the median (ignoring signs). If the mean deviation is computed from a mode that is also not scientific because the value of mode cannot always be determined. Thus, statement (a) is correct.

In a symmetrical distribution , the mean deviation equals 4/5 of standard deviation. Thus, statement (c) is correct.

76(C). The meaning of the acronym HRM is Human Resource Management. Human resource management (HRM) is the practice of recruiting, hiring, deploying and managing an organization's employees. HRM is really employee management with an emphasis on those employees as assets of the business.

77(D). According to the given passage,

A tax is an amount of money that governments require to be paid to support the government. Taxes have been around for a long time. In fact, there is a very old saying that in this world nothing is certain but death and taxes.

Thus, we can conclude that, taxes are the money that goes to support the government.

78(B). According to the given passage,

Many centuries ago people were already paying taxes. Six-thousand-year-old clay tablets were found, in what is now modern day Iraq, containing the earliest known tax records.

Thus, we can conclude that, 6000 years long have taxes been in existence.

79(B). According to the given passage,

Nobles revolted against King John in 1215 because he asked for payment of new taxes, made current taxes greater, and tried to tax people to pay for a war effort. King John's leadership was not trusted by the people who felt they had no obligation to pay to support this war.

Thus, we can conclude that, the nobles revolted against King John because he made them pay taxes they hated.

80(C). According to the given passage,

The American Revolution was in part caused by what the colonists in America considered unfair taxation. The colonists had to pay taxes to England but were not represented in the English government. Their battle cry was, 'No taxation without representation.'

Thus, we can conclude that, 'No taxation without representation' was the battle cry of the American Revolution.

Mock Test 04

1. Company images and brand equity is the factor affecting business:
(a) Externally (b) Internally
(c) Government Policy (d) None of these

2. When a company taken over another one and clearly becomes the new owner, the action is called
(a) Merger (b) Strategic Alliance
(c) Acquisition (d) None of the above

3. An indent house is one which:
(a) Serves as a middleman between importer and exporter of goods for getting orders
(b) Packs and forwards the goods
(c) Guarantees the payments for good
(d) Performs custom formalities on behalf of importer

4. A letter of credit (L/C) is produced by:
(a) An exporter (b) An importer
(c) Custom authorities (d) Shipping company

5. First Auditor of a Company is appointed by the–
(a) Shareholders (b) Central Government
(c) Company Law(d) Board of Directors
Board

6. Which of the following is not qualified to be a Company Auditor?
(a) A body corporate
(b) An employee of the company
(c) A person who is indebted to the company for an amount exceeding Rs. 1000
(d) All of the above

7. Which of the following statement is correct about the balance of trade?
(a) Balanced balance of trade exports> imports
(b) Adverse balance of trade exports = imports
(c) Favourable balance of trade exports < imports
(d) None of the above

8. The continuous audit is suitable for:
(a) Big institutions (b) Small institutions
(c) General institutions (d) None of the above

9. Social Accounting means:
(a) Accounting for social benefits and social costs
(b) Accounting for Government Revenue & Govt. Cost
(c) Accounting for private revenue and private cost
(d) None of the above

10. The technique of "Carrot and Stick" is used in business organization for__________.
(a) Reducing absenteeism
(b) Motivation
(c) Effective leadership
(d) Rewarding workers

11. The clearing agent is appointed by the-
(a) Shipping company (b) Custom's Authority
(c) Importer (d) Exporter

12. Risk per unit of return or stand-alone risk is represented by-
(a) Coefficient of standard
(b) Coefficient of return
(c) Coefficient of variation
(d) Coefficient of deviation

13. In Marine Insurance, the existence of insurable interest is necessary–
(a) When the loss is caused
(b) When the policy is taken
(c) Both when the policy is taken and when the loss is caused
(d) Throughout the period of contract

14. The policy of 'anticipate no profit and provide for all possible losses' is followed due to–
(a) Convention of consistency
(b) Convention of conservation
(c) Convention of disclosure
(d) None of the above

15. Receipts and Payments Account is prepared by–
(a) Companies
(b) Banks
(c) Partnership firms
(d) Non-trading organizations

16. Audit Programme is prepared by–
(a) The Auditor (b) The Company
(c) Internal Auditor (d) Financial Controller

17. Under the head 'Secured Loans' the following are disclosed:
(a) Loans and Advances from banks
(b) Debentures
(c) Loans and Advances from subsidiaries
(d) Other loans and advances

18. Which of the following statements is incorrect Regarding the sales budget?
(a) Sales budget is a functional budget.
(b) Usually the sales budget is stated in terms of quantity and value.
(c) Starting point of the development of master budget is preparation of sales budget.
(d) Sales budget is based on production budget.

19. Accounting for Intangible Assets are related to:
(a) AS - 10 (b) AS - 12
(c) AS - 24 (d) AS - 26

20. Indian Accounting Standard - 28 is related to:
(a) Accounting for taxes on income
(b) Financial Reporting of Interests in Joint Venture
(c) Impairment of Assets
(d) Provisions, Contingent Liabilities and Contingent Assets

21. Bad loans in banking terminology are generally known as–
(a) BPOs (b) Prime Asset

(c) NPAs (d) CBS

22. An association of cement manufacturers is an example of–
(a) Diagonal combination
(b) Vertical combination
(c) Horizontal combination
(d) Lateral combination

23. The product range is widest in case of–
(a) Chain store (b) Departmental store
(c) Speciality shop (d) One price shop

24. A public corporation is set up–
(a) By Special Act of Parliament
(b) By special order of the Government
(c) Under Indian Companies Act, 1956
(d) By none of the above

25. Financial securities that can be converted into cash at closing to their book value price are classified as:
(a) Inventories
(b) Short-term investments
(c) Cash equivalents
(d) Long-term investments

26. A large amount spent on special advertisement is–
(a) Capital Expenditure
(b) Revenue Expenditure
(c) Revenue Loss
(d) Deferred Revenue Expenditure

27. Which one of the following statements is correct?
(a) Internal audit and Management audit are the same
(b) Internal audit and statutory audit are the same
(c) Internal audit is optional in all cases
(d) Statutory audit of company accounts is compulsory

28. Discounted cash flow analysis is also classified as:
(a) Time value of stock
(b) Time value of money
(c) Time value of bonds
(d) Time value of treasury bonds

29. CHUNK Sampling is known as:
(a) Quota sampling
(b) Convenience sampling
(c) Judgement sampling
(d) Cluster sampling

30. When a population is heterogeneous, it is divided into groups, so that there is homogeneity within the group and heterogeneity between the groups, and some items are selected at random from each group. It is a case of-
(a) Cluster Random Sampling
(b) Systematic Random Sampling
(c) Quota Sampling
(d) Stratified Random Sampling

31. Which one among the following is a small sample?
(a) 5 (b) 10
(c) 29 (d) All the above

32. Which one of the following software is used for Research Analysis?
(a) SAP (b) ERP
(c) SPSS (d) TALLY

33. Classification of respondents only on the basis of gender is an application of:
(a) Ordinal scale (b) Nominal scale
(c) Interval scale (d) Ratio scale

34. Karl Pearson's coefficient of correlation between two variables is:
(a) the product of their standard deviations
(b) the square root of the product of their regression coefficients
(c) the covariance between the variables
(d) None of the above

35. Statistical software packages for research in social sciences include-
(a) SPSS (b) STATA
(c) MiniTab (d) All of the above

36. Given the following tests:
(i) 'Z' test
(ii) 't' test
(iii) F' test
(iv) 'χ^2' test
The concept of degrees of freedom is associated with:
(a) (i) and (ii) (b) (ii) and (iii)
(c) (iii) and (iv) (d) (ii), (iii) and (iv)

37. The structure of an organization in which there is a separation of ownership and management is called:
(a) Sole proprietorship (b) Partnership
(c) Company (d) Cooperative society

38. When a person transacts with a company on matters which is beyond the power of the company, the person will be governed by the Doctrine of-
(a) Management by Exception
(b) Constructive Notice
(c) Indoor Management
(d) Self Management

39. The appropriate sequence of the formation of a company are in the following order:
(a) Promotion, the commencement of business and incorporation
(b) Promotion, incorporation, capital subscription and commencement of business
(c) Capital subscription, promotion, incorporation and commencement of business
(d) Incorporation, capital subscription, the commencement of business and promotion

40. Delegation of authority makes the size of the organization:
(a) Smaller organization
(b) Larger organization
(c) Very big organization
(d) It does not affect the size of the organization

41. **Direction:** Given below are two statements - one is labelled as Assertion (A) and the other is labelled as Reason (R). Choose the correct option.
Assertion (A): MBO is an effective way of planning and

organizing the work.
Reason (R): Employees participate in setting the objectives.
(a) Both (A) and (R) are true.
(b) Both (A) and (R) are false.
(c) (A) is true, but (R) is false.
(d) (A) is false, but (R) is correct.

42. 'No ideas are ever criticized' and 'the more radical the ideas are the better' – are the rules of which is the decision-making process?
(a) Programmed decision-making
(b) Non-programmed decision making
(c) Brainstorming
(d) Group discussion

43. The people to adopt a new product first are called-
(a) Early adopters (b) First users
(c) Initial adopters (d) Innovators

44. Manufacturers of cars and motorcycles typically seek_____ distribution.
(a) selective (b) intensive
(c) exclusive (d) restrictive

45. Which method of setting an advertising budget is most scientific and logical?
(a) All-you-can afford method
(b) Competitive parity method
(c) Objective-and-task method
(d) Percentage-of-sales method

46. Which of the following is not the major component of holistic marketing?
(a) Relationship marketing
(b) Integrated marketing
(c) Customer satisfaction
(d) Socially-responsible marketing

47. Which of the legislations listed below do not form part of the marketing environment of India?
(a) The Drugs and Cosmetics Act, 1940
(b) The Prevention of Food and Adulteration Act, 1954
(c) The Monopolies and Restrictive Trade Practices Act, 1969
(d) Both (B) and (C)

48. The set of all actual and potential buyers of a product is known as-
(a) Customer group (b) Industry
(c) Market (d) None of the above

49. In case of every sale, there is an implied condition that the seller has the right to:
(a) Acquire the goods (b) Recover the price
(c) Sell the goods (d) Refuse to sell goods.

50. Given below are two statements.
Statement I: A sale has the immediate effect of transferring property, whereas in an agreement to sell the property is to pass at some future time.
Statement II: A sale makes the buyer the owner of goods but an agreement to sale does not make the buyer the owner of goods.
In light of the above statements, choose the correct answer from the options given below:
(a) Only Statement I is true
(b) Only Statement II is true
(c) Both Statements are true
(d) Both statements are false

51. Which of the following is/are true about the Negotiable Instruments Act, the Promissory Note is:
(I) Definition of Promissory Note is given in section 8 of the Negotiable Instrument Act
(II) Containing an unconditional undertaking
(III) To pay a certain sum of money only to a specific person or the bearer
(IV) The seller is bound to accept the promissory note
(V) A document was written and signed by the payer/maker
(a) (I), (II) and (III) (b) (II), (III) and (V)
(c) (II), (III), and (IV) (d) (I), (III) and (IV)

52. The registered office clause of memorandum of association contains-
(a) The name of the city/town only and not that of the state
(b) The complete postal address
(c) The name of the state in which the registered office of the company is to be situated
(d) The name of the registrar of companies

53. What is consent under the Indian Contract Act, 1872:
(a) When acceptance of the proposal is made by the party to whom the proposal is made
(b) When the acceptance is made by another person other than the person to whom the proposal is made
(c) When they agree upon the same thing in the same sense
(d) When both the parties agree upon a thing in the way it is understood by them

54. **Direction:** Match the columns and choose the correct pairs from the options.

Column-1	Column-2
A. Competition Act	E. 2005
B. Right to Information Act	F. 1930
C. Indian Contract Act	G. 1872
D. Sales of Goods Act	H. 2002

(a) A-G, B-E, C-F, D-H (b) A-H, B-E, C-G, D-F
(c) A-E, B-F, C-G, D-H (d) A-F, B-H, C-E, D-G

55. Tax is imposed irrespective of the exact amount of service rendered to the taxpayer in return and not imposed as a ________ for any legal offence.
(a) penalty (b) rule
(c) law (d) cost

56. Which types of taxes are levied directly on the entity meant to bear the burden?
(a) Indirect Tax (b) Direct Tax
(c) Custom Tax (d) Export Duty

57. The charging section of the income under the head capital gains is:
(a) Section 15 (b) Section 10
(c) Section 17 (d) Section 45 (2)

58. The income of the previous year is taxed in at the rates prescribed by the relevant finance Act-

(a) assessment year (b) previous year
(c) action year (d) last year

59. In most countries with income taxation, corporate entities are subject to tax on their profits and, in addition, are taxed in the hands of shareholders-
(a) surcharges (b) dividends
(c) shares (d) assets

60. The base of the corporate income tax is commonly the accounting profits derived with reference to ____.
(a) historical costs (b) records
(c) registers (d) databases

61. Rent received by an original tenant from sub-tenant is taxable under the head________.
(a) Income from House Property
(b) Income from Other Sources
(c) Income from Capital Gain
(d) None of the above

62. Which of the following is a part of Tele - Marketing?
(a) Viral marketing
(b) Social marketing
(c) Direct marketing
(d) Relationship marketing

63. The National Bank for Agriculture and Rural Development (NABARD) is a top-level development financial institution in India, established in __ to provide agricultural and rural credit.
(a) In 1990 (b) In 1982
(c) In 1985 (d) In 1987

64. The Committee of Directors of state-owned Indian Bank has given approval for raising fund up to what amount through share sale?
(a) 2000 crore (b) 1500 crore
(c) 4000 crore (d) 1000 crore

65. Which financial statement presents a summary of the Assets, Liabilities, and Owners' Equity of a firm?
(a) General ledger (b) Work sheet
(c) Balance sheet (d) None of these

66. If the impact and incidence of tax is imposed on one and the same person, then it is known as:
(a) Direct Tax (b) Indirect Tax
(c) Progressive Tax (d) Regressive Tax

67. ANBC is the net bank credit plus investments made by banks in non-SLR bonds held in the held-to-maturity category or credit equivalent amount of off-balance-sheet exposure, whichever is higher. What does 'C' stand-in ANBC?
(a) Credit (b) Cash
(c) Category (d) Commerce

68. ____________ is a part of business environment.
(a) Public debt
(b) Lifestyle of people
(c) Technological changes
(d) Level of education

69. Liberalization, globalization and privatization are the aims of:
(a) Economic planning
(b) Land reforms
(c) Socialistic pattern of society
(d) Economic reforms

70. Demand for LED TV are increasing day by day. Thus, TV manufacturers have started making LED TVs instead of LCD. Identify the significance of business environment being portrayed in the given case.
(a) Helpful in tapping useful resources
(b) Helps the firm to identify threats and early warning signals
(c) Helps in coping with rapid changes
(d) All of the above

71. ____________ indicates the importance of business environment.
(a) Identification
(b) Improvement in performance
(c) Coping with rapid changes
(d) All of the above

72. Which of the following item provides the important function of shielding part of income from taxes?
(a) Inventory (b) Supplies
(c) Machinery (d) Depreciation

Ques (73-76): Direction: Read the following passage and solve the question based on it.

While hotels have traditionally held a firm grip on the market of vacation-goers, the emergence of companies fostering short-term rentals are dramatically changing the landscape of the travel industry. Before the advent of the modern online forum, short-term rentals were an arrangement limited by sheer logistics. Information about the availability of (and desire for) a short-term rental was difficult to transmit and share. However, with the current explosion of social media and cyber enterprise, the business model of short-term rentals has blossomed.

In 2011, 40% of travelers reported that they would be staying in a short-term rental during the year, as opposed to a traditional hotel. By 2013, this figure had jumped up to a staggering 49%. The short-term rental business is a $24 billion market, holding 8% of the total market of U.S. travel. Rapidly expanding and growing with the innovations of creative renters, the question that hangs in the air is what this means for communities. Short-term rentals have had a polarizing effect in many ways, becoming a source of joy for venturists and cause of dismay for many homeowners.

There have been incredible scandals in which short-term renters have abused the property loaned to them, causing thousands of dollars' worth of property damage. Other accusations include disturbing the peace and the commission of criminal acts. Homeowners' Associations (HOAs) have been up in arms, and the legal backlash has been significant. New York enacted firm restrictions on short-term renters, and many HOAs now embed limits on the purposes that a space may be used for, barring short-term rentals.

However, this reaction is an over-reaction, and a detrimental one at that. Cities and towns that set hard limits against short-term rentals are halting the economic growth that would otherwise accompany them. Vacationers are likely to be deterred from venturing out to towns that have banned more affordable short-term rentals. While some vacationers might opt to stay at a hotel in desirable locations, as the short-term rental industry continues to grow, it will become more and more likely that vacation-goers will simply choose alternative destinations that actually allow for short-term rentals.

This is not to say, however, that short-term rentals should be completely unregulated. The key is imposing useful regulations that are mutually beneficial to both communities and to the proprietors of short-term rentals. One potential solution would be to impose reasonable taxes on visitors that use short-term rentals; having requirements for minimum stays could also ensure more consistency for the communities. This also has the added benefit of generating income for towns and cities. There is no reason why communities should see the short-term rental industry as an adversary, when it can just as easily be made into an ally.

73. The purpose of this passage is to ________.
- (a) rationalize a negative phenomenon
- (b) point out the weaknesses in a widely accepted point of view
- (c) provide an objective and unbiased point of view on a complex topic
- (d) advocate for a particular position

74. The author would most likely agree with which of the following statements?
- (a) In general, regulations have proven to do a disservice to travel industry, as the red tape prevents commerce from moving freely, and discourages travel as a whole.
- (b) Although short-term rentals are popular right now, it is likely that they will diminish in value as more restrictions are enstated against them.
- (c) Communities should see short-term rentals as an adversary, when they can just as easily be made an ally.
- (d) While short-term rentals and communities would mutually benefit from regulations, a hard ban against them would be counterproductive.

75. Which of the following most likely explains why Homeowners' Associations do not tend to support short-term rentals?
- (a) Homeowners' Associations see short-term rentals as being competition for the market of vacationers.
- (b) Short-term rentals do not confer a benefit on the Homeowners' Association that is comparable to that conferred on the proprietor of a short-term rental.
- (c) Short-term rentals, due to the transitory nature of their inhabitants, can make the members of a community feel uncomfortable, thereby negatively impacting the Homeowners' Association.
- (d) Short-term rentals directly confer extra fees on Homeowners' Associations.

76. The primary purpose of the second paragraph is to ________.
- (a) Argue that short-term rentals have reached their peak, and that they will never command more eminence than that which they currently have.
- (b) Convince the reader that short-term rentals are the most significant development in the realm in which the housing industry and the travel industry intersect.
- (c) Emphasize the impact that short-term rentals have had on the travel industry, thereby transitioning betwen the first and third paragraphs.
- (d) Provide a roadmap for the rest of the passage, given that the first paragraph served as an introductory paragraph to acquaint the reader with the topic.

77. The demand for necessities is usually:
- (a) Highly elastic
- (b) Highly inelastic
- (c) Unit elasticity
- (d) Relatively inelastic

78. When supply of a commodity decreases on a fall in its price, its is called:
- (a) Expansion of supply
- (b) Increase in supply
- (c) Contraction of supply
- (d) Decrease in supply

79. Which utility approach suggests that utility can be measured and quantified?
- (a) Ordinal
- (b) Cardinal
- (c) Diminishing marginal utility
- (d) None of these

80. ________ of a commodity is the additional utility derived by a consumer, by consuming one more unit of that commodity.
- (a) Marginal utility
- (b) Total utility
- (c) Average utility
- (d) Maximum utility

// Smart Answer Sheet //

Correct Percentage of students who answered correctly.

Skipped Percentage of students who skipped.

Q.	Ans.	Correct	Skipped	Q.	Ans.	Correct	Skipped	Q.	Ans.	Correct	Skipped
1	A	62.87%	37.01%	2	C	88.38%	11.09%	3	A	52.04%	42.42%
4	B	48.43%	45.85%	5	D	58.09%	32.95%	6	D	12.82%	81.94%
7	D	16.44%	73.11%	8	A	21.45%	73.31%	9	A	50.45%	48.06%
10	B	83.84%	12.39%	11	D	86.06%	11.27%	12	C	48.87%	32.55%
13	A	82.8%	12.89%	14	B	57.7%	38.59%	15	D	81.66%	15.01%
16	A	78.93%	16.02%	17	D	66.34%	33.59%	18	D	65.33%	33.28%
19	D	45.99%	48.83%	20	C	48.69%	49.95%	21	C	62.56%	37.2%
22	C	49.18%	36.6%	23	B	43.97%	30.72%	24	B	87.08%	12.75%
25	C	89.22%	10.05%	26	D	66.52%	33.34%	27	D	40.93%	37.55%
28	B	69.64%	30.08%	29	B	55.68%	32.89%	30	D	61.85%	30.35%
31	D	76.55%	11.09%	32	C	80.46%	19.04%	33	B	89.69%	10.03%
34	B	89.35%	10.49%	35	A	60.74%	37.31%	36	D	77.93%	21.77%
37	C	68.64%	30.24%	38	B	29.45%	69.6%	39	B	55.15%	44.65%
40	B	40.32%	57.97%	41	C	27.83%	69.77%	42	C	58.74%	36.41%
43	D	62.17%	30.31%	44	C	31.67%	67.99%	45	C	82.0%	16.3%
46	C	17.21%	76.52%	47	A	56.14%	40.92%	48	C	64.91%	32.03%
49	C	68.93%		50	C	25.77%		51	B	79.32%	

		30.77%			70.85%			10.13%
52	C	81.35% 16.88%	53	C	47.85% 38.04%	54	B	79.31% 11.01%
55	A	43.29% 41.77%	56	B	60.56% 34.22%	57	D	80.84% 16.53%
58	A	83.12% 11.82%	59	A	44.4% 54.14%	60	A	86.27% 10.72%
61	B	84.79% 13.9%	62	C	53.67% 43.98%	63	B	62.46% 37.49%
64	C	49.76% 39.25%	65	C	82.27% 14.63%	66	A	63.59% 31.93%
67	A	80.24% 16.01%	68	A	79.13% 12.66%	69	D	63.18% 30.59%
70	D	13.42% 74.19%	71	D	69.57% 30.36%	72	D	58.91% 31.85%
73	D	63.96% 33.27%	74	D	25.96% 73.98%	75	C	55.92% 37.14%
76	C	60.78% 36.78%	77	B	55.4% 37.47%	78	C	52.62% 37.1%
79	B	59.2% 36.34%	80	A	57.66% 33.88%			

// Hints and Solutions //

1(A). Company images and brand equity is the factor affecting business externally.

Company Image:

1. A company identity or company image is the manner in which a corporation, firm, or business enterprise presents itself to the public (such as customers and investors as well as employees).
2. The company identity is typically visualized by branding and with the use of trademarks, but it can also include things like product design, advertising, public relations, etc.
3. Company identity is a primary goal of corporate communications, in order to maintain and build the identity to accord with and facilitate the corporate business objectives.

Brand Equity:

1. Brand equity is a phrase used in the marketing industry that refers to the perceived worth of a brand in and of itself i.e., the social value of a well-known brand name.
2. It is based on the idea that the owner of a well-known brand name can generate more revenue simply from brand recognition, as consumers perceive the products of well-known brands as better than those of lesser-known brands.
3. In other words, brand equity refers to "the branding of a product name on an attention-deficit public."
4. Companies can create brand equity for their products by making them memorable, easily recognizable, and superior in quality and reliability.
5. Since both company image and brand equity mainly affect the perception of external stakeholders like consumers and investors, they affect business externally.

2(C). When a company taken over another one and clearly becomes the new owner, the action is called Acquisition.

Acquisition:

1. An acquisition is when one company purchases most or all of another company's shares to gain control of that company.
2. Purchasing more than 50% of a target firm's stock and other assets allows the acquirer to make decisions about the newly acquired assets without the approval of the company's shareholders.
3. When one company takes over another entity, and establishes itself as the new owner, the purchase is called an acquisition.

3(A). An indent house is one that serves as a middleman between importer and exporter of goods for getting orders.

Indent House import of goods from a foreign country can be affected in two ways. The import of goods can take place directly or through a middleman. The import of goods through an intermediary is called an Indent House. Indent Houses are of two types. They may be representative or agents of foreign producers or exporters or they may be independent firms engaged in foreign trade. At the time of securing order, the indent firm requests the merchant to sign an Indent Form which services as a letter of authority by the merchant to the Indent House to go for an order of the specified items stated in the form.

4(B). A letter of credit (L/C) is produced by an importer.

A Letter of Credit is a written undertaking by the Importer's bank, known as the Issuing Bank, on behalf of its customer, the Importer (Applicant), promising to effect payment in favour of the Exporter (Beneficiary) up to a stated sum of money, within a prescribed time limit and against stipulated documents. A key principle underlying Letters of Credit is that banks deal only in documents and not in goods. The decision to pay under a Letter of Credit will be based entirely on whether the documents presented to the bank appear on their face to be in accordance with the terms and conditions of the Letter of Credit. It would be prohibitive for the banks to physically check whether all merchandise has been shipped exactly as per each letter of Credit.

The documentary credit letter of credit or commercial letter of credit is an arrangement whereby the applicant (the importer) requests and instructs the issuing bank (the importer's bank) or the issuing bank acting on its own behalf-

Pays the beneficiary (the exporter) or accepts and pays the draft (bill of exchange) drawn by the beneficiary, or authorizes the advising bank or the nominated bank to pay the beneficiary or to accept and pay the draft drawn by the beneficiary, or authorizes the advising bank or the nominated bank to negotiate.

5(D). The First auditor of a company, other than a Government Company, shall be appointed by the BOARD OF DIRECTORS WITHIN THIRTY DAYS OF THE DATE OF INCORPORATION of a company. The auditor so appointed, shall hold office until the conclusion of the first annual general meeting.

IF THE BOARD FAILS to appoint the first auditor, it shall inform the MEMBER of the company, who shall within 90 days at an Extra-Ordinary General Meeting appoint an auditor.

6(D). The following persons shall not be qualified for appointment as the auditor of a company:

1) A body is corporate.

2) An officer or employee of the company.

A person who is a partner or who is in the employment of an officer or employee of the company.

4) A person who is indebted to the company for an amount exceeding Rs. 1000.

5) A person who has given any guarantee or security in connection with the indebtedness of any third person to the company for an amount exceeding Rs. 1,000.

A person who is disqualified for appointment as auditor of the company's subsidiary or holding company or a subsidiary of that company's holding company, cannot be appointed auditor of the company.

If an auditor after his appointment suffers from any of the disqualifications, he shall be deemed to have vacated his office as an auditor from the date he has become so disqualified.

7(D). **Balance of trade:**

- The difference between a nation's imports of goods and services and its exports of them is named as Balance of Trade.
- It is the most important element of the Balance of payments.
- There are mainly three assumptions or possibilities exists in the balance of trade are as follows:

1. Balanced balance of trade i.e. exports = imports.
2. Favourable balance of trade i.e. exports > imports.
3. Adverse balance of trade i.e. exports < imports.

Points that can influence the balance of trade include:

- The value of production (land, labour, capital, taxes, etc.) in the exporting economy.
- The cost and availability of raw materials and intermediate goods.
- Currency exchange cost movements.
- Non-tariff barriers such as environmental and health standards.
- Prices of goods i.e. manufactured at home.

8(A). The continuous audit is suitable for organisations where business is very large and large numbers of transactions are needed to be checked. So, it will be suitable for big institutions.

Continuous auditing is an automatic method used to perform auditing activities, such as control and risk assessments, on a more frequent basis. Technology plays a key role in continuous audit activities by helping to automate the identification of exceptions or anomalies, analyze patterns within the digits of key numeric fields, review trends, and test controls, among other activities.

The "continuous" aspect of continuous auditing and reporting refers to the real-time or near real-time capability for financial information to be checked and shared. Not only does it indicate that the integrity of information can be evaluated at any given point of time, it also means that the information is able to be verified constantly for errors, fraud, and inefficiencies. It is the most detailed audit.

Each instance of continuous auditing has its own pulse. The time frame selected for evaluation depends largely on the frequency of updates within the accounting information systems. Analysis of the data may be performed continuously, hourly, daily, weekly, monthly, etc. depending on the nature of the underlying business cycle for a given assertion.

9(A). Social Accounting is the process of measuring, monitoring, and reporting to stakeholders the social and environmental effects of an organization's actions.

The Social Audit Network (SAN) outlines social accounting as:

"The process whereby the organisation collects, analyses and interprets descriptive, quantitative and qualitative information in order to produce an account of its performance."

10(B). "Carrot and Stick" Approach of Motivation is a traditional motivation theory that asserts, in motivating people to elicit desired behaviours, sometimes the rewards are given in the form of money, promotion, and any other financial or non-financial benefits and sometimes the punishments are exerted to push an individual towards the desired behaviour.

11(D). The clearing agent is appointed by the exporter. Clearing and forwarding agents, also known as freight forwarders, perform a number of functions on behalf of the exporter. They provide specialized help in the exporter's warehouse to the importer's warehouse by undertaking the procedural and documentary formalities lie helps in packing, marking, and labeling of consignment, arrangement for transport to the port arrangement for shipment overseas, and customs clearance of cargo, procurement of transport and other documents. However, the main function of the agent is to obtain customs clearance of goods, ship them and procure the relevant transport document (Bill of Lading or Airway Bill).

12(C). Risk per unit of return or stand alone risk is represented by coefficient of variation. The coefficient of variation (CV) is a statistical measure of the dispersion of data points in a data series around the mean.

13(A). In Marine Insurance, the existence of insurable interest is necessary when the loss is caused.

If an individual wants to ensure property, he/she must have an insurable interest in the property; i.e. loss or damage to the property should affect the person financially.

Marine insurance is based on the insurable interest in the property. Although it is important to note that it is not essential for the insured to have an insurable interest at the time of effecting the insurance. Instead, he/she should have such an interest in due course of time. Otherwise, he will not become entitled to indemnification.

14(B). The policy of 'anticipate no profit and provide for all possible losses' is followed due to convention of conservation.

The rule of the accountant is 'anticipate no profit but provide for all possible losses' at the time of recording the business transactions and preparation of annual financial statements. The accountant wants to be on the safer side by not taking some profits which may be received but which is not yet received and providing for losses which he thinks may happen but which has not yet happened. This is because he thinks the chances of non-receipt of anticipated profit and the incurring of losses anticipated are higher. If he is very optimistic regarding receipt of profits and non -incurring of losses, the financial statements may present a very rosy picture of the state of affairs of the entity which may not subsequently materialise. So he acts conservatively by not taking anticipated profits and but taking anticipated losses in the

preparation of the financial statements.
Because of the convention of conservatism inventory is valued at 'lower of cost or market price and provision is made for bad and doubtful debts out of current year's profits. But the reckless application of this convention may lead to the creation of 'secret reserves' and the financial statements may fail to disclose a true and fair view of the state of affairs of the business.

15(D). The receipts and payments account summarizes receipts and payments made by a non-trading concern during a particular period of time (usually one year). Its is used to prepare income and expenditure account of non-trading concerns.
The receipts and payments account is prepared from transactions recorded in the cash book and can also be termed as a summarized version of the cash book of non-trading concerns. The various cash transactions recorded in cash book that can be grouped together are shown under one account head in receipts and payments account.

16(A). Audit Programme is prepared by the Auditor.
The goal of an audit program is to create a framework that is detailed enough for any outside auditor to understand what official examinations have been completed, what conclusions have been reached and what the reasoning is behind each conclusion. The framework should explain the audit's objectives, its scope and its timeline. The audit program should also describe how working papers the documented evidence of the audit will be collected, reviewed and reported.

17(D). Under the head 'Secured Loans' the following are disclosed Other loans and advances.
When you borrow money, the lender sometimes requires the loan to be 'secured'. This means that if you default on the loan, the lender can repossess and sell specified items of yours (eg your home, car or another personal asset) to recover the debt. With unsecured loans, the lender does not require you to list specific items for security, so if you default on the loan they can't take any of your possessions.
Secured loans include:
credit sales (formerly called hire purchase), i.e. where you buy products and pay for them later in instalments. The security is the items you bought on finance personal loans secured by one or some of your possessions mortgages, where your home secures the mortgage loan.
To protect their interest, the lender will usually register a security interest in the specified items until you finish paying the loan. This means you can't sell them or give them away.
They may also attach a disabling device, also called an immobilizer, to a property on finance (usually a vehicle). This immobilizer can be activated to disable the vehicle or other device. Activating an immobilizer can only be done under strict conditions and if you have been given reasonable notice in advance.

18(D). A sales budget is the estimated number of units and potential income that a company expects to sell over a specific period of time. Organizations typically measure this on a monthly, quarterly, or annual basis. Companies take into account variables including past sales trends, rival activity, and the current or anticipated economic conditions when forecasting a sales budget.

19(D). Intangible Assets are related to AS 26.
An intangible asset is a non-physical non-monetary asset which is held for use in the production or supply of goods and services, or for rentals to others, etc.
AS 26 should be applied by all enterprises in the accounting of intangible assets, except:
1. Intangible assets that are within the scope of another standard financial asset
2. Rights and expenditure on the exploration for or development of minerals, oil, natural gas and similar non-regenerative resources
3. Intangible assets arising in insurance enterprise from contracts with policyholders
4. Expenditure in respect of termination benefits

20(C). AS - 28 deals with the impairment of assets i.e. the carrying amount of the assets should not be more than the recoverable amount of the assets. This calculation has to be done at the end of each financial year. The objective of this Standard is to set out principles and procedures for accounting for interests in joint ventures and reporting of joint venture assets, liabilities, income and expenses in the financial statements of venturers and investors.

21(C). Bad loans in banking terminology are generally known as NPA's. A Non - performing Asset (NPA) is defined as a credit facility in respect of which the interest and instalment of the principal have remained 'past due' for a specified period of time.

22(C). An association of cement manufacturers is an example of Horizontal combination. It refers to the combination of businesses engaged in the production of the same type of product or engaged in the same trade.
For e.g. Cement companies joining together (acquisition of Gujarat Ambuja Cement by Lafarge of France) or steel manufacturers joining together (Tata Iron and Steel Co., acquiring Natsteel of Singapore) etc. It is also known as parallel or unit or trade combination.

23(B). A department store is a retail establishment offering a wide range of consumer goods in different product categories known as "departments". In modern major cities, the department store made a dramatic appearance in the middle of the 19th century, and permanently reshaped shopping habits, and the definition of service and luxury.

24(B). A public corporation is set up by special order of the Government.
In India, a public corporation is a business that's created by the legislature or an act of parliament, and its name is notified in the official gazette of the state or central government. There are many businesses that were created in India by the government in the form of a service organization.

25(C). Financial securities that can be converted into cash at closing to their book value price are classified as cash equivalents. Cash equivalents are investments securities that are meant for short-term investing; they have high credit quality and are highly liquid.

26(D). Deferred Revenue Expenditure is an expenditure which is revenue in nature and incurred during an accounting period, but its benefits are to be derived in multiple future accounting periods.

These expenses are unusually large in amount and, essentially, the benefits are not consumed within the same accounting period.
Part of the amount which is charged to profit and loss account in the current accounting period is reduced from total expenditure and rest is shown in the balance sheet as an asset (fictitious asset, i.e. it is not really an asset.

27(D). A statutory audit is a legally required review of the accuracy of a company's or government's financial statements and records. The purpose of a statutory audit is to determine whether an organization provides a fair and accurate representation of its financial position by examining information such as bank balances, bookkeeping records, and financial transactions.
Statutory Audit as the name suggests is a compulsory audit for all companies. Every entity which is registered under the Companies Act, as a Private Limited or a Public Limited company has to get its books of accounts audited every year. This type of audit is not conditional, it depends upon the entity type.
Thus, if your entity is a company, you need to get a statutory audit conducted from a Chartered Accountant, for your company.

28(B). Discounted cash flow analysis is also classified as time value of money. The time value of money (TVM) is the concept that money available at the present time is worth more than the identical sum in the future due to its potential earning capacity.

29(B). CHUNK sampling is also known as Convenience sampling.
Sampling is done because it is not possible for a researcher to take a survey of the whole population of respondents, so they choose a random sample of individuals that represent the whole population, and those individuals are considered as the sample size of the research.
Convenience sampling:

- When a sample is drawn randomly from a readily available list according to the convenience of the researcher.
- It is the most commonly used method as it is an economical, prompt, and uncomplicated technique.
- This method is also known as CHUNK Sampling.
- A CHUNK refers to that fraction of the population being investigated neither by probability nor by judgment but on the basis of convenience only.

30(D). Sampling is done because it is not possible for a researcher to survey the entire population of respondents, so they choose a rating sample of individuals who represent the entire population, and those individuals are considered to be the sample size of the research.
Stratified Random Sampling:

- This method of sampling involves dividing a heterogeneous population into small groups called strata.
- These sub-groups / groups are based on some symmetry of the members in the group.
- Then finally some items from each group are selected on the chart.
- This process of classifying groups is also known as stratification.

31(D). It is not possible for a researcher to take a survey of the whole population of respondents, so they choose a random sample of individuals that represent the whole population, and those individuals are considered as the sample size of the research.
Small sample size:

- There are some researchers who think with a small sample size they cannot use statistics but this is a misconception.
- There have been appropriate statistical methods to deal with small sample sizes.
- We can all agree that one researcher's small size can be other researcher's large but typically small sample sizes refer to 5 to 30 respondents , a sample size very common in usability studies.
- It is said that " statistical analysis with small samples is like making astronomical observations with binoculars" i.e. there are limitations for researchers to see big things but it does not mean that if you don't have a high-tech telescope then you cannot conduct astronomy.

Therefore, all of the above are small samples.

32(C). Research analysis refers to analyzing a topic/ concept by breaking it down into small parts, in order to understand and research it in a way that makes sense to the researcher. There is various software that can be used while doing research analysis.
SPSS:

- SPSS is an abbreviation of Statistical Package for Social Sciences.
- It is a statistical package used in the analysis of data of research.
- It was originally developed by SPSS Inc. but was acquired by IBM in 2009 and it was renamed IBM SPSS Statistics in 2014.
- This software was originally prepared for research in social science fields but now it has become popular in other fields also like health science, market research, marketing, data mining, etc.

Therefore, SPSS is one of the software used for Research Analysis.

33(B). The classification of respondents only on the basis of gender is an application of the Nominal scale.
Classification is used to group respondents to see how they are different from one another such as age, gender, income, class, location of household, etc.
Nominal Scale:

- It is a scale which neither ranks nor measures data and only assigns objects into discrete categories.
- It only helps in distinguishing or classifying data according to different parameters.
- The nominal scale doesn't take into consideration the numeric values or any other ranking categories.
- Some examples which use a nominal scale are which city you live in, gender, religion, etc.

34(B). Karl Pearson's coefficient of correlation between two variables is the square root of the product of their regression coefficients.
Karl Pearson's coefficient of correlation:

- It is used to find out the linear relationship between two related variables and it is denoted by 'r'.

- It is also known as the Pearsonian coefficient of correlation and is mostly used quantitative method in practice.
- The correlation of coefficient is independent of its origin and scale.
- If the relationship between two variables X and Y is to be obtained then by origin, it means subtracting any non-zero constant from the value of X and Y the value of 'r' remains unchanged. By scale it means, there is no effect on the value of 'r' if the value of X and Y is divided or multiplied by any constant.
- The geometric mean of two regression coefficients is equal to the coefficient of correlation.
- The geometric mean formula is the square root of the product of their regression coefficients.

35(A). Statistical software packages for research in social sciences include SPSS.

SPSS:

- SPSS is an abbreviation of Statistical Package for Social Sciences.
- It is a statistical package used in the analysis of data.
- It was originally developed by SPSS Inc. but was acquired by IBM in 2009 and it was renamed IBM SPSS Statistics in 2014.
- This software was originally prepared for research in social science fields but now it has become popular in other fields also like health science, market research, marketing, data mining, etc.

36(D). The degree of freedom is the number of observations that are free to vary while estimating the statistical analysis. Degrees of freedom is significant to find out critical cutoff values for inferential statistical tests.

'F' test:

- F-test is any statistical test in which the test statistic has an F-distribution under the null hypothesis.
- The parameters used in the F-test are mean and variances due to which parametric tests are used here as well.
- F-test of overall significance indicates whether your linear regression model provides a better fit to the data than a model that contains no independent variables.
- F-test uses two sample variances, or two squares s_1 and s_2, by dividing them.
- Mean squares are variances that account for the degree of freedom that uses estimates of variance.
- Here, there are two sets of the degree of freedom: one for the numerator and one for the denominator.

't' test:

- The particular form of t distribution in the t-test is determined by its degree of freedom.
- This test is used in hypothesis testing to find out whether a process actually has an effect on the population, or whether the groups are different from one another.
- A test is necessary for small sample sizes (n<30) where distributions are not normal.

' χ^2 ' test (Chi-square test):

- It is a statistical hypothesis test that compares two variables of a contingency test to check how they are related.
- It is a nonparametric test and this test normally applies to qualitative data.
- There are two types of chi-square test:

1. Chi-square goodness of fit test that determines if sample data matches with the population.
2. A chi-square test for independence tests to see whether the distribution of categorical variables differs from each other.

- The chi-square test of independence determines whether there is a significant relationship between the variables, and it also incorporates a degree of freedom.
- The general rule in this test of calculating the degree of freedom with a table having rows (r) and columns (c) is (r-1)(c-1).

Therefore, 'F' test, 't' test and ' χ^2 ' test are associated with the concept of degree of freedom.

37(C). The structure of an organization in which there is a separation of ownership and management is called Company.

Company:

- A company refers to a group of people, whether natural, legal or a mixture of both, with a specific objective.
- A company is defined as, "an incorporated association which is an artificial person, having a separate legal entity, with a perpetual succession, a common seal (if any), and a common capital compromised of transferable shares and limited liability."
- A company having a separate legal entity means that it is recognized by law as a 'legal person' and has its own separate legal existence.
- In a company, owners are the Shareholders and management is in the hands of the Board of Directors.

38(B). when a person transacts with a company on matters which is beyond the power of the company, the person will be governed by the Doctrine of Constructive Notice.

The doctrine of Constructive Notice:

- Constructive notice is an indirect notice that is not received in reality but in the eyes of law, it has been served.
- It is presumed that the person has knowledge about a particular fact on which the law is putting obligations.
- For example, when a person logs in to the site of an organization, the information regarding the Memorandum of Association and other incorporation certificates are clearly stated there so if anybody wants to read they can read it, because if afterwards, any problem arises then that person cannot say that he was not aware of the policies or limitations or drawbacks of the company as it is their duty to read the documents of which company you want to deal in.
- The doctrine of Constructive Notice is nothing but a legal fiction that states the person transacting with a company should have known of a legal action taken or to be taken, even if they have no idea regarding it at the moment.

39(B). The formation of a company is a lengthy process and is carried out in a proper given sequence.

The sequence of the formation of a company involves 4 stages and they are as follows:

1. Promotion stage:

- Promotion is the first stage in the formation of a company.
- Promotion of a company refers to the sum total of activities required to participate in the building of an organization and completion of a plan to execute the idea.
- The execution is based on top-level management's serious consideration of the idea on which the business will be based.
- Promotion presupposes the technical processing of a commercial proposition with reference to its potential profitability.
- According to Guthmann and Dougall, "Promotion starts with the conception of the idea from which the business is to evolve and continues down to the point at which the business is full, ready to begin operations in a going concern."

2. Incorporation stage:

- Incorporation is the second stage in the formation of a company.
- It refers to registration that brings a company into existence.
- A company is properly incorporated when it is registered under the Act and a Certificate of Incorporation has been obtained from the Registrar of Companies.

3. Capital Subscription stage:

- A public or private company that is not having share capital can directly commence their business after the incorporation stage.
- This stage is only relevant in the case of a public company having a share capital.
- Only such companies need to pass these remaining two stages in order to commence a business.
- Such companies need to do some formalities regarding the pattern of capital subscription, then the directors of the company file a copy of the 'prospectus' with the Registrar and invite the public to subscribe to the shares of the company by putting the 'prospectus' in circulation.
- After that, the application and allotment of share take place.

4. Commencement of business:

- After getting the certificate of incorporation, a private company can start its business but a public company can start its business only after getting a certificate of commencement of business'.
- After getting the certificate of incorporation a company needs to:
- A public company issues a prospectus of inviting the public to subscribe to its share capital,
- A minimum subscription is fixed, and
- The company is required to sell a minimum number of shares mentioned in the prospectus.
- After completion of this process if the Registrar is satisfied then they issue the certificate of Commencement of business.

Therefore, the appropriate sequence of the formation of a company is in the following order Promotion, incorporation, capital subscription, and commencement of business.

40(B). Delegation of authority is the process by which a manager delegates his part of the workload to his subordinate, granting authority and creating accountability.

Characteristics of Delegation of Authority:

- Delegation takes place at all the levels of the organization where a superior-subordinate relationship exists.
- Delegation involves the transfer and not surrendering of authority.
- It is only possible when the delegator has the authority to pass on the work.
- Delegation is not abdication, ultimately the responsibility for the proper discharge of authority and completion of the task remains of the manager or delegator.
- A manager will never delegate his overall work to his subordinate because there are some tasks that should be performed by himself only.
- Delegation of authority makes the size of an organization a larger organization because in the smaller organization the workload is low and the tasks can be performed easily by the manager himself so there is no need for delegation.
- The authority delegated can be withdrawn or revoked whenever the delegator feels so.

Therefore, the delegation of authority makes the size of the organization a larger organization.

41(C). The statement is an effective way of planning and organizing an MBO task, so the statement is true, but the reason employees participate in the setting of objectives is false.

Management by Objectives (MBO):

- The term MBO was first outlined by Peter Drucker in 1954 in his book The Practice of Management.
- Management by objectives is also known as management by results.
- MBO is a strategic approach of planning and organizing the work that aims to improve the performance of an organization by clearly defining the objectives which are agreed upon by both the management and the employees.
- In this process, the management takes decisions regarding setting the objectives that are supposed to be achieved and conveys them to the other employees of the organization and then employees perform their tasks to achieve those objectives.
- An MBO system allows the organization to link the company's financial goals, such as sales projections, profits, and reduced costs, with the goals and performance measures for each manager.

42(C). 'No ideas are ever criticized' and 'the more radical the ideas are the better' - are the rules of the Brainstorming decision-making process.

The decision-making process mostly starts because there is some sort of problem recognized that needs to be solved. It is a step-by-step cognitive process that can help you make more appropriate decisions by defining alternatives and by evaluating relevant information.

Brainstorming:

- Brainstorming is a group activity in which teams generate some creative ideas spontaneously to solve a specific problem.
- They come up with a vast collection of ideas without any fear of criticism and draw links between them to find out the potential solution.
- At first, even if the ideas seem a bit unrealistic, they are taken into consideration.
- In brainstorming sessions, the greater the

number of ideas generated there is bigger the chance of producing radical and effective solutions.

43(D). Innovators are the people to adopt a new product first:
- Innovators are the first customers to try a new product.
- They are, by nature, risk-takers and are excited by the possibilities of new ideas and new ways of doing things.
- Products tend to be more expensive at their point of release (though some products do defy this trend) and as such innovators are generally wealthier than other types of adopters.

44(C). Manufacturers of cars and motorcycles typically seek Exclusive distribution.

Exclusive distribution:
1. If a company wants to give a big region to one single distributor then it is known as an exclusive distribution strategy.
2. In some cases, a distributor might be appointed for a complete country.
3. There would be no one other than that distributor operating in that company.
4. Typical examples are designer wear, major domestic appliances, and even automobiles.
5. By granting exclusive distribution rights, the manufacturer hopes to have control over the intermediaries' price, promotion, credit inventory, and service policies.
6. The firm also hopes to get the benefit of aggressive selling by such outlets.

45(C). Objective-and-task method is the most scientific and logical method.

Objectives and Task Method:
1. This is the most appropriate advertising budget method for any company. It is a scientific method to set an advertising budget.
2. The method considers the company's own environment and requirements.
3. Objectives and task method guide the manager to develop his promotional budget by
- defining specific objectives,
- determining the task that must be performed to achieve them, and
- estimating the costs of performing the task.

The sum of these costs is the proposed amount for an advertising budget.

46(C). Customer satisfaction is not a major component of holistic marketing.

Holistic marketing refers to a marketing strategy that considers the whole of a business. And all the different marketing channels as a system. Under this approach, a business with different departments comes together. As a result, departments collaborate in interconnected marketing activities.

Although strategies for implementation differ from one company to the next, every holistic marketing approach includes four main components: relationship marketing, integrated marketing, internal marketing, and societal marketing.

47(A). The Drugs and Cosmetics Act, 1940 is not part of India's marketing environment.

The market environment is a marketing term and refers to all of the forces outside of marketing that affects marketing management's ability to build and maintain successful relationships with target customers.

The Law is for the purpose of protecting customers from exploitation by the businessman, to protect the interest of society, and also to protect companies from unfair competition. Examples of laws in India - Consumer Protection Act, Environment Protection Act Indian Contract Act, Competition Law, etc.

48(C). A Market is a set of all actual and potential buyers of a product.
1. Potential buyers are those who might be in the market to review what is available at what price ranges, and something they might consider buying as soon as they decide on buying.
2. Actual buyer is those who make the transaction and purchases the product.
3. Market refers to the group of consumers or organizations that is interested in the product, has the resources to purchase the product, and is permitted by law and other regulations to acquire the product.

49(C). In every contract of sale, the first implied condition on the part of the seller is that: in case of a sale, he has a right to sell the goods, and in the case of an agreement to sell, he will have the right to sell the goods at the time when the property is to pass.

50(C). **Statement I:** A sale has the immediate effect of transferring property, whereas an agreement to sell the property is to pass at some future time.

Statement II: A sale makes the buyer the owner of goods but an agreement to sale does not make the buyer the owner of goods.

Here Both the statements are correct.

51(B). According to section 13 of the Negotiable Instrument Act, 1881 - A 'negotiable instrument' means a promissory note, bill of exchange, or cheque payable either to order or to bearer.

A Promissory Note:
- Section 13 of the Negotiable Act defines a promissory note as a financial instrument that includes a written agreement made by one party i.e. the issuer or maker to pay another party i.e. the payee a certain sum of money, either on-demand or at a specific date.
- A promissory note is an instrument containing an unconditional undertaking.
- It is signed by the maker to pay a certain sum of money only to a specific person or the bearer of the instrument.
- A promissory note must be written and signed by the maker or else it is of no effect.
- If a promissory note does not have a date, it is assumed to have been made when it was delivered.
- Most importantly it must be stamped under the Indian Stamp Act and it is not stamped then that promissory note is considered null.

52(C). The registered office clause of the memorandum of association contains the name of the state in which the registered office of the company is to be situated.

A Memorandum of Association contains the following clauses:
- Name Clause
- Registered Office Clause
- Object Clause

- Liability Clause
- Capital Clause

Registered Office Clause:

- This clause specifies the name of the state in which the registered office of the company is to be situated.
- It helps to determine the jurisdiction of the Registrar of Companies.
- The company is required to inform the Registrar of Companies about the registered office within 30 days from the date of incorporation or commencement of business.

53(C). The Indian Contract Act, 1872 defines the term Contract under its section 2(h) as "An agreement enforceable by law". This Act is based upon the principles of English Common Law. All agreements are contracts if they are made by the free consent of parties that are involved in the contract, for a lawful consideration with a lawful object, and are not hereby expressed to be void.

54(B).

Column-1	Column-2
A. Competition Act	H. 2002
B. Right to Information Act	E. 2005
C. Indian Contract Act	G. 1872
D. Sales of Goods Act	F. 1930

Competition Act, 2002:

- Competition is the act of the sellers individually seeking to acquire the patronage of buyers in order to achieve profits or market share.
- The Competition Act, 2002 was enacted by the Parliament of India.
- Two of the main features of the Competition Act, 2002 is the framework it provides for the establishment of the Competition Commission, and the tools it provides to prevent anti-competitive practices and to promote positive competition in the Indian market.

Right to Information Act(RTI Act), 2005:

- It is an Act to provide for setting out the practical regime of right to information for citizens to secure access to information under the control of public authorities, in order to promote transparency and accountability in the working of every public authority, the constitution of a Central Information Commission and State Information Commissions and for matters connected therewith or incidental thereto.

The Indian Contract Act, 1872:

- It prescribes the law relating to contracts in India and is the key act regulating Indian contract law.
- The objective of the Contract Act is to ensure that the rights and obligations arising out of a contract are honoured and that legal remedies are made available to an aggrieved party against the party failing to honour his part of the agreement.

Sale of Goods Act 1930:

- It was introduced with the objective of balancing the rights, duties, claims, and expectations arising in the process of transferring property from one person to another i.e of buyers and sellers.

55(A). Tax is defined by Hugh Dalton, as a compulsory contribution imposed by a public authority, irrespective of the exact amount of service rendered to the taxpayer in return, and not imposed as a penalty for any legal offence.

Tax penalty:

- A tax penalty is a punishment imposed for a violation of the law.
- It is charged on an individual when he did not pay enough of his or her total estimated tax or withholding.
- If in case, an individual has underpaid the estimation of his tax, then he or she may be required to pay the penalty.

56(B). In direct tax, a unit that performs highly direct processing is taxed.

Direct Tax:

- Direct tax is the income tax paid directly to the government and is levied on the income of an individual.
- Direct tax includes income tax, poll tax, land tax, personal property tax.
- Such direct taxes are computed based on the ability of the taxpayer to pay, which means the higher the income, the higher their taxes are.
- It is computed as a percentage of the total income.

57(D). Section 45 (2) of Income Tax Act, 1961 provides that any profits or gains arising from the transfer of a capital asset effected in the previous year will be chargeable to income-tax under the head 'Capital Gains'. Such capital gains will be deemed to be the income of the previous year in which the transfer took place. In this charging section, two terms are important. One is "capital asset" and the other is "transfer".

58(A). The income of the previous year is taxed at the rates of the assessment year determined by the respective Finance Act.

The Finance Act includes all the necessary amendments in the direct taxes i.e. income tax and wealth tax, and indirect taxes i.e. custom duty, excise duty, service tax; signifying the policy decisions of the Union Government. Through this act, the Central Government gives effect to the financial proposals at the beginning of every financial year.

Assessment year:

- It is the year in which one files income tax returns of the prior fiscal year.
- This is the time in which the income earned during the previous year is assessed and taxed.
- The income of the previous year is assessed in the assessment year following the previous year.
- For instance, the income of the previous year 2020-21 is taxed in 2021-22 at the rate of the assessment year prescribed by the relevant finance act.

59(A). A surcharge is an additional charge or tax to the tax being already levied. The separate taxation of the incomes of corporations and their shareholders follows the legal principle that corporations and shareholders are distinct entities. A surcharge of 10% on a tax rate of 30% effectively increases the combined tax rate to 33%. Marginal reliefs are also provided to individuals as sometimes an increase in tax liability after factoring surcharge becomes more than the increase in income above Rs 1 crore. Marginal relief is given to both domestic and foreign companies in case the net income exceeds Rs 1 cr and Rs 10 cr.

60(A). Corporate tax is a tax on the profits of the corporation. It is also known as company tax or corporation tax. Accounting profit is a profit or loss for a period before deducting tax expense. Tax expense (tax income) is an aggregate amount included in the determination of profit or loss for the period in respect of current tax or deferred tax.

Basis of corporate income:

- The tax basis of workability or liability is the amount that is liable for that purpose or liability for tax purposes.
- The tax base of a punitive one is the amount that will be deductible for tax purposes against a taxable pecuniary gain which will flow into an entity upon recovery of the autonomous financing amount.
- If those economic benefits are not taxable, then the tax basis of succession is equal to its treatment amount.
- Let us understand this with an example: For tax purposes, the historical cost of the machine is Rs 100, depreciation of Rs 20 has already been deducted in the current and previous period and the remaining cost is either in the form of depreciation in future period or at Deductions will be made through the cut. The revenue generated using the machine is taxable, any profit on the machine's profit will be taxable and loss on anyone will be taxable for tax purposes.
- The basis of the county physics of the machine is Rs 80 in the above example.

61(B). Rent received by the original tenant from the sub-tenant is taxable under the head Income from other sources. Subletting is when a tenant lets out part of the property they are renting to another tenant. Rental income in the hands of the owner is charged to tax under the head "Income from house property". Rental income of a person other than the owner cannot be charged to tax under the head "Income from house property". Hence, rental income received by a tenant from sub-letting cannot be charged to tax under the head "Income from house property". Such income is taxable under the head "Income from other sources".

62(C). Tele-marketing is a part of Direct marketing.
Direct marketing:

- Direct marketing gives the opportunity of promoting goods and services directly to the customers who need them the most.
- Direct marketing helps in building relationships with new customers.
- All promotional information is relayed without intermediaries and any third parties.
- Emails, newspapers, outdoor advertising, SMS marketing, Tele-marketing, websites, catalog distribution, etc. are various types of direct marketing strategies.

63(B). The National Bank for Agriculture and Rural Development (NABARD) is a top-level development financial institution in India, established in 1982 to provide agricultural and rural credit.
Food stocks are maintained by the Central Government for three purposes:

- Maintaining prescribed buffer stock norms for food security,
- Monthly supply through Public Distribution System (PDS),
- Market intervention to stabilize open market prices.

64(C). The Committee of Directors of state-owned Indian Bank has given approval for raising up to ₹4,000 crores through share sale.

- The fund raising would be subject to all statutory and regulatory approvals.
- The bank required to increase its public shareholding to at least 25% within a period of three years from August 3, 2018.

65(C). Balance sheet is a financial statement presents a summary of the Assets, Liabilities, and Owners' Equity of a firm.
Financial statements are written document contains a company's operations and financial performance and financial position. Financial statements include:

- Balance Sheet: The balance sheet is a picture of an organization's assets, liabilities, and stockholders' equity.
- Income Statement: The income statement is primarily concerned with a company's revenues and costs over a certain time period. The statement creates a company's profit amount termed net income after costs are reduced from sales.
- Cash Flow Statement: The cash flow statement (CFS) assesses a company's ability to generate cash to pay debts, cover operational expenditures, and make investments.

66(A). Direct tax is a type of tax where the incidence and impact of taxation fall on the same entity.

- In the case of direct tax, the burden can't be shifted by the taxpayer to someone else. These are largely taxes on income or wealth. Income tax, corporation tax, property tax, inheritance tax, and gift tax are examples of direct tax.
- Some important direct taxes imposed in India are Income Tax, Corporation Tax, Property Tax, Inheritance Tax, and Gift Tax.

67(A). C Stands for Credit in ANBC.
ANBC stands for Adjusted Net Bank Credit.
ANBC is the net bank credit plus investments made by banks in non-SLR bonds held in the held-to-maturity category or credit equivalent amount of off-balance-sheet exposure, whichever is higher.

68(A). Public debt is a part of business environment. Public debt is the total amount, including total liabilities, borrowed by the government to meet its development budget. It has to be paid from the Consolidated Fund of India.

69(D). Liberalization, globalization and privatization are the aims of economic reforms. Liberalization in economics means minimizing the government's restrictions and regulations in an economy, in return for higher involvement of private organizations. Globalization refers to businesses operating internationally or on a global scale. This involves most of the world's economies working together to provide and produce goods and services. Privatization occurs when a government-owned business, operation, or property becomes owned by a private, non-government party.

70(D). Demand for LED TV are increasing day by day. Thus, TV manufacturers have started making LED TVs instead of LCD. Then the significance of business environment being portrayed in the given case are:

- Helpful in tapping useful resources

- Helps the firm to identify threats and early warning signals
- Helps in coping with rapid changes

The business environment also will provide various inputs (resources) like finance, machines, raw materials, power and water, labour etc. The business enterprise provides outputs such as goods and services to the customers, payment of taxes to the government, interest/dividend to investors and so on.

71(D). The importance of business environment:

- Identification
- Improvement in performance
- Coping with rapid changes
- Enables firms to analyze their competitors' strategies and actions.
- Helps strengthen the firm and use its resources effectively
- Giving Direction for Growth
- Continuous Learning
- Image Building
- Meeting Competition

72(D). Depreciation expenses are deducted from net income for tax purpose.
Depreciation expenses are subtracted from the company's revenue as a part of the net income calculations. On the other hand, for tax purposes, depreciation is considered as a tax deduction for the recovery of the costs of assets employed in the company's operations.

73(D). This passage is written to support short-term rentals and provide arguments as to why they should be supported. Therefore, the correct answer is "advocate for a particular position." The passage is not objective and unbiased, as it clearly has a particular agenda. While the intersection of business and community is a theme discussed in the passage, it is not the primary purpose. Short-term rentals are not a negative phenonmen, and so the answer choice, "rationalize a negative phenomenon," is also incorrect. The passage also does not "point out the weaknesses in a widely accepted point of view."

74(D). The author would most likely agree with the statement "While short-term rentals and communities would mutually benefit from regulations, a hard ban against them would be mutually counter-productive." This is because the author explicitly states that communities and short-term rentals should be allies as opposed to enemies. Thus, mutually beneficial regulations would serve them both well.
This answer choice says the exact opposite, and so it is incorrect: "Communities should see short-term rentals as an adversary, when they can just as easily be made an ally."
There is no evidence to suggest that the author supports this statement: "Although short-term rentals are popular right now, it is likely that they will diminish in value as more restrictions are enstated against them."
The author implies that hotels and short-term rentals are competitors, so this statement is not correct: "Hotels and short-term rentals complement each other and can contribute to one another's mutual development."
The author believes that some regulations are beneficial, so this statement is incorrect: "In general, regulations have proven to do a disservice to travel industry, as the red tape prevents commerce from moving freely, and discourages travel as a whole."

75(C). The best answer is "Short-term rentals, due to the transitory nature of their inhabitants, can make the members of a community feel uncomfortable, thereby negatively impacting the Homeowners' Association." Given that the patrons of short-term rentals are constantly coming and going, the nature of short-term rentals can upset members of a Homeowners' Association, who usually strive for consistency and stability.
While short-term rentals may be competition for hotels, there is no evidence that they are competition for Homeowners' Associations. Therefore, this answer choice is wrong: "Homeowners' Associations see short-term rentals as being competition for the market of vacationers."
The fact that short-term rentals experience success would not be an upsetting factor for Homeowners' Associations. Therefore, this answer choice is wrong: "Short-term rentals do not confer a benefit on the Homeowners' Association that is comparable to that conferred on the proprietor of a short-term rental."
There is no evidence in the passage to support either "Short-term rentals directly confer extra fees on Homeowners' Associations" or "Homeowners' Associations, as a general policy, have always looked down upon short-term rentals because they are unsanitary."

76(C). While the first paragraph provides background on the short-term rental phenomenon, explaining how the internet aided its spread, the third paragraph addresses the controversies that it has sparked. As a means of transitioning between these two topics, the second paragraph explains the significance of short-term rentals in order to allow the full impact of the controversial issues to be comprehended by the reader. Therefore, the correct answer is "Emphasize the impact that short-term rentals have had on the travel industry, thereby transitioning betwen the first and third paragraphs."
A tempting wrong answer is "Convince the reader that short-term rentals are the most significant development in the realm in which the housing industry and the travel industry intersect." While this sounds like it could be accurate, there is no evidence in the passage to indicate that short-term rentals are "the most significant development in the realm in which the housing industry and the travel industry intersect." The author does not provide sufficient information to justify use of the superlative "most."

77(B). The demand for necessities is usually Highly inelastic.
The demand for necessities is inelastic. By inelastic demand we mean that as the price of the commodity changes the quantity demand does not change. The consumer will not buy lesser of the commodity of the price increases.

78(C). When supply of a commodity decreases on a fall in its price, its is called Contraction of supply.
A contraction of supply occurs when the supply of a commodity reduces solely as a result of a decrease in the price of that commodity. The downward

trend to the left on the same supply curve indicates contraction.

79(B). The Cardinal Utility approach is propounded by neo-classical economists, who believe that utility is measurable, and the customer can express his satisfaction in cardinal or quantitative numbers, such as 1,2,3, and so on.

80(A). Marginal utility of a commodity is the additional utility derived by a consumer, by consuming one more unit of that commodity.
Marginal Utility derives its value from the consumption of extra unit. It is the satisfaction level of a consumer which he gains from the use of successive units of commodity. In simple words the utility derived from an extra unit of consumption is called Marginal Utility.

Mock Test 05

1. Advance Income-tax is shown in the:
   (a) Debit side of Profit and Loss Account
   (b) Liability side of the Balance Sheet
   (c) Credit side of Profit and Loss Account
   (d) Assets side of the Balance Sheet

2. Match List-I with List-II and select the correct answer from the codes given below.

List-I	List-II
(a) Planning	1. Training
(b) Staffing	2. Forecasting
(c) Directing	3. Evaluating
(d) Controlling	4. Motivating

   (a) 2, 4, 1, 3 (b) 1, 2, 3, 4
   (c) 2, 1, 4, 3 (d) 3, 4, 2, 1

3. Memorandum of Association contains–
   (a) Objective clause (b) Name clause
   (c) Capital clause (d) All of the above

4. The 'Doctrine of Indoor Management' provides protection to the:
   (a) Board of Directors (b) Shareholders
   (c) Managing Director (d) Outsiders

5. In foreign trade, what is the price quoted by a supplier which includes all charges incurred up to door delivery of goods to the buyer, called?
   (a) Loco price (b) C.I.F. price
   (c) Franco price (d) Landed price

6. Under which principle, all the rights of an insured are transferred to the insurance company after making payment of claim?
   (a) Subrogation (b) Utmost good faith
   (c) Contribution (d) Average clause

7. In marine insurance, when must the insurable interest exist?
   (a) At the time of making contract
   (b) At the time of loss of subject matter
   (c) Both at the time of making contract and at the time of loss of subject matter
   (d) At the time of termination of the policy

8. Henry Fayol is known for–
   (a) Scientific Management
   (b) Rationalisation
   (c) Industrial Psychology
   (d) Principles of Management

9. The headquarters of the ASEAN is located in which of the following country?
   (a) Indonesia (b) Vietnam
   (c) Thailand (d) Singapore

10. Which of these companies uses the tagline 'Think Different'?
    (a) Apple (b) Amazon
    (c) Facebook (d) Google

11. The sum total of the values of two variables 'X' and 'Y' is equal for all the observations. The value of the coefficient of correlation between 'X' and 'Y' is:
    1. +1 (perfectly positive)
    2. -1 (perfectly negative)
    3. Zero (No correlation)
    4. > 0 < 1 (Imperfect correlation)
    (a) 1 (b) 2
    (c) 3 (d) 4

12. Which one among the following is not true for Special Economic Zones?
    (a) No routine examination of cargo for export/import by customs authorities
    (b) No license is required for import
    (c) Manufacturing and service activities are allowed
    (d) No permission for subcontracting

13. Which one among the following is not true of the planning Commission?
    (a) It indicates the factors which tend to retard economic development.
    (b) It is an advisory body and makes recommendations to the cabinet.
    (c) It is responsible for the formulation of a plan for the most effective and balanced utilization of the country's resources.
    (d) It is responsible for the execution of development programs and plans.

14. Which one of the following statements is true about RBI ?
    (a) RBI maintains the foreign exchange reserves of India
    (b) RBI is the regulator of Banks and Securities market in India
    (c) RBI started functioning from 1870
    (d) None of these

15. Control function of management implies:
    (a) To bring harmony in various activities
    (b) To keep the workforce satisfied
    (c) To take corrective course of action
    (d) To dictate the subordinates

16. Maslow's needs hierarchy theory relates to–
    (a) Motivation (b) Leadership
    (c) Communication (d) Directing

17. A listed company opting for buyback of shares under the Companies Act, 1956 has to submit return, after completion of such buy-back within which one of the following periods ?
    (a) 6 months of such completion to the Registrar of Companies only
    (b) 45 days of such completion to the SEBI only
    (c) 30 days of such completion to the Registrar of Companies and SEBI
    (d) 30 days of such completion to the SEBI only

18. Private equity investors invest in a company based mainly on:
    (a) the creditability and the valuation of the company
    (b) the age of the company
    (c) the location of the company

(d) the activity undertaken by the company

19. 'Oligopoly' refers to:
(a) Many sellers, Few buyers
(b) Many sellers, Many buyers
(c) Few sellers, Many buyers
(d) Few sellers, Few buyers

20. To appoint new auditor in place of retiring auditor, to adopt the procedure, which section of Companies' Act, 1956 is applicable ?
(a) 223 (b) 224
(c) 225 (d) 226

21. According to ownership, Government Company means .... share.
(a) Whose paid-up share capital's 48%, shares are owned by Government
(b) Whose paid-up share capital's 49% shares are owned by Government
(c) Whose paid-up share capital's 50% shares are owned by Government
(d) Whose paid-up share capital's 51% shares are owned by Government

22. Which of the following Sections of the Companies' Act 1956 relates to the maintenance of proper books of accounts ?
(a) Section-211 (b) Section-217
(c) Section-209 (d) Section-205

23. Liability of partners in respect of the firm's debt is–
(a) Limited to the amount of his capital in the business
(b) Unlimited
(c) Limited to the amount of guarantee given by the partner
(d) Limited to the amount of capital and the loan to the firm, if any

24. A Government Company is one in which at least the following percentage of share capital is held by the Central and/or State Government?
(a) 25% (b) 26%
(c) 50% (d) 51%

25. 'Span of Management' means–
(a) A good organization should consist of five departments
(b) Authority of each person must be clearly defined
(c) Each subordinate should have one superior
(d) A manager can supervise a limited number of executives

26. Which of the following organisation makes "Doing Business Report" every year?
(a) WTO (b) World Bank
(c) UNCTAD (d) IMF

27. What does payout ratio mean?
(a) Ratio of debtors to creditors
(b) Ratio of profit distributed to profit retained
(c) Ratio of dividends per share and earnings per share
(d) Retained earnings

28. Consider the following statements–
1. Premium on issue of shares is transferred to General Reserve Account.
2. For declaration of bonus shares out of General Reserve, a resolution in the shareholders' meeting is necessary.
Which of the statements given above is/are correct ?
(a) 1 only (b) 2 only
(c) Both 1 and 2 (d) Neither 1 nor 2

29. Which one of the following correctly signifies the purpose of an Organization Chart?
(a) Office Décor
(b) Indication of available Office services
(c) Flow of Authority
(d) High Morale

30. Increase in the installation of Personal Computer is mainly due to–
(a) Monotony of work
(b) Reduction of fatigue
(c) Improvement of efficiency
(d) Lowering work load

31. With regard to the rate of return on investment (ROI), which one of the following statements is not valid?
(a) It is an overall indicator of the profitability of an enterprise
(b) It is a triangular relationship in the sense that ROI = Profit margin ×Asset turnover
(c) It is a superior measure compared to the cash flow generated per share
(d) It was first developed by Dupont, USA

32. When the audit is carried out during the accounting period with some interval it is called-
(a) Periodic audit (b) Partial audit
(c) Continuous audit (d) Interim audit

33. Which of the following is called Backbone of auditing?
(a) Routine checking (b) Vouching
(c) Internal check (d) Internal control

34. Which of the following are related to vouching of sales?
A. Dispatch of goods
B. Sales Book
C. Direct notes
D. Credit notes
Choose the correct answer from the options given below:
(a) B and D only (b) A and D only
(c) A and B only (d) B and C only

35. Which one of the following is not a tax saving investment?
(a) Home loan principal repayment
(b) Public Provident Fund (PPF)
(c) Life insurance premium
(d) Fixed Deposits

36. Which one the following document is prepared for documentary evidence by business?
(a) Invoice (b) Voucher
(c) Receipt (d) All of above

37. The area of intellectual property includes:
1. Copyrights and related rights

2. Trademarks including service marks
3. Industrial designs
4. The lay-out designs of integrated circuits
Choose the correct codes:

(a) Only 1 (b) Both 1 and 2
(c) 1, 2 and 3 (d) All of the above

38. Right to information includes the right to:
1. Inspect works, documents, records
2. Take notes, extracts or certified copies of documents or records
3. Take certified samples of material
4. Obtain information in forms of printouts, diskettes, floppies, tapes, video cassettes or in any other electronic mode or through printouts
Choose the correct codes:

(a) 1, 2 and 3 (b) 1, 2 and 4
(c) 1, 3 and 4 (d) All of the above

39. Section 6 of the Negotiable Instruments Act defines:
(a) Cheque
(b) Bill of Exchange
(c) Promissory Notes
(d) Dishonour by non-acceptance

Ques (40-43): Direction : Read the passage and answer the question that follows:

Business news does not repeat itself but it sometimes rhymes. In 2007 Walmart, America's biggest grocer, crowed that it would crack the coveted Indian market by being the first global retailer to set up shop there, pipping envious rivals in the process. On May 9th it announced much the same thing: its time in India has come, this time by virtue of paying $16bn for a majority stake in Flipkart, India's largest ecommerce outfit, which had also been coveted by its vast online rival, Amazon. The sense of déjà vu owes to the fact that its original foray proved a disappointment. Walmart's hopes of somehow circumventing rules to protect local shopkeepers, which have long prevented most foreign retailers from opening stores, have been repeatedly dashed. A decade on it has a meagre 21 wholesale stores in India, generating just 0.1% of its $500bn in global revenues and a small loss to boot. Somehow that has not dissuaded the beast of Bentonville from undertaking the biggest foreign acquisition in Indian history.

The Indian e-commerce market is as different from America's brick-and-mortar retail landscape as Walmart's Arkansas home is from Bangalore. Walmart probably has too many stores in its mature home market. Flipkart operates online and in quasi-virgin commercial territory: 95% of Americans shop at Walmart at least once a year, but only 5-10% of Indians have ever bought anything online. The deal is a departure in other ways, too. Walmart has already swooped on companies it thinks will help it grow its ecommerce presence. In 2016 it paid out $3bn for Jet.com, a putative rival to Amazon in America; it has also bagged Bonobos, a purveyor of tailored trousers. But Flipkart, which was founded in 2007 by two former Amazon employees, is in a different league in terms of price tag.

Walmart will own around 77% of the company, which is valued at over $20bn in total. Even for Walmart, that is a lot of money: $20bn is roughly the cash it generates every year net of capital expenditure, say, or 8% of its market capitalisation. Connoisseurs of the Indian tech scene have raised eyebrows at the price tag, given that Flipkart raised money at a valuation of under $12bn just a year ago. SoftBank, a Japanese telecoms and internet giant which became its biggest shareholder after investing $2.5bn just nine months ago, stands to walk away with $4bn. Walmart's new acquisition will not produce quick returns. Analysts reckon Flipkart loses money on each shipment. Margins are unlikely to improve soon given Amazon's incursion into the market (having committed $5bn to India, it probably ranks a close second to Flipkart, which is thought to account for just under half of India's online sales). Paytm Mall, a newish rival backed by Alibaba of China, is also ambitious.

40. How would Wamart's business in America be different from its Indian venture?
I. The business is America is mostly brick and mortar while it is online in nature in India.
II. Walmart owns about 88% of the market share in America but hardly any in the Indian market.
III. The market is vastly under penetrated in India.

(a) Only II (b) Only I and II
(c) Only II and III (d) Only I and III

41. What does the line- 'Business news does not repeat itself but it sometimes rhymes' refer to?
(a) It refers to Walmart beating rivals in the e-commerce space.
(b) It refers to Walmart entering India via e-commerce to avoid getting caught up in the huge number of regulations India has imposed on retailers.
(c) It refers to Walmart's entry in India via a majority stake buyout in Flipkart in 2018 after being unsuccessful in 2007.
(d) It refers to Walmart being the first global retailer to set up shop in India.

42. Which of the following is/are true as per the passage?
I. Softbank is the largest shareholder of Flipkart.
II. India's e-commerce market as a whole is worth about $15bn only.
III. Indian regulations dictate that e-commerce sites must sell stuff mainly from third-parties rather than from their own inventory.

(a) Only II (b) Only I
(c) Only I and III (d) Only II and III

43. As per your understanding of the passage, which of the following shows that the decision by Walmart to enter Indian e-commerce may not be as lucrative as it appears to be?
I. Analysts reckon Flipkart loses money on each shipment and at one point it was thought to guzzle $2m a day subsidising shipping and using discounts to lure buyers.
II. Venture capitalists in India complain about the lack of exits from dozens of investments in the Indian e-commerce industry.
III. The entire sector was flat in 2016 and grew at perhaps only 10% last year.

(a) Only II (b) Only I and II
(c) Only I and III (d) All of the above

Ques (44-47): Direction : Read the following passage carefully and answer the question that follows.

Insurance regulator IRDAI has allowed distribution of all micro-insurance products through point-of-sales (PoS), with an aim further increase insurance penetration in the country. The Insurance Regulatory and Development Authority of India (IRDAI) has created a special category of insurance policies called micro-insurance policies to promote insurance coverage among economically vulnerable sections of society. A micro-insurance policy is a general or life insurance policy with a sum assured of Rs 50,000 or less. Agreeing to the suggestions of insurance companies, IRDAI in a circular has done away with the practice of pre-fixing the word 'PoS' on life, general and health products sold through PoS. The regulator said it has received representations from insurance companies requesting to do away with the prefix 'POS' in the product name. Insurers made representations to change the norms that made it mandatory for every policy sold through the 'Point of Sales Persons' to be separately identified and pre-fixed by the name 'POS'. IRDAI said the requirement was to identify the person involved in the sales process.

The IRDAI (Protection of Policyholder's Interest) Regulations, 2017, under the matters to be stated in life, general and health insurance policy, makes it mandatory to give the details of the person involved in the sales process. "By virtue of this requirement, the need to have the prefix 'PoS' becomes redundant as the insurance policy itself will carry the details of the person selling such a policy," the regulator said. The Authority, "hereby, discontinues requirements" of using the word 'PoS' prefixed before the PoS product name for life, general and health products. Similarly, IRDAI said it has been observed that advantages such as higher insurance penetration, lower prices, increased choice to customers, which would otherwise accrue to the policyholder by making micro-insurance products available through POS channel are being lost. "Therefore, the Authority after reviewing the position, hereby allows all Micro Insurance products of Life, General and Health insurance to be distributed through the POS also," the circular said. On the manner of dealing with cases of health/personal accident (PA) policies where sum insured crosses the limit specified under the POS guidelines, IRDAI said the sponsoring entity is allowed to recognise such policies as being sourced by the POS and pay the fees to the POS.

44. Which among the following is/are correct regarding the Micro Insurance policies issued by insurance companies in India?
I. Micro Insurance policies are meant to give coverage to people who belong to the underprivileged section of society.
II. Micro Insurance policies are such that the sum assured in these policies is Rs 50000 or less than that.
III. Micro Insurance policies are only issued by banks and insurance companies because others are not authorized by IRDAI to issue such policies.
(a) Both I and II (b) Only II
(c) Only III (d) Both I and III

45. Which among the following is correct regarding the objective of IRDAI to allow the distribution of micro insurance policies through the POS delivery channel?
(a) POS channel is the most popular distribution network in the country and that is why most of the people are relying on this only.
(b) Banks and insurance companies are very much interested in ensuring that the micro insurance products sold in India are not the global ones.
(c) The IRDAI has understood that micro insurance policies are not popular as the normal policies and they should be done away with.
(d) The IRDAI is interested in extension of insurance coverage to more and more people in the country.

46. Which among the following is/are correct as per the information given the passage?
I. The POS channel can also be used to distribute policies of insurance beyond the permissible limit of coverage.
II. The insurance companies are mainly responsible behind the decision of the IRDAI to remove the prefix 'POS' from the names of the insurance products.
III. The POS channel of distribution of insurance products will be used by IRDAI only and no insurance company will be able to use it.
(a) Both II and III (b) Both I and II
(c) Both I and III (d) Only II

47. Which among the following is/are correct regarding the benefits that were not there before the decision of the IRDAI allowing the micro insurance products to be sold through the POS channel?
(a) There was fewer choices available to the policyholders to choose from the insurance products available in the market.
(b) The policyholders were not able to get benefitted from lower and competitive premiums offered by insurance companies.
(c) The insurance companies were not after the policyholders to take their policies without making any kind of customizations on the part of the insurance companies.
(d) Both (A) and (B)

48. Under Section 54 of the Income Tax Act, 1961, the deduction for capital gain can be claimed only if:
(a) Any long-term capital asset is transferred
(b) Any capital asset is transferred
(c) Any short-term capital asset is transferred
(d) Residential house is transferred

49. Which of the following is an indirect tax?
(a) Corporation tax (b) Excise tax
(c) Wealth tax (d) Capital Gains tax

50. Which of the following is an example of direct tax?
(a) Custom duty (b) Service tax
(c) Excise tax (d) Income tax

51. The objectives of tax planning is to minimise:
(a) Tax liability (b) Finance liability
(c) Tax return (d) None of these

52. Tax management deals with:
(a) Filing of return in time
(b) Getting the accounts audited
(c) Deducting tax at source
(d) All of the above

53. Higher the price of certain luxurious articles, higher will be the demand, this concept is called:
(a) Giffen effects
(b) Veblen effects
(c) Demonstration effects
(d) All of the above

54. __________ demand forecasting is related to the business conditions prevailing in the economy as a whole
(a) Macro level (b) Industry level
(c) Firm level (d) None of these

55. ________ is the change in total revenue irrespective of changes in price or due to the effect of managerial decision on revenue.
(a) Average revenue (b) Total revenue
(c) Marginal revenue (d) Incremental revenue

56. Regarding the sales budget, which of the following

statements is incorrect?

(a) Sales budget is a functional budget
(b) Usually the sales budget is stated in terms of quantity and value
(c) Starting point of the development of master budget is preparation of sales budget
(d) Sales budget is based on production budget

57. Marketing is a process which aims at _______.

(a) Production
(b) Profit-making
(c) The satisfaction of customer needs
(d) Selling products

58. The term marketing refers to ______.

(a) Advertising, Sales Promotion, Publicity and Public Relational activities
(b) A new product needs ideas, Developments, concepts and improvements
(c) Sales Planning, Strategy and Implementation
(d) A philosophy that stresses customer value and satisfaction

59. Marketing is the activity, set of _________ & processes for creating, communicating, delivering & exchanging offerings that have value for customers, clients, partners & society.

(a) Institutions (b) Organizations
(c) Companies (d) Enterprises

60. Marketing is ______, there is a constant tension between the formulated side of marketing and the management side.

(a) An art
(b) A Science
(c) Both an "art" and a "science"
(d) Selling

61. Marketers often use the term _______ to cover various groupings of customers.

(a) Buying power
(b) Demographic segment
(c) Market
(d) People

62. Which of the following defines marketing management?

(a) The art and science of choosing target markets and getting, keeping, and growing customers through creating, delivering, and communicating superior customer value.
(b) The development of planning, policies and various marketing strategies to move the company forward to achieve the goal of profit through selling the product and services.
(c) The process of identifying and managing all marketing process to sell product and service to the end users at low price.
(d) The process of developing and monitoring profit of companies products and services.

63. Which of the following is not a function of marketing?

(a) Bending the customers according to product
(b) Marketing planning
(c) Product designing and development
(d) Gathering and analysing market information

64. What are the Considerations in designing capital structure of a corporate?

(a) Trading on Equity (b) Cost of Capital
(c) Profitability (d) All of the above

65. In a unimodal and symmetric distribution, the relationship between averages is like this:

(a) mean > median > mode
(b) mean < median < mode
(c) mean = median = mode
(d) mean > median < mode

66. In a predominantly illiterate area consisting of 10,000 population, data has to be collected from 10% of them. The appropriate technique for data collection would be:

(a) Questionnaire (b) Schedule
(c) Interview (d) All the above

67. Given the following tests:
(i) 'Z'-test
(ii) 't'-test
(iii) 'F'-test
(iv) 'X^2'-test
The concept of degrees of freedom is associated with

(a) (i) and (ii) (b) (ii) and (iii)
(c) (iii) and (iv) (d) (ii), (iii) and (iv)

68. Given below are two statements:
Statement I : Deficit financing cannot create inflation in an economy.
Statement II : If RBI reduces the cash reserve ratio, the credit creation will decline.
In the light of the above statements, choose the most appropriate answer from the options given below:

(a) Both Statement I and Statement II are correct
(b) Both Statement I and Statement II are incorrect
(c) Statement I is correct and Statement II is incorrect
(d) Statement I is incorrect and Statement II is correct

69. The heavy initial expenditure on advertising the launch of a new product should be classified as:

(a) Capital expenditure
(b) Revenue expenditure
(c) A loss
(d) Deferred revenue expenditure

70. Compute the cash flow from operating activities from the following details by the indirect method:

Particulars	**2021 Rs.**	**2020 Rs.**

Profit and Loss A/c	1,10,000	1,20,000
Debtors	50,000	62,000
Outstanding Rent	24,000	42,000
Goodwill	80,000	76,000
Prepaid Insurance	8,000	4,000
Creditors	26,000	38,000

(a) (54,000) (b) 43,000
(c) (32,000) (d) 28,000

71. In Dow theory, if the primary trend of a security is downwards, it is called a _______ phase of the market.
(a) Bullish (b) Bearish
(c) Stagflation (d) Inflation

72. Which of the following measures of money supply is known as 'Broad money'?
(a) M 1 (b) M 2
(c) M 3 (d) M 4

73. Which of the following have a positive effect on exchange rate of domestic currency?
(a) Higher inflation rate (b) Lower interest rate
(c) Increase in Exports (d) Increase in Imports

74. Any statistical measure computed from population data is known as ______.
(a) Statistic (b) Parameter
(c) Standard error (d) Sampling frame

75. Class : 10 - 25 25 - 40 40 - 55
f : 6 20 44
Class : 55 - 70 70 - 85
f : ? 3
If the mode of the above distribution is 48.6, then the missing frequency will be:
(a) 29 (b) 32
(c) 26 (d) 13

76. Consider the following statements with respect to the Foreign Trade of India:
1. Financial services account for the majority of export services.
2. India is suffering from a capital account deficit in recent years.
3. Crude Petroleum is the highest imported commodity.
Which of the statements given above is/are incorrect ?
(a) 1 and 2 only (b) 3 only
(c) 1 and 3 only (d) 1, 2 and 3

77. External drains leave which type of impact on commercial bank?
(a) Lowers the reserves of bank
(b) Increases further deposits
(c) Increases credit creation
(d) Creates demand deposits

78. In which year was the Securities Appellate Tribunal (SAT) established in India?
(a) 1990 (b) 1992
(c) 1994 (d) 1997

79. Depreciation in spirit is similar to:
(a) Depletion (b) Amortization
(c) Depression (d) None of these

80. Under Stock and Debtors System, all figures in Branch Stock Account are recorded at _______ price.
(a) Cost (b) Wholesale
(c) Market (d) Selling

// Smart Answer Sheet //

Correct Percentage of students who answered correctly.
Skipped Percentage of students who skipped.

Q.	Ans.	Correct	Skipped	Q.	Ans.	Correct	Skipped	Q.	Ans.	Correct	Skipped
1	D	42.27%	48.08%	2	C	88.83%	10.28%	3	D	80.95%	11.56%
4	D	78.14%	15.86%	5	C	42.2%	31.17%	6	A	44.39%	32.65%
7	B	46.5%	52.74%	8	D	87.31%	11.08%	9	A	68.7%	30.7%
10	A	47.58%	31.89%	11	B	54.7%	41.84%	12	D	41.99%	31.23%
13	A	77.95%	17.76%	14	A	42.59%	41.92%	15	C	57.17%	31.03%
16	A	40.46%	54.82%	17	C	44.89%	41.27%	18	A	46.87%	34.81%
19	C	63.79%	30.58%	20	B	53.66%	41.15%	21	D	53.51%	38.0%
22	C	51.99%	37.02%	23	B	61.91%	36.34%	24	D	49.76%	35.33%
25	D	61.47%	33.74%	26	B	11.6%	81.86%	27	C	88.73%	10.2%
28	B	51.19%	46.16%	29	C	46.15%	50.11%	30	C	79.48%	11.96%
31	C	13.06%	82.72%	32	C	65.15%	32.07%	33	B	63.54%	35.6%
34	C	60.24%	34.68%	35	D	56.95%	40.27%	36	D	46.41%	35.11%
37	C	56.22%	37.05%	38	D	62.95%	32.1%	39	A	64.1%	34.13%
40	D	64.14%	31.08%	41	C	64.7%	30.83%	42	B	16.38%	79.95%
43	D	67.31%	32.08%	44	A	60.81%	31.65%	45	D	82.62%	13.42%
46	B	21.65%	71.42%	47	D	67.14%	31.95%	48	D	45.99%	53.58%
49	B	62.29%	34.56%	50	D	86.86%	11.57%	51	A	61.17%	37.71%
52	D	62.95%	37.03%	53	B	64.45%	34.92%	54	A	46.75%	36.18%
55	D	56.76%	31.26%	56	D	54.39%	35.28%	57	C	66.29%	32.56%
58	D	85.34%	12.1%	59	A	63.75%	31.9%	60	C	83.73%	13.57%
61	C	54.87%	35.99%	62	A	58.66%	35.27%	63	A	56.29%	30.49%
64	D	54.36%	32.13%	65	C	41.46%	53.38%	66	B	64.31%	31.41%
67	D	31.83%	67.22%	68	B	43.26%	53.28%	69	D	55.99%	39.21%
70	C	27.35%	70.89%	71	B	40.39%	48.33%	72	C	52.41%	43.8%
73	C	45.83%	43.41%	74	B	41.4%	58.12%	75	C	41.79%	50.31%
76	A	26.83%	69.01%	77	A	42.45%	30.4%	78	B	64.56%	32.57%
79	B	53.95%	38.17%	80	D	41.57%	40.71%				

// Hints and Solutions //

1(D). Advance Income-tax is shown in the assets side of the balance sheet.
While the tax liability will appear as an expense in the profit and loss account, the provision for income-tax will be shown in the Balance Sheet as a current liability and the Advance Tax of Rs. 3,50,000 paid will be shown as an advance on the asset side of the balance sheet.

2(C).

List-I	List-II
(a) Planning	2. Forecasting
(b) Staffing	1. Training
(c) Directing	4. Motivating
(d) Controlling	3. Evaluating

Planning is the process of thinking about the activities required to achieve the desired goal. It is the first and foremost activity to achieve the desired results.
Staffing is an operation of recruiting the employees by evaluating their skills and knowledge before offering them specific job roles accordingly. The staffing model refers to data that measures work activities, how many labour hours are needed, and how employee time is spent.
Directing is the heart of the management function. All other functions of management such as planning, organizing, and staffing have no importance without directing. Leadership, motivation, supervision, communication are various aspects of directing.
Control is a function of management which helps to check errors in order to take corrective actions. This is done to minimize deviation from standards and ensure that the stated goals of the organization are achieved in the desired manner.

3(D). A memorandum of association (MOA) contains a name clause, registered office or business location clause, objective or objects clause, liability clause, capital clause, as well as an association clause. MOAs are legal documentation that are prepared prior to the registration of limited liability companies (LLCs).

4(D). The 'Doctrine of Indoor Management' provides protection to the outsiders.
The 'Doctrine of Indoor Management' also known as Turquand rule is a 150-year old concept, which protects the outsiders against the actions done by the company. Any person who enters into a contract with the company shall ensure that the transaction is authorized by the articles and memorandum of the company.

5(C). In foreign trade, what is the price quoted by a supplier which includes all charges incurred up to door delivery of goods to the buyer, called Franco price.
Franco price: Also known as free price, this quotation includes all charges for delivery of goods to the buyer's warehouse. It implies the free delivery of good.

6(A). Subrogation is "the principle under which an insurer that has paid a loss under an insurance policy is entitled to all the rights and remedies belonging to the insured against a third party with respect to any loss covered by the policy".

7(B). Insurable interest, in a marine policy, must exist at the time of the loss though it is not necessary that it should be in existence at the time of effecting the policy. So long as the seller of a ship or of the goods retains any interest in the property, he can insure it to the extent of his interest.

8(D). Henry Fayol (1841 – 1925) was a french coal-mine engineer, director of mines, and modern management theoretician. His scientific management theory forms the base for business administration and business management. In the academic world, this is also known as Fayolism. Henri Fayol provided one of the most influential modern management concepts of his time. He is the founder of the 14 Principles of management and the five functions of management.

9(A). The Association of Southeast Asian Nations, or ASEAN , was established on 8 August 1967 in Bangkok, Thailand. Currently, there are 10 permanent members of this association. Its headquarter is in Jakarta (Indonesia) .
The creation of ASEAN was motivated by a common fear of communism. The Association of Southeast Asian Nations is a regional intergovernmental organization comprising ten countries in Southeast Asia, which promotes intergovernmental cooperation and facilitates economic, political, security, military, educational, and sociocultural integration among its members and other countries in Asia.

10(A). "Think different" is an advertising slogan used by Apple Computer Inc, now named Apple Inc.

- The slogan was taken as a response to IBM's slogan Think.
- The company was founded on April 1, 1976, by *Steve Jobs, Steve Wozniak, Ronald Wayne.*
- Steve Jobs, the co-founder of the company wished to build an advertising campaign that would remind people about the loyal fan-base of apple and it made him use the slogan "Think different".
- The headquarters of the company is in California US.

1. Amazon

- Amazon company was founded on 5th July 1994 by Jeff Bezos.
- The headquarters of the company is in Seattle, Washington, U.S.
- Amazon company is an E-commerce company that provides *web hosting, online shopping, and content distribution services.*
- The Tagline of the company is " Work Hard, Have fun".

2. Facebook

- Facebook was founded on 4th July 2004 by *Mark Zuckerberg, Chris Hughes, Andrew McCollum, Eduardo Saverin, Dustin Moskovitz.*
- The headquarters of the company is in Menlo Park, California, U.S
- Facebook provides social networking services.

3. Google

- Google was founded on 4th September 1998 by Larry Page & Sergey Brin.
- The headquarters of the company is in *Googleplex, Mountain View, California, U.S.*
- Google is an internet computer software industry.
- The *parent company of Google is Alphabet Inc.*
- The Tagline of the company is "Don't be evil".

11(B). When two variables are related in such a way that a change in the value of one variable affects the value of another variable, then variables are said to be correlated or there is a correlation between these two variables.

According to the direction of change in variables, there are two types of correlation: 1. Positive Correlation 2. Negative Correlation

1. Positive Correlation: Correlation between two variables is said to be positive if the values of the variables deviate in the same direction i.e. if the values of one variable increase (or decrease) then the values of another variable also increase (or decrease). Some examples of positive correlation are correlation between:

1. Heights and weights of a group of persons;
2. Household income and expenditure;
3. Amount of rainfall and yield of crops; and
4. Expenditure on advertising and sales revenue.

In the last example, it is observed that as the expenditure on advertising increases, sales revenue also increases. Thus, the change is in the same direction. Hence the correlation is positive. In the remaining three examples, usually the value of the second variable increases (or decreases) as the value of the first variable increases (or decreases).

2. Negative Correlation: Correlation between two variables is said to be negative if the values of variables deviate in opposite direction i.e. if the values of one variable increase (or decrease) then the values of another variable decrease (or increase). Some examples of negative correlations are correlation between:

1. Volume and pressure of perfect gas;
2. Price and demand for goods;
3. Literacy and poverty in a country; and
4. Time spent on watching TV and marks obtained by students in the examination.

In the first example, pressure decreases as the volume increases or pressure increases as the volume decreases. Thus the change is in opposite direction. Therefore, the correlation between volume and pressure is negative. In the remaining three examples also, the values of the second variable change in the opposite direction of the change in the values of the first variable.

Now, since the sum total of the values of two variables 'X' and 'Y' is equal for all the observations. i.e. x + y = 'z' (equal), for 'z' to remain same (equal) for all observations, if 'x' increases, 'y' should decrease and vice-versa. Thus, option (B) is the correct answer.

12(D). The Special Economic Zones (SEZs) policy was launched in April, 2000. The Special Economic Zones Act, 2005, was passed by Parliament in May, 2005 which received Presidential assent on the 23rd of June, 2005. The SEZs Rules, 2006 came into effect on 10th February, 2006 providing for drastic simplification of procedures and for single window clearance on matters relating to central as well as state governments.

The salient features of the SEZ scheme are:

1. A designated duty-free enclave to be treated as a territory outside the customs territory of India for the purpose of authorized operation in the SEZ.
2. No license required for import.
3. Manufacturing or service activities allowed.
4. The Unit shall achieve Positive Net Foreign Exchange to be calculated cumulatively for a period of five years from the commencement of production.
5. Domestic sales subject to full customs duty and import policy in force.
6. SEZ units will have freedom for subcontracting.
7. No routine examination by customs authorities of export/import cargo.
8. SEZ Developers/Co-Developers and Units enjoy Direct Tax and Indirect Tax benefits as prescribed in the SEZs Act, 2005.

13(A). The Planning Commission was an institution in the Government of India, which formulated India's Five-Year Plans, among other functions.

In his first Independence Day speech in 2014, Prime Minister Narendra Modi announced his intention to dissolve the Planning Commission. It has since been replaced by a new institution named NITI Aayog.

It is an advisory body and makes recommendations to the cabinet. It is responsible for the formulation of a plan for the most effective and balanced utilization of the country's resources. It is responsible for the execution of development programs and plans.

14(A). The Reserve Bank of India (RBI) is India's central bank, also known as the banker's bank. The RBI controls the monetary and other banking policies of the Indian government. The Reserve Bank of India (RBI) was established on April 1, 1935, in accordance with the Reserve Bank of India Act, 1934. The Reserve Bank is permanently situated in Mumbai since 1937.

The primary objectives of RBI are to supervise and undertake initiatives for the financial sector consisting of commercial banks, financial institutions, and non-banking financial companies (NBFCs). RBI maintains the foreign exchange reserves of India.

15(C). Control function of management implies to take corrective course of action.

Control is a function of management which helps to check errors in order to take corrective actions. This is done to minimize deviation from standards and ensure that the stated goals of the organization are achieved in a desired manner.

16(A). Maslow's hierarchy of needs is used to study how humans intrinsically partake in behavioural motivation. Maslow used the terms "physiological", "safety", "belonging and love", "social needs" or "esteem", and "self-actualization" to describe the pattern through which human motivations generally move.

17(C). A listed company opting for buyback of shares under the Companies Act, 1956 has to submit return, after completion of such buy-back within 30 days of such completion to the Registrar of Companies and SEBI.

18(A). Private equity investors invest in a company based mainly on the creditability and the valuation of the company.

Private equity is an alternative form of private financing, away from public markets, in which funds and investors directly invest in companies or engage in buyouts of such companies. Private equity firms make money by charging management and performance fees from investors in a fund.

19(C). Oligopoly is a commodity market that occurs when

there are a small number of firms producing a homogenous commodity. A few sellers, many buyers is the basic character of Oligopoly. In a market situation in which there are only a few firms in the industry producing either the homogeneous product or maybe having product differentiation in a given line of production is termed oligopoly. *The special case of oligopoly* where there are exactly two sellers is termed duopoly. Economic, legal, and technological factors can contribute to the formation and maintenance, or dissolution, of oligopolies. It is difficult to enter an oligopoly industry and compete as a small start-up company.
Monopoly: In the market structure where there is only one seller in the market who controls the entire market supply.
Monopsony: It is the market situation in which there is only one single buyer of the product in the market.

20(B). Proposing a new person to be appointed as auditor of the company under section 224 of the Companies Act, 1956.

21(D). A "Government company" is defined under Section 2(45) of the Companies Act, 2013 as "any company in which not less than 51% of the paid-up share capital is held by the Central Government, or by any State Government or Governments, or partly by the Central Government and partly by one or more State Governments.

22(C). Section-209 is one of the most important sections in the Companies Act, 1956. This section deals with the requirements of maintenance of books of accounts and penalties for non-compliance. A detailed analysis of the provisions of Section 209 and its implication on other related sections is brought out in this article.

23(B). A typical partnership form of the business suffers from the problem of unlimited liability. Liabilities of partners of a firm extend right up to their personal assets. This makes regular partnerships undesirable for a lot of entrepreneurs. One solution for this issue exists in the form of Limited Liability Partnerships, better known as LLP.

24(D). A Government Company is one in which at least 51% of share capital is held by the Central and/or State Government.
Government Company is also called Public Enterprise, State Enterprise. It works as other companies registered under the Companies Act.

25(D). 'Span of Management' means a manager can supervise a limited number of executives.
The span of management, also known as 'span of control', refers to the number of people a manager directly manages. In a wider span of control, a manager has many subordinates who report to him.

26(B). World Bank makes "Doing Business Report" every year.
Doing Business Report is an annually published report which was developed by a team led by Djankov in 2003. It has been elaborated by the World Bank Group since 2003 every year that is aimed to measure the costs to firms of business regulations in 190 countries.

27(C). Payout ratio mean r atio of dividends per share and earnings per share.
The payout ratio is a financial metric showing the proportion of earnings a company pays shareholders in the form of dividends, expressed as a percentage of the company's total earnings.

28(B). For declaration of bonus shares out of General Reserve, a resolution in the shareholders' meeting is necessary is the correct statement.
Bonus shares are additional shares given to the current shareholders without any additional cost, based upon the number of shares that a shareholder owns. These are company's accumulated earnings which are not given out in the form of dividends, but are converted into free shares.

29(C). Flow of Authority correctly signifies the purpose of an Organization Chart.
An organizational chart , also called organigram or organogram, is a diagram that shows the structure of an organization and the relationships and relative ranks of its parts and positions/jobs.

30(C). Increase in the installation of Personal Computer is mainly due to i mprovement of efficiency.
A personal computer (PC) is a multi-purpose computer whose size, capabilities, and price make it feasible for individual use and also its improve efficiency.

31(C). With regard to the rate of return on investment (ROI), ' It is a superior measure compared to the cash flow generated per share' is not a valid statement.
Return on Investment (ROI) is a performance measure used to evaluate the efficiency of an investment or compare the efficiency of a number of different investments.

32(C). When the audit is carried out during the accounting period with some interval it is called "Continuous Auditing".
It is also called as each and every time audit because all the transactions are checked up to date.

33(B). Vouching is called Backbone of auditing.
Vouching is a procedure followed in the auditing process to authorize the credibility of the entries entered in the books of accounts.

34(C). A sales voucher is a form of a receipt or documentation commonly given to a buyer of supplies or goods. It typically serves as proof of purchase when a provider must order or deliver the goods at a later point.
Vouching of sales includes:
Sales Book:
- Sales book records only credit sales of goods to the customer.
- When the goods are sold, invoices are sent out and that only becomes the source document or voucher for recording transactions in the sales book.

Dispatch of goods:
- Dispatching of goods refers to an act of sending goods to a particular place which is undertaken by a logistic unit.
- The term "lead time" can be used to refer to the time elapsed between order and dispatch of goods.
- The document of dispatch clarifies that the goods have been transported or dispatched under the conditions specified.

An auditor verifies and vouches for both the Sales Book and Dispatch of goods documents to check that they support the entries made in them and the inventory is maintained accordingly or not.

35(D). Interest income from Fixed Deposits is fully taxable.
This Tax is Deducted at source by the bank at the time they credit the interest to the account, and not when the FD matures. Suppose a person has an FD for 3 years - banks shall deduct TDS at the end of each year.

36(D). Invoice, Voucher, and Receipt are the documents which are prepared for documentary evidence by business.
- A documentary evidence also known as source document is the original document containing the information about a commercial transaction.
- A source document contains crucial details regarding a transaction, such as the names of the persons involved, the sums paid (if any), the date, and the transaction's substance.
- Invoice, voucher, cash memo, credit and debit note, receipt, etc. are some examples of source document.

37(C). Intellectual property (IP) is a category of property that includes intangible creations of the human intellect. There are many types of intellectual property, and some countries recognize more than others. The most well-known types are copyrights, patents, trademarks, and trade secrets.
- Copyright refers to the legal right of the owner of intellectual property. In simpler terms, copyright is the right to copy. This means that the original creators of products and anyone they give authorization to are the only ones with the exclusive right to reproduce the work.
- A trademark is a word, phrase, symbol, and/or design that identifies and distinguishes the source of the goods of one party from those of others. A service mark is a word, phrase, symbol, and/or design that identifies and distinguishes the source of a service rather than goods.
- Industrial design (ID) is the professional service of creating and developing concepts and specifications that optimize the function, value, and appearance of products and systems for the mutual benefit of both user and manufacturer.

38(D). The Right to Information Act passed in 2005 extends to all states and union territories of India excepting the state of Jammu and Kashmir. This act gives Indian citizens the right to access information about any public authority or institution, including non-government organizations substantially funded by the government.
The main aims of the RTI Act are to provide clarity of the information to the citizens of India, to contain corruption, and to promote accountability in the working of every public authority.
This includes the right to:
- Inspect works, documents, records
- Take notes, extracts, or certified copies of documents or records
- Take certified samples of material
- Obtain information in form of printouts, diskettes, floppies, tapes, video cassettes or in any other electronic mode or through printouts

39(A). Section 6 of the Negotiable Instruments Act 1881 defines "Cheque".
- A Cheque is a bill of exchange drawn on a specified banker and not expressed to be payable otherwise than on demand.
- A cheque is a document that orders a bank to pay a specific amount of money from a person's account to the person in whose name the cheque has been issued.

40(D). From the given statements, statements I and III are correct.
Refer to: 'The Indian e-commerce market is as different from America's brick-and-mortar retail landscape as Walmart's Arkansas home is from Bangalore. Walmart probably has too many stores in its mature home market. Flipkart operates online and in quasi-virgin commercial territory: 95% of Americans shop at Walmart at least once a year, but only 5-10% of Indians have ever bought anything online.'

41(C). This line refers to the fact that Walmart had plans to enter the Indian retail space n 2007 which did not see the light of the day. However, it has fulfilled its ambition of foraying into India's e-commerce space via a majority stake buyout of Flipkart in 2018.
- Options (A) and (D) are incorrect as per the meaning of the statement.
- Option (B) is absurd and nowhere mentioned in the passage.

42(B). From the given statements, statement I is correct.
Refer to: 'SoftBank, a Japanese telecoms and internet giant which became its biggest shareholder after investing $2.5bn just nine months ago, stands to walk away with $4bn.'

43(D). All of the statements showcase the negative side of the e-commerce sector and are correct.

44(A). Refer to, "The Insurance Regulatory and Development Authority of India (IRDAI) has created a special category of insurance policies called micro-insurance policies to promote insurance coverage among economically vulnerable sections of society. A micro-insurance policy is a general or life insurance policy with a sum assured of Rs 50,000 or less."
Statement I is correct since it is mentioned that micro insurance policies are meant to be given to the people from the backward section of the society.
Statement II is also correct since it is also true that micro insurance policies are meant to give coverage of up to Rs 50000 or less.
Statement III is not correct since it is not mentioned anywhere if banks and insurance companies are only authorized to sell the micro insurance policies in the country but the Point of Sales persons are also eligible and that is the main theme of the passage.
So, both Statements I and II are correct.

45(D). Refer to, "Insurance regulator IRDAI has allowed distribution of all micro-insurance products through point-of-sales (PoS), with an aim further increase insurance penetration in the country."
It is clear that the only objective of the IRDAI to allow the distribution of the micro insurance policies through the POS channel is the aim of the authority to increase the insurance coverage in the

country and moreover micro insurance policies are meant for backward people only, so, it would be great to make them available through this channel of distribution.

46(B). Statement I is correct since it is given in the passage that the POS channel of distribution will be used in order to provide policies which cross the permissible limit of coverage applicable to such channel by the IRDAI. Refer to, "On the manner of dealing with cases of health/personal accident (PA) policies where sum insured crosses the limit specified under the POS guidelines, IRDAI said the sponsoring entity is allowed to recognise such policies as being sourced by the POS and pay the fees to the POS."
Statement II is correct since it is true that the insurance companies made representations to do away with the provision of addition of the prefix POS to all the insurance products sold through this channel of distribution. Refer to, "Insurers made representations to change the norms that made it mandatory for every policy sold through the 'Point of Sales Persons' to be separately identified and pre-fixed by the name 'POS'."
Statement III is not correct since there is no reference in the passage that IRDAI can only use the POS channel of distribution to sell the insurance policies and not the insurance companies. This is absurd because IRDAI is the regulator and it does not sell any policy itself.
So, statements I and II are correct according to the information given in the passage.

47(D). Refer to, "Similarly, IRDAI said it has been observed that advantages such as higher insurance penetration, lower prices, increased choice to customers, which would otherwise accrue to the policyholder by making micro-insurance products available through POS channel are being lost. "Therefore, the Authority after reviewing the position, hereby allows all Micro Insurance products of Life, General and Health insurance to be distributed through the POS also," the circular said."
Now, statement A is correct since IRDAI has accepted that the choices were fewer for the policyholders before since the micro insurance products were not available through the POS channel of distribution.
Statement B is also correct since with the availability of the micro insurance products through the POS channel of distribution, the premiums will become lower and more competitive as every insurance company will try to woo the customers with lower premium.
Statement C is not correct since there is no reference in the passage that the insurance companies used to offer the policies without any kind of customization before the decision of the IRDAI to allow micro insurance products to be sold through the POS channel of distribution. This can be eliminated.

48(D). Under Section 54 of the Income Tax Act, 1961, the deduction for capital gain can be claimed only if residential house is transferred.
According to Section 54 of the Income Tax Act, if a person or HUF sells a residential property and uses the proceeds to buy or build another residential property, they are exempted from paying capital gains tax on such gains. Section 54 prohibits taxpayers, including partnership firms, LLPs, corporations, and other associations or bodies, from claiming a tax exemption.

49(B). Excise tax is an indirect tax.
Excise taxes can be used to price an externality or discourage consumption of a product that imposes costs on others. They can also be employed as a user fee to generate revenue from people who use particular government services, revenue which should be used to maintain that government service.

50(D). Income tax is an example of direct tax.
The tax that is directly paid to the Government, is directly imposed on the taxpayer and the liability of tax cannot be passed on to other taxpayers. Some of the examples of Direct taxes are Income-tax, Corporate tax, Minimum Alternate Tax, Dividend Distribution Tax, Securities Transaction Tax, Capital gains Tax .etc.

51(A). The objectives of tax planning is to minimise tax liability.
Tax planning is a focal part of financial planning. It ensures savings on taxes while simultaneously conforming to the legal obligations and requirements of the Income Tax Act, 1961. The primary concept of tax planning is to save money and mitigate one's tax burden.

52(D). Tax management refers to the management of finances, for the purpose of paying taxes. Tax Management deals with filing Returns in time, getting the accounts audited, deducting tax at source etc. Tax Management helps in avoiding payment of interest, penalty, prosecution.
The objective of Tax Management is to comply with the provisions of Income Tax Law and its allied rules. Tax Management deals with filing of Return in time, getting the accounts audited, deducting tax at source etc. Tax Planning relates to future.

53(B). Higher the price of certain luxurious articles, higher will be the demand, this concept is called Veblen effects.
A Veblen good is a good for which demand increases as the price increases. Veblen goods are typically high-quality goods that are made well, are exclusive, and are a status symbol. Veblen goods are generally sought after by affluent consumers who place a premium on the utility of the good.

54(A). Macro level demand forecasting is related to the business conditions prevailing in the economy as a whole.
Macro-level sociology looks at large-scale social processes, such as social stability and change. Micro-level sociology looks at small-scale interactions between individuals, such as conversation or group dynamics.

55(D). Incremental revenue is the change in total revenue irrespective of changes in price or due to the effect of managerial decision on revenue.
Incremental revenue is the additional revenue that a company generates from selling new products or services or from expanding into new markets. It is the revenue that a company would not have otherwise earned if it had not taken these actions.

56(D). Regarding the sales budget sales budget is based on production budget is incorrect.
A sales budget is the estimated number of units

and potential income that a company expects to sell over a specific period of time. Organizations typically measure this on a monthly, quarterly, or annual basis. Companies take into account variables including past sales trends, rival activity, and the current or anticipated economic conditions when forecasting a sales budget.

57(C). Marketing is a process which aims at t he satisfaction of customer needs.
Selling focuses on sale and profit only but marketing has broader goal. Marketing achieves his goal of profit through the customer need satisfaction. In simple words, marketing identifies customer's or market's needs. Then, it tries to fulfill i.e. satisfy that needs by offering right combination of products and services.

58(D). The term marketing refers to a philosophy that stresses customer value and satisfaction.
Marketing mainly emphasizes on customer value and satisfaction. Marketing includes all other elements mentioned in option (A), (B) & (C), but the term mainly deals with customer satisfaction. To satisfy customers, marketer need to offer right combination of benefits and price i.e. value.

59(A). Marketing is the activity, set of institutions & processes for creating, communicating, delivering & exchanging offerings that have value for customers, clients, partners & society.
Marketing is the activity, set of institutions, and processes for creating, communicating, delivering, and exchanging offerings that have value for customers, clients, partners, and society at large.

60(C). Marketing is Both an "art" and a "science" there is a constant tension between the formulated side of marketing and the management side.
Marketing is a science because marketing is about understanding and influencing behaviors. Psychology, the science of behaviors, studies how people react to certain stimuli in predictable ways. This is similar to Newton's' third law - cause and effect. For every marketing action there is a reaction. The science is in anticipating the reactions to your actions. Marketing is an art because marketing is about appreciating the nuances of human behaviors.

61(C). Marketers often use the term market to cover various groupings of customers.
Marketers often use the term market to cover various groupings of customers. They view the sellers as constituting the industry and the buyers as constituting the market. They talk about need markets, product markets, demographic markets, and geographic markets or they extend the concept to cover other markets, such as voter markets.

62(A). The art and science of choosing target markets and getting, keeping, and growing customers through creating, delivering, and communicating superior customer value.
The process of marketing management is as follows.

- The first is choosing a target market.
- Create demand for the product so that the customers in the target market will purchase those products.
- Lastly, it is to create superior value in its product.

63(A). Marketing function types within a larger business might include performing market research, producing a marketing plan, and product development, as well as strategically overseeing advertising, promotion, distribution for sale, customer service and public relations.

64(D). Capital structure represents only long-term funds and excludes all short-term loans and advances. It is a set of patterns in which a company decides to finance its activities with a particular combination of debt, equity, or securities.
Considerations in designing capital structure of a corporate:
(A) Trading on Equity:
Trading on equity refers to taking advantage of equity capital base i.e. by keeping equity in a small proportion against the preference share capital and loan capital.
(B) Cost of Capital:
The cost of capital is also important in designing the capital structure of a corporate.
The expected returns should be more than the expected cost in any investment activity and the cost of capital is the rate of return that capital can expect to earn in an alternative investment of equivalent risk.
(C) Profitability:
An optimum capital structure must provide adequate profits.

65(C). In a unimodal and symmetric distribution, the relationship between averages is like mean = median = mode.
A unimodal distribution has only one clear peak. Initially, the value goes on increasing up to a certain highest point and then starts decreasing. A unimodal distribution can either be symmetric or unsymmetric distribution.

66(B). In a predominantly illiterate area consisting of 10,000 population, data has to be collected from 10% of them. The appropriate technique for data collection would be schedule.
There are two main methods of data collection namely primary and secondary data. Primary data refers to the collection of data directly from the respondents with the help of different techniques like questionnaires, experiments, interviews, observations, etc. and secondary data refers to the collection of data from readily available sources like books, journals, web pages, articles, etc.

67(D). The concept of degrees of freedom is associated with 't'-test, 'F'-test, 'X^2'-test.
The degree of freedom is the number of observations that are free to vary while estimating the statistical analysis. Degrees of freedom is significant to find out critical cutoff values for inferential statistical tests.

68(B). Both Statement I and Statement II are incorrect.

- Fiscal deficit is defined as the excess of total expenditures over the total receipts, excluding the borrowings in a year.
- The gap is covered by borrowing from the public through the sale of bonds or by printing new money.
- Deficit financing may lead to inflation. Due to deficit financing money supply increases & the purchasing power of the people also increase which increases the aggregate demand and the

prices also increases.

- Cash Reserve Ratio (C. R. R.) refers to the number of money banks have to keep with the central bank. If RBI reduces the cash reserve ratio, credit creation will increase.

69(D). The heavy initial expenditure on advertising the launch of a new product should be classified as Deferred Revenue Expenditure.

- Deferred revenue expenditure is an expenditure which is incurred in the present accounting period but its benefits are incurred in the following or the future accounting periods. This expenditure might be written off in the same financial year or over a period of a few years.
- The benefit of such expenditure generally lasts between 3 to 7 years.
- The whole expenditure is not debited to the Profit and Loss Account of the current year but spread over the years for which the benefit is likely to last, only a part of such expenditure is taken to the Profit & Loss Account every year and the unwritten off portion is allowed to stand on the assets side of the Balance Sheet.
- For Example, Amount spent of Rs. 5,00,000 on advertising to introduce a new product in the market and it is estimated that the benefit will last for 5 years, then Rs. 1,00,000 will be charged every year to the profit & loss account and balance amount shown on the Assets side of the Balance Sheet.

70(C). Cash Flow from Operating Activities:

- The operations of a firm directly engaged with providing its commodities and services to the marketplace are known as operating activities.
- Producing, assigning, selling, and promoting a good or service are examples of the enterprise's primary trading pursuits.
- Operating activities are a company's primary source of revenue and expenditure.

Calculation of cash flow from operating activities (Indirect Method):

Particulars	Rs.
Net Loss as per Profit & Loss A/c (1,10,000 - 1,20,000) (+) Decrease in Current Assets: Debtors Operating profit before working capital changes (-) Increase in Current Assets: Prepaid Insurance Decrease in Current Liabilities: Outstanding Rent Creditors Cash used in operating activities	(10,000) 12,000 2,000 (4,000) (18,000) (12,000) (32,000)

71(B). In a bearish phase, the overall trend is that of a decline in share values. After each fall, there is a slight rise but the subsequent fall is even sharper.

- The primary trend lasts from one to three years.
- Over this period, the markets exhibit definite upward or downward movement which is punctuated by shorter spans of a trend reversal in the opposite directions.
- The trend reversal is called the secondary trend.
- The primary trend is indicative of the overall pattern of movement.
- In Dow Theory, the primary trend is the major trend of the market, which makes it the most important one to determine.

72(C). M 3 is known as 'Broad money'.

- In economics, broad money is a measure of the money supply that includes more than just physical money such as currency and coins.
- Broad money is the most inclusive method of calculating a given country's money supply.
- Central Bank tracks the growth of broad money to help forecast inflation.

Broad money (M 3) includes:

- Currency and Coins
- Deposits with an agreed maturity of up to two years, Deposits in checking accounts, savings accounts, and small-time deposits
- Deposits redeemable at notice of up to three months and
- Repurchase agreements
- Money market fund shares/units and
- Debt securities up to two years

73(C). An increase in Exports has a positive effect on the exchange rate of the domestic currency.

- An increase in imports will lead to higher demand for foreign currency and hence the demand for domestic currency reduces.
- This will negatively affect the exchange rate.
- The lower interest rate will attract less foreign investors to invest in the country and thus the demand for currency will decrease, resulting in depreciation in the value of the currency.
- The higher inflation rate will make the country uncompetitive in the international market. The exports will fall resulting in decreased demand for the currency and hence lower value.

74(B). Any statistical measure computed from population data is known as Parameter.

- Parameters are descriptive measures of an entire population.
- However, their values are usually unknown because it is infeasible to measure an entire population.
- Because of this, you can take a random sample from the population to obtain parameter estimates.
- One goal of statistical analyses is to obtain estimates of the population parameters along with the amount of error associated with these estimates.
- These estimates are also known as sample statistics.

75(C). Steps to calculate missing frequency:

- Step 1 - Determine class in which mode lies - As mode given in the question is 48.6, the class in which mode lies is 40-55.
- Step 2 - Find the value of Z, I, h, f_0, f_1, f_2 -
- Z is the value of mode i.e. 48.6

- l is the lower class limit of modal class 40-55 i.e. 40
- h is the class interval of modal class. Class interval = Upper class limit - Lower class limit i.e. 55-40 = 15
- f_0 is the frequency preceding the modal class i.e. 20
- f_1 is the frequency of the modal class i.e. 44
- f_2 is the frequency succeeding the modal class i.e. x.
- Step 3 - Put the data of step 2 in the formula of mode-

Formula of Mode:

$$Z = l + \frac{f_1 - f_0}{2f_1 - f_0 - f_2} \times h$$

Now,

$$Z = l + \frac{f_1 - f_0}{2f_1 - f_0 - f_2} \times h$$

$$\Rightarrow 48.6 = 40 + \frac{44-20}{2\times 44 - 20 - x} \times 15$$

$$\Rightarrow 48.6 - 40 = \frac{24}{68-x} \times 15$$

$$\Rightarrow \frac{8.6}{15} = \frac{24}{68-x}$$

$$\Rightarrow 8.6(68 - x) = 15 \times 24$$

$$\Rightarrow 584.8 - 8.6x = 360$$

$$\Rightarrow 8.6x = 224.8$$

$$\Rightarrow x = 26.1$$

So the value of missing frequency f_2 is 26 (approx).

76(A). From the given statements, statements 1 and 2 are incorrect.
India has a significant presence in the services sector exports. It remained among the top ten trading countries in commercial services in 2019 accounting for 3.5 per cent of world services exports. Notwithstanding the setback witnessed in the wake of the pandemic, India's services sector remained relatively resilient when compared to merchandise trade. The resilience of the services sector was primarily driven by software services, which accounted for 49 per cent (largest component) of total services export. So, statement 1 is not correct.
According to Economics Survey 2020-21, net capital flows was modest in H1: FY 2020-21 at US$ 16.5 billion, as against US$ 40.0 billion in HI: FY 2019-20, mainly accounted for by net repayments of external commercial borrowings (ECBs) and decline in banking capital. During April-October, 2020, net FDI flows recorded an inflow of US$27.5billion, 14.8per cent higher as compared to the first seven months of 2019-20. According to RBI statistics, it can be said that India has been maintaining a capital account surplus in recent years. So, statement 2 is not correct.
Crude Petroleum continues to be the highest imported commodity in April-November, 2020, accounting for 14.3 per cent share vis-à-vis 21.0 per cent in April-November, 2019. The share of gold imports reduced to 5.6 per cent in April-November, 2020 from 6.3 per cent in the corresponding period a year ago, slipping to the third position from the second earlier. So, statement 3 is correct.

77(A). External drains refer to the withdrawal of cash from the banking system by the public. It lowers the reserve of the banks and limits credit creation.

78(B). Securities Appellate Tribunal is a statutory body established under the provisions of Section 15K of the Securities and Exchange Board of India Act, 1992.

- Securities Appellate Tribunal deals with cases with respect to SEBI, IRDAI and PFRDA.
- The jurisdiction of the Securities Appellate Tribunal is the whole of India.
- The Securities Appellate Tribunal has only one bench which sits in Mumbai.

79(B). Depreciation in spirit is similar to Amortization because both depreciation and amortization have the same characteristics except that depreciation is used for tangible assets and amortization for intangible assets.

80(D). Stock and Debtors System is followed where the goods are invoiced to the branch at the selling price.
Under Stock and Debtors System, the Head Office does not open a Branch Account in its books. It maintains a few control accounts for recording the various branch transactions. The Head Office maintains (i) Branch Stock Account, (ii) Branch Expenses Account, (iii) Goods Sent to Branch Account, and (iv) Branch Fixed Assets Account.
At the end of the accounting period, it prepares Branch Adjustment Account and Branch Profit and Loss Account for ascertaining the branch gross profit/ gross loss and the net profit/net loss respectively.

Mock Test 06

1. By which act government checks restrictive trade?
   (a) Industrial Policy Act 1991
   (b) MRTP Act
   (c) FEMA Act
   (d) None of these

2. Liberalization means
   (a) Reducing number of reserved industries from 17 to 8
   (b) Liberating the industry, trade and economy from unwanted restrictions
   (c) Opening up of economy to the world by attaining international competitiveness
   (d) Free determination of interest rates

3. **Direction:** Choose the correct alternatives from the following options as given below for the Assertion (A) and Reason (R).
   Assertion (A): It is wrong to blame the economic policies of India for the unprecedented depreciation of the Indian rupee. Indian rupee falls to a record low against US Doller owing to the increased demand for US Doller in the international market.
   Reason (R): During the pandemic, the US government provided fiscal stimulus to keep the economy on track. The increased demand paved the way for inflation. The US government responded to the inflation by increasing interest rates, consequently, many investors around the globe withdrew their money from other economies and invested in the US economy to earn better profit.
   (a) Both (A) and (R) are true and (R) is the correct explanation of (A).
   (b) Both (A) and (R) are true but (R) is not the correct explanation of (A).
   (c) (A) is true but (R) is false.
   (d) (A) is false but (R) is true.

4. Which of the following statements is/are correct about the new FDI policy?
   1. An entity of a country, which shares a land border with India or where the beneficial owner of investment into India is situated in or is a citizen of any such country, can invest only under the Government route.
   2. This revised FDI policy aims to curb opportunistic takeovers/acquisitions of Indian companies due to the current Covid-19 pandemic.
   (a) Only 1 (b) Only 2
   (c) Both 1 and 2 (d) Neither 1 nor 2

5. Laissez Faire policy is adopted in:
   (a) Socialist Economic system
   (b) Capitalist Economic system
   (c) Mixed Economic System
   (d) Communist Economic System

6. FEMA signifies
   (a) Free Export Management Act
   (b) Foreign Exchange Management Act
   (c) Foreign Exchange Monitoring Act
   (d) Free Export Marketing Act

7. Consumer protection in India is ensured by
   (a) Consumer protection Act, 1946
   (b) Consumer protection Act, 1986
   (c) Consumer protection Act, 1990
   (d) Consumer protection Act, 1968

8. Micro factors of external business environment does not include
   (a) Competitors (b) Customers
   (c) Government Policies (d) None of these

9. Match the following:

List - A	List - B
a) Perfect competition	i) No substitutes
b) Pure monopoly	ii) Homogenous Product
c) Monopolistic competition	iii) Price rigidity
d) Oligopoly	iv) Product differentiation

   (a) (a) - (ii), (b) - (i), (c) - (iv), (d) - (iii)
   (b) (a) - (i), (b) - (ii), (c) - (iii), (d) - (iv)
   (c) (a) - (ii), (b) - (iii), (c) - (iv), (d) - (i)
   (d) (a) - (iii), (b) - (ii), (c) - (iv), (d) - (i)

10. When indifference curves are shaped as right angles?
    I. In the case of perfect complementary products
    II. When MRS is zero
    III. When MRS is infinite
    IV. When prices are declining
    Select the correct code:
    (a) IV only (b) I and II
    (c) I, II and III (d) I, II, III and IV

11. IS and LM curve analysis explain
    A. Product market equilibrium
    B. Money market equilibrium
    C. Capital market equilibrium
    D. Foreign trade equilibrium
    Choose the correct answer from the options given below:
    (a) A and C only (b) A and D only
    (c) A and B only (d) C and D only

12. Market with one buyer and one seller is called
    (a) Monopsony (b) Monopoly
    (c) Bilateral Monopoly (d) None of the above

13. **Direction:** Choose the correct alternatives from the following options as given below for the Assertion (A) and Reason (R).
    Assertion (A): The demand curve of FMCG products in usually relatively inelastic.
    Reasoning (R): FMCG companies usually follow skimming pricing as a strategy to fix the price.
    (a) Both (A) and (R) are incorrect
    (b) Both (A) and (R) are correct
    (c) (A) is incorrect and (R) is correct
    (d) (A) is correct and (R) is incorrect

14. Match the cost concepts in List I and their description in List II

List I (Cost concept s)		List II (Description)	
a.	Sunk cost	i)	Change in total cost for a unit c hange in output
b.	Marginal c ost	i i)	Value of inputs owned and use d in production
c.	Investmen t cost	ii i)	Costs that are unaffected by a fi rm decision
d.	Implicit co st	i v)	The total increase in costs resul ting from a decision

Choose the correct answer from the options given below:

(a) a-ii, b-i, c-iv, d-iii (b) a-i, b-iii, c-iv, d-ii
(c) a-iv, b-ii, c-iii, d-i (d) a-i, b-ii, c-iii, d-iv

15. Match the following:

List - I	List - II
a. Joint Demand	i. Beef and Hide
b. Joint Supply	ii. Pepsi and Coco-cola
c. Derived Demand	iii. Tea and Sugar
d. Competitive Demand	iv. Computer and Operat or

(a) a - iii, b - i, c - iv, d - ii (b) a - iv, b - ii, c - iii, d - i
(c) a - ii, b - i, c - iii, d - iv (d) a - iii, b - iv, c - i, d - ii

16. Demand Analysis includes:
(a) Demand Forecasting
(b) Demand Differentials
(c) Demand Determinations
(d) All of the above

17. Match the following :

List – I	List – II
1. Market segme ntation	i. Pricing high of a new product i nitially.
2. Skimming pric e	ii. Process of disaggregating a ma rket into a number of submarket s.
3. Multilevel mar keting	iii. Translation of the marketing p lan into marketing performance.
4. Sales manage ment	iv. Modified version of direct mar keting.

(a) 1-ii 2-i 3-iv 4-iii (b) 1-iii 2-i 3-ii 4-iv
(c) 1-i 2-ii 3-iii 4-iv (d) 1-iv 2-ii 3-iii 4-i

18. Holistic marketing does not include
(a) Internal Marketing
(b) Integrated Marketing
(c) Performance Marketing
(d) Financial Marketing

19. In the buying decision process, what is the term used for a person who first suggests buying the product or service?
(a) Influencer (b) Initiator
(c) Decider (d) Buyer

20. Which method of setting an advertising budget is most scientific and logical?
1. Objective method
2. Task method
3. Percentage of sales method
(a) Only 1 (b) Only 2
(c) 1, 2 and 3 (d) Both 2 and 3

Ques (21-24): Direction: Read the information carefully and give the answer of the following questions.
Apple decided to slow down some of its old devices but did not inform their customers about it. Although they may have had an understandable reason for this action, their failure to notify customers led to an outrage from users. Apple on their behalf said that the action was taken to save the battery life in the older phones. Now, this reason might have been valid but in reality, it was the lack of transparency that triggered the customers. The brand ended up apologizing to customers and had to offer discounted battery replacements as a way to make up for the anger of customers. If Apple on the first hand had told the customers that their devices would eventually slow down then it might have been less of a scandal. But as the customers got to know about it on their own, it left them feeling suspicious about how else the company might be lying to them about different things. Hence, customer service is an integral component of any successful brand. Bad customer service costs organizations more than any other default they do.

21. Statement I: Customer equity is about the feelings of the customers whether they feel that they received the benefits in accordance with what they paid or not.
Statement II: Customer value is the total combined customer lifetime values of all of the company's customers.
Choose the correct option from those below:
(a) Statement I is correct, Statement II is incorrect.
(b) Statement I is incorrect, Statement II is correct.
(c) Both Statement I and Statement II are correct.
(d) Both Statement I and Statement II are incorrect.

22. Which of the following statements regarding the Teboul model of customer satisfaction is incorrect?
(a) The circle in the Teboul model stands for company's offer
(b) The square in the Teboul model stands for company's offer
(c) The circle in the Teboul model stands for customer needs
(d) The overlapping part of the square and the circle in Teboul models represents customer satisfaction

23. Choose the incorrect statement regarding levels of customer satisfaction:

(a) Dissatisfiers are what customer takes for granted and expect it to be present
(b) There are basically three levels of customer satisfaction and those are Basic, Performance, and Excitement needs
(c) Satisfiers become the benchmarks in the competitive markets
(d) The absence of excitement needs results in customer dissatisfaction and its presence leads to customer satisfaction

24. Statement I: The supplementary elements in the flower model consist of billing, payment, information, and order-taking.
Statement II: The enhancing elements of the flower model consist of expectations, hospitality, safekeeping, and consultation.
Choose the correct option from those below:
(a) Statement I is correct, Statement II is incorrect.
(b) Statement I is incorrect, Statement II is correct.
(c) Both Statement I and Statement II are correct.
(d) Both Statement I and Statement II are incorrect.

Ques (25-28): Direction: Read the following passage and answer the questions given at the end by picking up the appropriate answer from the given alternatives.
Talent management refers to the strategic approach, which involves the process of placing the right people in the right jobs at the right time in order to meet the objectives of the firm. It consists of a number of activities that depend on one another. The two main objectives of all the activities of talent management are attracting suitable candidates from internal and external sources and making them travel with the organization for a longer period of time, i.e., retention. The retention of super keepers is a major task for the talent management team. These people always exceed the expectations of the management, and they expect the work to be challenging.
All the companies formulate separate strategies to deal with super keepers, solid citizens, and misfits. In the long run, misfits become a liability to the company, and to avoid this; the company should work on imparting sufficient training to them and make them compete with solid citizens to some extent. The super keepers and solid citizens should be assigned challenging tasks to keep them engaged with the work process.

25. Among the following, whose performance is quite satisfactory and can meet the expectations of the organization?
(a) Super keepers (b) Keepers
(c) Solid citizens (d) Misfits

26. Talent management involves the identification of what jobs to be filled. Which of the following states the duties, responsibilities, reporting, or subordinating relations of a job?
(a) Job analysis (b) Job description
(c) Job specification (d) Workflow analysis

27. Which of the following refers to the extent to which the individuals are realistic about their careers?
(a) Career resilience (b) Career insight
(c) Career counselling (d) Career identity

28. Which of the following involves training and educating the subordinates?
(a) Career planning (b) Career management
(c) Career development (d) Career coaching

29. Planning function is mainly performed at
(a) Top management level
(b) Middle management level
(c) Lower management level
(d) All of the above

30. The main advantage of functional organization is
(a) Specialization (b) Simplicity
(c) Expert advice (d) Experience

31. Staffing includes:
1. Training
2. Appraisal
3. Placement
4. Directing

Choose the correct answer using the codes given below:
(a) 1 and 3 (b) 2 and 3
(c) 1, 2 and 3 (d) 1, 2, 3 and 4

32. Upward appraisal is done by
(a) Immediate Supervisor
(b) Peers
(c) Subordinates
(d) None of the given options

33. Which of the Following Issue is NOT covered by the 'investment' area of finance?
A. Best Mixture of Financial Investment
B. International Aspects of Corporate Finance
C. Associated Risks and Rewards
D. Pricing Financial Assets
(a) Only A and B (b) Only B
(c) A, B, and D (d) Only D

34. **Direction:** Choose the correct alternatives from the following options as given below for the Assertion (A) and Reason (R).
Assertion (A): Weighted average cost of capital should be used as a hurdle rate for accepting or rejecting a capital budgeting proposal.
Reason (R): It is because by financing in the proportions specified and accepting the project, yielding more than the weighted average required return, the firm is able to increase the market price of its stock.
(a) Both (A) and (R) are false.
(b) Both (A) and (R) are true.
(c) (A) is true, while (R) is false.
(d) (A) is false, while (R) is true.

35. Cash Flow from assets involves which of the following component(s)?
A. Operating Cash Flow
B. Capital Spending
C. Change in Net Working Capital
(a) Only A (b) Only B
(c) Only A and C (d) A, B, and C

36. Which of the following refers to the cash flows that result from the firm's day-to-day activities of producing and selling?
A. Operating Cash Flows
B. Investing Cash Flows
C. Financing Cash Flows

(a) Only A (b) Only B
(c) Only A and C (d) A, B, and C

37. Match the following:

List - I	List - II
(a) Matching Principle	(i) Ignores future profit estimations
(b) Materiality Principle	(ii) Normal basis for valuing assets
(c) Conservatism Principle	(iii) Revenues and expenses of a particular period
(d) Cost Principle	(iv) Relates to relative size or importance of item or event

(a) (a)- i (b)- iv (c)-ii (d)-iii
(b) (a)-ii (b)-iii (c)-iv (d)-i
(c) (a)-iii (b)-iv (c)-i (d)-ii
(d) (a)-iv (b)-iii (c)-ii (d)-i

38. Choose the correct statement regarding Capital structure:
Statement - I: Capital structure refers to the composition of long-term funds.
Statement - II: These include equity share capital, preference share capital, debentures, all debts, and all reserves.
(a) Both Statements I and II are correct.
(b) Statement I is correct but Statement II is incorrect.
(c) Statement I is incorrect but Statement II is correct.
(d) Both Statements I and II are incorrect.

39. Match the items of the following two lists and suggest the correct code:

List – I	List – II
a. Pay-back Rate of Return	i. Discounted Cash Flow Technique
b. Internal Rate of Return	ii. Compounded values of investments and returns
c. Benefit-Cost Ratio	iii. Crude method for project evaluation
d. Net Terminal Value Method	iv. Varying sized projects evaluation

(a) a-ii, b-iii, c-i, d-iv (b) a-iii, b-i, c-iv, d-ii
(c) a-i, b-iv, c-ii, d-iii (d) a-iv, b-ii, c-iii, d-i

40. Match the items of the following two lists and suggest the correct code:

List – I	List – II
a. Realised yield method	i. Cost of equity share capital
b. Taxation	ii. Cost of equity capital
c. Cost of total capital employed	iii. Cost of debt capital
d. Dividend growth is a consideration	iv. Weighted cost of capital

(a) a-iv b-iii c-ii d-i (b) a-ii b-iv c-i d-iii
(c) a-ii b-iii c-iv d-i (d) a-i b-ii c-iii d-iv

41. A stipulation in a bond for payment of compound interest on failure to pay simple interest at the same rate as was payable upon the principal is not a penalty within the meaning of this section:
(a) Section 74 of the Indian Contract Act, 1872
(b) Section 75 of the Indian Contract Act, 1872
(c) Section 76 of the Indian Contract Act, 1872
(d) None of these

42. The agreement made with an alien enemy is:
(a) Valid (b) Voidable
(c) Unlawful (d) Difficult

43. What is known as a charter of a Company?
(a) Memorandum of Association
(b) Bye-laws
(c) Articles of Association
(d) Prospectus

44. A who owes Rs. 10000 to B dies leaving an estate of Rs. 6000. The legal representation of A are –
(a) Liable for Rs. 10000 (b) Liable for Rs. 6000
(c) Not liable at all (d) Liable for Rs. 3000

45. Standing offer means
(a) Offer allowed to remain open for acceptance over a period of time
(b) Offer made to the public in general
(c) When the offeree offers to qualified acceptance of the offer
(d) Offer made to a definite person

46. Holding company is defined in section __________ of the companies Act.
(a) 2(46) (b) 2(26)
(c) 3(46) (d) 3(16)

47. The chairman of the company has __________ vote.
(a) 1 (b) 3
(c) 2 (d) None of these

48. Minimum __________ and maximum __________ members constitute a private limited company.
(a) 2, 10 (b) 7, unlimited
(c) 2, 15 (d) 2, 50

49. Punjab National Bank was established i n which year ?

(a) 1880 (b) 1887
(c) 1894 (d) 1900

50. Match the following:

List - A	List - B
a) RBI	i) Governing Debentures
b) FEMA	ii) Bank rate
c) Company Law	iii) Mutual Funds
d) SEBI	iv) Forex activities

(a) (a) - (iv), (b) - (iii), (c) - (ii), (d) - (i)
(b) (a) - (ii), (b) - (iv), (c) - (i), (d) - (iii)
(c) (a) - (ii), (b) - (iii), (c) - (i), (d) - (iv)
(d) (a) - (iii), (b) - (iv), (c) - (ii), (d) - (i)

51. Which of the following is not a quantitative tool of money supply used by the RBI?
(a) Bank rate
(b) Repo rate
(c) Open market operation
(d) Margin requirement

52. Match the following:

List - A	List - B
(a) Masala b ond	(i) Convertible bond
(b) Euro bo nd	(ii) Issued by non – Japanese compani es in Japan
(c) Samurai bond	(iii) Issued outside India but denomin ated in Indian rupees
(d) FCCB	(iv) Denominated in a currency other than the home currency

(a) (a) - (iv), (b) - (i), (c) - (ii), (d) - (iii)
(b) (a) - (iv), (b) - (ii), (c) - (i), (d) - (iii)
(c) (a) - (iii), (b) - (iv), (c) - (i), (d) - (ii)
(d) (a) - (iii), (b) - (iv), (c) - (ii), (d) - (i)

53. What is the proportion of the Central government's ownership of capital in Regional Rural Banks?
(a) 50% (b) 60%
(c) 45% (d) 55%

54. Non-Banking Financial Companies (NBFCs) are Financial Intermediaries engaged primarily in the business of:
i. Accepting Deposits
ii. Lending loans and advances
iii. Leasing
iv. Hire purchasing
Codes:
(a) i and ii (b) iii and iv
(c) i and iii (d) i, ii, iii and iv

55. Which one of the following is not an objective of fiscal policy of Indian Government?
(a) Full employment
(b) Regulation of Inter-State-trade
(c) Price stability
(d) Equitable distribution of wealth & income

56. Which among the followings are correct statements with regard to NBFC in India?
(A) All NBFCs should be registered with RBI.
(B) NBFCs cannot accept demand deposits.
(C) NBFCs do not form part of the payment and settlement system and cannot issue cheques drawn on itself.
(D) Deposit insurance facility of Deposit Insurance and Credit Guarantee Corporation is not available to depositors of NBFCs.
Choose the correct from the options given below:
(a) (A), (B), (C) only (b) (A), (B), (C), (D)
(c) (A), (B), (D) only (d) (A), (D) only

57. Match List-I with List-II and select the correct code:

List – I	List – II
A. Voluntary Return of income	1 Section 139 (5)
B. Return of Loss	2. Section 139 (4)
C. Belated Return	3. Section 139 (3)
D. Revised Return	4. Section 139 (1)

(a) A - 2, B - 3, C - 4, D - 1
(b) A - 3, B - 4, C - 1, D - 2
(c) A - 1, B - 2, C - 3, D - 4
(d) A - 4, B - 3, C - 2, D - 1

58. Which amongst the following is Artificial Juridical Person?
(a) Corporation (b) Local Fund
(c) District Board (d) None of these

59. A citizen of India who goes abroad for the purpose of employment, he must stay in India at least for ____ days to become a resident.
(a) 90 days (b) 162 days
(c) 180 days (d) 182 days

60. Section______ of the Income Tax Act deals with exempted incomes.
(a) Section 2 (b) Section 7
(c) Section 10 (d) Section 80

61. Central Board of Direct Taxes launched e-nivaran facility to help the taxpayers. e-nivaran relates to:
(a) Income Tax Refunds
(b) Income Tax Returns
(c) Tax Deducted at Source
(a) All (a), (b) and (c) are true.
(b) (a) is true and (b) is false.
(c) (b) is true and (c) is false.
(d) (c) is true and (a) is false

62. When a population is heterogeneous, it is divided into groups, so that there is homogeneity within the group and heterogeneity between the groups, and some items are selected at random from each group. It is a case of:
1. Cluster Random Sampling

2. Systematic Random Sampling
3. Quota Sampling
4. Stratified Random Sampling

(a) Only 1 (b) Both 2 and 3
(c) Both 1 and 3 (d) Only 4

63. Graphical and numerical methods are specialized processes utilized in:
(a) Education Statistics (b) Descriptive Statistics
(c) Business Statistics (d) Social Statistics

64. Action research means
(a) A longitudinal research
(b) An applied research
(c) A research initiated to solve an immediate problem
(d) A research with socioeconomic objective

65. In a unimodal and symmetric distribution the relationship between averages is like:
(a) Mean > Median > Mode
(b) Mean < Median < Mode
(c) Mean = Median = Mode
(d) Mean > Median < Mode

66. Linear programming models solve problems dealing with ________.
(a) Relatives and absolutes
(b) Routes and mixes
(c) Dispersions and similarities
(d) Rupees and percentages

67. What is the device through which the functional relationship is studied and forecasting is made called?
(a) Correlation (b) Regression
(c) Time Series (d) None of the above

68. If the probability of inclusion of every unit of the population in the sample is equal, it is called:
(a) Simple Random Sampling
(b) Stratified Random Sampling
(c) Systematic Sampling
(d) None of these

69. The accounting equation (i.e., Assets = Liabilities + Capital) is an expression of:
(a) Cost Concept
(b) Business Entity Concept
(c) Money Measurement Concept
(d) Matching Concept

70. The main objective of providing depreciation is:
(a) To calculate true profit
(b) To show the true financial position in the balance sheet
(c) To reduce tax burden
(d) To provide funds for replacement of fixed assets

71. Which accounting standard deals with accounting for amalgamations?
(a) AS-24 (b) AS-10
(c) AS-20 (d) AS-14

72. In accounting equation approach for recording business transactions all accounts are divided into three categories, namely:
(a) Personal, Real and Nominal
(b) Assets, Liabilities and Capital
(c) Expenditure, Revenue and Loss
(d) None of the above

73. Cash flows denominated in foreign currency are reported in a manner consistent with:
(a) AS-3 (b) AS-5
(c) AS-11 (d) AS-21

74. As per Section 143 (9) of the Companies Act 2013, every auditor is required to _____.
(a) attend any general meeting
(b) report fraud
(c) comply with accounting standards issued by ICAI
(d) sign the report

75. Any amount to be written off after the admission of a partner is transferred to the capital accounts of all partners in:
(a) Their capital ratio
(b) New profit sharing ratio
(c) Old profit sharing ratio
(d) Sacrificing ratio

76. What is the item that appears below the line in the Profit and Loss Account?
(a) Proposed Dividend
(b) Provision for Taxation
(c) Contribution to Provident Fund
(d) Miscellaneous expenditure written off

77. Mohan, has rendered his services in India and retired in 2015. He then shifted and settled in Singapore. The pension received by him for such services would be ____?
(a) Deemed to accure or arise outside India
(b) Deemed to accure or arise in India only when it is received in India
(c) Deemed to accure or arise in India only when it is received outside India
(d) Deemed to accure or arise in India

78. In the Income Tax Act, __ is a certificate which an employer gives to his employees. It certifies the amount of tax deducted by the employer from the salary of the employee.
(a) Form 16 (b) Form12
(c) Form 15 (d) Form 26AS

79. For the Assessment Year 2020-21, Section 192A provides for deduction of tax at the rate of ______ on premature taxable withdrawal from the employees' provident fund scheme.
(a) 15 percent (b) 20 percent
(c) 10 percent (d) 5 percent

80. If the mode of the following data is 7, then the value of k in the data set 3, 8, 6, 7, 1, 6, 10, 6, 7, $2k + 5$, 9, 7, and 13 is:
(a) 3 (b) 7
(c) 4 (d) 1

// Smart Answer Sheet //

Correct Percentage of students who answered correctly.

Skipped Percentage of students who skipped.

Q.	Ans.	Correct	Skipped	Q.	Ans.	Correct	Skipped	Q.	Ans.	Correct	Skipped
1	B	53.81%	40.83%	2	B	81.8%	13.21%	3	A	17.98%	81.73%
4	C	41.0%	31.63%	5	B	50.62%	45.89%	6	B	21.99%	73.56%
7	B	15.36%	71.48%	8	C	57.51%	40.9%	9	A	64.96%	30.11%
10	C	22.81%	67.45%	11	C	29.99%	67.78%	12	C	68.8%	30.2%
13	D	29.58%	67.7%	14	A	22.73%	74.22%	15	A	55.37%	39.83%
16	D	28.16%	67.82%	17	A	40.67%	35.43%	18	D	55.19%	40.56%
19	B	82.17%	10.87%	20	C	25.37%	73.66%	21	D	65.96%	33.4%
22	A	86.77%	12.12%	23	D	21.48%	70.51%	24	B	45.18%	37.18%
25	C	60.33%	36.77%	26	B	82.44%	11.73%	27	B	88.04%	11.61%
28	D	32.65%	67.09%	29	D	79.53%	18.88%	30	A	44.58%	53.4%
31	C	79.41%	18.13%	32	C	43.51%	44.52%	33	B	23.41%	71.04%
34	B	52.77%	36.6%	35	D	48.93%	44.05%	36	A	54.43%	37.48%
37	C	60.4%	32.75%	38	B	49.29%	48.94%	39	B	80.92%	13.46%
40	C	49.63%	32.03%	41	A	21.75%	72.43%	42	C	89.01%	10.92%
43	A	77.73%	11.8%	44	B	58.18%	32.36%	45	A	48.02%	34.4%
46	A	24.52%	67.16%	47	C	27.15%	68.05%	48	D	63.49%	32.0%
49	C	31.63%	67.22%	50	B	61.06%	33.53%	51	A	17.07%	77.57%
52	D	88.99%	10.2%	53	A	51.0%	43.66%	54	D	14.49%	80.26%
55	B	65.62%	34.33%	56	B	26.84%	72.53%	57	A	30.88%	67.16%
58	A	52.79%	40.96%	59	D	64.95%	33.26%	60	C	12.28%	72.57%
61	A	23.71%	67.88%	62	D	63.27%	30.17%	63	B	29.88%	69.79%
64	C	76.28%	14.48%	65	C	29.34%	68.84%	66	B	49.84%	46.71%
67	B	22.42%	74.93%	68	C	18.02%	67.96%	69	B	77.55%	10.3%
70	B	82.75%	11.28%	71	D	12.91%	71.45%	72	B	78.24%	16.25%
73	C	26.43%	72.93%	74	C	45.27%	38.41%	75	B	77.3%	21.68%
76	A	42.99%	37.73%	77	A	52.49%	40.36%	78	A	15.21%	68.07%
79	C	52.37%	33.38%	80	D	67.4%	31.51%				

// Hints and Solutions //

1(B). The government checks restrictive trade by MRTP Act.

The Monopolistic and Restrictive Trade Practices Act, 1969, was enacted

- To ensure that the operation of the economic system does not result in the concentration of economic power in hands of few.
- To provide for the control of monopolies.
- To prohibit monopolistic and restrictive trade practices.

2(B). Liberalization means liberating the industry, trade and economy from unwanted restrictions.

Core features of liberalization are:

- A change in the attitude of the state towards an industrial society.
- A change from a centrally-planned economy to a market led country.
- A change from excessive government intervention to minimal intervention.
- A change from nationalization to privatization.

3(A). Both (A) and (R) are true and (R) is the correct explanation of (A).

The assertion is correct.

- We know that the value of any currency depends on many factors such as interest rate differentiation, inappropriate monetary policies, and excessive inflation. So, it is wrong to blame economic policy for the deprecation of the Indian rupee. As the US dollar is getting stronger, the values of other currencies may not remain constant.

The reason is correct.

- During the pandemic, many countries infused money in economies to protect them from crumbling. The US too did this. It is a basic principle that if cash flow increases it will lead to inflation. Generally, central banks respond to inflation by increasing interest rates to encourage people to save and invest. The US economy is one of the most reliable economies. Hence, it is an attractive destination for many investors. As the US has increased the interest rates, investors around the globe have started to withdraw their money from other economies (including India) and invest it in the US. This is the reason for the depreciation of the Indian rupee. (Government policies are not responsible for the situation)

4(C). FDI is allowed in India under two modes: the automatic route and the government route. Companies don't need government approval for Automatic Route. Companies need Government approval in Government mode. Provisions of the New FDI policy:

-
- An entity of a country, which shares a land border with India or where the beneficial owner of investment into India is situated in or is a citizen of any such country, can invest only under the Government route. Hence, Statement 1 is correct.
- A transfer of ownership in an FDI deal that benefits any country that shares a border with India will also need government approval.
- Investors from countries not covered by the new policy only have to inform the RBI after a transaction rather than asking for prior permission from the relevant government department.
- India shares land borders with Pakistan, Afghanistan, China, Nepal, Bhutan, Bangladesh, and Myanmar .
- This revised FDI policy aims to curb opportunistic takeovers/acquisitions of Indian companies due to the current Covid-19 pandemic. Hence, Statement 2 is correct.

5(B). Laissez Faire policy is adopted in Capitalist

Economic system.

A capitalist economic system is one characterized by free markets and the absence of government intervention in the economy.

The driving principle behind laissez-faire, a French term that translates to "leave alone" (literally, "let you do"), is that the less the government is involved in the economy, the better off business will be, and by extension, society as a whole.

6(B). FEMA signifies Foreign Exchange Management Act.

The Foreign Exchange Management Act, 1999 (FEMA) is an Act of the Parliament of India "to consolidate and amend the law relating to foreign exchange with the objective of facilitating external trade and payments and for promoting the orderly development and maintenance of foreign exchange market in India".

7(B). Consumer protection in India is ensured by Consumer protection Act, 1986.

The Consumer Protection Act, 1986 was an Act of the Parliament of India enacted in 1986 to protect the interests of consumers in India.

8(C). Micro factors of external business environment does not include government policies.

Competitors and customers are included in micro factors of external business environment.

9(A). The correct match code is (a) - (ii), (b) - (i), (c) - (iv), (d) - (iii).

Perfect competition - Homogenous Product:

- Perfect competition is a theoretical market structure in which the number of buyers and sellers is very large, all are engaged in buying and selling a homogeneous product without any artificial restrictions and all are possessing perfect knowledge of the market at a time.

Pure monopoly - No substitutes:

- A pure monopoly means a single seller with no competitors and no substitute available for his product. Monopoly power is the extent to which a firm can influence the market price or quantity supplied to the market and also the extent to which conditions of business are influenced by a single firm.

Monopolistic competition - Product differentiation:

- Monopolistic competition is a type of imperfect competition such that there are many producers competing against each other, selling differentiated products that are not perfect substitutes. Barriers to entry and exit are low and the decisions of any one firm do not directly affect its competitors.

Oligopoly - Price rigidity:

- Oligopoly is a market structure with a small number of firms, each seller having a high percentage of the market and cannot afford to ignore the actions of the others. Under an oligopoly, after a certain point, there is no increase in demand for the firm which changes its price, thus firms stick to the same price over a period of time leading to price rigidity.

10(C). The correct answer is 'I, II, and III'.

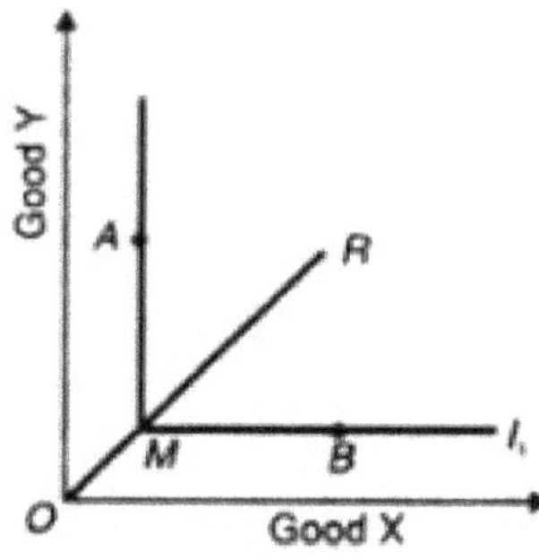

- When MRS is infinite the indifference curve is vertically parallel to the Y-axis.
- When MRS is 0 the indifference curve is horizontally parallel to the X-axis.
- If the two goods are perfect complements the indifference curve is right-angled or L shaped , as shown in Figure.
- The vertical portion of the I_1, curve reveals that no amount of reduction in good Y will lead even to a slight increase in good X.
- For example, points A, M, and B are all on the curve but point B involves the same amount of Y but more of X than point M.
- Thus MRS $_{XY}$ is zero . The two goods X and Y are consumed in the desired ratio, as indicated by the slope of the ray OR at point M. Such complementary goods are left and right shoes which are used in the 1 : 1 fixed ratio.

11(C). The correct answer is A and B only.

Analysing the options:

- Product Market Equilibrium: The goods market equilibrium schedule is the IS curve (schedule). It shows combinations of interest rates and levels of output such that planned (desired) spending (expenditure) equals income.
- Money Market Equilibrium: The LM curve is the schedule of combinations of interest rates and levels of income such that the money market is in equilibrium.
- Capital Market Equilibrium: Capital market equilibrium represents a point where supply and demand meet for investments. Capital market equilibrium may be difficult to reach as the price for various investments can change quickly for a host of reasons. IS or LM curve have no relation to these.
- Foreign Trade Equilibrium: In a two-country trade equilibrium model it is supposed that there are two countries A and B and they produce two commodities: X and Y. The trade equilibrium of these countries can be analysed under constant, increasing, and decreasing cost conditions. Again this has nothing to do with the IS/LM curve.

12(C). Market with one buyer and one seller is called bilateral monopoly.

A bilateral monopoly is a market structure consisting of both a monopoly and a monopsony.

A monopoly exists when a specific person or enterprise is the only supplier of a particular commodity.

A monopsony is a market structure in which a single buyer substantially controls the market as the major purchaser of goods and services offered by many sellers.

13(D). Here (A) is correct and (R) is incorrect.

Assertion (A): The demand curve of FMCG products is usually relatively inelastic.
The price elasticity of demand is an indicator of the impact on the demand for a product in relation to its price change. Some types of consumer goods show a higher price elasticity of demand than others. For example, non-essential goods have a high elasticity of demand, while essential goods or consumer staples have a low elasticity of demand. Factors that affect the price elasticity of demand include the availability of competitive substitutes and the brand recognition of products. Relatively inelastic demand is one when the percentage change produced in demand is less than the percentage change in the price of a product.
Reasoning (R): FMCG companies do not follow skimming pricing as a strategy to fix the price, they follow penetration pricing.
Price skimming is a product pricing strategy by which a firm charges the highest initial price that customers will pay and then lowers it over time. As the demand of the first customers is satisfied and competition enters the market, the firm lowers the price to attract another, more price-sensitive segment of the population. This approach contrasts with the penetration pricing model, which focuses on releasing a lower-priced product to grab as much market share as possible.

14(A). The correct match code is a-ii, b-i, c-iv, d-iii.
Sunk Cost - Value of inputs owned and used in production:
- Sunk costs are those which have already been incurred and which are unrecoverable. In business, sunk costs are typically not included in consideration when making future decisions, as they are seen as irrelevant to current and future budgetary concerns. Sunk costs are in contrast to relevant costs, which are future costs that have yet to be incurred.

Marginal Cost - Change in total cost for a unit change in output:
- Marginal cost can help an organization optimize its production through economies of scale. Marginal cost is the change in the total cost that arises when the quantity produced is incremented by one unit; that is, it is the cost of producing one more unit of a good. A company that is looking to maximize its profits will produce up to the point where marginal cost (MC) equals marginal revenue (MR). Fixed costs are constant regardless of production levels, so higher production leads to a lower fixed cost per unit as the total is allocated over more units. Variable costs change based on production levels, so producing more units will add more variable costs.

Investment Cost - Total increase in costs resulting from a decision:
- The cost of an investment includes acquisition charges such as brokerage, fees, and duties. If an investment is acquired in exchange, or part exchange, for another asset, the acquisition cost of an investment is determined by reference to the fair value of the asset given up.

Implicit cost - Costs that are unaffected by firm decision:
- An implicit cost is a cost that exists without the exchange of cash and is not recorded for accounting purposes. Implicit costs represent the loss of income but do not represent a loss of profit. These costs are in contrast to explicit costs, which represent money exchanged or the use of tangible resources by a company.

15(A). The correct match code is a - iii, b - i, c - iv, d - ii.
Joint Demand - Tea and Sugar:
- Joint demand refers to the relationship between two commodities or services when they are demanded together. For example, there is a joint demand for tea and sugar, car and petrol, pens and ink, etc.

Joint Supply - Beef and Hide:
- Joint supply refers to a product that can result in at least two other types of goods. For example, cows can be used for beef and hide; sheep can be utilized for milk products, wool, etc.

Derived Demand - Computer and Operator:
- Derived demand refers to the demand for a good or service that results from the demand for a different related good or service. For example, computers and operators, mobile phones, and lithium batteries.

Competitive Demand - Pepsi and Coca-Cola:
- Competitive demand occurs when there is an alternative product or service a customer can choose from i.e. the demand for products that have close substitutes. For example, Pepsi and Coca-cola, tea and sugar, meat and fish, etc.

16(D). Demand Analysis includes Demand Forecasting, Demand Differentials and Demand Determinations.
Demand analysis is the process of understanding the customer demand for a product or service in a target market.

17(A). The correct match code is 1-ii 2-i 3-iv 4-iii.
Market Segmentation - Process of disaggregating a market into a number of submarkets:
- Market segmentation is a marketing term that refers to disaggregating prospective buyers into groups or segments with common needs and who respond similarly to a marketing action.

Skimming Price - Pricing high of a new product initially.:
- Price skimming is a product pricing strategy by which a firm charges the highest initial price that customers will pay and then lowers it over time. As the demand of the first customers is satisfied and competition enters the market, the firm lowers the price to attract another, more price-sensitive segment of the population.

Multilevel Marketing - Modified version of direct marketing:
- Multi-level marketing is a distribution model companies use to get their product to consumers. Instead of directly offering their products to consumers online or in brick-and-mortar stores, they use sales representatives to distribute and sell their products. It is a modified version of direct marketing.

Sales Management - Translation of the marketing plan into marketing performance:
- Sales management specifically contributes to achieving the marketing objectives of a firm. In fact, sales managers set their personal selling objectives and formulate personal selling policies and strategies.

18(D). Holistic marketing does not include financial marketing.

Holistic marketing refers to a marketing strategy that considers the whole of a business and all the different marketing channels as a system.

19(B). An Initiator is a person who first suggests buying the product or service.
An Influencer is someone in your niche or industry with sway over your target audience.
A Decider is the person who ultimately determines any part of or the entire buying decision-whether to buy, what to buy, how to buy, or where to buy.
A Buyer is the person who handles the paper work of the actual purchase.

20(C). The objective method, task method, and percentage of sales method is the most scientific and logical method.
Objectives and Task Method:
This is the most appropriate advertising budget method for any company. It is a scientific method to set an advertising budget. The method considers the company's own environment and requirements. Objectives and task methods guide the manager to develop his promotional budget.
Percentage of Sales Method:
It is a commonly used method to set an advertising budget. In this method, the amount for advertising is decided on the basis of sales. The advertising budget is a specific percentage of sales. The sales may be current or anticipated. Sometimes, past sales are also used as the base for deciding on an ad budget.

21(D). Both Statement I and Statement II are incorrect.
Customer equity is the total combined customer lifetime values of all of the company's customers. In a simpler way, this concept says that the more loyal a customer will be, the more will be customer equity.
Customer value, in short, is about the feelings of the customers and that if they feel that they received the benefits in accordance with what they paid or not.

22(A). The statement 'The circle in the Teboul model stands for company offer' regarding the Teboul model of customer satisfaction is incorrect.
The square in the Teboul model stands for company offer. The circle in the Teboul model stands for customer needs. The overlapping part of the square and the circle in the Teboul models represents customer satisfaction.

23(D). The statement 'Absence of excitement needs results in customer dissatisfaction and its presence leads to customer satisfaction' is incorrect regarding levels of customer satisfaction.
There are basically three levels of customer satisfaction those are Basic needs (Dissatisfiers), Performance needs (Satisfiers), and Excitement needs (Delighters). Dissatisfiers are what customer takes for granted and expect it to be present. Satisfiers become the benchmarks in the competitive markets. The absence of excitement needs does not result in customer dissatisfaction but its presence adds to customer satisfaction.

24(B). Statement I is incorrect, and Statement II is correct.
The flower model in service marketing consists of Core and Supplementary elements. The supplementary elements are again of two types which are facilitating and enhancing elements. The facilitating elements consist of billing, payment, information, and order-taking and the enhancing elements consist of expectations, hospitality, safekeeping and consultation.

25(C). The performance of solid citizens is quite satisfactory and can meet the expectations of the organization.
The performance of the super keepers is above the expectations of the management.
Keepers perform very well, but when compared with the performance of the super keepers, their performance is quite low.
The performance of misfits is not up to the expectations of the management and occupies the lowermost level in the performance pyramid of the organization.

26(B). Job description includes all the duties and responsibilities to be performed by an individual as a part of the job.
Job analysis is the process of determining the nature of the job by studying its duties, responsibilities, skills, knowledge, and qualification required to accomplish the job in an effective manner.
Job specifications include all the educational qualifications, certifications, skills, qualities, etc. that are required for the job.
Workflow analysis refers to a detailed study of the flow of work from job to job in a work process.

27(B). The three facets of career motivation are as follows:
- Career insight: It refers to the extent to which individuals are realistic about their careers.
- Career resilience: It is the ability to adapt to changes to match the market demand even though the circumstances are discouraging.
- Career identity: It refers to the extent to which a job or work of a person defines that person.

28(D). Career coaching is an activity that focuses on teaching, educating, instructing, and training subordinates.
Career planning is a process in which an employee becomes aware of personal skills, interests, knowledge, motivation, and other characteristics and establishes an action plan to attain specific goals.
Career management is a process of enabling employees to understand and develop their skills and interests and to use these skills and interests more effectively.
Career development refers to the long life series of activities that contribute to a person's career, exploration, establishment, success, and fulfillment.

29(D). Planning function is mainly performed at all the management levels.
Top level managers make long-term plans, middle level managers make departmental plans and lower level managers make operating plans.

30(A). The main advantage of functional organization is specialization.
A functional organization is a common type of organizational structure in which the organization is divided into smaller groups based on specialized functional areas, such as IT, finance, or marketing.

31(C). Staffing includes:
1. Training
2. Appraisal

3. Placement

Staffing is the process of hiring eligible candidates in the organization or company for specific positions.

32(C). Upward appraisal is done by subordinates.

In organizations that use upward appraisal, after the manager has finished preparing and discussing their performance appraisals with each subordinate, the subordinates individually and anonymously complete a questionnaire about how well the manager manages them.

33(B). International Aspects of Corporate Finance is not covered by 'investment' area of finance.

The three major areas of business finance are:

- Best Mixture of Financial Investment
- Associated Risks and Rewards
- Pricing Financial Assets

34(B). Both (A) and (R) are true.

Weighted Average Cost of Capital (WACC):

- WACC is referred to as a company's cost of capital.
- When each category of cost of capital employed is calculated proportionately then it is known as the Weighted Average Cost of Capital.
- The purpose of WACC is to the determine cost of capital structure based on the proportion of debt, equity, and preference stock it has.
- The company pays interest on its debts, a fixed yield on its preferred stock, and gives a dividend to its equity holders.
- WACC is used as a hurdle rate in order to accept or reject a capital budgeting proposal.
- After accepting the proposal using this method, financing activities take place in the proportions specified, which leads to yielding more returns on the basis of the cost spent on that project, which ultimately helps the firm to see an increase in the market price of its stock.

Therefore, both Assertion and Reason are true, and also Reason is the correct explanation of Assertion.

35(D). Cash Flow from assets involves:

- Operating Cash Flow
- Capital Spending
- Change in Net Working Capital

Cash flow from assets is the aggregate total of all cash flows related to the assets of a business.

36(A). Operating Cash Flows refers to the cash flows that result from the firm's day-to-day activities of producing and selling.

Operating cash flow is a measure of the amount of cash generated by a company's normal business operations.

37(C). The correct match code is (a)-iii (b)-iv (c)-i (d)-ii.

Matching Principle - Revenues and expenses of a particular period:

- This principle states that businesses must incur expenses in order to gain revenues. In other words, revenues and expenses of a particular period.

Materiality Principle - Relates to relative size or importance of item or event:

- This principle concerns the importance of information, the size, and the nature of transactions that reports in the financial statement. In other words, it relates to the relative size or importance of an item or event.

Conservatism Principle - Ignores future profit estimations:

- This principle records all probable losses when they are discovered, while gains are recorded when they are fully realized. This principle ignores future profit estimates.

Cost Principle - Normal basis for valuing assets:

- This principle states that all the assets acquired by the company must be recorded at their cost price. It follows a normal basis for valuing assets.

38(B). Statement I is correct but Statement II is incorrect.

Capital structure:

- The capital structure represents only long-term funds and excludes all short-term loans and advances.
- It is a set of patterns in which a company decides to finance its activities with a particular combination of debt and equity-like equity share capital and preference share capital and other long-term reserves .
- Capital structure is a part of the financial structure.
- Capital structure refers to only long-term debts and equity in the total capital of the company whereas financial structure refers to the owner's equity and all debts i.e. long-term and short-term.

Therefore, Statement I: Capital structure refers to the composition of long-term funds is correct but Statement II: These include equity share capital, preference share capital, debentures, all debts, and all reserves is incorrect.

39(B). The correct match code is a-iii, b-i, c-iv, d-ii.

Pay-back Rate of Return - Crude method for project evaluation:

- It is the time required to recover the funds invested initially. This method is used to evaluate a project whose payback period is minimum.

Internal Rate of Return - Discounted Cash Flow Technique:

- It is used to estimate the rate of return of the investment after accounting for all discounted cash flows together with the time value of money.

Benefit-Cost Ratio - Varying sized projects evaluation:

- It is used to determine the overall value of money for undertaking the evaluation of different-sized projects.

Net Terminal Value Method - Compounded values of investments and returns:

- This method is used in valuing a company by taking the sum of all cash flows from an investment on a specified rate of return. In other words, compounded values of investments and returns.

40(C). The correct match code is a-ii b-iii c-iv d-i.

Realised yield method - Cost of equity capital:

- It refers to the actual return earned during the holding period of investment. The cost of equity is calculated using this method.

Taxation - Cost of debt capital:

- Taxation is a part of the Cost of debt. The after-tax cost of debt formula is an effective interest rate multiplied by (1 - tax rate).

Cost of total capital employed - Weighted cost of capital:

- When each category of cost of capital employed is calculated proportionately then it is known as the Weighted cost of capital.

Dividend growth is a consideration - Cost of equity share capital:

- It is used to calculate the Cost of equity share capital. Formula: $R_e = (D_1 / P_0) + g$ Where, Re = Cost of equity share, D_1 = Dividend/share next year, P_0 = current share price, g = dividend growth rate.

41(A). A stipulation in a bond for payment of compound interest on failure to pay simple interest at the same rate as was payable upon the principal is not a penalty within the meaning of Section 74 of the Indian Contract Act, 1872.
The Indian Contract Act, 1872 prescribes the law relating to contracts in India and is the key act regulating Indian contract law.

42(C). The agreement made with an alien enemy is Unlawful.
In India, a contract with an alien enemy is void but a contract with an alien friend is valid under the Indian Contract Act.

43(A). Memorandum of Association is known as a charter of a Company.
Memorandum of Association is a legal document prepared during the formation and registration process of a company to define its relationship with shareholders and it specifies the objectives for which the company has been formed.

44(B). A who owes Rs. 10000 to B dies leaving an estate of Rs. 6000. The legal representation of A are liable for Rs. 6000.

45(A). Standing offer means offer allowed to remain open for acceptance over a period of time.
Standing Offer is an agreement between a supplier and buyer where supplier agrees to provide the desired goods and services to the buyer as and when asked at a predetermined price.

46(A). Holding company is defined in section 2(46) of the Companies Act.
Section 2(46) of the Companies Act, 2013 defines a Holding Company. The company is said to be the holding company if that particular company holds/ owns at least 50% of the other companies and has the authority to make management decisions, influence, and control the company's board of directors. If one company holds more than 50% of the shares of another or appoints a majority of the other company's directors, the second company is a subsidiary of the first. The first company is called the holding company. If the holding company owns 100% of the shares of the subsidiary, the subsidiary is known as a wholly owned subsidiary (WOS).

47(C). The chairman of the company has 2 vote.
A chairman is an executive elected by a company's board of directors who is responsible for presiding over board or committee meetings. A chairman often sets the agenda and has significant sway as to how the board votes.

48(D). Minimum 2 and maximum 50 members constitute a private limited company.
A private company is owned entirely by a relatively small group of individuals or other entities providing capital.

49(C). Punjab National Bank was established in 1894.
Punjab National Bank, abbreviated as PNB, is an Indian public sector bank headquartered in New Delhi, India. The bank is the second largest public sector bank in India, both in terms of business and its network.

50(B). The correct match code is (a) - (ii), (b) - (iv), (c) - (i), (d) - (iii).
RBI - Bank rate:

- The formulation, framework, and institutional architecture of monetary policy in India have evolved around these objectives – maintaining price stability, ensuring adequate flow of credit to sustain the growth momentum, and securing financial stability.

FEMA - Forex activities:

- The main objective behind the Foreign Exchange Management Act (1999) is to consolidate and amend the law relating to foreign exchange with the objective of facilitating external trade and payments.

Company Law - Governing Debentures:

- The basic objectives of the Company law are A minimum standard of good behavior and business honesty in company promotion and management.

SEBI - Mutual Funds:

- The fundamental objective of SEBI is to safeguard the interest of all the parties involved in trading. It also regulates the functioning of the stock market.

51(A). The bank rate is not a quantitative tool of money supply used by the RBI.
The bank rate is the rate charged by the central bank for lending funds to commercial banks. In the event of a fund deficiency, a bank can borrow money from the central bank of a country. In India's case that would be the Reserve Bank of India. The borrowing is done on the basis of the monetary policy of that country.

52(D). The correct match code is (a) - (iii), (b) - (iv), (c) - (ii), (d) - (i).
Masala bond - Issued outside India but denominated in Indian rupees:

- Masala Bonds are rupee-denominated bonds issued outside India by Indian entities. They are debt instruments that help to raise money in local currency from foreign investors.

Euro bond - Denominated in a currency other than the home currency:

- A Eurobond is a debt instrument that's denominated in a currency other than the home currency of the country or market in which it is issued.

Samurai bond - Issued by non – Japanese companies in Japan:

- A samurai bond is a yen-denominated bond issued in Tokyo by non-Japanese companies and is subject to Japanese regulations.

FCCB - Convertible bond:

- A foreign currency convertible bond (FCCB) is a type of convertible bond issued in a currency different than the issuer's domestic currency.

53(A). The proportion of the Central government's ownership of capital in Regional Rural Banks is 50%.
The shareholding pattern of Regional Rural Banks

among the three sponsoring entities is 50: 35: 15 among the central government, sponsoring bank, and state government, respectively. Regional Rural Banks are financial institutions that ensure adequate credit for agriculture and other rural sectors. The Reserve bank of India (RBI) has no ownership of Regional Rural Banks.

54(D). Non-Banking Financial Companies (NBFCs) are Financial Intermediaries engaged primarily in the business of Accepting Deposits, Lending loans and advances, Leasing, and Hire purchasing.
NBFCs (Non-Banking Financial Companies) play an important role in promoting inclusive growth in the country, by catering to the diverse financial needs of bank excluded customers. Further, NBFCs often take a lead role in providing innovative financial services to Micro, Small, and Medium Enterprises (MSMEs) most suitable to their business requirements. NBFCs do play a critical role in participating in the development of an economy by providing a fillip to transportation, employment generation, wealth creation, bank credit in rural segments, and supporting financially weaker sections of society.

55(B). Regulation of Inter-State-trade is not an objective of fiscal policy of Indian Government.
Fiscal policy in India is the guiding force that helps the government decide how much money it should spend to support the economic activity, and how much revenue it must earn from the system, to keep the economy running smoothly.

56(B). NBFC is defined as a company registered under the Companies Act, 2013, and also under the RBI act 1934 under section 45-IA . These type of companies provides banking services without holding any banking license. NBFCs lend and make investments and hence their activities are akin to that of banks; however, there are a few differences as given below:
i. NBFC cannot accept demand deposits ;
ii. NBFCs do not form part of the payment and settlement system and cannot issue cheques drawn on themselves ;
iii. T he deposit insurance facility of Deposit Insurance and Credit Guarantee Corporation is not available to depositors of NBFCs, unlike in the case of banks .
Hence, the correct option is (A).

57(A). The correct match code is A - 4, B - 3, C - 2, D - 1.
Voluntary Return of income - Section 139 (1):
- Section 139(1) deals with two types of belated income returns i.e. Mandatory Returns and Voluntary Returns.

Return of Loss-Section 139 (3):
- Section 139(3) states that if an individual has suffered a loss in a year, he is not mandated to file an ITR for that particular assessment year.

Belated Return-Section 139 (4):
- If the ITR could not have been filed within the due date even then the same can be filed validly as a belated return within the time limit given u/s 139(4) of the IT Act.

Revised Return-Section 139 (5):
- An assessee who is required to file a return of income is entitled to revise of return of income u/s 139(5), filed by him to make such amendments, additions, or changes as may be found necessary by him.

58(A). Corporation is an Artificial Juridical Person.
A public corporation established under special Act of legislature and a body having juristic personality of its own are known to be Artificial Juridical Persons.

59(D). A citizen of India who goes abroad for the purpose of employment, he must stay in India at least for 182 days to become a resident.
This condition will apply only if his total income (other than foreign sources) exceeds Rs. 15 lakh.

60(C). Section 10 of the Income Tax Act deals with exempted incomes.
As per the Income Tax Act, 1961, every Indian citizen who earns above a certain threshold of income is liable to pay taxes. Hence, with the drawdown of each financial year, taxpayers seek out ways to minimize their tax liabilities.

61(A). The correct answer is All (a), (b) and (c) are true.
e-Nivaran is a scheme launched by the Central Board of Direct Taxes to help taxpayers. Its aim is to promote a paperless environment. It is an electronic system of lodging one's complaint, fast-tracking taxpayer grievances, and ensuring early resolution or redressal of their complaint. Through this e-portal, taxpayers can register all complaints related to delay in refunds, filing of e-returns, Tax Deducted at Source (TDS), PAN issues, and those pertaining to their Assessing Officer (AO).

62(D). When a population is heterogeneous, it is divided into groups, so that there is homogeneity within the group and heterogeneity between the groups, and some items are selected at random from each group. It is a case of Stratified Random Sampling.
Stratified Random Sampling:
- This method of sampling involves dividing a heterogeneous population into small sub-groups called strata. These sub-groups/strata are based on some homogeneity of the members in the group. Then lastly some items are selected at random from each group. This process of classifying groups is also known as stratification.

Cluster Random Sampling:
- This sampling technique is used in an area or geographical cluster sampling for market research.

Systematic Random Sampling:
- This method of probability sampling is used when there is a low risk of data manipulation.

Quota Sampling:
- A quota sample allows researching a subgroup that shares great interests with the topic of research.

63(B). Graphical and numerical methods are specialized processes utilized in Descriptive Statistics.
A descriptive statistic is a summary statistic that quantitatively describes or summarizes features from a collection of information, while descriptive statistics is the process of using and analyzing those statistics.

64(C). Action research means a research initiated to solve an immediate problem.
Action research is an interactive inquiry process that balances problem-solving actions implemented in a collaborative context with data-driven collaborative analysis or research to understand underlying causes enabling future

predictions about personal and organizational change.

65(C). In a unimodal and symmetric distribution the relationship between averages is like mean = median = mode.
A unimodal distribution is a distribution that has one clear peak. A symmetrical distribution is one where the mean, mode, and the median are all equal.

66(B). Linear programming models solve problems dealing with routes and mixes.
Linear programming is a method to achieve the best outcome (such as maximum profit or lowest cost) in a mathematical model whose requirements are represented by linear relationships.

67(B). The device through which the functional relationship is studied and forecasting is made is called regression.
Regression is a statistical method used in finance, investing, and other disciplines that attempts to determine the strength and character of the relationship between one dependent variable and a series of other variables.

68(C). If the probability of inclusion of every unit of the population in the sample is equal, it is called systematic sampling.
Systematic sampling is a statistical method that researchers use to zero down on the desired population they want to research.

69(B). The accounting equation (i.e., Assets = Liabilities + Capital) is an expression of business entity concept.
The business entity concept states that the transactions associated with a business must be separately recorded from those of its owners or other businesses.

70(B). The main objective of providing depreciation is to show the true financial position in the balance sheet.
Depreciation is an accounting method of allocating the cost of a tangible or physical asset over its useful life or life expectancy.

71(D). AS-14 specifically deals with the accounting for amalgamations and the treatment of any resultant difference arising on amalgamation in the books of Transferee Company.

72(B). In accounting equation approach for recording business transactions all accounts are divided into three categories, namely Assets, Liabilities and Capital.
The accounting equation is considered to be the foundation of the double-entry accounting system. On a company's balance sheet, it shows that a company's total assets are equal to the sum of the company's liabilities and shareholders' equity.

73(C). Cash flows denominated in foreign currency are reported in a manner consistent with AS-11.
The standard deals with the principal issue with respect to accounting for foreign operations and foreign currency transactions in deciding which exchange rate to be used and a guidance on recognizing the financial effect of changes in exchange rates in the financial statements.

74(C). As per Section 143 (9) of the Companies Act 2013, every auditor is required to comply with accounting standards issued by ICAI.
An auditor is an authorized person who verifies and reviews the financial records and financial statements of a company and ensures that they are prepared in accordance with the norms. He also checks whether any tampering or manipulation has been done with the financial data with the aim of hiding any fraud or malpractice within the company.

75(B). Any amount to be written off after the admission of a partner is transferred to the capital accounts of all partners in new profit sharing ratio.
New profit sharing ratio is the proportion in which the old partners, as well as the new partners of a firm, agree to distribute the future profit of that organization.

76(A). Proposed Dividend appears below the line in the Profit and Loss Account.
Proposed dividend is the dividend declared or proposed to be distributed among the shareholders of the company during a financial year which will be paid in the next financial year.

77(A). Any pension payable outside India to a person residing permanently outside India shall be deemed to accrue or arise outside India.
Following incomes are treated as incomes deemed to have accrued or arisen in India:

- Capital gain arising on transfer of property situated in India.
- Income from a business connection in India.
- Income from salary in respect of services rendered in India.

78(A). In the Income Tax Act, From 16 is a certificate which an employer gives to his employees. It certifies the amount of tax deducted by the employer from the salary of the employee.
Form 16 is the salary TDS certificate. If your income from salary for the financial year is more than the basic exemption limit of Rs 2,50,000 your employer is required, by the Income Tax Act, to deduct TDS on your salary and deposit it with the government.

79(C). TDS will be deducted at 10 percent, provided PAN is submitted. However, if the provident fund holder furnishes Form No. 15G or 15H, then no tax will be deducted at source. If a person fails to submit PAN or Form No 15G or 15H, then tax will be deducted at source at the maximum marginal rate.

80(D). Given data values are $3, 8, 6, 7, 1, 6, 10, 6, 7, 2k+5, 9, 7$, and 13
In the above data set, values 6,7 have occurred more times i.e., 3 times
But given that mode is 7 .
So, 7 should occur more times than 6 .
Then the variable $2k+5$ must be 7
$\Rightarrow 2k+5=7$
$\Rightarrow 2k=2$
$\therefore k=1$

Mock Test 07

1. **Direction** : Match List-I and List-II and indicate the correct code:

List-I	List-II
(a)Job specifications	(i)The procedure for determi ning the duties and skill requ irements of a job and the kin d of pe who should be hired f or it.
(b)Job description	(ii) A list of human requirem ents.
(c)Job analysis	(iii) A list of job's duties, resp onsibilities, reporting relatio nships, working conditions a nd supervisory responsibiliti es.

Code: (a) (b) (c)
(a) (i) (ii) (iii) (b) (ii) (iii) (i)
(c) (iii) (ii) (i) (d) (ii) (i) (iii)

2. What are the Considerations in designing the capital structure of a corporate?
(a) Trading on Equity (b) Cost of Capital
(c) Profitability (d) All of the above

3. To become a director in a company the person must obtain:
(a) Business Licence (b) Director's Licence
(c) TIN (d) DIN

4. As per the RBI Act, 1934, the following functions are described as the functions of a Central Bank :
(i) Banking functions
(ii) Advisory functions
(iii) Supervisory functions
(iv) Promotional functions
Identify the correct combination:
(a) (i), (iii) and (iv) (b) (i), (ii) and (iv)
(c) (ii), (iii) and (iv) (d) Only (i) and (iii)

5. **Direction** : Match the items of List-I with List-II and indicate the correct code:

List-I	List-II
(a)Fiscal Policy	(i) Mitigation of National haz ards
(b)Technology Policy	(ii) Balance of Payments
(c)Macro-Economic Po licy	(iii) Fiscal Federalism
(d)Monetary Policy	(iv) Inflation

Codes: (a) (b) (c) (d)
(a) (i) (ii) (iii) (iv) (b) (iii) (i) (ii) (iv)
(c) (iv) (iii) (i) (ii) (d) (ii) (i) (iv) (iii)

6. Which of the following factor is not directly responsible for slowing down the growth of infrastructure?
(a) High level of perceived political risk.
(b) High level of sunk cost.
(c) High probability of time and cost over-run.
(d) Introduction of competition in all sectors.

7. Out of the following which is not a major component of Gross Domestic Product (GDP)?
(a) Personal Consumption Expenditure
(b) Gross Private Domestic Investment
(c) Net Personal Income
(d) Net Exports

8. Which of the following is required while vouching Sales?
(i) Examine sales book
(ii) Examine sales Invoices
(iii) Examine Cut off Points
(iv) Examine the numerical sequence of source documents generated within the organization
(a) (i), (ii), (iii) and (iv) (b) (i), (ii)
(c) (ii), (iv) (d) (i), (iii)

9. The amount of depreciation charged to Profit and Loss Account varies every year under:
(a) Fixed installment method
(b) Annuity Method
(c) Diminishing method
(d) Insurance policy method

10. **Direction** : For the following statements of Assertions (A) and Reasoning (R) indicate the correct code:
Assertion (A) : Price Reduction normally leads to an increase in the demand for a commodity.
Reasoning (R) : Price reduction leads to the entry of new buyers of the commodity in the market.
(a) (A) is correct but (R) is not correct
(b) (A) is not correct but (R) is correct.
(c) Both (A) and (R) are correct and (R) offers full explanation of (A).
(d) Both (A) and (R) are correct and (R) does not offer full explanation of (A).

11. The minimum Long Run Average Cost (LAC) can be determined on:
(I) LAC curve for a normal production function
(ii) LAC curve for a linear production function
(iii) Planning curve
(iv) Envelope curve
(a) (i), (ii), (iii), (iv) (b) (ii), (iii), (iv)
(c) (i), (iii), (iv) (d) (i), (ii), (iv)

12. Monopoly is not considered desirable from the point of view of the society mainly because of the monopolist endeavors to:
(a) Earn net revenue on the sale of all goods including those involving no cost of production.
(b) Earn net revenue on the sale of goods in short_run as well as long run.
(c) Charge different prices for the same product from the different categories of buyers.
(d) Produce below the economic capacity level when he exhibits satisfaction with normal profit only.

13. When the date is classified only on the basis of descriptive characteristics that cannot be quantified is known as:
(a) Geographical classification
(b) Chronological classification
(c) Qualitative classification
(d) Quantitative classification

14. Which one of the following is a false description?

(a) In a moderately asymmetrical distribution, the empirical relationship between Mean, Mode and Median suggested by Karl Pearson is Mean – Mode = 3 (Mean – Median).
(b) The coefficient of variation is an absolute measure of dispersion.
(c) The measure of skewness indicates the direction in the distribution of numerical values in the data set.
(d) Kurtosis refers to the degree of flatness of peakedness in the region around the mode of a frequency curve.

15. In economics, _______ is a period where some factor inputs are fixed, while the others are variable.
(a) long run (b) short-run
(c) very long period (d) None of the above

16. Computers that recognize data as discrete signals are called?
(a) Analog computers (b) Digital computers
(c) Hybrid computers (d) Super computers

17. ________ are those cost which does not change with change in output.
(a) Variable cost (b) Fixed cost
(c) Semi-variable cost (d) Semi-fixed cost

18. **Direction** : Match List-I and List-II and choose the correct code:

List-I	List-II
(a)Equity theory	(i) Motivation depends on ratio s of inputs and outcomes of self and others.
(b)Vroom's theory	(ii) People are motivated to ach ieve a goal to the extent that th ey expect that certain activities will help them to reach the goa l.
(c)Porter and Law yer Model	(iii) There exists a complex rela tionship among motivation, per formance and satisfaction.
(d)Herzberg's theo ry	(iv) A challenging job that has o pportunities for achievement, r ecognition, responsibility and g rowth will motivate employees.

Code: (a) (b) (c) (d)
(a) (i) (ii) (iii) (iv) (b) (ii) (i) (iii) (iv)
(c) (iii) (ii) (i) (iv) (d) (i) (iii) (ii) (iv)

19. Marginal product is ____________.
(a) produced when all factors of production are employed at optimum efficiency
(b) the extra output obtained from employing an additional unit of the factor
(c) left to the entrepreneur after he has paid all his expenses
(d) the annual output of the most efficient producer in the industry

20. Which type of differentiation is used to gain a competitive advantage through the way a firm designs its distribution coverage, expertise and performance?
(a) Channel differentiation
(b) Services differentiation
(c) People differentiation
(d) Product differentiation

21. **Direction** : For the following statements of Assertions (A) and Reasoning (R) indicate the correct code:
Assertion (A) : Too many stimuli make a person accommodated to those sensations, Sensory adaption is a problem that concerns many advertisers, which is why they try to change their advertising campaigns regularly.
Reasoning (R) : To cut through the advertising clutter and to ensure that consumers perceive advertisement, marketers try to increase sensory input.
Codes:
(a) (A) is right and (R) is wrong.
(b) (A) is wrong and (R) is right
(c) Both (A) and (R) are right but (R) does not explain (A).
(d) Both (A) and (R) are right and (R) explains (A).

22. Which of the following is not a feature of payback period method?
(a) It is simply a method of cost recovery and not of profitability
(b) It does not consider the time value of money.
(c) It does not consider the risk associated with the projects.
(d) It is very difficult to calculate.

23. Which of the following is not a source of credit information of prospective customers?
(a) Letter of credit (b) Bank Reference
(c) Trade Enquiry (d) Credit Bureau

24. Select the correct code regarding motives for holding inventories by firms:
(a) Transaction motive
(b) Environmental motive
(c) Precautionary motive
(d) Speculative motive
(e) Competitive motive
(a) (a),(b),(c),(d) (b) (a),(b),(d),(e)
(c) (a),(d),(e) (d) (a),(c),(d)

25. **Direction** : Match the items of List-I with the items of List-II and select the correct code:

List-I	List-II
(a)Golden parachute s	(i)The right to purchase a sta ted number of shares of com pany stock at today's price at some time in the future.
(b)Gainsharing	(ii)An incentive plan that eng ages employees in a common effort to achieve productivity objectives and share the gain s.
(c)Stock-option	(iii) Payments companies ma ke in connection with a chan ge in ownership or control of a company.
(d)Annual bonus	(iv) Plans designed to motiva te short term performance of managers and are tried to pr ofitability.

Code: (a) (b) (c) (d)
(a) (iii) (i) (ii) (iv) (b) (i) (ii) (iii) (iv)

(c) (ii) (iii) (i) (iv) (d) (iii) (ii) (i) (iv)

26. Which Government co-owns 'OneWeb', a Low Earth Orbit (LEO) satellite communications operator?

(a) India (b) United Kingdom
(c) Canada (d) Switzerland

27. **Direction** : For the following statements of Assertions (A) and Reasoning (R) indicate the correct code:
Assertion (A) : "Banks globally are facing more challenges now and Macro sustainability is a necessity but not sufficient for sustainable economic growth."
Reason (R) :"Putting regulations in place is only one part and their implementation is equally important for achieving growth and sustainability."

(a) (A) and (R) both are true and (R) is the correct explanation of (A).
(b) (A) and (R) both are true but (R) is not the correct explanation of (A).
(c) (A) is true and (R) is false.
(d) (A) is false and (R) is true.

28. **Direction** : Match the items of Column-I with the items in Column-II and suggest the correct code:

Column-I	Column-II
(a)Interbank call market	(i) Money market
(b)Commercial Bills	(ii) Promissory note
(c)Commercial paper market	(iii) Short-term maturity
(d)Treasury bills	(iv) Government papers

Codes: (a) (b) (c) (d)

(a) (i) (ii) (iv) (iii) (b) (iii) (i) (ii) (iv)
(c) (i) (iii) (iv) (ii) (d) (iv) (iii) (ii) (i)

29. **Direction** : Match the items of List-I with List-II with regard to Balance of Payments equilibrium:

List-I	List-II
(a)Exchange control.	(i) Exporters surrender foreign exchange to the central bank.
(b)Trade Policy Measure	(ii) Bank rate raised by the central bank
(c)Expenditure reducing policy	(iii) Reduction in foreign exchange
(d)Expenditure switching policy	(iv) Enhancing exports by granting

(a) (i) (iv) (ii) (iii) (b) (i) (ii) (iii) (iv)
(c) (iii) (ii) (iv) (i) (d) (iv) (iii) (ii) (i)

30. What is not correct about the International Development Association(IDA)?
(a) Following the earthquake in 2015, IDA has helped Nepal rebuild and recover.
(b) IDA ranks as the highest performing multilateral development bank in 2016.
(c) IDA is a subsidiary bank of IBRD.
(d) India has procured the highest amount of international loans from IDA.
Codes:

(a) (a) and (b) (b) Only (c)
(c) Only (d) (d) (a) and (c)

31. Which payment system is set to be made available round the clock from December 2020?

(a) NEFT
(b) RTGS
(c) Bharat Bill Payment System
(d) Aadhar Enabled Payment System

32. Which of the following will not enter the profit and loss account of the bank?

(a) Interest expense on deposits
(b) Interest earned on advances.
(c) Profit/loss on sale of assets
(d) Income from investment banking related activities

33. **Direction** : Match the items of Column-I with those of Column-II:

Column-I	Column-II
(a)Exchange control	(i) Adverse BOP
(b)Price Control	(ii) Domestic firms
(c)Import control	(iii) Mass Consumption product
(d)Legislative control	(iv) Industrial location

Code: (a) (b) (c) (d)

(a) (ii) (i) (iii) (iv) (b) (iv) (ii) (iii) (i)
(c) (iii) (ii) (i) (iv) (d) (ii) (iii) (i) (iv)

34. **Direction** : Match the items of Column-I with those of Column-II:

List-I	List-II
(a)Provision for taxation	(i) Adverse BOP
(b)Live-stock	(ii) Domestic firms
(c)Sundry Debtors	(iii) Mass Consumption product
(d)Interest accrued	(iv) Industrial location

Code: (a) (b) (c) (d)

(a) (iv) (iii) (i) (ii) (b) (iv) (iii) (ii) (i)
(c) (iii) (iv) (ii) (i) (d) (ii) (i) (iii) (iv)

35. What is the reason for net omissions and errors account?

(a) Reduces errors (b) It is a balancing item
(c) Increases errors (d) None of the above

36. Which of the following is not a cash in-flow?

(a) Decrease in creditors (b) Decrease in debitors
(c) Issues of shares (d) Sales of a fixed asset

37. Which one of the following is not the characteristic of normal distribution?

(a) Mean, median and mode for the normal distribution are equal.
(b) The two tails of the normal curve extend to infinity in both directions but never touch the horizontal axis.
(c) For different values of standard deviation, the height of the mean ordinate remains the same.
(d) The number of independent constraints of the normal distribution are N, X and σ.

38. **Direction** : Consider the following statements. Which of the statements are correct?
Statement-I: Non-parametric tests are based on some assumptions about the parent population from which

the sample has been drawn.
Statement-II: The standard deviation of the sampling distribution of means is called standard error of means.

(a) Both the statements are true
(b) Both the statements are false
(c) Statement-I is true but Statement-II is false
(d) Statement-II is true but Statement-I is false

39. Which of the following is a deterioration of mental efficiency, reality testing and moral judgment that results from in-group pressure?

(a) Harassment (b) Groupthink
(c) Group Burnout (d) Group control

40. Tax Evasion attracts a penalty at _______ under Section _______ of Income Tax Act, 1961.

(a) 200%, 269 A (b) 200%, 270 A
(c) 200%, 271 A (d) 100%, 265 A

41. Which of the following is related to the practical means of determining a moral course of action?

(a) Meta ethics (b) Virtue ethics
(c) Normative ethics (d) Applied ethics

42. Who is the head of the committee for Analysis of QR (Quick Response) Code, set up by the Reserve Bank of India?

(a) D.B. Phatak (b) Narasimhan
(c) Y. V. Reddy (d) D. K. Mohanty

43. Sales of a firm are Rs. 74 Lakh, variable costs Rs. 40 lakh, fixed costs Rs 8 lakh. Operating leverage of the firm will be :

(a) 1.48 Lakh (b) 1.78 Lakh
(c) 1.31 Lakh (d) 2.42 Lakh

44. Which Indian bank has launched a special card named 'Shaurya KGC Card', for armed forces?

(a) ICICI Bank (b) HDFC Bank
(c) Axis Bank (d) Yes Bank

45. On which emission standards Bharat Stage emission is based on?

(a) European emission standards
(b) American emission standards
(c) Russian emission standards
(d) None of the above

46. What is the share of Indian capital goods in world exports?

(a) 2% (b) 0.8%
(c) 3% (d) 5%

47. Amount of Calls in Arrears is shown in the balance sheet ____________.

(a) as deduction from issued capital
(b) as addition to issued capital
(c) as deduction from subscribed capital
(d) as addition to subscribed capital

48. "A company remains free from the hazards of all personal misfortunes of its member" is derived from the benefit of incorporation of the company being_____.

(a) Limited liability
(b) Perpetual succession
(c) Infinite membership
(d) Independent legal entity

49. Which combination of the following methods indicate quantitative methods of control of credit creation practiced by the Reserve Bank of India?
(a) Bank Rate
(b) Open Market Operations
(c) Variable Reserve Ratios
(d) Credit Rationing

(a) (a), (b) and (c) (b) (a), (b) and (d)
(c) (b), (c) and (d) (d) (a), (c) and (d)

50. Which one of the following development financial institutions in India have started the special refinance scheme for the resettlement and rehabilitation of voluntary retired workers of the National Textile Corporation of India?

(a) IDBI (b) SIDBI
(c) ICICI (d) None of the above

51. Where a company purchases its own shares out of reserves or securities premium account, a sum equal to the nominal value of the shares so purchased is transferred to the _______ and details of such transfer are disclosed in the balanced sheet.

(a) Capital Reserve Account
(b) Reserve Capital Account
(c) General Reserve
(d) Capital Redemption Reserve Account

52. Which of the following approaches is adopted for the valuation of human resources according to the economic concept?

(a) Replacement cost approach
(b) Opportunity cost approach
(c) Historical cost approach
(d) None of the above

53. Who has the sole authority to issue currency in India?

(a) Finance Ministry (b) RBI
(c) SBI (d) NITI Aayog

54. Accounting Standard-6 is meant for :

(a) Accounting for Fixed Assets
(b) Accounting treatment for goodwill
(c) Depreciation Accounting
(d) Disclosure of Accounting policies

55. Which of the following is not a feature of OTCEI?

(a) Quick transfer and disposal system
(b) Nationalised computerized networking
(c) Ringless trading system
(d) Fragmentation of regional stock exchanges.

56. What is the objective of Public Distribution System in India?

(a) To provide food security to poor
(b) To stop Hoarding and Black marketing
(c) To prevent traders to take excess price
(d) All the above

57. **Direction** : Consider the following statements. Which of the statements are correct?
Statement-I: Marketing is the process by which a firm profitably translates customer needs into revenue

Statement-II: Marketing is the messages and/or actions that cause messages and/or actions.

Codes :

(a) (I) is correct but (II) is not correct.

(b) (II) is correct but (I) is not correct.

(c) (I) and (II) both are correct.

(d) (I) and (II) both are incorrect.

58. The advertising method in which an advertisement is broadcasted simultaneously on several radio stations and/or television channels is known as :

(a) Black-out (b) Consolidation

(c) Roadblock (d) Cornering

59. As per section 80G maximum deduction allowed for any cash donation is upto:

(a) Rs. 1,000 (b) Rs. 2,000

(c) Rs. 5,000 (d) Rs. 10,000

60. The rights of the consumer as enunciated under section 6 of the consumer protection Act, 1986 include:

(A) To be protected against the marketing of goods and services which are hazardous to life and property

(B) To be assured the competitive price and low-cost quality products and services

(C) To be assured that consumers' interests will service the due consideration at appropriate forums

(D) To be protected for multiple use of products, profits, diversity, and equity.

(E) To be informed about the quality, potency, purity, and price of goods or service

Choose the correct answer from the options given below:

(a) (A), (B) and (C) only (b) (B), (C) and (D) only

(c) (C), (D) and (E) only (d) (A), (C) and (E) only

Ques (61-64): Direction: Read the following passage carefully and answer the questions that follow.

Start-ups are heaving a sigh of relief as the Finance Minister announced measures to do away with the long pending contentious issue of Angel Tax, which many of them had to cough up for raising Angel funding under Section 56 of the Income Tax Act.

Also, special administrative arrangements will be made by the Central Board of Direct Taxes for pending assessments of start-ups and redressal of their grievances. Start-ups have been assured that no inquiry or verification in such cases can be carried out by the Assessing Officer without obtaining approval of his supervisory officer. This provision will do away with much of the angst among start-ups who were subjected to aggressive questioning by the Income Tax department.

A TV channel exclusively for start-ups under the Doordarshan boutique will be designed and executed by start-ups themselves and will also serve as a platform for promoting them, discussing issues affecting their growth, match making with VCs and for funding and tax planning, came as a pleasant surprise to many. Although it remains to be seen how it will be executed on the ground.

The Budget sounded the bugle for fostering rural entrepreneurship for those depending on agriculture and traditional industries by announcing the setting up of 80 Livelihood Business Incubators and 20 Technology Business Incubators this fiscal with the aim to develop 75,000 skilled entrepreneurs in agro-rural industry sectors. "The Government has tried to broad base and foster entrepreneurship beyond metros to Tier 2 and 3 cities which is a good sign. And doing away with Angel Tax is welcome" said Bhaskar Majumdar, Managing Partner, Unicorn India Ventures.

61. Which among the following is correct regarding the attitude of the government towards the startup economy of the country?

(a) The economy of the country has been given a lifeline but there are a lot of questions to ponder over that.

(b) The economy of the country is mainly concerned about the startups of the nation though the government has not done anything for them.

(c) The country is still reliant on big industrial houses so that they can pay taxes as much as possible.

(d) The government has understood the importance of the startups in the economy and is positive about the development of this economy.

62. Which among the following is /are correct regarding the TV channel that has been announced by the government in the Budget?

I. This new channel will be run by the government with the experts from the government organizations.

II. This new channel will be financed by the public sector banks with a fresh round of capital from the government only.

III. This new channel will attempt at saving the taxes of the startup founders by the experts.

(a) Both II and III (b) Both I and III

(c) Both I and II (d) Only III

63. What is the opinion of the author regarding the TV channel that has been proposed to be set up by the government?

(a) The author is excited about the new TV channel since it will bring a lot of interest in the sector.

(b) The author has nothing to say regarding the new TV channel that has been proposed in the Union Budget.

(c) The author is cautious in his reaction because he wants to see if the government is able to make it work actually.

(d) The author is disappointed with this decision for the fact that the government should have done something more worthwhile for the startups in India.

64. Which among the following is/are correct regarding the Angel Tax levied by the government on the startups in India?

I. Angel Tax is levied on companies that raise capital from the angel investors only and not from others sources.

II. Angel Tax is not defined in the Income Tax legislation and the government had to implement it separately.

III. Angel Tax is not going to be levied on the companies that go out of business from this year onwards.

(a) Both I and II (b) Only I

(c) Both II and III (d) Both I and III

Ques (65-68): Direction: Read the passage carefully and answer the questions given beside.

Across the world, organisations are increasingly offering the gift of flexibility to their employees. A study by the Society of Human Resource Management shows that 17% of the organisations in the United States allow sabbaticals. We see this as a rising trend in India, particularly in the last 5 years.

Most of these are "leave without pay" and offered to employees having a strong performance track record. This is how it works. Organisations invest significant amount of resources in training and development of their employees. The returns on the investments are realised over a long period of time. As the employee keeps performing, there is an increasing acclimatisation and cultural alignment with the beliefs of the organisation. One may be able to spot a pair of trained hands with the competition, but the commitment that a performer brings to work each day is irreplaceable. So, for companies to have a sustainable future, they must retain not only the top performers but also all the people who meet expectations consistently. When one of the good employees wants a long leave either to explore a new world of opportunity or deal with something personal, sabbaticals come in handy. By granting a long vacation, an organisation can win a star performer's heart and ensure he/she is in for the long haul.

Sabbaticals do create unpredictability and inject instability into the organisation. Typically, the boss has to find someone to fill in the role vacated by the person going on a sabbatical. Often, the person proceeding on a sabbatical does not offer a long notice period and hence, the replacement has to happen quickly. This further adds to the pressure of finding a replacement. Secondly, such replacements are risky because of the high stakes involved with an external stakeholder such as a key client, a government body or a strategic partner.

For employees, it is a great benefit. They do not have to scratch their heads after they complete their switch-off period. They have the same job and a workplace that recognises them. The risk of not finding a new job is non-existent and hence, the person can easily take the bold step of moving away from the din and bustle of day-to-day work. Sabbaticals give them the space to reflect, the opportunity to shape their dreams and craft the path ahead. People proceed for higher studies, go for medical treatment, take up social work, pursue a passion, write a book, attend to personal emergencies in family and so on without worrying about a place and job to resume after the break.

Sometimes, sabbaticals are misused by people. One could moonlight during that period of time with another organisation in a similar area of work and hence, act against the spirit of taking a sabbatical. Companies try to mitigate the risk by drawing up the terms of the sabbatical such as eligibility in terms of duration of employment, level in the organisation and performance track record; they also define the period of sabbatical considering these factors.

There are hidden costs associated with a sabbatical. For example, employee benefits such as health insurance and accident cover have to continue. Another challenge with a long sabbatical, say six months, is to accommodate the employee in a role which is commensurate with his or her capabilities and commensurate with the pay. Small organisations do not have the elbow room required for a successful sabbatical programme. Many United States and United Kingdom headquartered multinational companies operating in India offer such programmes. Many large Indian companies and mid-sized progressive companies in India, particularly in the services sector, such as IT, consulting and healthcare have been offering sabbaticals. This helps the employer brand stand tall in the crowd and attract bright talent.

65. Which of the following is a valid assumption with reference to the passage?

(a) The concept of 'Sabbaticals' exists only in the west.

(b) Happiness of employees is valued by the organizations which offer 'Sabbaticals' to them.

(c) No organization offers 'Sabbaticals' to its employees willingly.

(d) All of the above

66. Which of the following benefits 'Sabbaticals' offer to employees?

I. Employees do not have risk of losing their jobs.

II. They can find time to follow their passion.

III. They can attend to personal emergencies without bothering anything about their jobs.

(a) Only I (b) Only III

(c) I and II (d) All I, II and III

67. Which of the following can be inferred as a valid reason/reasons as in why the 'sabbatical programme' isn't a success as far as small organizations are concerned?

I. Small organizations do not follow a fair leave management policy.

II. Small organizations in general do not have a heavy budget that can support 'sabbatical programme'.

III. Small organizations have a high attrition rate.

(a) Only I (b) I and III

(c) Only II (d) All I, II and III

68. Which of the following is given as an example of a possible misuse of 'Sabbaticals' offered to employees?

I. Employees on sabbaticals can divulge secret information of their organization to rival companies.

II. Employees can get themselves indulge in criminal activities.

III. Employees availing themselves of sabbaticals can join rival companies in the market.

(a) Only I (b) Only III

(c) I and III (d) All I, II and III

69. What is the CORRECT sequence of the following?

A. Uruguay Round

B. Kennedy Round

C. Doha Round

D. Geneva Round

Choose the correct answer from the options given below:

(a) D, B, A, C (b) B, D, C, A

(c) A, B, C, D (d) C, A, B, D

70. Which of the following are the methods of marketing new issues of securities ?

1. Listing of securities
2. Jobbers and brokers
3. Private placement of securities
4. Privileged subscriptions

(a) 1 and 2 (b) 2 and 3

(c) 3 and 4 (d) 1, 2, 3 and 4

71. Consider the following statements with respect to Foreign Exchange Reserves of India:

1. India is the second largest foreign exchange reserves holder in the world.
2. Gold constitutes the largest component of the foreign exchange reserves.
3. Under the Reserve Bank of India Act, RBI is prohibited from investing Foreign exchange reserves in debt instruments.

Which of the statements given above is/are not correct?

(a) 1 only (b) 2 and 3 only

(c) 1 and 3 only (d) 1, 2 and 3

72. Consider the following statement about the Call Money market -

1. It is an inter-bank money market which is borrowed and lent for one day.
2. Collateral is not required to borrow money to call money market.

Select the correct answer using the code given below-

(a) Only 1 (b) Only 2
(c) Both 1 and 2 (d) Neither 1 nor 2

73. Given below are two statements.

Statement I: A sale has the immediate effect of transferring property, where as in an agreement to sell the property is to pass at some future time.

Statement II: A sale makes the buyer the owner of goods but agreement to sale does not make the buyer the owner of goods.

(a) Only Statement I is true
(b) Only Statement II is true
(c) Both Statements are true
(d) Both Statements are false

74. Statement I: It is a pre-condition of right of stoppage in transit that seller must have parted with possession of goods.

Statement II: Unpaid seller can exercise his rights of resale when goods are in his possession.

Statement III: When property in goods has been passed to the buyer, seller can file a suit against buyer for recovery of price.

Which of the above statement (s) is/are true?

(a) Only I (b) Only III
(c) Both I and II (d) All of the above

75. Mr. Murthy was appointed on 20 th August 2014 as an Assistant Professor in a college on temporary basis. He was confirmed on January 1, 2015. What would be the duration of his previous year for the Assessment Year 2015-16?

(a) 20.8.2014 to 31.3.2015
(b) 01.01.2015 to 31.03.2015
(c) 01.04.2014 to 31.3.2015
(d) 20.08.2014 to 19.08.2015

76. Which Section governs the deduction in respect of medical insurance premiums under the Income Tax Act 1961?

(a) 80DDB (b) 80DD
(c) 80E (d) 80D

77. Logically sequence the following in the process of entering international markets outlined in the uppsala model.

(A) Sporadic (Ad hoc) exports
(B) Foreign production and manufacturing
(C) Establishing a foreign sales subsidiary
(D) Domestic operations and production
(E) Exporting via an independent representative

Choose the correct answer from the options given below:

(a) (A), (B), (C), (D), and (E)
(b) (C), (B), (D), (A), and (E)
(c) (D), (A), (E), (C), and (B)
(d) (E), (B), (D), (C), and (A)

78. Which one of the following is the correct difference between Realisation and Revaluation Account?

1. Realisation account is prepared at the time of change in profit sharing ratio, while Revaluation account is prepared on admission of partner.
2. Revaluation account may be prepared multiple times, while realisation account is prepared only once in the lifetime of business.
3. Revaluation is prepared for adjustment of Assets and Liabilities, while realisation is prepared for calculating profit or loss on realisation of them.

(a) Only 2 (b) Both 1 & 2
(c) Both 2 & 3 (d) Both 1 & 3

79. Zero-Based Budgeting (ZBB) lays emphasis on:

A. Allocation of resources based on cost-benefit terms
B. Unlimited deficit financing
C. Preparing a new budget right from the scratch
D. Preparing the budget, neglecting the history of expenditure

Choose the correct answer from the options given below:

(a) A, B and C only (b) A, C and D only
(c) B, C and D only (d) A, B and D only

80. Which of the following statements are true?

(i) In marginal costing, fixed costs are treated as product costs.
(ii) Marginal costing is not an independent system of costing.
(iii) Marginal costing is not a technique of cost analysis.
(iv) In marginal costing, all costs are divided into fixed and variable.

(a) (i) and (ii) (b) (ii) and (iii)
(c) (i) and (iv) (d) (ii) and (iv)

// Smart Answer Sheet //

Correct Percentage of students who answered correctly.

Skipped Percentage of students who skipped.

Q.	Ans.	Correct	Skipped	Q.	Ans.	Correct	Skipped	Q.	Ans.	Correct	Skipped
1	B	51.97%	45.5%	2	D	82.78%	10.65%	3	D	62.71%	33.41%
4	A	29.19%	67.93%	5	B	50.81%	42.3%	6	D	83.67%	13.1%
7	C	83.49%	15.33%	8	A	77.31%	20.32%	9	C	67.76%	31.66%
10	D	45.41%	54.39%	11	A	46.59%	52.44%	12	A	83.13%	10.03%
13	C	58.92%	32.38%	14	B	87.63%	11.18%	15	B	86.54%	12.83%
16	B	87.49%	12.19%	17	B	85.1%	12.25%	18	A	47.69%	38.23%
19	B	88.86%	10.42%	20	A	55.53%	37.04%	21	D	52.03%	30.33%
22	C	68.0%	30.98%	23	C	86.54%	10.36%	24	D	60.23%	37.76%
25	D	52.2%	39.39%	26	B	42.76%	32.93%	27	B	24.13%	73.97%
28	B	12.67%	85.66%	29	A	12.19%	82.34%	30	C	49.89%	36.55%
31	B	69.46%	30.29%	32	C	55.58%	38.68%	33	D	25.2%	72.85%
34	A	19.76%	71.15%	35	B	85.15%	10.51%	36	A	88.97%	10.63%
37	A	84.65%	12.52%	38	A	15.04%	75.16%	39	B	58.19%	37.53%
40	B	62.47%	36.22%	41	C	77.59%	15.9%	42	A	50.39%	35.81%
43	C	82.71%	14.21%	44	B	87.25%	10.75%	45	A	76.8%	12.51%
46	B	79.7%		47	C	85.93%		48	D	66.12%	

		14.24%			12.67%			32.67%
49	A	21.89% 72.71%	50	B	51.78% 32.32%	51	D	88.8% 10.91%
52	B	58.17% 39.0%	53	B	82.04% 12.98%	54	C	53.41% 39.9%
55	D	89.42% 10.53%	56	A	82.09% 12.18%	57	C	30.63% 69.07%
58	C	79.78% 10.19%	59	B	40.29% 35.83%	60	D	60.93% 36.48%
61	D	54.83% 39.96%	62	D	43.78% 44.88%	63	C	50.86% 40.41%
64	B	56.96% 39.42%	65	B	88.83% 10.95%	66	D	40.44% 36.01%
67	C	55.36% 40.76%	68	B	61.59% 37.77%	69	A	63.95% 30.53%
70	C	58.11% 34.16%	71	D	59.33% 31.09%	72	C	40.38% 38.82%
73	C	65.29% 34.28%	74	C	47.5% 50.14%	75	C	31.96% 67.31%
76	D	83.89% 14.63%	77	C	45.89% 33.51%	78	C	59.46% 30.89%
79	B	56.23% 30.41%	80	D	53.52% 42.01%			

// Hints and Solutions //

1(B). A job specification is a detailed description of the role, including all responsibilities, objectives and requirements. A person specification is a profile of your ideal new employee, including skills, experience and personality type.

A job description or JD is a written narrative that describes the general tasks, or other related duties, and responsibilities of a position.

Job analysis is the process of gathering and analyzing information about the content and the human requirements of jobs, as well as, the context in which jobs are performed. This process is used to determine the placement of jobs. Under NU Values the decision-making in this area is shared by units and Human Resources.

2(D). The capital structure represents only long-term funds and excludes all short-term loans and advances. It is a set of patterns in which a company decides to finance its activities with a particular combination of debt, equity, or securities.

(1) Trading on Equity:
- Trading on equity refers to taking advantage of equity capital base i.e. by keeping equity in a small proportion against the preference share capital and loan capital.
- The surplus earnings are distributed over the equity capital to maximize the equity dividends.
- The high dividends will directly lead to the high market value of equity share which will indirectly increase the goodwill of the organization.

(2) Cost of Capital:
- The cost of capital is also important in designing the capital structure of a corporate.
- The expected returns should be more than the expected cost in any investment activity and the cost of capital is the rate of return that capital can expect to earn in an alternative investment of equivalent risk.
- A company's securities typically include both debt and equity, so one must therefore calculate both the cost of debt and the cost of equity to determine a company's cost of capital.
- After this, the company's weighted average cost of capital will be known which would help in further activities.

(3) Profitability:
- An optimum capital structure must provide adequate profits.
- Hence the profitability aspect needs to be verified by performing an EBIT-EPS analysis which will help the firm know various financial alternatives at different levels of EBIT where EPS would be different for each alternative.
- From these, the alternative that gives the highest EPS will be selected.

Therefore, All of the above are Considerations in designing the capital structure of a corporate.

3(D). DIN is a unique Director identification number allotted by the Central Government to any person intending to be a Director or an existing director of a company. It is an 8-digit unique identification number that has lifetime validity. Through DIN, details of the directors are maintained in a database.

4(A). The central bank is an apex bank that controls the entire banking system of a country. It is the sole agency of note-issuing and controls the supply of money in the economy.

It performs the following functions as per the Reserve Bank of India Act, 1934:

1. Banking functions:
- The Reserve Bank acts as the Banker, Agent, and Adviser to the Government of India and states. It performs all the banking functions of the State and Central Government and it also tenders useful advice to the government on matters related to economic and monetary policy. It also manages the public debt of the government.
- It performs the same functions for the other commercial banks as the other banks ordinarily perform for their customers. RBI lends money to all the commercial banks of the country.

2. Supervisory functions: It supervises other banks and governments into various economic conditions and guides them at the time of inflation or deflation in the economy.

3. Promotional functions: The central bank also performs promotional functions which include integrating with world economies and maintaining foreign reserves. They represent the country's economy internationally.

5(B). The correct code is (a)-(iii), (b)-(i), (c)-(ii), (d)-(iv).

Fiscal policy is the means by which a government adjusts its spending levels and tax rates to monitor and influence a nation's economy. It is the sister strategy to monetary policy through which a central bank influences a nation's money supply.

Technology policy is a form of "active industrial policy", and effectively argues, based on the empirical facts of technological development as observed across various societies, industries and time periods, that markets rarely decide industrial fortunes in and of their own and state-intervention or support is required to overcome standard cases of market-failure (which may include, for example, under-funding of Research & Development in highly competitive or complex markets).

Macro-Economic Policy is a branch of economics dealing with the performance, structure, behaviour, and decision-making of an economy as a whole.

Monetary policy is a policy adopted by the monetary authority of a nation to control either the interest rate payable for very short-term borrowing (borrowing by banks from each other to meet their short-term needs) or the money supply, often as an attempt to reduce inflation or the interest rate to ensure price stability and general trust of the value and stability of the nation's currency.

6(D). Infrastructure is basically the base on which economic growth is built upon. Roads, water systems, mass transportation, airports and utilities are all examples of infrastructure. It covers those supporting services that help the growth of directly productive activities like agriculture and industry.

7(C). The four components of the gross domestic product are personal consumption, business investment, government spending, and net exports. That tells you what a country is good at producing. GDP is the country's total economic output for each year.
Therefore, net personal income does not come in GDP.

8(A). The correct answer is (i), (ii), (iii) and (iv).

- A Sales book is a record of all credit sales made by a business. It is required to be examined.
- A sales Invoice is a written document issued by a seller to inform the detail of the transaction to their customers. It is required to be examined
- A cut-off point means that transactions and events have been recorded in the correct accounting period.. Audit procedures are used to determine whether transactions have been recorded within the correct reporting period. It is r equired to be examined.
- The numerical sequence of source documents generated within the organization is required to be examined.

9(C). Under this method, the amount of depreciation is calculated as a fixed percentage of the reducing or diminishing value of the asset standing in the books at the beginning of the year, so as to bring down the book value of the asset to its residual value. The amount of depreciation goes on decreasing every year.

10(D). **Assertion:**
Price reduction normally leads to an increase in the demand for a commodity- this is a correct statement since price and demand possess an inverse relationship.
Reason:
Price reduction leads to the entry of new buyers of the commodity in the market- this is the correct explanation for assertion since more consumers can buy the commodity when the price falls.
Both (A) and (R) are correct and (R) does not offer a full explanation of (A).

11(A). The minimum Long Run Average Cost (LAC) can be determined on:

- LAC curve for a normal production function
- LAC curve for a linear production function
- Planning curve
- Envelope curve

The long-run is that time period when a firm can change all its inputs. In fact, there are no fixed inputs in the long run; all inputs are variable. Thus, in the long run, there is no fixed cost; all costs are variable. That is why, in the long run, a firm can change its scale of production according to its needs.

12(A). Monopoly is not considered desirable from the point of view of the society mainly because the monopolist endeavors to earn net revenue on the sale of all goods including those involving no cost of production. A market structure characterized by a single seller, selling a unique product in the market.

13(C). When the date is classified only on the basis of descriptive characteristics from which quantification cannot be determined it is called qualitative classification.
Qualitative Classification - The qualitative classification of the data emphasizes the certain qualitative phenomenon of the data. Under this type of data classification, data is classified on the basis of qualitative measurements.

14(B). We can obtain a relative measurement by the ratio of absolute variability or percentage of absolute variability to the mean value. They are also known as coefficients of dispersion. The coefficient of mean deviation is known as the coefficient of standard deviation and the coefficient of variation.

15(B). In economics, short-run is a period where some factor inputs are fixed, while the others are variable.
The short-run, as economists use the phrase, is characterized by at least one fixed factor of production so the proportion of inputs can be changed, the law of variable proportion will only operate in the short run. It is in the long run all factors are variable as producers have enough time to organize all factor inputs in the appropriate proportions to achieve the minimum efficient scale.

16(B). Digital computers recognize data by calculating a discrete signal of type (binary number system - 0 or 1), these are high-speed programs; They calculate the values and store the results. They work on computer digital signals. These signals are used to represent data as a sequence of discrete values; At any time it can take a finite number of values.

17(B). Fixed costs do not change even after changes in output. Fixed costs are indirect costs and have to be paid irrespective of the level of production. Even if zero output is being produced these costs have to be incurred. These costs include rent of the factory, interest payments on borrowed financial capital, payment on the lease for factory equipment.

18(A). The correct code are (i) (ii) (iii) (iv).

- Equity theory focuses on determining whether the distribution of resources is fair to both relational partners. Equity is measured by comparing the ratio of contributions (or costs) and benefits (or rewards) for each person. Considered one of the justice theories, equity theory was first developed in the 1960s by J.
- Vroom's expectancy theory assumes that behaviour results from conscious choices among alternatives whose purpose is to maximize pleasure and to minimize pain. Vroom realized that an employee's performance is based on individual factors such as personality, skills, knowledge, experience and abilities.
- The Porter and Lawler theory of motivation is based on the assumption that rewards cause satisfaction and that sometimes performance produces a reward.
- The two-factor theory (also known as Herzberg's motivation-hygiene theory and dual-factor theory) states that there are certain

factors in the workplace that cause job satisfaction while a separate set of factors cause dissatisfaction, all of which act independently of each other.

19(B). Marginal product is the extra output obtained from employing an additional unit of the factor.
Marginal productivity or marginal product refers to the extra output, return, or profit yielded per unit by advantages from production inputs. Inputs can include things like labor and raw materials.

20(A). Firms that practice channel differentiation gain a competitive advantage through the way they design their channel's coverage, expertise, and performance. Such factors as the level of customer service, speed of delivery, packaging, transportation type, and so on may play a role in channel differentiation.

21(D). Assertion (A): Too many stimuli make a person accommodated to those sensations, Sensory adaption is a problem that concerns many advertisers, which is why they try to change their advertising campaigns regularly.
Reasoning (R): To cut through the advertising clutter and to ensure that consumers perceive advertisement, marketers try to increase sensory input.
Both (A) and (R) are right and (R) explains (A).

22(C). It does not consider the risk associated with the projects is not a feature of the payback period method.
The payback period method is used to quickly evaluate the time it should take for an investor to get back the amount of money put into a project. Those investments with even cash flows are computed by dividing the cost of the investment by the annual net cash flow.

23(C). Trade enquiry is a written request by an importer to the exporter for the supply of required information. So option C is not a source of credit information for prospective customers.

24(D). The correct code regarding motives for holding inventories by firms:
(a) Transaction motive.
(b) Precautionary motive.
(d) Speculative motive.

25(D). The correct code is (iii) (ii) (i) (iv).
- Golden parachutes are lucrative severance packages inked into the contracts of top executives that compensate them when they are terminated.
- Gainsharing is a system of management used by a business to increase profitability by motivating employees to improve their performance through involvement and participation. As their performance improves, employees share financially in the gain (improvement).
- A stock option gives an investor the right, but not the obligation, to buy or sell a stock at an agreed-upon price and date. There are two types of options: puts, which is a bet that a stock will fall, or calls, which is a bet that a stock will rise.
- Annual Bonus. Usually, a lump-sum payment (cash, shares, etc.) made once a year in addition to an employee's normal salary or wage for a fiscal or calendar year. Generally non-discretionary and not based on predetermined performance criteria or standards.

26(B). The Low Earth Orbit (LEO) satellite communications operator is co-owned by Bharti Global and the United Kingdom government.
The Operator has recently launched 36 satellites from a cosmodrome in Russia. This step will expedite the launch of high-speed internet services in India by mid-2022. At present, a foreign satellite operator should go through Antrix (ISRO's commercial arm), for selling bandwidth capacity to users in India.

27(B). "Banks globally are facing more challenges now and Macro sustainability is a necessity but not sufficient for sustainable economic growth." is true. "Putting regulations in place is only one part and their implementation is equally important for achieving growth and sustainability." is true but is not the correct explanation of (A).

28(B). The correct code is (iii) (i) (ii) (iv).
- The interbank call money market is a short-term money market which allows for large financial institutions, such as banks, mutual funds, and corporations, to borrow and lend money at interbank rates, the rate of interest that banks charge when they borrow funds from each other.
- Commercial bills are unsecured, short-term debt issued by a corporation, oftentimes for the financing of short-term liabilities and inventory. Meanwhile, a Treasury bill (T-Bill) is short-term debt backed by the U.S. government with a maturity of under one year.
- Commercial paper is a money-market security issued (sold) by large corporations to obtain funds to meet short-term debt obligations (for example, payroll) and is backed only by an issuing bank or company promise to pay the face amount on the maturity date specified on the note.
- Treasury Bills (T-bills) 1.3 Treasury bills or T-bills, which are money market instruments, are short-term debt instruments issued by the Government of India and are presently issued in three tenors, namely, 91 days, 182 days and 364 days. Treasury bills are zero-coupon securities and pay no interest.

29(A). Exchange controls are government-imposed limitations on the purchase and/or sale of currencies. These controls allow countries to better stabilize their economies by limiting in-flows and out-flows of currency, which can create exchange rate volatility.
These instruments include many forms of non-tariff measures (NTMs) such as quotas, licensing, pre-shipment inspections, imports and export regulations, as well as technical barriers to trade (TBT) and sanitary and phytosanitary measures (SPS).
Reducing overall spending in the economy (including on imports) by raising income taxes and reducing government spending (contractionary fiscal policies) can improve the trade balance.
Expenditure switching is a macroeconomic policy that affects the composition of a country's expenditure on foreign and domestic goods. More specifically it is a policy to balance a country's

current account by altering the composition of expenditures on foreign and domestic goods (see Balance of payments account).

30(C). India has procured the highest amount of international loans from IDA is not correct about the International Development Association(IDA).
The International Development Association (IDA) is an international financial institution that offers concessional loans and grants to the world's poorest developing countries. The IDA is a member of the World Bank Group and is headquartered in Washington, D.C. in the United States. It was established in 1960 to complement the existing International Bank for Reconstruction and Development by lending to developing countries that suffer from the lowest gross national income, from troubled creditworthiness, or from the lowest per capita income. Together, the International Development Association and International Bank for Reconstruction and Development are collectively generally known as the World Bank, as they follow the same executive leadership and operate with the same staff.

31(B). The Reserve Bank has announced that the Real Time Gross Settlement System or the RTGS facility will be available round the clock, from December 14, 2020.
As per the RBI, RTGS can be used for both domestic payments in Indian financial markets and cross-border payments.

32(C). Profit/loss on the sale of assets is an entry in the manufacturing company's P & L account under the heading other income. In banks, the other income includes income from distribution of financial products, income from investment banking related activities, treasury gains and other fee incomes.

33(D). The correct code is (ii) (iii) (i) (iv).

- A governmental restriction on the movement of currency between countries.
- Price controls are government-mandated minimum or maximum prices that can be charged for specified goods.
- Import and Export Control is essential to enforce health, environmental, security and safety, and technical standards that arise from domestic laws and international agreements.
- The principle of legislative control, on the contrary, involves the legislature in administration to the extent that it scrutinizes, and has some formal power to influence, the administrative activities of the executive.

Exchange control	Domestic firms
Price Control	Mass Consumption product
Import control	Adverse BOP
Legislative control	Industrial location

34(A). The correct code is (iv) (iii) (i) (ii).

- A provision for income taxes is the estimated amount that a business or individual taxpayer expects to pay in income taxes for the current year.
- Livestock is commonly defined as domesticated animals raised in an agricultural setting to produce labour and commodities such as meat, eggs, milk, fur, leather, and wool.
- Sundry Debtor. A person who receives goods or services from a business in a credit or does not make the payment immediately and is liable to pay the business in the future is called a Sundry Debtor.
- Accrued interest is the amount of interest earned on a debt, such as a bond, but not yet collected. Interest accumulates from the date a loan is issued or when a bond's coupon is made.

List-I	List-II
(a)Provision for taxa tion	(iv) Industrial location
(b)Live-stock	(iii) Mass Consumption pr oduct
(c)Sundry Debtors	(i) Adverse BOP
(d)Interest accrued	(ii) Domestic firms

35(B). A balancing item is the reason for net omissions and errors account. The balance of payment of a country must always be in equilibrium a surplus on one account must be met with a deficit of equal magnitude on the other. Thus, the sum of the capital account and the current account must always be 0. In order for the sum to be exactly equal to 0, the component net commission and errors are added to the calculations.

36(A). Decrease in creditors is not a cash in-flow. Funds received by a company due to sales, financing, or investments. Cash inflows are used to gauge the overall financial health of a business, and a company with a large and stable cash inflow can be considered to be in a good financial position.

37(A). Normal distributions are symmetric, unimodal, and asymptotic, and the mean, median, and mode are all equal. A normal distribution is perfectly symmetrical around its center. That is, the right side of the center is a mirror image of the left side.

38(A). Both statements are true.
Those tests both assume that the population data has a normal distribution. Non-parametric do not assume that the data is normally distributed. For example, the Kruskal Willis test is the non-parametric alternative to the One way ANOVA and the Mann Whitney is the non-parametric alternative to the two-sample t-test
The standard error of the mean is the standard deviation of the sampling distribution of the mean. It is, therefore, the square root of the variance of the sampling distribution of the mean and can be written as: The standard error is represented by a σ because it is a standard deviation

39(B). Groupthink is a psychological phenomenon that occurs within a group of people in which the desire for harmony or conformity in the group results in an irrational or dysfunctional decision-making outcome.

40(B). Tax Evasion attracts a penalty at 200% under Section 270 A of Income Tax Act, 1961.
Penalty u/s 270A is required to be levied from A.Y. 2017-18 onwards.
Penalty u/s 270A is leviable for:

Under-reporting of inco me	Penalty @ 50% of amo unt of tax payable on u nder-reported income
Under-reported income is in consequence of any misreporting thereof	Penalty @ 200% of am ount of tax payable on under-reported incom

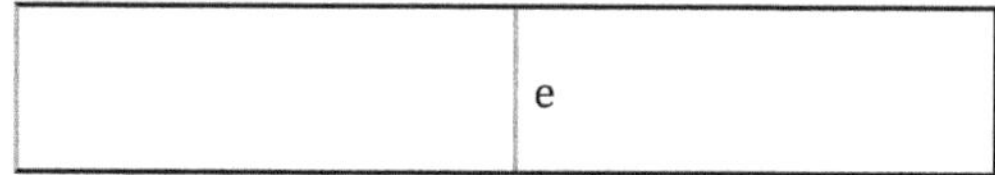

41(C). Normative ethics is the study of ethical action. It is the branch of philosophical ethics that investigates the set of questions that arise when considering how one ought to act, morally speaking.

42(A). The Committee was constituted by RBI in December 2019 under the Chairmanship of Prof. D.B. Phatak, to review the present system of QR Codes in India in digital payments. The Reserve Bank of India has released the 'Report of the Committee for Analysis of QR (Quick Response) Code'.
The report asked the Government to provide incentive schemes to popularise QR code transactions among consumers. It also recommended phasing out proprietary and closed loop QR codes.

43(C). Operating leverage = $\frac{\text{Contribution}}{\text{Earnings Before Tax}}$
Contribution = Sales − Variable Cost = 74 − 40 = Rs. 34 Lacs .
Earnings Before Tax = Contribution − Fixed Cost = 34 − 8 = Rs. 26 Lacs.
Thus, Operating leverage = $\frac{\text{Contribution}}{\text{Earnings Before Tax}}$
$= \frac{34}{26}$
= 1.3 lakh
Sales of a firm are Rs. 74 Lakh, variable costs Rs. 40 lakh, fixed costs Rs 8 lakh. The operating leverage of the firm will be 1.31 Lakh.

44(B). India's leading private sector bank, HDFC Bank has recently announced the launch of "Shaurya KGC Card" for the armed forces.
This card has been designed based on the Kisan Credit Card guidelines by the Government. More than 45 lakh Indian armed force personnel would get a life cover ranging from Rs 2 lakh to Rs 10 lakh. It also requires simple documentation suited to the job nature of the armed force personnel.

45(A). The Bharat Stage emission is based on the European emission standards. The European emission standards define the acceptable limits for exhaust emissions of new vehicles sold in the European Union and EEA member states.

46(B). The share of the Indian capital goods industry in the world exports is 0.8%. Indian capital goods industry. The capital goods exports are about 27% of total manufactured in India.

47(C). The amount of calls in arrears is shown in the balance sheet as deduction from subscribed capital.
- A company issues stock in the market, and the general public buys it. The company may call the entire amount or only a portion of it.
- When funds are required within a specified time frame, the company solicits funds from shareholders.
- If a shareholder is unable to pay the call amount due on an allotment or any calls according to the conditions before or on the designated payment date, the amount is considered call in arrears.
- An amount of calls in arrears is recorded on the liabilities side of the balance sheet by subtracting it from the subscribed capital.

48(D). "A company remains free from the hazards of all personal misfortunes of its member" is derived from the benefit of incorporation of the company being independent legal entity.
A legal entity, typically a business that is defined as detached from another business or individual with respect to accountability. A separate legal entity may be set up in the case of a corporation or a limited liability company, to separate the actions of the entity from those of the individual or other company.

49(A). Bank Rate, Open Market Operations, Variable Reserve Ratios are the methods indicate quantitative methods of control of credit creation practiced by the Reserve Bank of India.
Credit control is an important tool used by the Reserve Bank of India, a major weapon of the monetary policy used to control the demand and supply of money (liquidity) in the economy. Central Bank administers control over the credit that the commercial banks grant. Such a method is used by RBI to bring "Economic Development with Stability". It means that banks will not only control inflationary trends in the economy but also boost economic growth which would ultimately lead to an increase in real national income stability. In view of its functions such as issuing notes and custodian of cash reserves, credit not being controlled by RBI would lead to Social and Economic instability in the country.

50(B). Small Industries Development Bank of India (SIDBI) is a development financial institution in India, headquartered at Lucknow and having its offices all over the country. Its purpose is to provide refinance facilities and short term lending to industries and serves as the principal financial institution in the Micro, Small and Medium Enterprises (MSME) sector. SIDBI also coordinates the functions of institutions engaged in similar activities. It was established on April 2, 1990, through an Act of Parliament. It is headquartered in Lucknow. SIDBI operates under the Department of Financial Services, Government of India.

51(D). Where a company purchases its own shares out of reserves or securities premium account, a sum equal to the nominal value of the shares so purchased is transferred to the Capital Redemption Reserve Account and details of such transfer are disclosed in the balanced sheet.
A share buyback is when a company buys back previously issued shares. It's a business activity in which a company makes a public announcement about a buyback offer to acquire existing shareholders' shares within a set period of time.

52(B). Opportunity cost approach is approaches is adopted for the valuation of human resources according to the economic concept.
Human resource valuation means the identification and measurement of the value of human resources and then supplying this information to interesting parties. It is sometimes also defined as a method of assigning value to the employees on the basis of their future economic services to the organization.

53(B). Reserve Bank of India (RBI) is the issuer of currency. The Reserve Bank is the nation's sole note-issuing authority. Along with the Government of India, they are responsible for the design, production, and overall management of the nation's currency, with the goal of ensuring an adequate supply of clean and genuine notes.

54(C). Accounting Standard-6 is meant for Depreciation Accounting.
1. This Standard deals with depreciation accounting and applies to all depreciable assets, except the following items to which special considerations apply:—
(i) forests, plantations and similar regenerative natural resources;
(ii) wasting assets including expenditure on the exploration for and extraction of minerals, oils, natural gas and similar non-regenerative resources;
(iii) expenditure on research and development;
(iv) goodwill and other intangible assets;
(v) livestock. This standard also does not apply to land unless it has a limited useful life for the enterprise.
2. Different accounting policies for depreciation are adopted by different enterprises. Disclosure of accounting policies for depreciation followed by an enterprise is necessary to appreciate the view presented in the financial statements of the enterprise.

55(D). Fragmentation of regional stock exchanges is not a feature of OTCEI.
Over The Counter Exchange of India (OTCEI) can be defined as a stock exchange without a proper trading floor. All stock exchanges have a specific place for trading their securities through counters. But the OTCEI is connected through a computer network and the transactions are taking place through computer operations.

56(A). Public Distribution System (PDS) is an Indian food security system, to distribute subsidized food and non-food items to items to India's poor. Major commodities distributed include staple food grains such as wheat, rice, sugar, and Kerosene through PDS shops.

57(C). Marketing is the study and management of exchange relationships. Marketing is the business process of creating relationships with and satisfying customers. With its focus on the customer, marketing is one of the premier components of business management. Both the statement are correct.

58(C). Roadblock advertising is where all placements on the site are "roadblocked" with the same creative for the advertiser. Roadblock advertising allows advertisers to own 100% of voice for a given period, usually a day or could be the first-page impression of the day. When this is run across multiple sites concurrently, roadblock advertising provides a wide-reaching media buy with similar metrics to those of TV media buy. In other words, an advertising campaign would run exclusively across all the advertising units on a page reinforcing the advertising message. Ideal for a brand or product launch when the aim is to gain brand awareness quickly.

59(B). As per section 80G maximum deduction allowed for any cash donation is up to Rs. 2000.
Finance Act, 2017 amended section 80G so as to provide that no deduction shall be allowed under section 80G in respect of donation of any sum exceeding Rs. 2,000/- unless such sum is paid by any mode other than cash. Earlier this limit was Rs. 10,000.

60(D). The correct answer is (A), (C), and (E) only
Consumer Protection Act, 1986:

- To resolve consumer complaints in an easier and faster way, the Consumer Protection Act of 1986 was passed.
- The Act aims to advance and safeguard consumer interests against shortcomings and flaws in goods and services.
- Additionally, it aims to protect consumer rights from unfair business practises that suppliers and sellers might engage in.
- A consumer forum's goals are to offer assistance to all parties and deter protracted legal disputes.
- Officials from the forum mediate between the two parties and encourage compromise in a procedure known as "informal adjudication."

1. Right to Safety: A consumer has the right to safety against such goods and services as are hazardous to his health, life and property.
2. Right to be heard: Means that consumer's interests will receive due consideration at appropriate forums. It also includes the right to be represented in various forums formed to consider the consumer's welfare.
3. Right to be Informed: Means right to be informed about the quality, quantity, potency, purity, standard and price of goods to protect the consumer against unfair trade practices.
4. Right to choose: Means the right to be assured, wherever possible of access to a variety of goods and services at a competitive price.
5. Right to consumer education: Means the right to acquire the knowledge and skill to be an informed consumer throughout life. Ignorance of consumers, particularly of rural consumers, is mainly responsible for their exploitation.
6. Right to Seek redressal: Means right to seek redressal against unfair trade practices or unscrupulous exploitation of consumers. It also includes the right to fair settlement of the genuine grievances of the consumer.

61(D). It has been described in the passage that the government has announced a number of steps in order to boost the startup economy of the country. The government has announced tax exemptions and also more networking in order to help the startups develop more and more. Among the given options, we can easily pick up Option D whereas Option A is correct in the first part but for the second part, we can say that no question has been put forward by the government for the startup sector of the country. Other options can be eliminated since they do not at all follow from the passage.

62(D). Statement I is not correct for the fact that the new channel has been proposed to se set up and run by the startup companies themselves so that they can utilize the platform properly. Refer to, " A TV channel exclusively for start-ups under the Doordarshan boutique will be designed and executed by start-ups themselves and will also serve as a platform for promoting them, discussing issues affecting their growth, match making with VCs and for funding and tax planning, came as a pleasant surprise to many."

Statement II is also not correct because it is said that the new channel will be financed by the public sector banks whereas there is no such reference in the passage to that effect. It can be eliminated.
Statement III is correct because from the above quoted lines it can be understood that the new channel will try to match the startup founders with the VCs so that they can raise capital and also plan the taxes so that there is tax saving by these small companies.

63(C). We can see from the passage that the author is not overjoyed with the fact that the government has announced a new channel that will be dedicated to the startup sector of the country. He wants to see if the government is actually able to execute this idea at the end as it will be difficult to bring everything in one place to get this going. Among the given options, Option (C) explains this reaction of the author whereas the rest can be eliminated because they do not follow from the passage.

64(B). Statement I is correct for the fact that Angel Tax is a kind of tax that is levied on the startups that raise capital from the angel investors. So, it is correct that the companies that raise capital from this source only will be subjected to this particular tax.
Statement II is not correct because it is said that Section 56 of the Income Tax Act is regarding the Angel Tax that is levied on companies raising capital from angel investors. So, it cannot be said that there is no such provision in the Income Tax Act of the country.
Statement III is not correct for the fact that the Angel Tax is not going to be levied on any startup from now onwards as has been announced in the recent Budget of the government. So, it is applicable for each and every company and not for them who have decided to shut down the business.

65(B). Refer to: Across the world, organisations are increasingly offering the gift of flexibility to their employees.
The very first sentence of the passage as taken above as reference implies that when an organization brings a concept of 'Sabbaticals' for its employees, it clearly shows that it values their happiness.
No other statement is a valid assumption with reference to the passage.

66(D). Refer to: For employees, it is a great benefit. They do not have to scratch their heads after they complete their switch-off period. They have the same job and a workplace that recognises them. The risk of not finding a new job is non-existent and hence, the person can easily take the bold step of moving away from the din and bustle of day-to-day work. Sabbaticals give them the space to reflect, the opportunity to shape their dreams and craft the path ahead. People proceed for higher studies, go for medical treatment, take up social work, pursue a passion, write a book, attend to personal emergencies in family and so on without worrying about a place and job to resume after the break.
The above line confirms the points mentioned in points I, II and III.

67(C). Refer to: There are hidden costs associated with a sabbatical. For example, employee benefits such as health insurance and accident cover have to continue. Another challenge with a long sabbatical, say six months, is to accommodate the employee in a role which is commensurate with his or her capabilities and commensurate with the pay. Small organisations do not have the elbow room required for a successful sabbatical programme.
The above two sentences clearly implies that small organizations do not have much freedom to spend on 'sabbaticals' and therefore the concept is not successful with them.
The other two statements are nowhere mentioned or can be inferred from the passage.

68(B). Refer to: Sometimes, sabbaticals are misused by people. One could moonlight during that period of time with another organisation in a similar area of work and hence, act against the spirit of taking a sabbatical.
The above line confirms statement III.
Neither of the other two statements is mentioned anywhere in the passage.

69(A). **GATT:** General Agreement on Tariffs and Trade (GATT), set of multilateral trade agreements aimed at the abolition of quotas and the reduction of tariff duties among the contracting nations. The General Agreement on Tariffs and Trade (GATT) covers international trade in goods.
During the GATT (General Agreement on Tariffs and Trade) years 9 rounds of tariff negotiations were held between 1947 and 1994:
- Geneva (1947)
- Annecy (1949)
- Torquay (1950-51)
- Geneva (1956)
- Geneva (1960-61)
- Kennedy Round (1964-67)
- Tokyo Round (1973-79)
- Uruguay Round (1986-94)
- Doha Round (2001 - 2015)

70(C). Private placement of securities and Privileged subscriptions are the methods of marketing new issues of securities.
Share issues:
- New issues, whether stocks or bonds are a means of raising capital for a company.
- New equity shares are often issued via an initial public offering (IPO), allowing investors to buy the stock of a previously private company for the first time.
- Bonds preferred, and convertible securities may also be disseminated as new issues to raise debt capital for a firm.
- Investors should be aware of the "hype" surrounding a new issue like an IPO, as it could go one way or the other.
- Companies that are already public can make a new issue through a secondary offering .

Methods of Marketing Securities:
1. Pure Prospectus Method 2. Offer for Sale Method 3. Private Placement Method 4. Initial public Offers (IPOs) Method 5. Rights Issue Method 6. Bonus Issue Method 7. Book-building Method 8. Stock Option Method and 9. Bought-out Deals Method

71(D). India's forex reserves comprise foreign currency assets (FCAs), gold reserves, special drawing rights (SDRs), and the country's reserve position with the International Monetary Fund (IMF). Foreign exchange reserves reached an all-time high of US$ 583.8 billion as of February 19, 2021, covering about 18 months of imports. At present, India is the fifth-largest foreign exchange reserves holder among all countries of the world after China, Japan, Switzerland and Russia. So, statement 1 is not correct.

Foreign Currency Assets (US$ 542.1 billion) constitute the largest component of the forex reserves followed by Gold (US$ 35.2 billion) and Special Drawing Rights (US$ 1.5 billion). So, statement 2 is not correct.

The Reserve Bank of India Act, 1934 provides the overarching legal framework for the deployment of reserves in different foreign currency assets and gold within the broad parameters of currencies, instruments, issuers and counterparties. In brief, the law broadly permits the following investment.

Categories:

- Deposits with other central banks and the Bank for International Settlements (BIS);
- Deposits with commercial banks overseas;
- Debt instruments representing sovereign/ sovereign-guaranteed liability with residual maturity for the debt papers not exceeding 10 years;
- Other instruments/institutions as approved by the Central Board of the Reserve Bank.
- So, statement 3 is not correct.

72(C). Call money market (CMM):

- The call money market (CMM) the market where overnight loans can be availed by banks to meet liquidity.
- It is an inter-bank money market which is borrowed and lent for one day. So statement 1 is correct.
- Banks who seek to avail liquidity approach the call market as borrowers and the ones who have excess liquidity participate there as lenders.
- No collateral security is required to borrow from the money market. So statement 2 is correct.

73(C). Statement I : A sale has the immediate effect of transferring property, whereas an agreement to sell the property is to pass at some future time.

Statement II : A sale makes the buyer the owner of goods but an agreement to sale does not make the buyer the owner of goods.

Here Both statements are correct.

74(C). Statement I: It is a pre-condition of the right of stoppage in transit that the seller must have parted with possession of goods.

Statement II: Unpaid seller can exercise his rights of resale when goods are in his possession.

Statement III: When the property in goods has been passed to the buyer, the seller can file a suit against the buyer for recovery of price only when the buyer wrongfully neglects or refuses to pay for the goods.

Here Statement I, Statement II are correct, but Statement III is incorrect.

75(C). 01.04.2014 to 31.3.201 5 would be the duration of his previous year for the Assessment Year 2015-16

.

Previous year:

For the purposes of this Act, "previous year" means—

- (a) the financial year immediately preceding the assessment year; or
- (b) if the accounts of the assessee have been made up to date within the said financial year, then, at the option of the assessee, the twelve months ending on such date; or
- (c) in the case of any person or business or class of persons or business not falling within clause (a) or clause (b), such period as may be determined by the Board or by any authority authorized by the Board in this behalf; or
- (d) in the case of a business or profession newly set up in the said financial year, the period beginning with the date of the setting up of the business or profession and—

A ssessment year:

1. The assessment year (AY) is the year that comes after the FY.
2. This is the time in which the income earned during FY is assessed and taxed. Both FY and AY start on 1 April and end on 31 March.
3. For instance, FY 2019-20 and AY 2020-21 are one and the same.
4. The Assessment Year is the financial year of the Govt. of India during which the income of a person relating to the relevant previous year is assessed to tax. Every person who is liable to pay tax under this Act . files return of income by prescribed dates.
5. These returns are processed by the income tax department officials and officers. This processing is called assessment. Under this income returned by the assessee is checked and verified.
6. Tax is calculated and compared with the amount paid and an assessment order is issued. The year in which the whole of this process is undertaken is called an assessment year.

76(D). Section 80D of the Income Tax Act, 1961 explains the deductions applicable for the premium paid for Medical Insurance.

Eligibilit y	An individual or HUF can claim a ded uction under section 80D
Conditio ns	• Premium paid for Medical Insuran ce for self, spouse, and dependent children. • Additional deduction for insuranc e of parents is available
Amount of Deduc tion	• Rs.25,000 (for self, spouse, and de pendent children) • Rs. 25,000 (insurance of parents l ess than 60 years of age) • Rs. 50,000 (insurance of parents more than 60 years of age) • Rs. 1,00,000 (if both taxpayer and parent(s) are 60 years or above)

- Section 80DDB: This Section is related to a deduction for Medical Expenditure on Self or Dependent Relative
- Section 80DD: This Section is related to a deduction for Rehabilitation of Handicapped Dependent Relatives.
- Section 80E: This Section is related to the deduction of Interest paid on loans taken for pursuing higher education.

77(C). The correct answer is (D), (A), (E), (C), and (B).

Uppsala Model:

- Swedish scholars (Johanson and Wiedersheim-Paul, 1975; Johanson and Vahlne, 1977) developed the Uppsala Internationalization Model as a result of their interest in the internationalisation process.
- They constructed a model of the firm's choice

of market and type of entrance when moving abroad after studying the internationalisation of Swedish manufacturing enterprises.

- The Uppsala model is one of the best known models of how firms set about the internationalization process.
- It presents a sequential approach, meaning that the firm internationalizes incrementally.
- The model assumes that there is a lack of knowledge of the foreign market which is detrimental to internationalization.

Sequence of process of entering international markets:

1. Domestic operations and production
2. Sporadic (Ad hoc) exports
3. Exporting via an independent representative
4. Establishing a foreign sales subsidiary
5. Foreign production and manufacturing

78(C). **Difference between Revaluation Account and Realisation Account:**

Basis	Revaluation Account	Realisation Account
Meaning	Revaluation account records the reassessment of the assets and liabilities	Realisation account records the effect of the realisation of assets and settlement of liabilities
Purpose	Revaluation account is prepared for adjustment in the value of assets and liabilities from time to time. So, Statement 2 is correct	Realisation is prepared for ascertainment of profit and loss that arises from realisation of assets and liabilities. So, Statement 2 is correct
Time	It is prepared at the time of admission, retirement, or death of a partner and, change in profit sharing ratio. So, Statement 1 is incorrect	It is prepared only at the time of dissolution of the partnership firm. So, Statement 1 is incorrect
Contents	Includes only those Assets and Liabilities which are revalued.	Includes all the Assets (except fictitious assets, cash/bank and loan to partners) and outsiders liabilities of the firm.
Effect on assets & liabilities	All the assets & liabilities accounts recorded in the Revaluation A/C are just revalued and not closed.	All the assets & liabilities accounts recorded in Realisation A/C are closed.
Frequency	This account can be prepared multiple times during the life of a business. So, Statement 3 is correct	This account is prepared only once, during the dissolution of the firm. So, Statement 3 is correct

79(B). **Zero-Based Budgeting (ZBB):** With zero-based budgeting (ZBB), instead of starting with the prior budget and making adjustments as needed, all expenses must be justified for a new period or year starting from scratch with a zero base.

Features of Zero-Based Budgeting (ZBB):

- Any decision unit's management must first provide justification for the budget allocation to that decision unit. Without mentioning the previous amount of spending in his decision unit, he should explain his request.
- Decision packages are assessed through a methodical study that links them to expressly stated company objectives.
- Preparing the budget, neglecting the history of expenditure.

Advantages of Zero-Based Budgeting (ZBB):

- It gives the business a methodical means to assess operations and activity programmes, and it enables management to allocate resources in accordance with the importance of various programmes.
- It makes it possible to approve departmental budgets using as a foundation.
- Instead of being susceptible to any arbitrary cuts or increases in budget estimates, consider cost-benefit ratios.

80(D). Marginal cost is a technique of cost analysis wherein the marginal cost i.e. the variable cost is charged to units of cost, while the fixed cost for the period is completely written off against the contribution.

- Note that variable costs are those which change as output changes - these are treated under marginal costing as costs of the product. Fixed costs, in this system, are treated as costs of the period.
- Marginal costing is a technique of analysis and presentation of costs that helps management in taking many managerial decisions and is not an independent system of costing such as process costing or job costing.
- Marginal cost implies the additional cost involved in producing an extra unit of output, which can be reckoned by the total variable cost assigned to one unit.
- In marginal costing, all costs are divided into fixed and variable.
- Break-even analysis is an integral and important part of marginal costing.
- When valuing the finished goods and work in progress, only variable costs are taken into account but the variable selling and distribution overheads are not included in the valuation of inventory.
- It is calculated as Marginal cost = Direct Material + Direct Labour + Direct Expenses + Variable Overheads.

Therefore, statements (ii) and (iv) are true.

Mock Test 08

1. Which of the following statements denote(s) the structural changes in the Indian economy?
   (a) Primary sector contribution has gone down.
   (b) Service sector contribution has gone up.
   (c) Secondary sector has not changed much.
   (d) All of the above

2. Goods and Service Tax was implemented in India from.
   (a) 1-Jun-2017 (b) 1-Jul-2017
   (c) 1-Aug-2017 (d) 1-Sep-2017

3. Counter Vailing Duties (CVD) are often imposed on imports to offset the impact of:
   (a) Predatory pricing (b) Export subsidies
   (c) Dumping (d) Low cost financing

4. Conversion cost is the sum of:
   (a) Indirect wages and factory overhead
   (b) Direct wages, direct expense, and factory overheads
   (c) Direct material cost and indirect wages
   (d) Prime cost and selling and distribution overheads

5. Arrange these ratios in sequence to reflect the liquidity in descending order:
   (i) Basic defensive and interval ratio
   (ii) Current ratio
   (iii) Superquick ratio
   (iv) Quick ratio
   (a) (ii), (iv), (iii) and (i) (b) (i), (ii), (iv) and (iii)
   (c) (iv), (ii), (iii) and (i) (d) (iii), (iv), (i) and (ii)

6. Match the items of List - I with the items in List - II according to the code given below the lists:

List - I	List - II
(a) Error of Principle	(i) A purchase of Rs. 1000 has not be recorded.
(b) Error of Commission	(ii) Treating repair charges as addition to assets
(c) Error of Omission	(iii) A sale of Rs. 563 was posted as Rs. 653.
(d) Compensatory error	(iv) Sales book is undercast by Rs. 1000 and return inward book is overcast by Rs. 1000.
	(v) Return inward book is undercast by Rs. 1000 and purchase book is overcast by Rs. 1000.

   (a) (a) - (ii), (b) - (iii), (c) - (i), (d) - (iv)
   (b) (a) - (ii), (b) - (iii), (c) - (iv), (d) - (v)
   (c) (a) - (iv), (b) - (ii), (c) - (i), (d) - (iii)
   (d) (a) - (ii), (b) - (iii), (c) - (i), (d) - (v)

7. Which of the following is not a type of inflation based on speed or intensity?
   (a) Rapid inflation (b) Cost-push inflation
   (c) Runaway inflation (d) Low inflation

8. Which of the following points refer(s) to perfect competition?
   Under perfect competition-
   (i) There are restrictions on buyers and sellers.
   (ii) There are no restrictions on movement of goods.
   (iii) There are no restrictions on factors of production.
   (a) Only (i) and (ii) (b) Only (ii) and (iii)
   (c) Only (i) and (iii) (d) Only (i)

9. Consider the following oligopoly models and arrange them in the correct sequence as per the order of evolution.
   (i) Sweezy's Kinked Demand Curve Model
   (ii) Newman and Morgenstern Game Theory Model
   (iii) Cournot's Duopoly Model
   (iv) Baumol's Sales Maximisation Model
   (a) (iv), (iii), (ii), (i) (b) (ii), (i), (iii), (iv)
   (c) (iii), (i), (ii), (iv) (d) (i), (iii), (ii), (iv)

10. Average revenue curve will not touch x-axis because it cannot be:
    (a) Positive (b) Zero
    (c) Negative (d) None of the above

11. Which of the following is not a restricted random sampling technique?
    (a) Stratified sampling
    (b) Simple random sampling
    (c) Systematic sampling
    (d) Multistage sampling

12. Classification of respondents on the basis of gender alone is an application of ________.
    (a) Ordinal scale (b) Nominal scale
    (c) Interval scale (d) Ratio scale

13. Statistical software packages for research in Social Sciences include:
    (a) SPSS (b) Stata
    (c) Minitab (d) All of the above

14. The F-test is used to test the significance of the difference between ________.
    (a) two sample means
    (b) more than two sample means
    (c) variances of two samples
    (d) (B) and (C)

15. Match List I with List II and c hoose the correct answer from the options given below:

	List I (Market Forms)		List II (Distinctive featured)
a.	Perfect competition	i)	Price rigidity
b.	Monopoly	ii)	Product improvements
c.	Monopolistic competition	iii)	Homogeneous products
d.	Oligopoly	iv)	Price discrimination

    (a) a-ii, b-i, c-iv, d-iii (b) a-iv, b-iii, c-i, d-ii
    (c) a-iii, b-iv, c-ii, d-i (d) a-i, b-ii, c-iii, d-iv

16. Identify the correct sequence of steps involved in planning:
    (i) Selecting the best course of action
    (ii) Establishing the sequence of activities
    (iii) Establishment of objectives
    (iv) Evaluating alternative actions

(v) Determining alternative actions

(a) (i), (ii), (iii), (iv) and (v)

(b) (iii), (v), (iv), (ii) and (i)

(c) (v), (iv), (iii), (ii) and (i)

(d) (iii), (v), (iv), (i) and (ii)

17. Howard-Sueth Model of Consumer Behaviour is popularly known as:

(a) Machine Model (b) Human Model

(c) Marketing Model (d) Purchase Model

18. Generating and facilitating any exchange to satisfy human needs is the satisfaction of these wants with minimum harmful effect on the natural environment, which is known as______.

(a) Aggressive marketing

(b) Operational marketing

(c) Green marketing

(d) All of the above

19. All the activities involved in selling goods or services directly to final consumers for personal non-business uses are done by?

(a) Wholesalers (b) Retailers

(c) Mediators (d) Commission agents

20. DAGMAR approach in marketing is used to measure?

(a) Public relations

(b) Advertising results

(c) Selling volume

(d) Consumer satisfaction

21. Which of the following refers to cash inflow under the Payback Period method?

(a) Cash flow before depreciation and taxes

(b) Cash flow after depreciation and taxes

(c) Cash flow after depreciation but before taxes

(d) Cash flow before depreciation and after taxes

22. The concept of present value is based on the__________.

(a) Principle of compounding

(b) Principle of discounting

(c) (A) and (B)

(d) None of the above

23. Match the following:

(a) Modigliani-Miller Appro ach	(i) Commercial papers
(b) Net Operating Income A pproach	(ii) Working Capital M anagement
(c) Short term Money Mark et Instrument	(iii) Capital Structure
(d) Factoring	(iv) Arbitrage

(a) (a) - (iv), (b) - (iii), (c) - (i), (d) - (ii)

(b) (a) - (iii), (b) - (iv), (c) - (i), (d) - (ii)

(c) (a) - (iii), (b) - (ii), (c) - (i), (d) - (iv)

(d) (a) - (iii), (b) - (ii), (c) - (iv), (d) - (i)

24. Which of the following is an incorrect statement?

(a) The issue of bonus shares is subject to sanction from SEBI.

(b) The prior approval of capitalization of reserves up to Rs.1 crore is totally exempted.

(c) Bonus issues beyond the ratio of 1:1 are not permitted.

(d) Partly paid equity shares are issued as bonus shares.

25. Direction: Read the given statements carefully and choose the correct option accordingly.

Statement I: Data material held in any electronic form is 'information' under RTI Act, 2005.

Statement II: IT Act, 2000 came into force on 10th October, 2000.

Choose the correct code:

(a) Only Statement I is correct.

(b) Only Statement II is correct.

(c) Both Statements are correct.

(d) Both Statements are incorrect.

26. Performance appraisal means evaluating the performance of an employee relative to _______.

(a) Established goods

(b) Fellow employees

(c) Job description requirements

(d) Performance standards

27. Broad money can be sensitized by?

(a) CRR (b) SLR

(c) Repo Rate (d) All of the above

28. Imperial Bank was established on January 27, 1921, on the advice of?

(a) J. M. Keynes (b) Lord Illingworth

(c) King George V (d) Winston Churchill

29. In India, the commercial banks are given the license of operation by the_______.

(a) Government of India

(b) Ministry of Finance

(c) Reserve Bank of India

(d) Banking Companies Regulation Act, 1949

30. The provisions of General Reserve in banking companies are made keeping in view the provisions of_______.

(a) Indian Companies Act, 1956

(b) Banking Companies Act, 1949

(c) SEBI Act, 1992

(d) All of the above

31. Which of the following is not an objective of IMF?

(a) To promote international monetary co-operation

(b) To ensure balanced international trade

(c) To finance productive efforts according to the peace-time requirement

(d) To ensure exchange rate stability

32. Donation to National Children & aposs Fund will come under which of the following deductions under Section 80 G of Income Tax Act, 1961?

(a) 100 percent deduction without any qualifying limit.

(b) 50 percent deduction without any qualifying limit.

(c) 100 percent deduction subject to qualifying limit.

(d) 50 percent deduction subject to qualifying limit.

33. Liberalization means:

(a) reducing the number of reserved industries from 17 to 8

(b) freeing the economy trade and industry from unwanted restrictions

(c) opening up of the economy to the world market by attaining international competitiveness

(d) free determination of interest rates

34. Match the following items of List - I with List - II.

	List - I		List - II
(i)	Bretton Woods Conference	a	1958
(ii)	General Agreement on Trade and Tariffs	b	1964
(iii)	ACCRA conference	c	1944
(iv)	United Nations Conference on Trade and Development	d	1947

(a) i - (c), ii - (d), iii - (a), iv - (b)

(b) i - (b), ii - (d), iii - (c), iv - (a)

(c) i - (b), ii - (c), iii - (d), iv - (a)

(d) i - (c), ii - (a), iii - (b), iv - (d)

35. HRM is viewed as a management process consisting of four functional activities.

(i) Acquisition

(ii) Motivation

(iii) Development

(iv) Resolution of industrial disputes

(v) Maintenance

Select the correct combination.

(a) (i), (ii), (iii) and (iv) (b) (i), (ii), (iii) and (v)

(c) (i), (ii), (iv) and (v) (d) (i), (iii), (iv) and (v)

36. Cost audit is to be conducted by a cost auditor who is a ________.

(a) qualified cost and management accountant

(b) qualified chartered accountant

(c) qualified company secretary

(d) any Indian resident

37. Subsequent expenditures that extend useful life, improve quality of output, or reduce operating costs of an existing asset beyond their originally estimated levels are called________.

(a) Capital expenditures

(b) Revenue expenditures

(c) Deferred revenue expenditures

(d) None of the above

38. Match the statements in List - I with dividend models in List - II:

	List - I		List - II
a.	Dividend capitalisation approach	1.	Traditional model
b.	Dividend Policy has a bearing on the share valuation.	2.	Gardon model
c.	Stock Market places more weight on dividends than on retain earnings.	3.	Walter model
d.	Dividend payout is irrelevant to the value of the firm.	4.	Modigliani and Miller model

(a) a - 2, b - 3, c - 1, d - 4 (b) a - 1, b - 2, c - 4, d - 3

(c) a - 4, b - 1, c - 3, d - 2 (d) a - 3, b - 4, c - 2, d - 1

39. What is NOT included in Internet Banking?

(a) Withdrawal of cash anywhere in India

(b) Statement of account for a specific period

(c) Transfer of funds from one account to another account

(d) Balance enquiry

40. Match the following List - I with List - II

List – I	List – II
1. Market segmentation	i. Pricing high of a new product initially.
2. Skimming price	ii. Process of disaggregating a market into a number of submarkets.
3. Multilevel marketing	iii. Translation of the marketing plan into marketing performance.
4. Sales management	iv. Modified version of direct marketing.

(a) 1-ii 2-i 3-iv 4-iii (b) 1-iii 2-i 3-ii 4-iv

(c) 1-i 2-ii 3-iii 4-iv (d) 1-iv 2-ii 3-iii 4-i

41. Which of the following is the most popular approach for accomplishing results?

(a) Management by exception

(b) Reward system

(c) Management by objectives

(d) Mentor system

42. Match the statements in List - I with the types of lease in the List - II as follows.

	List - I		List - II
I.	Lessor transfers all risks and rewards of an asset to the lessee.	1.	Indirect lease
II.	Lessor transfers the assets to the lessee but bears the cost of maintenance	2.	Operating lease
III.	The owner of the asset sells it to the lessor who in turn leases it back to the owner (now lessee)	3.	Finance lease
IV.	Lessor owns/acquires the assets that are leased to a given lessee.	4.	Direct lease

(a) I - 2, II - 3, III - 4, IV - 1

(b) I - 1, II - 4, III - 2, IV - 3

(c) I - 3, II - 2, III - 1, IV - 4

(d) I - 4, II - 1, III - 3, IV - 2

43. The method that is applied where work is undertaken to customers special requirements is;

(a) unit costing (b) batch costing

(c) job order costing (d) terminal costing

44. In India, which of the following pricing practices is notpermissible?

(a) Penetrating pricing (b) Skimming pricing

(c) Predatory pricing (d) None of the above

45. According to which one of the following theories, differences in nominal interest rates will be eliminated in the exchange rate?
   (a) Leontief Paradox Trade Theory
   (b) Fisher Effect Economic Theory
   (c) Purchasing Power Parity Theory
   (d) Combined Equilibrium Theory

46. The financial system consists of:
   I. Well established network of financial institutions
   II. Well developed financial markets
   III. Well established network of financial subsidiaries
   IV. Well developed system of financial assets
   Choose the correct option from those below:
   (a) I, II, III (b) I, III, IV
   (c) I, II, IV (d) II, III, IV

47. Match the items of List - I with the items of List - II.

	List - I		List - II
i.	Economic profi t	a.	Total Revenue Explicit cost
ii.	Accounting pro fit	b.	Buyers and sellers exchang ing
ii i.	Collusion/Cart el	c.	Total revenue - Total cost
i v.	Market	d.	Oligopoly

   (a) i - c, ii - a, iii - d, iv - b
   (b) i - a, ii - b, iii - c, iv - d
   (c) iv - a, iii - b, ii - c, i - d
   (d) ii - a, iv - b, i - d, iii - c

48. The European Union benefited its member nations:
   (a) By reducing barriers to trade and travel
   (b) By sharing the expense of a common defence
   (c) By promoting the use of a common language
   (d) By providing funds and materials for education

49. Which one of the following is not the basic function of WTO?
   (a) To facilitate the implementation, administration and operation of trade agreements
   (b) To settle differences and disputes among its member countries
   (c) To facilitate the expansion and balanced growth of international trade
   (d) To carry out periodic reviews of the trade policies of its member countries

50. Match the items of List - I with the items of List-II and select the correct answer.

	List - I		List - II
i.	The political and legal env ironment	(a)	Important for industries dire ctly depending on imports
i i.	Demographi c environme nt	(b)	A close relationship with the economic system and econo mic policy.
ii i.	Economic en vironment	(c)	Related to natural resources
i v.	Geographical and ecologic al environme nt	(d)	Occupational and spatial mo bilities of the population hav ing implications for business

   (a) i - (b), ii - (d), iii - (c), iv - (a)
   (b) i - (b), ii - (d), iii - (a), iv - (c)
   (c) i - (a), ii - (b), iii - (c), iv - (d)
   (d) i - (a), ii - (b), iii - (d), iv - (c)

51. Which of the following types of complaints are not to be entertained by Consumer Forums under the Consumer Protection Act, 1986?
   (a) A defective product purchased 1× years back
   (b) Misleading advertisement in a newspaper
   (c) Services provided free of cost
   (d) Tie in sales

52. Selection means-
   (a) Elimination (b) Testing
   (c) Recruitment (d) None of the above

53. Which of the following is not true with regard to the RTI Act, 2005?
   (a) The objective behind RTI is to maintain transparency in government operations
   (b) RTI is a key for empowering citizens
   (c) Containment of corruption in Government units is the important objective of the RTI Act.
   (d) RTI Act appoints NITI Aayog responsible for channelizing, regulating and maintaining the RTI Act in India.

54. Performance appraisal is related to ________.
   (a) 360 degrees appraisal
   (b) Open-door method
   (c) Autocratic method
   (d) All of the above

55. Which of the following is false regarding merchant banks?
   (i) They can accept deposits.
   (ii) They can advance loans.
   (iii) They can do other banking activities.
   (iv) They can be managers to a public issue.
   (a) Only (iv) (b) Only (i), (ii) and (iii)
   (c) Only (i), (iii) and (iv) (d) Only (ii) and (iv)

56. ECGC is concerned with:
   (a) Credit (b) Insurance
   (c) Transport (d) All of the above

57. Which of the following statements is true?
   (a) The currency notes issued by RBI are legal tender throughout the world.
   (b) Treasury bills are sold by the RBI for raising its working capital.
   (c) All commercial banks, including those owned by the Government, need a licence from the RBI to do banking business.
   (d) The RBI is a banker to both central and state governments.

58. The amount of gold, reserve currencies and special drawing rights available to finance international trade is known as ______.
   (a) International liquidity
   (b) Special drawing rights

(c) International monetary finance
(d) None of the above

59. The Double Taxation Avoidance Convention (DTAC) pact was signed between?
(a) India and China
(b) India, Serbia and Montenegro
(c) Australia and China
(d) None of the above

60. **Direction:** Given below are two statements. Choose the correct statement.
Statement I: A sale has the immediate effect of transferring property, where as in an agreement to sell the property is to pass at some future time.
Statement II: A sale makes the buyer the owner of goods but agreement to sale does not make the buyer the owner of goods.
(a) Only Statement I is true.
(b) Only Statement II is true.
(c) Both Statements are true.
(d) Both Statements are false.

61. Tax Evasion attract a penalty at _______ under Section _______ of Income Tax Act 1961.
(a) 200%, 269 A (b) 200%, 270 A
(c) 200%, 271 A (d) 100%, 265 A

62. In the contract of agency, Implied agency may arise by:
A. Agency by Estoppel
B. Agency of Necessity
C. Agency by Ratification
D. Agency by Holding out
(a) Both A and B (b) A, B and C
(c) Both B and D (d) All of the above

63. The maximum rate for CGST is?
(a) 28 (b) 12
(c) 18 (d) 14

64. Which of the following receipt is revenue in nature as per Income Tax Act?
1. When any contract is entered into in the ordinary course of business, any compensation received for its termination would be a revenue receipt.
2. A receipt under a general insurance policy may be a revenue receipt, if the policy relates to circulation asset.
3. Forfeited security deposits would be revenue receipt's, where they are related to the assessee's trading activity.
Select the correct answer using the codes given below:
(a) Both 1 and 2 (b) Only 3
(c) Both 2 and 3 (d) All of the above

65. Which of the following statements is/are correct?
1. An assessee may enjoy the residential status for different assessment year.
2. It is not necessary that a person, who is resident in India, cannot become resident in any other country for the same assessment year.
3. Where a person is in India only for a part of a day, it will be calculated as one complete day.
Select the correct answer using the codes given below:
(a) Only 1 (b) Both 1 and 2
(c) Both 1 and 3 (d) All of the above

66. Which of the following incomes are exempt from tax?
1. Dividend received from the foreign company.
2. Agricultural income.
3. Remuneration received by an individual who is not a citizen of India
4. Capital gain income.
5. Dividend received from an Indian company.
6. Rental income of house property.
(a) 2, 3, and 4 (b) 1, 3, 5, and 6
(c) 3, 4, and 6 (d) None of the above

67. Which of the following statement is true?
1. The tax rate of STCG is 10%
2. The tax rate of LTCG is 15%
3. The tax rate on casual income is 30%
4. The tax rate on dividend received from domestic company is 10%
(a) 1 and 2 are true
(b) 2 and 4 are true
(c) 3 and 4 are true
(d) All statements are true

68. Salary received by a Member of Parliament is taxable under the head ________.
(a) Income from salary
(b) Capital gains
(c) Profits and gains of business or profession
(d) Income from other sources

69. Which test we normally apply for Qualitative data?
(a) 't' test (b) 'F' test
(c) x^2 chi-square test (d) 'z' test

70. Chunk Sampling is known as:
(a) Quota sampling
(b) Convenience sampling
(c) Judgement sampling
(d) Cluster sampling

71. F-test is used to test the significance of the differences between/among:
(a) Two sample mean
(b) More than two samples mean
(c) Variance of two samples
(d) (B) and (C)

72. In a unimodal and symmetric distribution, the relationship between averages is like this:
(a) Mean > median > mode
(b) Mean < median < mode
(c) Mean = median = mode
(d) Mean > median < mode

Ques (73-76): Directions: Read the passage carefully and answer the questions that follow.
The government's move to infuse upfront an additional capital of Rs 70,000 crore into public sector banks (PSBs) is welcome. The promised removal of the Damocles' sword of punitive investigation of any banking decision hanging over the heads of bankers today will help banks lend the additional liquidity leveraging this capital would enable.
The moves to support non-banking financial companies (NBFCs) — such as enhancing additional liquidity support to housing finance companies to Rs 30,000 crore by National Housing Bank from Rs 20,000 crore and co-origination of loans by PSBs jointly with NBFCs that are reeling under a liquidity crunch — will provide a booster for fresh loans to the MSME sector.

A transparent one-time settlement policy being provided by banks to benefit MSMEs and retail borrowers in settling their overdues is pragmatic. But banks also must acquire the expertise to assess MSME loan viability and invest in data mining.

Making banks link their lending rates to the repo rates will help better transmission of monetary policy. But for this to work without impairing bank financial health, multiple structural rigidities in the system must be removed. Public sector pre-emption of the bulk of household financial savings must end, for the bond market to really take off to provide longer-term funds for infrastructure projects.

Steps such as further development of the credit default swap markets, facilitating increased trading for price discovery, and establishing an organisation to provide credit enhancement for infrastructure and housing projects make eminent sense, as does onshoring the offshore rupee derivative markets.

A coherent policy of managerial reform, including of remuneration, at public sector banks must accompany the measures announced, for them to take effect.

73. What is the meaning of the idiom "Damocles' sword", as used in the passage?

(a) Planned fraud
(b) Meticulous investigation
(c) Imminent danger
(d) Careless attitude

74. According to the passage, what will provide a booster for fresh loans to the MSME sector?

I. Loan waivers and collateral free loans.
II. Increasing additional liquidity support of Rs 20,000 cr by 50%.
III. Joint contribution of credit by PSBs and NBFCs.

(a) Only III (b) Only II and III
(c) Only I and III (d) All of I, II and III

75. With which of the following statements would the author most likely agree?

I. One-time settlement policy that will benefit MSMEs is impractical for banks and is unwise.
II. Banks have not yet developed the required proficiency in judging the sustainability of MSME loans.
III. Banks have made huge investments in data mining.

(a) Only I (b) Only II
(c) Only I and II (d) Only I and III

76. What is the tone of the passage?

(a) Acerbic (b) Vitriolic
(c) Indignant (d) None of the above

Ques (77-80): Directions: Read the passage and answer the questions that follow:

During the financial crisis, Western governments poured hundreds of billions of dollars into their banks to avert collapse. The search for ways to avoid future bail-outs started before the turmoil ended. One of the niftiest proposals was the "contingent convertible" (coco) bond, which turns into equity when the ratio of a bank's equity to risk-weighted assets falls below a predetermined danger point (since set at a minimum of 5.125% for cocos, although it can be up to around 7%). The ambition was grand. As the Squam Lake Group, composed of mostly American academics, put it in 2009, the automatic conversion of cocos would "transform an undercapitalised or insolvent bank into a well-capitalised bank at no cost to taxpayers".

At first, regulators were keen. In 2010 Mervyn King, then the governor of the Bank of England, said he wanted contingent capital to be a "major part of the liability structure of the banking system". Swiss regulators, too, pushed for coco issuance. The hybrid nature of cocos seemed a way to satisfy both regulators, who wanted banks to have bigger safety buffers, and bankers, who were reluctant to issue new shares because of the high cost of capital. The hope was that investors, too, might see the appeal of an asset that offered a higher yield than bank bonds but lower risk than bank shares.

Nine years after the first cocos were issued by Lloyds Banking Group in Britain, they have not fulfilled this promise. To be sure, they are now an established asset class, with around $155bn of issuance in 2017 in Dollars, Euros and Pounds. But this is a fraction of more than $1trn in bank debt issued that year. Cocos are issued by only around 50 banks in a dozen countries mostly in Europe. Although cocos are held by the world's largest asset managers, including BlackRock and PIMCO, few specialise in them. Exceptions include niche funds run by Algebris Investment and Old Mutual Global Investors.

The main reason is that, despite early enthusiasm, regulators did not throw their weight behind cocos. In 2011, the Financial Stability Board, a global grouping of regulators, decided that they would not count towards the capital "surcharge" the biggest banks would be required to hold. Only equity would do. Rules on "total loss absorption capacity" finalised in 2015 require banks to have liabilities that can take a haircut or be wiped out if they are liquidated or restructured. But a wide range of liabilities, from shares to subordinated and even senior debt, is included. Cocos became part of a spectrum of at-risk liabilities, rather than a neat, catch-all solution.

The result is that cocos are a specialised investment proposition. They still offer fairly high yields—currently 5.3% for dollar cocos and 3% for those in euros, according to indices compiled by Credit Suisse, a bank. And they offer a premium over junior debt. They have appealing technical characteristics, too. Unlike bonds with a fixed maturity, they are perpetual, but redeemable after five years. If not redeemed, their coupon resets with reference to the mid-swap rate, a widely used rate related to interbank lending rates. That offers some protection against inflation. In 2016 investor jitters caused a spike in coco yields. But since then, nerves have calmed and spreads have narrowed.

77. As per the passage, what is meant by 'coco'?

(a) Coco refers to convertible bonds which can be converted from debt to equity after a certain number of years.
(b) Coco refers to a special type of bond which gets converted to debt when the debt-to-equity ratio of the bank falls below a certain level.
(c) Coco is used to refer to a situation where in the government forces a company to liquidate some of its shares so as to pay back its debt.
(d) Coco is short for contingent convertible bonds which get converted to equity after the bank's equity to risk weighted assets fall below a certain level.

78. As per the Squam Lake Group, what was the biggest benefit of the coco bonds?

I. It would keep the costs to manage customer accounts to a bare minimum.
II. It was an off-balance sheet item and would not increase the liability of the banks.
III. It would help in capitalizing the undercapitalized banks without any extra costs.

(a) Only II (b) Only III
(c) Only I and II (d) Only II and III

79. As per the passage, why would investors want to invest in coco bonds?

I. As cocos could play a major part in helping the banks

become safer.
II. As they wanted banks to have bigger safety buffer.
III. As they were reluctant to invest in equity shares of the banks
IV. As cocos offered better yields than normal bank bonds with lesser risk.

(a) Only IV (b) Only I
(c) Only I, III and IV (d) Only II, III and IV

80. Refer to- 'Nine years after the first cocos were issued by Lloyds Banking Group in Britain, they have not fulfilled this promise.' What is meant by the author in the line above?
I. Cocos are not a reliable asset class.
II. Cocos form only a tiny fraction of the total bank debt issued.
III. Cocos do not seem to have made a big difference in the banking system.

(a) Only I (b) Only III
(c) Only II and III (d) Only I and II

// Smart Answer Sheet //

Correct Percentage of students who answered correctly.

Skipped Percentage of students who skipped.

Q.	Ans.	Correct	Skipped	Q.	Ans.	Correct	Skipped	Q.	Ans.	Correct	Skipped
1	D	79.67%	11.29%	2	A	51.53%	40.5%	3	B	60.12%	39.51%
4	B	49.39%	30.69%	5	A	84.75%	10.74%	6	D	67.28%	31.69%
7	B	69.43%	30.5%	8	B	44.48%	48.96%	9	C	47.07%	30.58%
10	B	41.55%	54.35%	11	B	20.14%	71.74%	12	B	63.28%	33.75%
13	D	41.54%	52.57%	14	D	48.93%	46.18%	15	C	69.52%	30.19%
16	D	79.0%	12.84%	17	A	46.84%	37.09%	18	C	50.19%	47.36%
19	B	88.34%	11.07%	20	B	29.48%	70.38%	21	D	53.91%	40.95%
22	B	66.28%	30.69%	23	A	66.66%	33.32%	24	D	88.68%	10.33%
25	A	47.93%	37.27%	26	D	63.85%	35.76%	27	D	66.24%	32.04%
28	A	85.41%	12.26%	29	C	67.62%	32.23%	30	B	54.73%	39.64%
31	C	80.54%	17.52%	32	A	69.12%	30.31%	33	B	87.64%	11.69%
34	A	11.37%	84.67%	35	B	53.58%	44.23%	36	A	57.38%	41.87%
37	A	64.26%	30.63%	38	A	41.61%	30.82%	39	A	77.68%	18.25%
40	A	64.11%	30.4%	41	C	69.26%	30.16%	42	C	43.48%	51.17%
43	C	19.37%	67.01%	44	C	63.45%	35.66%	45	B	26.27%	70.83%
46	C	58.02%	36.45%	47	A	11.13%	88.85%	48	A	18.2%	79.12%
49	C	68.34%	30.52%	50	B	15.83%	79.44%	51	C	54.28%	32.39%
52	D	79.9%	19.58%	53	D	41.08%	56.46%	54	A	60.44%	34.05%
55	B	40.04%	42.88%	56	B	84.36%	10.28%	57	D	64.08%	34.85%
58	A	57.59%	35.1%	59	D	57.36%	37.48%	60	C	67.41%	30.23%
61	B	63.98%	32.18%	62	C	52.67%	35.19%	63	D	65.53%	30.42%
64	C	60.67%	35.46%	65	D	42.75%	33.41%	66	A	63.21%	32.76%
67	C	67.69%	30.87%	68	D	55.79%	41.94%	69	C	63.99%	33.87%
70	B	57.56%	40.34%	71	D	65.23%	32.7%	72	C	68.99%	30.37%
73	C	56.69%	40.45%	74	B	41.35%	31.55%	75	B	50.62%	39.83%
76	D	50.24%	32.5%	77	D	69.7%	30.02%	78	B	51.0%	31.21%
79	A	57.13%	38.21%	80	C	60.58%	31.44%				

// Hints and Solutions //

1(D). Indian economy consists of three sectors: primary, secondary, and service. With the development process, the significance of the primary sector declines, while that of the secondary and service sector increases. Any changes in these sectors will lead to change in the Indian economy.

2(A). Goods and Service (GST) came into effect from 1 July 2017 through the implementation of the One Hundred and First Amendment of the Constitution.

- Goods and Services Tax (GST) is an indirect tax (or consumption tax) used in India on the supply of goods and services.
- It has subsumed almost all the indirect taxes except a few state taxes.
- Multi-staged as it is, the GST is imposed at every step in the production process but is meant to be refunded to all parties in the various stages of production other than the final consumer and as a destination-based tax, it is collected from point of consumption and not point of origin like previous taxes.
- Goods and services are divided into five different tax slabs for collection of tax - 0%, 5%, 12%, 18% and 28%.
- However, petroleum products, alcoholic drinks, and electricity are not taxed under GST and instead are taxed separately by the individual state governments, as per the previous tax system.
- There is a special rate of 0.25% on rough precious and semi-precious stones and 3% on gold.

3(B). Counter Vailing Duties are tariffs imposed on imported commodities to compensate for subsidies given to producers of these goods in the exporting country.
Countervailing duty (CVD) is a specific form of duty that the government imposes in order to protect domestic producers by countering the negative impact of export subsidies.

4(B). Conversion cost is the cost required for the conversion of raw material into the final output.
Conversion cost = direct wages + direct expense + manufacturing overheads (factory overheads)
Direct wages means monetary amounts paid by the contractor or its subcontractor(s) to its employees for straight time (non-overtime) hours worked, including shift differentials.
Direct expense is an expense incurred that varies directly with changes in the volume of a cost object.
Factory overhead is the total cost involved in operating all production facilities of a manufacturing business that cannot be traced directly to a product.

5(A). Liquidity measures a company's ability to pay short-term and long-term obligations.

Liquidity in descending order: Current ratio, quick ratio, superquick ratio, and basic defensive and interval ratio

The current ratio is more liquid than others.

- The defensive interval ratio (DIR), also called the defensive interval period (DIP) or basic defense interval (BDI), is a financial metric that indicates the number of days that a company can operate without needing to access noncurrent assets, long-term assets whose full value cannot be obtained within the current.
- The current ratio is a liquidity ratio that measures a company's ability to pay short-term obligations or those due within one year.
- The standard ratio of Super Quick Ratio is 0.5:1. It ensures most liquidity of the business concern.
- The quick ratio measures a company's capacity to pay its current liabilities without needing to sell its inventory or obtain additional financing.

6(D). The error of Principle is an error in which an entry is recorded in the incorrect account, i.e. treating repair charges as an addition to assets. Repair charges are revenue expenditure, it is to be shown in the P&L account. The error of Commission is an error of entering the wrong amount, i.e. a sale of Rs. 563 was posted as Rs. 653. The error of Omission is an error incurred by omitting an entry to record, i.e. purchase of Rs. 1000 has not to be recorded. Compensatory error is an error that is neutralized by an equal and opposite error, i.e. return inward book is undercast by Rs. 1000 and purchase book is overcast by Rs. 1000.

7(B). Cost-push inflation occurs when overall prices increases (inflation) due to the increase in the cost of wages and raw materials.

The most common cause of cost-push inflation starts with an increase in the cost of production or the cost of the raw of material. The cost of raw materials or inventory used in production might increase, leading to higher costs.

8(B). The following characteristics are essential for the existence of Perfect Competition:

- Large Number of Buyers and Sellers
- Homogeneity of the Product
- Free Entry and Exit of Firms
- Perfect Knowledge of the Market
- Perfect Mobility of the Factors of Production and Goods
- Absence of transportation cost

9(C). According to the oligopoly model when there are very few sellers in the market. This results in reduction of competition and increase in price.

- In Cournot's Duopoly Model, the firms simultaneously choose quantities.
- Sweezy's Kinked Demand Curve Model advocates that the behavior of oligopolistic organizations remains stable when the price and output are determined.
- Newman and Morgenstern Game Theory Model: Game theory is mainly used in economics, political science, and psychology.
- Baumol's Sales Maximisation Model represents the managerial theory of the firm based on sales maximization.

10(B). The average revenue curve will not touch the x-axis because it cannot be zero.

AR = Price

AR (price) can neither be zero or negative because TR(Total revenue) is always positive.

11(B). Simple random sampling is a non- probability random sampling where a simple random sample is a subset of individuals chosen from a larger set. Each individual is chosen randomly and entirely by chance, such that each individual has the same probability of getting selected. Therefore, it is free from all types of restrictions.

12(B). Classification of respondents on the basis of gender alone is an application of nominal scale.

Quantitative variables are categorized into ordinal scale, interval scale, and ratio scale. A qualitative variable is classified into nominal, dummy and preference, etc.

13(D). Departments use various types of statistical software packages, i.e Stata, SPSS, Minitab, etc. to analyze both quantitative and qualitative data.

- The computer program SPSS (Statistical Package for the Social Sciences) is used by market researchers, health researchers, survey companies, government, education researchers, and others.
- Stata is a complete, integrated statistical package that provides everything you need for data analysis, data management, and graphics.
- Minitab is a general statistics package.

14(D). F-test is used to test the significance of the differences among variances of two samples and more than two sample means. It is a ratio of variances of two samples.

The F-test is designed to test when two population variances are equal. It does this by comparing the ratio of two variances. Therefore, if the deviations are equal, the ratio of deviations will be 1. If the null hypothesis is true, then the F test-statistic above can be simplified.

15(C). "Market structures" refer to the different market characteristics that determine relations between sellers to each another, of sellers to buyers and more. There are four basic types of market structures.

Perfect Competition:

- All firms sell an identical product (the product is a "commodity" or "homogeneous").
- All firms are price takers (they cannot influence the market price of their products).
- Market share has no influence on prices.

Monopoly:

- Competitors are not able to enter the market as there are high barriers to entry.
- There is only one seller in the market, meaning the company becomes the same as the industry it serves.

Monopolistic Competition:

- It occurs when an industry has many firms offering products that are similar but not identical.
- Unlike a monopoly, these firms have little power to set curtail supply or raise prices to increase profits.
- Firms in monopolistic competition typically try to differentiate their products in order to achieve above-market returns.

Oligopoly:

- Oligopoly is when a small number of firms

collude, either explicitly or tacitly, to restrict output and/or fix prices, in order to achieve above normal market returns.

- Economic, legal, and technological factors can contribute to the formation and maintenance, or dissolution, of oligopolies.

16(D). The planning process is to determine what is to be accomplished during the planning period. Vision and mission statements provide long-term broad guidance on where the organization is going and how to get there. The planning process should define specific goals and show how the goals support the vision and mission.
The following are the steps involved in the planning process:
1. Establishment of Objectives:
This is the first step in the planning process. Objectives specify the expected results and indicate the endpoints of what is to be done, where the primary emphasis is to be placed, and what is to be accomplished by different types of plans.
2. Determination of alternative actions:
The second step in planning is to identify alternatives. Various alternatives can be identified depending on the organizational objectives and planning premises.
3. Evaluation of Alternative Actions:
Various alternative courses of action should be analyzed in the light of objectives and goals. Various techniques are available for evaluating alternatives.
4. Choosing the Best Course of Action:
Selecting the best course of action from alternatives is called decision making. Decision-making is a process of selecting from a set of alternative courses of action which are thought to meet the objective of the decision problem more satisfactorily than others.
5. Establishing Sequence of Activities:
After making basic and derivative plans, a sequence of activities is determined so that those plans are executed. After decisions are made and plans are laid down, budgets can be prepared for different periods and divisions to give more concrete meaning to the plans for implementation.
Thus, the correct answer is (iii), (v), (iv), (i) and (ii).

17(A). Howard-Sueth Model of Consumer Behaviour is the integration of social, psychological, and marketing influences on consumer choice. It shows the rational brand choice behavior by the buyer under conditions of incomplete information. Howard-Sueth Model of Consumer Behaviour is popularly known as Machine Model.

18(C). Green marketing is the marketing of products that is preferable to the environment. This is also called ecological/environmental marketing. Companies involved in green marketing make decisions relating to the entire process of the products based on environmental factors such as the method of processing, packaging, and distribution to satisfy human wants/needs with a minimal detrimental impact on the natural environment.

19(B). Retailers are the persons who sell goods in small quantities directly to the ultimate consumers through various distribution channels for the purpose of making profits.
These rules include all goods and services purchased or sold through direct selling, all models of direct selling, all direct selling entities providing goods and services to consumers in India, all forms of unfair trade practices in all models of direct selling, shall apply to a direct selling entity which is not established in India but provides goods or services to consumers in India.

20(B). DAGMAR (defining advertising goals for measured advertising results) is a marketing model used to establish clear objectives for an advertising campaign and measure its success. The DAGMAR model defines the four steps of an effective advertising campaign as causing awareness, comprehension, conviction, and action.

21(D). In this method, cash flow before depreciation, but after-tax, is taken as cash inflow. Depreciation is not taken because it is a non-cash expense. The payback period is the time required for the amount invested in an asset to be repaid by the net cash inflow generated by the asset.
Payback period = Initial investment/Cash inflow

22(B). The concept of present value is based on the principle of discounting.
Present value (PV) is the current worth of a future sum of money or stream of cash flows given a specified rate of return. Future cash flows are discounted at the discount rate, and the higher the discount rate, the lower the present value of the future cash flows. The concept of present value is based on the principle of discounting. It means to bring the value of inflows to be received in the future, at present value, i.e. today's value.

23(A). Modigliani Miller Approach is used in the arbitrage concept.
Net Operating Income Approach is used in the capital structure.
Commercial Papers are short term money market instruments.
Factoring is a concept of working capital management.

24(D). Partly paid-up shares cannot be issued as bonus shares. Bonus shares are issued free of cost. These are issued only when they are fully paid up. If shares are partly paid up, and these are to be issued as bonus shares, it is essential to make these shares fully paid up before issuing them as bonus shares.

25(A). Section 2(f) of the RTI Act, 2005 defines 'Information' as any material in any form, including records, documents, memos, e-mails, opinions, advice, press releases, circulars, orders, logbooks, contracts, reports, papers, samples, models, data material held in any electronic form and information relating to any private body which can be accessed by a public authority under any other law for the time being in force.
IT Act 2000

- To give legal recognition to any transaction which is done by electronic way or use of the internet.
- To give legal recognition to digital signature for accepting any agreement via computer.
- To provide the facility of filling in documents online.

26(D). Performance appraisal is a comprehensive evaluation of the employee's performance on the basis of performance standards set up by the organization. Whatever task is assigned to employees is evaluated to measure their efficiency by following the standards.

27(D). Broad money is a category for measuring the amount of money circulating in an economy. It is defined as the most inclusive method of calculating a given country's money supply, and includes narrow money along with other assets that can be easily converted into cash to buy goods and services.

- Cash Reserve Ratio is a minimum proportion of customer's deposits that are to be kept as a reserve by banks.
- Statutory Liquid Ratio is a portion of the deposits that banks have to be kept in form of gold.
- Repo Rate is a rate at which the central bank lends money to a commercial bank in case of a shortage of funds.

28(A). Imperial Bank was established on January 27, 1921, on the advice of J. M. Keynes. The Imperial Bank of India (IBI) was the oldest and the largest commercial bank of the Indian subcontinent and was subsequently transformed into the State Bank of India in 1955.

29(C). In India, the commercial banks are given the license of operation by the Reserve Bank of India. The Banking Regulation Act, 1949 gives the Reserve Bank of India (RBI) the power to license banks.

30(B). The provisions of General Reserve in banking companies are made keeping in view the provisions of Banking Companies Act, 1949. The Banking Regulation Act, 1949 is a legislation in India that regulates all banking firms in India.

31(C). To finance productive efforts according to the peace-time requirement is not an objective of IMF.
The International Monetary Fund (IMF) is an international organization working to foster global monetary co-operation, secure financial stability, facilitate international trade, promote high employment and sustainable economic growth, and reduce poverty around the world.

32(A). Donation to National Children & aposs Fund will come under 100 percent deduction without any qualifying limit.
Section 80G deduction of the Income Tax Act is allowed for amount paid by the taxpayer as donation to any fund or institution or charitable Trust. All donations are not treated equally under Income Tax Act. Donations to certain funds and institutions qualify for 100% or 50% deduction without any qualifying limit.

33(B). Liberalization means freeing the economy trade and industry from unwanted restrictions.
The removal or loosening of restrictions on something, typically an economic or political system. It is the removal or reduction of restrictions or barriers on the free exchange of goods between nations. These barriers include tariffs, such as duties and surcharges, and nontariff barriers, such as licensing rules and quotas.

34(A). The correctly matched pairs are-i - (c), ii - (d), iii - (a), iv - (b)
The Bretton Woods Conference, officially known as the United Nations Monetary and Financial Conference, was a gathering of delegates from 44 nations that met from July 1 to 22, 1944 in Bretton Woods, New Hampshire, to agree upon a series of new rules for the post-WWII international monetary system.
The General Agreement on Tariffs and Trade (GATT), signed on Oct. 30, 1947, by 23 countries, was a legal agreement minimizing barriers to international trade by eliminating or reducing quotas, tariffs, and subsidies while preserving significant regulations.
The All-Africa Peoples Conference was conceived to represent the position that Africa should be returned to the peoples and groups, such as ethnic communities, from who it was grabbed by colonialism. This was at the end of the first Africa Heads of State Conference in Accra Ghana in March 1958.
The first United Nations Conference on Trade and Development (UNCTAD) was held in Geneva in 1964.

35(B). Human resource management is an organizational function that deals with issues. According to Dale Yoder, "The management of the human resource is viewed as a system in which participants seeks to attain both individual and group goals" HRD is a process, which consists of a series of activities.
Functions of HRM: Acquisition, Motivation, Development, and Maintenance

36(A). Cost auditing is the thorough examination of the costing methodology, system, and accounts to confirm their accuracy and guarantee conformity to the goal of cost accounting.
The following credentials are required of a candidate for a position as a company's cost auditor:

- He or she must meet the requirements for the title of Cost Accountant as set forth in clause (a) of subsection (1) of section 2 of the Cost and Management Accountants Act, 1959. (23 of 1959).
- In accordance with Section 7 of the Cost and Works Accountants Act, 1959, he or she must possess a current certificate of practise granted by the Council of the Institute of Cost and Works Accountants of India.
- A partner in a firm of cost accountants who has a current certificate of practise is also eligible to be named the company's cost auditor. It is crucial that such a cost accountant or a partner of the cost accounting firm not hold another job.

So, a cost audit is to be conducted by a cost auditor who is a/an qualified cost and management accountant.

37(A). Subsequent expenditures that extend useful life, improve quality of output, or reduce operating costs of an existing asset beyond their originally estimated levels are called capital expenditures. Capital expenditure is the money spent by the government on the development of machinery, equipment, building, health facilities, education, etc.

38(A). The correctly matched pairs are- a - 2, b - 3, c - 1, d - 4
The Gordon Growth Model assumes a company exists forever and pays dividends per share that increase at a constant rate. To estimate the value of a stock, the model takes the infinite series of dividends per share and discounts them back into

the present using the required rate of return. According to Walter's Model, given by prof. James E. Walter, the dividends are relevant and have a bearing on the firm's share prices. If r=K, the firm's dividend policy does not affect the firm's value. Stock Market places more weight on dividends than on retained earnings. The weight attached to Dividends is equal to 4 times the weight attached to retained earnings.
Modigliani – Miller's theory is a major proponent of the 'Dividend Irrelevance' notion. According to this concept, investors do not pay any importance to the dividend history of a company and thus, dividends are irrelevant in calculating the valuation of a company.

39(A). Internet banking can be used for transacting online and has the limitation that cash cannot be withdrawn through the platform.

40(A). Market Segmentation:

- Market segmentation is the process of dividing a target market into smaller, more defined categories.
- It segments customers and audiences into groups that share similar characteristics such as demographics, interests, needs, or location.
- Market segmentation is a marketing term that refers to disaggregating prospective buyers into groups or segments with common needs and who respond similarly to a marketing action.

Skimming Price:

- Price skimming is a product pricing strategy by which a firm charges the highest initial price that customers will pay and then lowers it over time.
- As the demand of the first customers is satisfied and competition enters the market, the firm lowers the price to attract another, a more price-sensitive segment of the population.
- The skimming strategy gets its name from "skimming" successive layers of cream, or customer segments, as prices are lowered over time.

Multilevel Marketing:

- Multi-level marketing is a distribution model companies use to get their product to consumers.
- Instead of directly offering their products to consumers online or in brick-and-mortar stores, they use sales representatives to distribute and sell their products.
- It is a modified version of direct marketing.

Sales Management:

- Sales management is defined as the planning, direction, and control of personal selling including recruiting, selecting, equipping, assigning, routing, supervising, paying, and motivating as these tasks apply to the personal sales force.
- Sales management specifically contributes to achieving the marketing objectives of a firm. In fact, sales managers set their personal selling objectives and formulate personal selling policies and strategies.

41(C). Management by objectives is the most popular approach for accomplishing results. Management by objectives (MBO) is a strategic management model that aims to improve organizational performance by clearly defining objectives that are agreed to by both management and employees.

42(C). The correctly matched pairs are-I - 3, II - 2, III - 1, IV - 4
A lease is an agreement whereby the lessor conveys to the lessee in return for a payment or series of payments the right to use an asset for an agreed period of time.
A finance lease is a lease that transfers substantially all the risks and rewards incidental to ownership of an asset.
An operating lease is a contract that allows for the use of an asset but does not convey ownership rights of the asset. Operating leases are considered a form of off-balance-sheet financing—meaning a leased asset and associated liabilities (i.e. future rent payments) are not included on a company's balance sheet.
Indirect leasing is a three-party arrangement involving an asset's supplier (manufacturer or dealer), the asset's lessee, and a lessor that is unaffiliated with the asset's supplier. The lessee obtains contractual possession and use of the asset indirectly from the supplier after it has been purchased by the lessor.
Direct lease refers to a contractual arrangement between a lessor and a lessee where the lessor leases out some property (generally equipment) to the lessee.

43(C). Job order costing:

- It is a costing method used to determine the expense of producing each product according to the customer's special requirements.
- It includes direct material, direct labour, and manufacturing overhead of that particular job.
- Ex: A company that produces custom made laptops or other electronic devices.

Therefore, the method that is applied where work is undertaken to customer's special requirements is Job order costing.

44(C). In India, predatory pricing practice is not permissible. Predatory pricing is the illegal act of setting prices low in an attempt to eliminate the competition. Predatory pricing violates antitrust law, as it makes markets more vulnerable to a monopoly.

45(B). According to f isher effect economic theory differences in nominal interest rates will be eliminated in the exchange rate.
Fisher Effect Economic theory states the difference between countries' nominal interest rates is almost equal to their exchange rate and the differences thus, get eliminated. Instead of solely using inflation rates in the prediction of exchange rate shifts like the PPP Theory, it relates inflation and interest rates to a currency's appreciation or depreciation, thereby taking a combined view of the same.

46(C). The financial system consists of the following:

- Well-established system of financial institutions
- Well Developed Financial Markets
- Well developed system of financial assets

The financial system is concerned about money, credit, and finance for the promotion of faster economic growth.

47(A). The correctly matched pairs are- i - c, ii - a, iii - d, iv - b
Economic profit is the difference between total monetary revenue and total costs, but total costs

include both explicit and implicit costs. Economic profit includes the opportunity costs associated with production and is, therefore, lower than accounting profit.
Accounting profit is the total revenues minus explicit costs, including depreciation. Economic profit is total revenues minus total costs—explicit plus implicit costs. Explicit costs are out-of-pocket costs for a firm—for example, payments for wages and salaries, rent, or materials.
Collusion/Cartel can hold down industry output, charge a higher price, and divide up the profit among themselves. When firms act together in this way to reduce output and keep prices high, it is called collusion. A group of firms that have a formal agreement to collude to produce the monopoly output and sell at the monopoly price is called a cartel.
While parties may exchange goods and services by barter, most markets rely on sellers offering their goods or services (including labor) in exchange for money from buyers. It can be said that a market is a process by which the prices of goods and services are established.

48(A). The European Union benefited its member nations by Reducing barriers to trade and travel.

- When the EU was founded in 1957, the Member States concentrated on building a 'common market' for trade.
- Since 1957, the European Union has benefited its citizens by working for peace and prosperity.
- Free trade among its members was one of the EU's founding principles.
- The European Union was a group of 28 countries that operate as a cohesive economic and political block.
- After BREXIT (Britain's exit from EU), The Union currently counts 27 EU countries.
- 19 of these countries use the EURO as their official currency.
- 8 EU members (Bulgaria, Croatia, Czech Republic, Denmark, Hungary, Poland, Romania, Sweden) and the United Kingdom do not use the euro.
- In 2012, the EU received the Nobel Peace Prize for having "contributed to the advancement of peace and reconciliation, democracy, and human rights in Europe.
- Switzerland is not a member state of the European Union (EU).

49(C). World Trade Organization (WTO) was formed after the Uruguay Round(1986-1993). The pre-existing members of GATT signed an agreement of Uruguay round in April 1994 in Morocco paving way for the establishment of a new organization named WTO.

- To execute rules and provisions related to trade policies review mechanism.
- To provide a common platform to member countries to discuss and strategize the trade mechanism and tariff rate formulation.
- To aid facilities for administration and operation of multilateral agreements of the World Trade.
- To monitor and provide a forum to resolve dispute settlement among member Nations.
- To ensure the optimization of resource allocation through global trade.
- To achieve Universal Economic Policy determination by aiding International organizations such as the IMF & The World Bank.
- It provides protection to innovation and creative ideas by setting up proper trading protocols for 'Intellectual Property' Rights.

50(B). The correctly matched pairs are- i - (b), ii - (d), iii - (a), iv - (c)
The political-legal environment is a combination of a lot of factors such as the current political party in power, the degree of politicization of trade and industry, the efficiency of the current government, government policies, current legal framework, the public attitude towards the economy, etc.
The demographic environment is about the characteristics of the population in a specific area and includes multiple factors like age, race, income, etc. Every business can be concerned with different aspects of the demographic characteristics of a population.
The economic environment refers to all the economic factors that affect commercial and consumer behavior. The economic environment consists of all the external factors in the immediate marketplace and the broader economy. These factors can influence a business, i.e., how it operates and how successful it might become.
Environmental Geography is a branch of geography. It deals with the spatial distribution of various ecosystems, habitats, plants, animals, and human life.

51(C). The Consumer Protection Bill was passed by the Parliament on 24 December 1986 on the initiative of the then Prime Minister Rajiv Gandhi to protect the interests of the customers and then the Consumer Protection Act came into force nationwide after it was signed by the President. Important amendments were made to this Act later in 1993 and 2002.

52(D). Selection is the process of choosing the most suitable candidate for the vacant position in the organization. In other words, the selection means weeding out unsuitable applicants and selecting those individuals with prerequisite qualifications and capabilities to fill the jobs in the organization.

53(D). RTI Act appoints NITI Aayog responsible for channelizing, regulating and maintaining the RTI Act in India.

- In 1976, in the Raj Narain vs the State of Uttar Pradesh case, the Supreme Court ruled that the Right to information will be treated as a fundamental right under article 19.
- Thus the government enacted the Right to Information act in 2005 which provides machinery for exercising this fundamental right.
- All constitutional authorities, agencies, owned and controlled, also those organizations which are substantially financed by the government comes under the purview of the act.
- The act also imposes penalties if the authorities delay in responding to the citizen in the stipulated time.
- The act also mandates public authorities of union government or state government, to provide timely responses to the citizens' request for information.
- The act is one of the most important acts which empowers ordinary citizens to question the government and its work.

- This has been widely used by citizens and media to uncover corruption, progress in government work, expenses-related information, etc.

54(A). Performance appraisal or performance review is a systematic process in which employee performance at work is evaluated in relation to the projects on which employee has worked and his contribution to the organisation. It is also known as an annual review or performance review.

55(B). A merchant bank deals with international finance, business loans for companies and underwriting. The following points are not true with regard to merchant bank:
I. It can accept deposits.
ii. It can advance loans.
iii. It can do other banking activities.

56(B). ECGC (Export Credit Guarantee Corporation):
- Export Credit Guarantee Corporation of India is administered by the Government of India through the Ministry of Commerce and Industry.
- It is fundamentally an export promotion organization with a motive to enhance the competitiveness of Indian exports by offering them credit insurance covers.
- ECGC was set up for ensuring the smooth functioning of Indian exporters by minimizing the risk associated with the payments emanating from other nations.
- ECGC insurance covers also assist the Indian exporters with better access to credit facilities from banks and other financial institutions.
- ECGC is the 5th largest credit insurance company dealing with the exports of any country.
- It also offers Overseas Investment Insurance to the Indian companies investing in Joint Ventures abroad in the form of loans or equity.

Therefore, ECGC is concerned with insurance.

57(D). The statement RBI is a banker to both central and state governments is true.
The Reserve Bank may, by agreement, also act as a banker to the State Government. Presently, the Reserve Bank acts as a banker to all the states in India (including the Union Territory of Puducherry) except Sikkim.

58(A). The term 'International Liquidity' means all the financial resources and facilities that are available to the monetary authorities of individual countries for financing the deficits in their international balance of payments when all other sources of supply of foreign funds prove insufficient to ensure a balance in international payments.

59(D). The initial DTAC between India and Kazakhstan was signed on December 9, 1996, for the avoidance of double taxation and prevention of evasion with respect to taxes on income.

60(C). **Statement I:** A sale has the immediate effect of transferring property, whereas an agreement to sell the property is to pass at some future time.
Statement II: A sale makes the buyer the owner of goods but an agreement to sale does not make the buyer the owner of goods.
Here Both the statements are correct.

61(B). Tax evasion attracts a penalty of 200% under Section 270A of the Income Tax Act, 1961. Section 270A, which deals with penalty in cases where income is understated or misstated.
Sub-section 10 of section 270A provides that the tax payable on the under-stated income is either 50% or 200%. It will be calculated in the following ways:
- If no return is filed and the income is assessed for the first time, tax will be calculated on the lower income, which is not the maximum for tax, as if it were total income.
- If the total income is assessed in accordance with section 143 or reassessed in accordance with a previous order, tax shall be computed as if it were total income.

62(C). In the contract of agency, Implied agency may arise by a gency of necessity and a gency by holding out.
The Agency system is very popular in the current business scenario. There are two parties in the agency system one is the principal and the agent. An agent is a person acting on behalf of his principal. It's a connecting link between the principal and the third party. Herein we will discuss the creation of an agency under the Indian Contract Act, 1872.
Implied agency arises when there is any conduct, the situation of parties, or is necessary for the case.

63(D). The maximum rate for CGST is 14.
The full form of CGST is Central Goods and Services Tax under the GST law. It is called CGST Act 2017. CGST and SGST are levied on interstate supplies (intra-state supplies). IGST, the sum of CGST and SGST, is levied on inter-state supplies and is covered separately by the IGST Act. The maximum CGST rate on interstate supplies is capped at 14%. Alcoholic liquor for human consumption is outside the purview of GST; Hence, it will continue to come under the purview of the excise laws of the state.

64(C). Both 2 and 3 receipts are revenue in nature as per Income Tax Act.
Revenue receipts refer to those receipts which neither create any liability nor cause any reduction in the assets of the government. Revenue receipts are regular and recurring in nature and the government receives them in the normal course of activities.
It includes the proceeds from taxes and other duties levied by the Centre; the interest and dividend received on investments; and the fees and charges the government receives for its services. For the government, there are two sources of revenue receipts: tax revenues and non-tax revenues.

65(D). The residential status of an assessee is determined for each category of persons separately e.g. there are separate sets of rules for determining the residential status of an individual and separate rules for companies, etc.
The residential status is always determined for the previous year because we have to determine the total income of the previous year only. An assessee may enjoy the residential status for the different assessment years.
If a person is resident in India in a previous year relevant to an assessment year in respect of any source of income, he shall be deemed to be resident in India in the previous year relevant to the assessment year in respect of each of his other sources of income. A person may be a resident of

more than one country for any previous year.

66(A). An income earned which is not subject to income tax is called exempt income. As per Section 10 of the Income Tax Act, 1961, there are certain types of income that will be subjected to Income tax within a financial year, provided that they meet certain conditions and guidelines.

67(C). **Casual income:**
Income received from winning lotteries, puzzles, card games, crosswords, gambling, betting, horse racing, etc. is known as casual income. All these casual incomes are taxed at a flat rate of 30%. No expenditure is allowed as a deduction from casual income and also the benefit of the basic exemption limit is not available for casual income.
Dividend received from domestic company:
The dividend received from the domestic company was exempt until 31 March 2020 (FY 19-20). However, the Finance Act, 2020 changed the method of dividend taxation. Henceforth, all dividend received on or after 1 April 2020 is taxable in the hands of the investor/shareholder. The normal rate of TDS is 10% on dividend income paid in excess of Rs 5,000 from a company or mutual fund. However, as a COVID-19 relief measure, the government reduced the TDS rate to 7.5% for distribution from 14 May 2020 until 31 March 2021.
Therefore, statements 3 and 4 are true.

68(D). Salary received by a Member of Parliament is taxable under the head Income from other sources. Income from other sources, which is the last among the five heads of income sketched out in the Income Tax Act, is essentially a head of income that includes all receipts that cannot otherwise be classified under any of the other heads of income.

69(C). Qualitative testing of data is about understanding the cognitive process of participants i.e. understanding how the interaction affects their overall emotions and expectations.
x^2 Chi-square test:
It is a statistical hypothesis test that compares two variables of a contingency test to check how they are related. It is a nonparametric test and this test normally applies to qualitative data.
There are two types of chi-square test:
- Chi-square goodness of fit test that determines if sample data matches with the population.
- A chi-square test for independence tests to see whether the distribution of categorical variables differs from each other.

Therefore, the x^2 chi-square test normally applies to Qualitative data.

70(B). Chunk Sampling is known as Convenience sampling.
Sampling is done because it is not possible for a researcher to take a survey of the whole population of respondents, so they choose a random sample of individuals that represent the whole population, and those individuals are considered as the sample size of the research.

71(D). F-test is used to test the significance of the differences between More than two samples mean and Variance of two samples.
Hypothesis testing is a way to find out that the results of a survey or experiment are meaningful/ true and dependent or not. The alternative hypothesis assumes that there is some difference between the true mean and comparison value and the null hypothesis assumes that no difference exists.

72(C). If the distribution is symmetric then the mean is equal to the median and the distribution will have zero skewness. And in addition to this, if the distribution is unimodal then mean = median = mode.
Therefore, in a unimodal and symmetric distribution, the relationship between averages is like mean = median = mode.
A unimodal distribution:
- A unimodal distribution has only one clear peak.
- Initially, the value goes on increasing up to a certain highest point and then starts decreasing.
- A unimodal distribution can either be symmetric or unsymmetric distribution.

A symmetric distribution:
- A symmetric distribution is where all the values of mean, median, mode are equal.
- In such distribution, the interval of gains and losses display the same frequency.
- A distribution that differs from symmetrical distribution is known as unsymmetrical distribution and that is where we get positive skewness and negative skewness.

73(C). Meaning : Any imminent, impending, or eventual trouble, danger, or disaster.
In Greek mythology, the courtier Damocles was forced to sit beneath a sword suspended by a single hair to emphasize the instability of a king's fortunes.
Example: The new tax law is going to be Damocles' sword hanging over our very business model.

74(B). The moves to support non-banking financial companies (NBFCs) — such as enhancing additional liquidity support to housing finance companies to Rs 30,000 crore by National Housing Bank from Rs 20,000 crore and co-origination of loans by PSBs jointly with NBFCs that are reeling under a liquidity crunch — will provide a booster for fresh loans to the MSME sector.
Increasing 20,000 by 50% gives us 30,000 and co-origination of loans refers to joint contribution of credit. Hence, statements II and III are correct. However, nothing has been mentioned about loan waivers and collateral free loans. So the first statement is incorrect.

75(B). A transparent one-time settlement policy being provided by banks to benefit MSMEs and retail borrowers in settling their over-dues is pragmatic. But banks also must acquire the expertise to assess MSME loan viability and invest in data mining.
Statement I : One-time settlement policy that will benefit MSMEs is impractical for banks and is unwise.
The one-time settlement policy has been stated as being pragmatic which means that it is practical and sensible. Hence, statement I is invalid.
Statement II : Banks have not yet developed the required proficiency in judging the sustainability of MSME loans.
The author is urging banks to acquire the expertise of assessing MSME loan viability. This implies that he is likely to believe that banks have not yet mastered this skill. Hence, statement II is valid.

Statement III : Banks have made huge investments in data mining

76(D). Acerbic, vitriolic, indignant and belligerent are tones that correspond to negative passages. However, the given passage is not negative in nature. Hence, options A, B, C and D can be eliminated.

77(D). The search for ways to avoid future bail-outs started before the turmoil ended. One of the niftiest proposals was the "contingent convertible" (coco) bond, which turns into equity when the ratio of a bank's equity to risk-weighted assets falls below a predetermined danger poi.
As per the fragment highlighted above, only option D mentions all the relevant points.

78(B). As the Squam Lake Group, composed of mostly American academics, put it in 2009, the automatic conversion of cocos would "transform an undercapitalised or insolvent bank into a well-capitalised bank at no cost to taxpayers". ...
As per the fragment highlighted above, only III is correct while I and II have not been mentioned anywhere.

79(A). The hybrid nature of cocos seemed a way to satisfy both regulators, who wanted banks to have bigger safety buffers, and bankers, who were reluctant to issue new shares because of the high cost of capital. The hope was that investors, too, might see the appeal of an asset that offered a higher yield than bank bonds but lower risk than bank shares.
As per the highlighted fragment, only IV is the reason for investors to invest in the bonds.
I and II are reasons for regulators to prefer cocos while III is irrelevant and not mentioned in the passage.

80(C). To be sure, they are now an established asset class, with around $155bn of issuance in 2017 in Dollars, Euros and Pounds. But this is a fraction of more than $1trn in bank debt issued that year. Cocos are issued by only around 50 banks in a dozen countries mostly in Europe. Although cocos are held by the world's largest asset managers, including BlackRock and PIMCO, few specialise in them. Exceptions include niche funds run by Algebris Investment and Old Mutual Global Investors.
As per the fragments, I is clearly incorrect.
II and III are both correct. Cocos have not been able to fulfill the promise as they lack popularity and have not been effective.

Mock Test 09

1. **Direction:** Choose the correct option out of the following.
When a population is heterogeneous, it is divided into groups so that there is homogeneity within the group and heterogeneity between the groups and some items are selected at random from each group. It is a case of
(a) Cluster random sampling
(b) Systematic random sampling
(c) Quota sampling
(d) Stratified random sampling

2. Which of the following is not the salient feature of the industrial policy developments since 1991?
(a) The scope of the private sector has been enormously expanded.
(b) Public sector has been withdrawing partially or fully from several of the enterprises by divestment.
(c) The Indian industry is increasingly exposed to foreign competition.
(d) Monopoly or dominant position for the public sector in most of the industries and control of the commanding heights of the economy by the public sector.

3. **Direction:** For the Assertion (A) and Reason (R) given below, choose the correct alternative.
Statement (A): The demand for the product of a firm under Oligopoly is at prices higher than the prevailing market prices.
Reason (R): The Oligopolistic firm faces a kinked demand curve.
(a) Both (A) and (R) are false.
(b) Both (A) and (R) are true, but (R) is not the correct explanation of (A).
(c) (A) is true, but (R) is false.
(d) (A) is false, but (R) is true.

4. A rectangular hyperbola shaped demand curve on all its points has_________.
(a) Equal slopes and equal point elasticities
(b) Unequal slopes and unequal point elasticities
(c) Unequal slopes and equal point elasticities
(d) Equal slopes and unequal point elasticities

5. A marketing concern generally taps sources for financing its activities from_______.
(a) Owned capital (b) Bank credit
(c) Trade credit (d) All of the above

6. Which of the following liabilities are taken into account for acid-test ratio?
(i) Trade Creditors
(ii) Bank Overdraft
(iii) Bills Payable
(iv) Outstanding Expenses
(v) Redeemable Debentures
(a) (i), (ii), (iii), (iv) and (v)
(b) (i), (ii), (iii) and (iv)
(c) (i) and (ii) only
(d) (i), (iii) and (iv)

7. **Directions:** Read the given statements carefully and choose the correct alternative.
Statements:
(i) The objective of finance function is wealth maximisation.
(ii) The objective of finance function is profit maximisation.
(a) Both statements are correct.
(b) Both statements are incorrect.
(c) Statement (i) is correct, statement (ii) incorrect.
(d) Statement (i) is incorrect, statement (ii) is correct.

8. **Direction:** Read the given statements carefully and choose the correct alternative.
Statements:
(i) Dividends can be paid only when there are profits.
(ii) Dividends can be paid when there are losses.
(a) Both are correct.
(b) Both are incorrect.
(c) (i) is incorrect, (ii) is correct.
(d) (i) is correct, (ii) is incorrect.

9. If NPV is positive, then IRR will be?
(a) Positive (b) Equal to K
(c) Greater than K (d) None of the above

10. "Grapevine" is a word used in relation to ______.
(a) Formal communication
(b) Informal communication
(c) Both formal and informal communication
(d) None of these

11. Which one of the following softwares is used for Research Analysis?
(a) SAP (b) ERP
(c) SPSS (d) TALLY

12. Arrange the following in the correct chronological order:
(i) Value and Capital
(ii) Principles of Political Economy and Taxation
(iii) A Revision of Demand Theory
(iv) The General Theory of Employment, Interest, and Money
(a) (ii), (iv), (i), (iii) (b) (iii), (i), (iv), (ii)
(c) (iv), (iii), (i), (ii) (d) (i), (iv), (iii), (ii)

13. Which of the following is not a part of PEST?
(a) Political (b) Environmental
(c) Social (d) Technological

14. What does the statement of change in financial position show?
(a) Sources and uses of cash funds
(b) Assets and liabilities
(c) Income and expenses
(d) Losses and gains

15. **Directions:** Out of the statements given below, choose the correct alternative.
Statement 1: The law of demand always operates in the case of superior goods.
Statement 2: The substitution effect is always positive.
(a) Both are correct
(b) Both are incorrect

(c) Statement 1 is correct, 2 is incorrect
(d) Statement 1 is incorrect, 2 is correct

16. For-profit maximization of a firm,
(i) MC = MR
(ii) Marginal cost curve must cut the average cost curve from below.
Choose the correct option.
(a) Both are correct.
(b) Both are incorrect.
(c) (i) correct, (ii) incorrect
(d) (i) incorrect, (ii) correct

17. For a hypothesis test, alpha (α) is 0.05 and beta (β) is 0.10. The power of this test is _______.
(a) 0.95 (b) 0.90
(c) 0.80 (d) 0.15

18. If a sample is taken at random from a population, it is likely to possess almost the same characteristics as those of the population.
Which one of the following laws states the above theme?
(a) Law of inertia of large numbers
(b) Law of statistical regularity
(c) Law of persistence of small numbers
(d) Law of optimisation

19. Which of the following factors cause(s) non-sampling errors?
(a) Inappropriate statistical units
(b) Inadequate sampling frame
(c) Faulty process of selection
(d) All of the above

20. 360-degree method relates to?
(a) Performance appraisal
(b) Organisational climate
(c) Employees' morale
(d) Retrenchment of employees

21. **Directions:** For the Assertion (A) and Reason (R) given below, choose the correct alternative.
Assertion (A): Comparative Advantage theory states that each country should produce those goods in which it has a comparative advantage.
Reason (R): This is because of the presence of opportunity costs which gives the country a relative advantage in the production of one good. Choose the correct answer from the following code:
(a) Both (A) and (R) are correct, and (R) is the correct explanation of (A).
(b) Both (A) and (R) are correct, but (R) is not the correct explanation of (A).
(c) (A) is correct, but (R) is not correct.
(d) (A) is wrong, and (R) is correct.

22. From an investor's point of view, the cost of capital is:
(a) Interest Rate
(b) Market Value
(c) Yield of Capital Sacrifice
(d) Stock Exchange Value

23. Committees promoting worker's participation in management are usually set up only at ______.
(a) Corporate level (b) Plant level
(c) Shop-floor level (d) All of the above

24. Match the following:

List-I (Job Analysis)	List-II (Example)
(a) Task	i. Payroll processing
(b) Element	ii. Compensation policy adm inistrator
(c) Duty	iii. Compensation design ma nager
(d) Position	iv. Compensation specialist
(e) Job	v. Preparing forms
(f) Occupation	vi. Signing paycheques

(a) (a) - i, (b) - ii, (c) - iii, (d) - iv, (e) - v, (f) - vi
(b) (a) - v, (b) - vi, (c) - i, (d) - ii, (e) - iii, (f) - iv
(c) (a) - vi, (b) - v, (c) - iv, (d) - ii, (e) - iii, (f) - i
(d) (a) - vi, (b) - i, (c) - ii, (d) - iii, (e) - iv, (f) - v

25. The following steps relate to the shares of a company. What is the correct sequence of the steps?
(a) Issue, Application, Call, and Forfeiture
(b) Application, Call, Forfeiture, and Issue
(c) Call, Issue, Application, and Forfeiture
(d) Forfeiture, Application, Issue, and Call

26. In which year Accounting Standards Board was established in India?
(a) 1970 (b) 1972
(c) 1973 (d) 1977

27. When a bill is paid before the due date and the drawer gives some allowance to the drawee, this is called:
(a) Discount
(b) Retirement of the bill at a discount
(c) Rebate
(d) All of the above

28. The purpose of accountability accounting is to collect and report information on ____.
(a) Department-wise (b) Cost center-wise
(c) Function-wise (d) Product-wise

29. Which of the following is considered as the last stage in the new product development process?
(a) Test marketing
(b) Product development
(c) Commercialization
(d) Business analysis

30. Number of competitors are maximum at which stage of the life cycle of a product?
(a) Growth stage (b) Introductory stage
(c) Maturity stage (d) Declining stage

31. Which of the following is a supply strategy?
(a) Capacity sharing
(b) Creative pricing
(c) Reservation system
(d) Development of complementary services

32. Which of the following is not the example of only upward communication?
(a) Reports (b) Circulars
(c) Grapevine (d) Interviews

33. What is the communication between two members of

a project team from different functions, but the same level of authority called?

(a) Upward communication
(b) Downward communication
(c) Lateral communication
(d) Diagonal communication

34. The most important component of the promotion mix to be used for industrial goods is?

(a) Personal Selling (b) Advertisement
(c) Sales Promotion (d) Publicity

35. Which of the following performance appraisal techniques involve(s) highest emphasis on results?

(a) 360 degree (b) Graphic rating
(c) BARS (d) MBO

36. Match the following:

List-I	List-II
(a) Presence of fixed cost in the cost str ucture of a firm	(1). Super leverage
(b) Presence of fixed return funds in the capital structure of a firm	(2).Operat ing levera ge
(c) Impact of changes in sales on the ear nings available to shareholders	(3).Financ ial leverag e

(a) (a) - (1), (b) - (2), (c) - (3)
(b) (a) - (2), (b) - (3), (c) - (1)
(c) (a) - (3), (b) - (2), (c) - (1)
(d) (a) - (1), (b) - (3), (c) - (2)

37. In which of the following types of collective bargaining does one party gain at the expense of the other?

(a) Distributive bargaining
(b) Integrative bargaining
(c) Collective bargaining
(d) None of the above

38. Match the following:

List-I (Decisions regar ding branding)	List-II (Explanation)
(a) Diversification	(i) Preservation of produc t
(b) Quality	(ii) Production of one or more products
(c) Variety	(iii) Finding new products in the same line
(d) Packing	(iv) Various product

(a) (a) - (ii), (b) - (iv), (c) - (i), (d) - (iii)
(b) (a) - (ii), (b) - (iv), (c) - (i), (d) - (iii)
(c) (a) - (iii), (b) - (i), (c) - (iv), (d) - (ii)
(d) (a) - (iv), (b) - (iii), (c) - (ii), (d) - (i)

39. The full form of SWIFT is ___.

(a) Society for Worldwide Inter-bank Fund Transfer
(b) Society for Worldwide Inter-bank Fast Transmission
(c) Society for Worldwide Inter-bank Financial Telecommunications
(d) None of the above

40. Select from the following the techniques of monetary control adopted by RBI:

(a) Cash Reserve Ratio
(b) Statutory Liquidity Ratio
(c) Bank Rate
(d) Currency Rate

(a) (a), (b), (c) and (d) (b) (b), (c) and (d)
(c) (a), (c) and (d) (d) (a), (b) and (c)

41. **Direction:** For the statements given below, choose the correct alternative.

Statements:

(I) No gain from trade is shared between countries in accordance with their relative strength of demand.

(II) The terms of trade are against the primary producer unless it has a monopoly or the product has an inelastic demand abroad.

(a) Both are correct
(b) Both are incorrect
(c) I is correct, II is incorrect
(d) I is incorrect, II is correct

42. **Direction:** For the following two statements of Assertion (A) and Reason (R), indicate the correct code:

Assertion (A): The quantity of a commodity demanded invariably changes inversely to changes in its price.

Reason (R): The price effect is the net result of the positive substitution effect and a negative income effect.

(a) (A) and (R) both are correct.
(b) (A) is correct, but (R) is incorrect.
(c) (A) is incorrect, but (R) is correct.
(d) (A) and (R) both are incorrect.

43. Which of the following is/are necessary document(s) to file Income Tax Return for an employed person in India?

(a) Aadhar Card
(b) PAN Card
(c) Form No. 16 issued by the employer

(a) (a) only (b) (a) and (b)
(c) (a), (b) and (c) (d) (b) and (c)

44. The Carl Pearson and Epso's coefficient correlation measures the _____ between the X and Y variables.

(a) Covariance between the two
(b) The inverse of the products of their standard deviations
(c) Product of A and B
(d) None of the above

45. If the purchase consideration is calculated by adding the various payments to be made, the method is called:

(a) Lump-sum method
(b) Net-asset method
(c) Net-payment method
(d) Net-payment method

46. ____ is a progressive tax.

(a) Custom duty
(b) Sales tax
(c) Income tax
(d) Development Surcharge

47. Which of the following terminology are NOT related to income tax?

(a) Tax Deduction and Collection Account Number (TAN)
(b) Leave Travel Allowance (LTA)
(c) Dearness Allowance (DA)
(d) Taxpayer Identification Number (TIN)

48. The uncommitted pension received by a Government servant is ______.
(a) fully exempted (b) up to 50 percent off
(c) fully taxable (d) up to 20 percent off

Ques (49-52): Direction : Read the following passage carefully and answer the question that follows.

India's e-commerce sector, poised to grow four times to $150 billion by 2022, is still a work in progress when it comes to safeguarding customer interest. Consumers are still compelled to take wild chances in online transactions. There is little they can do if their calls go wrong. Returns and reimbursements are risky and cumbersome. There are no authentic ways to figure out if product reviews, ratings or even discounts are genuine. So, it is heartening to see the government coming up with a set of guidelines to protect interests of consumers. The guidelines released last week by the Consumer Affairs Ministry in this regard emphasize that an e-commerce entity shall not influence the price of the goods or services, adopt any unfair or deceptive methods to influence transactional decisions of consumers or falsely represent themselves as consumers and post reviews about goods and services. The guidelines on returns and refunds favour consumers. The message seems simple: If online companies want to dupe consumers to earn extra bucks, they're in trouble.

Clearly, the Ministry's thinking seems to be in line with the way the Centre's approach to regulating the fast-growing e-commerce sector. It is, however, worth considering whether the Department of Promotion of Industry and Internal Trade (then DIPP) will strike the right balance between regulating consumer interests and encouraging innovation and investment, without discriminating against a particular class of investors. Now marketplace entities won't be able to buy more than 25 per cent from a single vendor, give discounts on products or sell the goods of the companies in which there is equity participation by the marketplace entity. The changes had irked foreign e-tailers who felt the rules would ____ (A) ____ their business models and could cost them time and money. But anecdotal evidence does not entirely seem to bear that out.

The DPIIT is also framing an e-commerce policy and, like the Consumer Affairs Ministry, has put up the draft for comments. The draft talks about the country retaining ownership and control of data generated within the country, rigorous monitoring of cross-border imports, placing the responsibility of consumer protection on the intermediary and addressing the issue of piracy. That said, the element of indecision over data localisation requirement is still a worry. Attempts made by both the DPIIT and the MeitY in the e-commerce policy and the data protection policy, respectively, to make a case for storage of personal data locally (along with the RBI in the case of payment systems) have predictably resulted in a lot of protests from the EU and US entities. While the Centre is certainly on a sound wicket here, it should take a call soon — without succumbing to the recent tendency to over-regulate business.

49. Which among the following is correct regarding the prospect of the e-commerce sector in India?
(a) It is one of the dying sectors of the country with nothing to offer in the long run.
(b) It is one of the most promising sectors that will definitely grow in the years to come without any inhibition.
(c) It is one of the most promising sectors in the economy though the other sectors are also crossing them.
(d) It is of no use to regulate the e-commerce business in India since that will not help the cause of the business at all.

50. Which among the following is/are the problem(s) faced by e-commerce customers in India these days, as stated in the passage?
I. They do not get the money back easily in case they have to return the products delivered to them.
II. They have no credible information regarding the products and the feedback regarding them available to them.
III. They have to pay extra to ship the products directly to their homes as they do not need to come out for shopping.
(a) Both I and II (b) Both II and III
(c) Both I and III (d) All I, II and III

51. Which among the following is correct regarding the opinion of the government on the storage of data, as stated in the passage?
(a) There is nothing to say that the government is at all interested to take care of this thing in the present scenario.
(b) There is everything that can be found out from the issue at hand that we are losing on revenue here.
(c) There is demand that the government should restrict the storage of data from various electronic sources within the boundary of the country only.
(d) The government wants to explore foreign and better options for anything before taking the final call.

52. Which among the following can be inferred from the sentence – "It is, however, worth considering whether the Department of Promotion of Industry and Internal Trade (then DIPP) will strike the right balance between regulating consumer interests and encouraging innovation and investment, without discriminating against a particular class of investors"?
(a) It is very difficult to have the class necessary in everything within the country though others are there.
(b) It is not at all necessary to have something here since nothing can stop you from this.
(c) It can be said that the interests of the buyers and the sellers should be harmonized while formulating policy though that is pretty difficult.
(d) The government is in s position to understand the issue that it is nothing to stop the inevitable.

Ques (53-56): Direction : Read the passage and answer the question that follows.

Financial markets don't much like uncertainty. Thanks to Italy's politicians, in recent days they have had plenty. By May 30th some calm had returned: it seemed possible that a pair of populist parties, the Five Star Movement and the Northern League, would form a government after all. Markets had been in turmoil for two days, unsettled by a farcical back-and-forth between the populists and the country's president, who had rejected the parties' choice of a Eurosceptic economist as finance minister. The politicians may have done the markets a service, by shaking them out of complacency. Investors may have returned the favour, by shaking some sense into the politicians—at least for now. Italy is perennially slow-growing and groans under public debt of around $2.7trn, or132% of GDP. The drama reawakened dormant worries about those two problems—and the deeper fear that the euro zone's third-biggest member might be sneaking towards the exit. So the yield on Italian two-year bonds, negative as recently as May 15th, leapt to almost 1% on May 28th. It carried on climbing the next day, touching 2.73%, the highest since 2013, before retreating. Ten-year yields also rose, if less spectacularly. Yields on German Bunds, Europe's safest government bonds, declined. Share prices tumbled. Banks in Italy, holders of €600bn of government bonds, were hit hardest. UniCredit, the country's biggest, fell by 9.2% and Intesa Sanpaolo, the number two, lost 7.2% on May 28th and 29th. Other European banks' shares were also roughed up. The worries rippled across the Atlantic. The S&P 500 index slipped by 1.2% on May 29th, with banks again leading the way down. The yield on ten-year Treasury bonds fell from 2.93% to 2.77%, the biggest drop since the day after Britons voted for Brexit in June 2016. So far, this adds up to a nasty bout of the jitters rather than full-blown panic. Italy's two-year bond yield is far below the 7.6% it hit in November 2011, at the depths of the euro zone's previous crisis. The effect on the euro area's other problem members has been limited - even though yields in Greece, Portugal and Spain, where the prime minister faces a confidence vote on June 1st, reached their highest this year on May 29th.

Foreigners are also unlikely to have suffered much direct harm from the fall in bond prices (the corollary of rising yields). Nor has the run-up in yields yet threatened the sustainability of Italy's debt. On May 30th Italy sold a total of €5.6 bn-worth of five-, seven- and ten-year bonds at yields of 2.32%, 2% and 3% respectively. Granted, that is dearer than in the recent past, but it is well below the average coupon of 3.4% on its existing stock of debt. And the longish average maturity of its bonds, around seven years, gives it breathing space. Alberto Gallo of Algebris, an investment firm, estimates that yields would have to be at least 4-4.5% for several months before higher coupon payments would make debt unsupportable. That is not unimaginable, but is some way off. One reason for that is the backing of the European Central Bank. Under its quantitative-easing programme, which has held down borrowing costs across the euro area, the ECB has bought €340 bn worth of Italian bonds; it holds around a sixth of the stock. In effect, it has been a willing buyer as foreigners have quit. Yet none of this means that markets could not turn against Italy with greater violence—if, say, a populist government undid recent reforms, opened the fiscal taps or picked a fight with bureaucrats in Brussels or Frankfurt. Although the biggest banks are now in decent health (or getting there), they own lots of government bonds. One bank, Monte dei Paschi di Siena, is still in intensive care. The bad-loan burden, though reduced, remains heavy. Departure from the euro area would be unthinkably costly—for both Italy and the zone. Just like when Argentina abandoned dollar parity at the start of 2002, the value of Italians' bank deposits would plunge. Italy is not Greece, in that it is in far better shape. But it is not Greece, too, in that it is much, much bigger. In 2012 Mario Draghi, the ECB's president, quelled the crisis that looked likely to destroy the currency club by saying that the ECB would do "whatever it takes to preserve the euro".

53. Which of the following statements shows that investors were losing confidence in Italy?
I. Its debt hit a level of $2.7 trn, many times above its GDP.
II. Yield on Italian bonds rose in general.
III. Yields on German Bonds fell.
(a) Only II (b) Only III
(c) Only I and II (d) Only II and III

54. Which of the statements below strengthen the argument -'So far, this adds up to a nasty bout of the jitters rather than full-blown panic'?
I. The bond yields in Italy are still far below the levels reached during the 2011 Euro-zone crisis.
II. The effect of the issue has not impacted other members very hard.
III. The ratings given to many Italian Bank stocks by credit agencies has not changed at all.
(a) Only I (b) Only III
(c) Only I and II (d) All of the above

55. Which of the following could be a possible reason for the line- 'Foreigners are also unlikely to have suffered much direct harm from the fall in bond prices'?
I. Italy's huge public-debt market gives it a decent weight in global bond indices.
II. Foreign investors have cut their Italian holdings from €473bn to €250bn during the last year.
III. Exposure of banks outside Italy has fallen by almost half since 2009, to €133bn.
(a) Only II (b) Only I and II
(c) Only II and III (d) Only I and III

56. Which of the following does not adversely impact the sustainability of Italy's debt?
I. The rate offered on the bonds has increased when compared to the past.
II. The current rate offered on bonds is around the average rate of the existing debt.
III. Most of the debt is short to mature in terms of maturity.
(a) Only II (b) Only I and II
(c) Only III (d) Only II and III

57. Which is the Act which provides legal framework for e-Governance in India:
(a) IT (amendment) Act 2008
(b) Indian Penal Code
(c) IT Act 2000
(d) None of the above

58. Which of the statement (s) is/are true?
Statement I: As per Section 125 of the Indian Contract Act, a contract of indemnity is a contract by which one party promises to save the other party from loss caused to him.
Statement II: The person who promises to indemnify or make good the loss is called the indemnity holder and the person whose loss is made is called indemnifier.
(a) Only I (b) Only II
(c) Both I and II (d) None of the above

59. In the contract of agency, Implied agency may arise by:
A. Agency by Estoppel
B. Agency of Necessity
C. Agency by Ratification
D. Agency by Holding out
(a) Both A and B (b) A, B and C
(c) Both B and D (d) All of the above

60. Right to information includes the right to:
1. inspect works, documents, records.
2. take notes, extracts or certified copies of documents or records.

3. take certified samples of material
4. obtain information in forms of printouts, diskettes, floppies, tapes, video cassettes or in any other electronic mode or through printouts.
Choose the correct codes:

(a) 1, 2, and 3 (b) 1, 2, and 4
(c) 1, 3, and 4 (d) All of the above

61. Statement I: Data material held in any electronic form is 'information' under RTI Act, 2005.
Statement II: IT Act, 2000 came into force on 10th October, 2000.
Choose the correct code:

(a) Only Statement I is correct
(b) Only Statement II is correct
(c) Both Statements are correct
(d) Both Statements are incorrect

62. Match the columns and choose the correct pairs from the options.

Column (1)	Column (2)
(A) Competition Act	(1) 2005
(B) Right to Information Act	(2) 1930
(C) Indian Contract Act	(3) 1872
(D) Sales of Goods Act	(4) 2002

(a) A- 3, B- 1, C- 2, 4- H (b) A- 4, B- 1, C- 3, D- 2
(c) A- 1, B- 2, C- 3, D- 4 (d) A- 2, B- 4, C- 1, D- 3

63. Which Act was replaced with the introduction of Competition Act, 2002?

(a) FERA (b) FEMA
(c) MRTP (d) POTA

64. Section 2(36) of Companies Act is related to:

(a) Memorandum (b) Prospectus
(c) Articles (d) Incorporation

65. Mr. Shushant is the owner of a house, the details of which are given below the gross annual value would be ________ Municipal value Rs. 36,000 Actual rent Rs 32,000 Fair Rent Rs. 36,000 Standard Rent Rs. 40,000.

(a) 36,000 (b) 35,000
(c) 30,000 (d) 40,000

66. Among the following, identify the Direct Taxes.
A) Income Tax and Customs Duty
B) Income Tax and Corporate Tax
C) Corporate Tax and Sales Tax
D) Income Tax and Excise Duties

(a) A & C (b) B only
(c) C & D (d) A only

67. In the balance of payment account, the transfer payments are included in which one of the following?

(a) Capital Account
(b) Service Account
(c) Current Account
(d) Official Reserve Account

68. Which one of the following statements is false?

(a) IFC was established in July 1956
(b) IFC encourage the growth and development of Public Sector Enterprises in member countries
(c) IFC is an affiliate of the World Bank
(d) IFC encourages the growth of productive private enterprises in member countries

69. As per the RBI Act, 1934, the following functions are described as the functions of a Central Bank:
(i) Banking functions
(ii) Advisory functions
(iii) Supervisory functions
(iv) Promotional functions
Identify the correct combination:

(a) (i), (iii) and (iv) (b) (i), (ii) and (iv)
(c) (ii), (iii) and (iv) (d) Only (i) and (iii)

70. 'Chi square test' measures which of the following?

(a) Mean deviation (b) Goodness of fit
(c) Trend (d) Variation

71. The error committed by rejecting an applicant who would have been successful on the job is called:

(a) True negative error (b) False negative error
(c) False positive error (d) True positive error

72. Which of the following economies accrue all the firm in an industry?

(a) Managerial Economies
(b) Economies of Concentration
(c) Labour Economies
(d) Marketing Economies

73. Surcharge is levied when the total income exceeds for domestic corporation.

(a) 5 Crore (b) 10 Crore
(c) 1 Crore (d) 2 Crore

74. Which of the following is not the part of net invisibles of Balance of Payments Current Account?

(a) Services (b) Transfer
(c) External Assistance (d) Remittance

75. Consider the following statement:
Assertion (A): Primary and secondary capital markets are integrated after LPG reform in India.
Reason (R): Globalization integrates the domestic economy with the world economy.

(a) Both (A) and (R) are correct and (R) is the right explanation of (A)
(b) Both (A) and (R) are correct but (R) is not the right explanation of (A)
(c) Both (A) and (R) is incorrect
(d) (A) is incorrect but (R) is correct

76. Consider the following statement:
Statement (A): When a banker provides the locker facility to a customer, the relationship between them is that of bailor and bailee.
Statement (B): Debentures are governed by company law.

(a) Both the Statements are correct
(b) Both the Statements are wrong
(c) Statement (A) is correct and (B) is wrong
(d) Statement (B) is correct and (A) is wrong

77. Given below are two statements, One is labelled as Assertion A and the other is labelled as Reason R
Assertion (A): High powered money is the source of all other forms of money that impact the money supply
Reason (R): Credit is created by commercial banks.

(a) Both (A) and (R) are correct and (R) is the correct explanation of (A)
(b) Both (A) and (R) are correct but (R) is NOT the correct explanation of (A)
(c) (A) is correct but (R) is not correct
(d) (A) is not correct but (R) is correct

78. Under whose chairmanship the RBI appointed a committee on capital Account Convertibilty?
(a) S. S. Tarapore
(b) Dr. C. Rangrajan
(c) Dr. Y. Venugopal Reddy
(d) Abdul Hussain

79. ______ is useful for new auditors of the company.
(a) Salary report
(b) Commission report
(c) Audit programme
(d) Documents statement

80. Mainly to avoid ______ we conduct audit in the business concern.
(a) Wrong accounts
(b) More expenses
(c) Bad names of company
(d) Errors & frauds

// Smart Answer Sheet //

Correct Percentage of students who answered correctly.

Skipped Percentage of students who skipped.

Q.	Ans.	Correct	Skipped	Q.	Ans.	Correct	Skipped	Q.	Ans.	Correct	Skipped
1	D	59.79%	39.29%	2	D	86.25%	10.45%	3	D	48.54%	48.62%
4	C	41.71%	46.16%	5	D	43.96%	42.99%	6	B	21.1%	75.02%
7	A	83.03%	15.72%	8	D	21.22%	78.53%	9	C	55.74%	31.87%
10	B	88.18%	10.73%	11	C	52.97%	43.01%	12	A	55.06%	39.03%
13	B	83.1%	12.11%	14	A	40.21%	57.56%	15	C	49.86%	49.67%
16	A	69.38%	30.37%	17	B	58.94%	32.44%	18	B	66.12%	31.06%
19	C	54.0%	42.87%	20	A	81.36%	13.69%	21	A	55.71%	40.32%
22	C	80.98%	12.53%	23	D	24.9%	73.69%	24	B	59.16%	34.69%
25	A	51.6%	31.7%	26	D	11.05%	68.37%	27	D	76.63%	16.17%
28	B	23.1%	68.12%	29	C	29.48%	67.66%	30	C	53.61%	41.69%
31	A	52.64%	30.32%	32	B	83.52%	14.66%	33	C	80.1%	18.85%
34	A	43.41%	34.22%	35	D	64.91%	33.01%	36	B	46.68%	46.67%
37	A	48.06%	39.45%	38	D	28.73%	68.56%	39	C	43.02%	43.65%
40	D	21.06%	76.68%	41	D	53.95%	34.26%	42	C	24.28%	74.52%
43	C	41.1%	41.84%	44	A	49.31%	44.86%	45	C	45.78%	52.02%
46	C	44.17%	55.11%	47	D	42.26%	37.91%	48	C	63.21%	35.17%
49	B	77.95%	16.54%	50	A	44.68%	54.17%	51	C	45.63%	32.96%
52	C	11.87%	85.99%	53	D	29.24%	70.33%	54	D	52.65%	39.79%
55	C	40.25%	50.67%	56	A	79.81%	15.97%	57	C	48.52%	37.3%
58	D	85.13%	13.72%	59	B	15.33%	82.05%	60	D	26.42%	70.52%
61	A	18.39%	70.3%	62	B	57.36%	36.8%	63	C	53.06%	41.94%
64	B	52.77%	36.3%	65	A	50.52%	39.31%	66	B	63.65%	35.94%
67	C	53.86%	35.0%	68	B	41.75%	31.48%	69	B	43.71%	33.44%
70	B	53.04%	30.72%	71	B	57.47%	37.05%	72	B	60.78%	33.36%
73	C	65.21%	33.52%	74	C	44.63%	36.05%	75	D	32.28%	67.65%
76	D	54.34%	37.71%	77	B	50.83%	42.13%	78	A	76.37%	17.59%
79	C	76.56%	12.72%	80	D	54.14%	34.9%				

// Hints and Solutions //

1(D). Stratified random sampling is a method of sampling that involves the division of a population into smaller groups, known as strata. In stratified random sampling, the strata are formed based on members' shared attributes or characteristics. When a population is heterogeneous, it is divided into groups so that there is homogeneity within the group and heterogeneity between the groups and some items are selected at random from each group. It is a case of stratified random sampling.

2(D). "Industrial policy means such a formal declaration in which the government adopts a general policy towards the establishment and development of industries and includes state principles, rules and policies."
The steps taken by the government under the Industrial Policy from July 1991 onwards were aimed at bolstering the country's past industrial achievements and accelerating the process of making Indian industries internationally competitive.
In 1991, the Government of India introduced significant economic reforms, which were major efforts in the sense that they included foreign trade liberalization, financial liberalization, tax reforms and calls for foreign investment. These measures helped in giving impetus to the Indian economy. Since then the Indian economy has come a long way.

3(D). A is false, but R is true.
A is false that the demand for the product of a firm under an Oligopoly is at prices higher than the prevailing market prices. Demand can be above or below the prevailing price. The kink demand curve is formed at the prevailing price level.
The Demand curve above the prevailing price is highly elastic and below the prevailing price is less elastic. So, R is true that The Oligopolistic firm faces a kinked demand curve.

4(C). A rectangular hyperbola shaped demand curve on all its points has unequal slopes and equal point elasticities. Rectangular hyperbola is a curve under which the total area at all points will be the same.

5(D). A marketing concern can raise funds by availing credits from banks, trade credit, and owned capital, etc.

- Owned Capital refers to the Capital collected by issuing various types of shares.
- Bank credit is the total amount of funds a person or business can borrow from a financial institution.
- Trade credit is a type of commercial financing in which a customer is allowed to purchase goods or services and pay the supplier at a later scheduled date.

6(B). The acid-test ratio is a measure of how well a company can meet its short-term financial liabilities.
1. Trade Creditors
2. Bank Overdraft
3. Bills Payable
4. Outstanding Expenses are current liabilities, so they are taken into account, but redeemable debentures is a non-current liability, so it is not taken.

7(A). Both statements are correct. The objective of the finance function is profit maximisation and wealth maximisation. Profit maximisation states that the profit of the firm should be increased, while wealth maximisation aims at accelerating the worth of the entity.

8(D). Dividends can be paid only out of the current year's profit or free reserves available with the company relating to the current year. Dividends to the shareholders are declared out of the current year profits only.
It is correct that dividends can be paid only when there are profits and not in the case of losses.
So, statement (i) is correct but statement (ii) is incorrect.

9(C). If NPV (Net Present Value) is positive, then R (Internal Rate of Return) > K (Cost of Capital). The project should be accepted. IRR is the discount rate at which the NPV=0. If your IRR is positive, then your PV of future cash flows will also be positive.

10(B). Grapevine is related to informal/unofficial/ personal communication that takes place within the organization as a result of rumors and gossips. Grapevine communication is informal workplace dialogue in its purest form: it is characterized by conversations between employees and superiors that do not follow any prescribed structure or rule-based system.

11(C). SPSS is the Statistical Package for The Social Sciences. It is used for Research Analysis. SPSS Statistics is a software package that is used for statistical analysis. It is also used by market researchers and health researchers.

12(A). The correct chronological order will be (ii), (iv), (i), (iii).
- Principles of Political Economy and Taxation is a book by David Ricardo on economics, published in 1817.
- The General Theory of Employment, Interest, and Money was written by the English economist John Maynard Keynes, published in 1936.
- Value and Capital is a book by the British economist John Richard Hicks, published in 1939.
- Revision of Demand Theory was first published in 1956 written by the late Harry Johnson.

13(B). PEST analysis (political, economic, social, and technological) describes a framework of macro-environmental factors used in the environmental scanning component of strategic management. Therefore, no such factor named environmental exists in a PEST analysis.

14(A). The statement of changes in financial position (sometimes called a "cash flow statement") shows a company's net cash flow in a given period of time. Because it also indicates where the cash flowed from or to, it is often referred to as the "sources and uses of cash funds".

15(C). The law of demand always operates in the case of superior goods and the substitution effect is always negative. So, statement 1 is correct, 2 is incorrect.
The substitution effect states that when the price of a good decreases, consumers will substitute away from goods that are relatively more expensive to the cheaper good.
The law of demand is a fundamental principle of economics that states that at a higher price, consumers will demand a lower quantity of a good. Demand is derived from the law of diminishing marginal utility, the fact that consumers use economic goods to satisfy their most urgent needs first.

16(A). Both statements are correct.
The profit maximization rule formula is MC = MR.
Marginal Cost is the increase in cost by producing one more unit of the good.
Marginal cost (MC) is the extra cost incurred when one extra unit of output is produced. Average product (AC) is the total cost per unit of output. When the MC is smaller the AC, the AC decreases. This is because when the extra unit of output is cheaper than the average cost then the AC is pulled down. Similarly, when the MC is greater than the AC, the AC is pulled up. The point of intersection between the MC and AC curves is also the minimum of the AC curve.

17(B). The power of this hypothesis test will be
1 - beta = 1 - 0.10 = 0.90
Mathematically, power is 1 – beta. The power of a hypothesis test is between 0 and 1; if the power is close to 1, the hypothesis test is very good at detecting a false null hypothesis

18(B). The law of statistical regularity observes that samples taken from a large group of the test population tend to reflect the characteristics of the group.

19(C). Faulty process of selection causes non-sampling errors. Non-sampling errors can be defined as errors arising during the course of all survey activities other than sampling.

20(A). The 360-degree method relates to performance appraisal. The method provides each employee with the opportunity to receive performance feedback from his or her supervisor, peers, staff members, co-workers, and customers.

21(A). Comparative Advantage theory was given by David Ricardo who questioned Adam Smith's theory of Absolute Advantage stating that what if a country has absolute advantages in the production of more than one good.
Comparative Advantage theory states that each country should produce those goods in which it

has a comparative/relative advantage because of the presence of opportunity costs which gives the country a relative advantage in the production of one good.
Ricardo also stated the countries are identical in all respects, but there are differences in relative labor productivity.

22(C). From the investor's point of view, the yield of capital sacrifice is the required rate of return on capital invested. It can be said that cost of capital for the investor is the yield on the capital invested by investors.

23(D). The committees which promote worker's participation in management are usually established at all levels, i.e. corporate level, shop-floor level, and plant level.
A corporate-level strategy is a multi-tiered company plan that leaders use to define, outline and achieve specific business goals .
A plant generally consists of the physical capital, like the building and the equipment at a particular location that is used for the production of goods. A plant is also called a factory.
A shop floor is the area of a factory, machine shop, etc. where people work on machines, or the space in a retail establishment where goods are sold to consumers.

24(B). The correctly matched pairs are given below-
Task - Preparing forms
Element - Signing paycheques
Duty - Payroll processing
Position - Compensation policy administrator
Job - Compensation design manager
Occupation - Compensation specialist

25(A). Correct sequence: Firstly, shares are issued along with application money, then allotment and call money is demanded. In case of failure in payment of allotment money or call money, shares of default shareholders are forfeited by the company.

26(D). Indian Accounting Standards in India were issued under the supervision and control of the Accounting Standards Board (ASB) in the year 1977. On 21st April 1977, the Institute of Chartered Accountants of India as the premier accounting body in our country, set up "Accounting Standard Board" (ASB) to harmonize the diverse accounting policies and practice prevalent in our country.

27(D). Retiring a bill means making payment before the date of maturity. When the acceptor of a bill is prepared to make the payment of the bill before the due date, he may ask the holder to accept the payment, provided he receives some rebate or discount for the unexpired period. Such a rebate or discount is an expense to the party receiving the payment and gain to the party making the payment.

28(B). Responsibility accounting aims at collecting and reporting costing information cost center-wise. It helps exercise cost control.
There are 4 types of responsibility accounting: Cost, revenue, profit, and investment center.

29(C). Commercialization is the last stage in the new product development process that involves the launching of the product on a full scale. At this stage, new product developments have gone mainstream, consumers are purchasing the good or service, and technical support is consistently monitoring progress.

30(C). The number of competitors are maximum at the Maturity stage which is the longest stage in the product life cycle and where the product is already established. In this stage the primary focus of the companies shifts in maintaining their market share as there are large number of manufacturers competing for the same market share. Thus this stage has the most amount of competition.

31(A). Capacity sharing is a supply strategy in order to increase the supply of service. Capacity sharing is a common practice to align excessive capacity with excessive demand.

32(B). Circulars is not the example of only upward communication.
Upward communication means the flow of information from the lower levels of the organization to higher levels of authority. Examples of upward communication are:
(i) Reports (ii) Meetings (iii) Interviews (iv) Conferences (v) Letters (vi) Complaints (vii) Suggestions (viii) Surveys (ix) Union publication and (x) Grapevine etc. Circulars are not the example of upward communication as it is an example of downward communication that flows from a superior to a subordinate.

33(C). Lateral communication is defined as the exchange, imparting, or sharing of information, ideas, or feelings between people within a community, peer groups, departments, or units of an organization, who are at or about the same hierarchical level as each other, for the purpose of coordinating activities.
Upward communication is the flow of information from front-line employees to managers, supervisors, and directors. Downward communication is the flow of information from the upper level of the organization to the lower level of the organization. Diagonal communication is the sharing of information among different structural levels within a business.

34(A). Personal selling is a form of person-to-person communication in which a seller attempts to assist and/or persuade prospective buyers to purchase the company's products or services or to act on an idea. Personal selling is regarded as the most important tool for industrial goods because the products are technical in nature and costly, and persuasion is considered essential for their sale.

35(D). Management by objectives (MBO) is a result-oriented process and focuses on setting and controlling goals. It encourages managers to do detailed planning. Management by Objectives (MBO) method, as a method for performance appraisal (PA) in enhancing employees' effectiveness.

36(B). In operating leverage, the presence of fixed cost is there. The higher the fixed expense, the higher is the operating leverage.
In financial leverage, there is the use of fixed returned funds. The use of long term fixed income bearing debt and preference share capital along with the equity share capital is called financial

leverage or trading on equity.
In super leverage, there is an impact of changes in sales on the earnings available to shareholders.

37(A). In distributive bargaining, one party gains at the expense of the other. It is also known as win-lose bargaining. In this, it is to decide how to distribute the fixed resources, e.g money.

38(D). Diversification is the process of a company enlarging or varying its range of products or field of operation.
Quality is finding new products in the same line.
Variety refers to the production of one or more products.
Packing is the preservation of the product.

39(C). SWIFT stands for Society for Worldwide Inter-bank Financial Telecommunications. SWIFT provides secure financial messaging services to financial entities. SWIFT uses a standardized proprietary communications platform to facilitate the transmission of information about financial transactions.

40(D). The techniques of monetary control adopted by RBI are Cash Reserve Ratio, Statutory Liquid Ratio, and Bank Rate. CRR is the proportion of deposits of a commercial bank that is required to be kept with the central bank. SLR is the portion of the deposits that banks have to keep in liquid form all the time. Bank Rate is the rate at which a central bank gives loans to commercial banks in case of a shortage of funds.

41(D). It is true that no gain from trade is shared between countries in accordance with their relative strength of demand, but it is incorrect that the terms of trade are against the primary producer unless it has a monopoly or the product has an inelastic demand abroad. It is believed that the terms of trade for primary products will decline over time; that is, over time, it will take increasing amounts of an agricultural product to pay for a manufactured good. So, statement I is incorrect, II is correct.

42(C). As per the law of demand, if price increases demand for the commodity falls and vice versa. The assertion is wrong because the price is not related to the quantity of the commodity. Its relationship is with the demand for the commodity. The reason is true that the price effect is the net result of the positive substitution effect and negative income effect.

43(C). PAN Card, Aadhar Card, and Form No. 16 issued by the employer are necessary documents to file Income Tax Return for an employed person in India.

- PAN stands for Permanent Account Number. A PAN number is a ten-digit number in alphabets and numerical, or in 'alphanumeric' terms, that is allocated by the income tax department to all the taxpayers, and is unique with each individual.
- Form No. 16 is an acknowledgment which states your deducted tax has been deposited with the Income Tax department.
- Aadhar Card is an individual identification number issued by the Unique Identification Authority of India (UIDAI) on behalf of the Government of India to individuals for the purpose of establishing the unique identity of every single person.

44(A). Karl Pearson's Coefficient of Correlation between X and Y variables measures Covariance between the two. The correlation shows a specific value of a degree of a linear relationship between X and Y variables.

45(C). 'Purchase consideration' under the net payments method is taken as the aggregate of all payments made in the form of shares, debentures, other securities, and cash to the shareholders of the transferor company.

46(C). A progressive tax is directly related to the taxpayer's ability to pay.
Every year, we have to pay a fixed portion of our income to the central government in the form of income tax. As per the rule of the central government for Income tax, a certain tax is applicable on the income of all people as per slab. Every business and person is supposed to pay the tax and the return is to be submitted every year. Total funds collected through tax are used by the government for services as well as to fulfill the requirements for the country's development.

47(D). Taxpayer Identification Number is a number issued to individuals and organizations to track tax obligations and payments they make to the Internal Revenue Service (IRS).
TIN is issued by the federal government. TAN is to be obtained by all persons who are responsible for deducting tax at source (TDS) or who are required to collect tax at source (TCS).

48(C). The uncommitted pension received by a Government servant is fully taxable.
Uncommuted pension: The term "uncommuted pension" refers to a pension that is paid on a regular basis. The pension may be received monthly, quarterly or yearly.
Commuted Pension: When the amount of pension is received in a lump sum, it is referred to as Commuted Pension.

49(B). It is stated in the passage that the e-commerce industry in India is going to scale new heights in the years to come and that is why the government has also come out with a policy dedicated to this sector only. It implies the government has also understood that it is the future of commerce and business in the country and something should be there to protect the interests of the customers in this sphere.

50(A). Statement I is correct since it has been stated in the passage that the customers often do not get the refund if they have returned the products. Refer to, "Returns and reimbursements are risky and cumbersome."
Statement II is also correct for the fact that the reviews posted on the websites of the e-commerce companies are not always true and there is no way to find out if they are true or fake or even the discounts are not always for real. Refer to, "There are no authentic ways to figure out if product reviews, ratings or even discounts are genuine."
Statement III cannot said to be correct for the fact that it is not the case at all rather the reality is the opposite of what is being said here. The prices are generally lower in case of the ecommerce companies and that is the main reason they are

becoming popular day by day.

51(C). It is very clearly stated in the passage that the government has been recommended by the DPIIT that the data pertaining to the electronic transactions should be stored within the country only and no foreign intervention should be there in this regard. There should not be any involvement of anybody from other countries or foreign companies in the whole thing.

52(C). The author wants to make the point here that the DPIIT will have to strike the right balance between the investors and the buyers of the e-commerce industry so that there is no disparity in the policy. A policy should take into account the interests of each and everybody since that is the important approach here.

53(D). Statement I is merely a fact and merely states the debt conditions in the country.
Statement II is correct. When investors lose confidence in the markets, the bond yields increase.
Statement III is correct as investors have been shifting from Italian to German bonds which provide more safety. This led to a decrease in the yields of the bonds.
So, both II and III are correct.

54(D). As per the passage, bond yields rise when investors lose confidence in the ability of bonds to repay the debt. Here, the levels have not hit the heights that were achieved during the 2011 crisis and thus, statement I is correct.
Statement II is correct clearly.
Statement III is correct as a fall in the ratings would have indicated deterioration of conditions in the economy.

55(C). Statement I is incorrect as if the Italian debt market has a huge share in the global bond indices, it would have an adverse impact on foreigners.
Statement II and Statement III are both correct as if the banks and other foreign investors have cut down on Italian holdings, they would not suffer much from the current situation.

56(A). Refer to: 'Nor has the run-up in yields yet threatened the sustainability of Italy's debt. On May 30th Italy sold a total of €5.6bn-worth of five-, seven- and ten-year bonds at yields of 2.32%, 2% and 3% respectively. Granted, that is dearer than in the recent past, but it is well below the average coupon of 3.4% on its existing stock of debt. And the longish average maturity of its bonds, around seven years, gives it breathing space.'

- I is incorrect as an increase in rate would decrease the sustainability of Italy's debt.
- III is incorrect as the debt should be long term in nature so as to be sustainable. A short term maturity would put more burden in terms of repayment.
- II is correct.

57(C). The act that provides the legal framework for e-Governance in India is the IT Act 2000.
An Act to provide legal recognition for transactions carried out by means of electronic data interchange and other means of electronic communication, commonly referred to as "electronic commerce", which involve the use of alternatives to paper-based methods of communication and storage of information.

58(D). Section 125: The promisee in a contract of indemnity, acting within the scope of his authority, is entitled to recover from the promiser-

- (1) all damages which he may be compelled to pay in any suit in respect of any matter to which the promise to indemnify applies;
- (2) all costs which he may be compelled to pay in any such suit if, in bringing or defending it, he did not contravene the orders of the promiser, and acted as it would have been prudent for him to act in the absence of any contract of indemnity, or if the promiser authorized him to bring or defend the suit;
- (3) all sums which he may have paid under the terms of any compromise of any such suit, if the compromise was not contrary to the orders of the promiser, and was one which it would have been prudent for the promisee to make in the absence of any contract of indemnity, or if the promiser authorized him to compromise the suit.

However, As per Section 124 of the Indian Contract Act , a contract of indemnity is a contract by which one party promises to save the other party from loss caused to him.
There are generally two parties in indemnity contracts:

- The Indemnity holder is the one who is protected from any liability.
- The Indemnifier is the one who promises to reimburse the Indemnitee for any claims.

Therefore, the person who promises to indemnify or make good the loss is called the indemnified, and the person whose loss is made is called the indemnity holder.

59(B). The Agency system is very popular in the current business scenario. There are two parties in the agency system one is the principal and the agent. An agent is a person acting on behalf of his principal. It's a connecting link between the principal and the third party. Herein we will discuss the creation of an agency under the Indian Contract Act, 1872.

1. Agency by estoppel:
- The concept of agency by estoppel arises where one person acts in such a way that the other believes that a third person is authorized to act on his behalf and enters into a transaction with the third person, the person whose act induced him to do so, is liable for that agreement as if the third person acting on his behalf.
- It is based on principles of natural justice and equity.

2. Agency by necessity
- It is a type of legal relationship in which one party can make essential decisions for another party.
- The courts recognize agency by necessity during an emergency or urgent situation under which the beneficiary is unable to provide explicit authorization.

3. Agency by Ratification:
- A confirmation by the principal of an act or contract performed or entered into on his or her behalf by another, who assumed, without authority, to act as his or her agent.

60(D). The Right to Information Act passed in 2005 extends to all states and union territories of India excepting the state of Jammu and Kashmir. This act gives Indian citizens the right to access information about any public authority or institution, including non-government organizations substantially funded by the government.

The main aims of the RTI Act are to provide clarity of the information to the citizens of India, to contain corruption, and to promote accountability in the working of every public authority.

61(A). Data material held in any electronic form is 'information' under the RTI Act, 2005. IT Act, 2000 came into force on 17 October 2000.

Therefore, the only statement I is correct.

Section 2(f) of the RTI Act, 2005 defines 'Information' as any material in any form, including records, documents, memos, e-mails, opinions, advice, press releases, circulars, orders, logbooks, contracts, reports, papers, samples, models, data material held in any electronic form and information relating to any private body which can be accessed by a public authority under any other law for the time being in force.

62(B). The correct pair is: A- 4, B- 1, C- 3, D- 2.

Competition Act, 2002

- Competition is the act of the sellers individually seeking to acquire the patronage of buyers in order to achieve profits or market share.
- The Competition Act, 2002 was enacted by the Parliament of India.

RTI Act, 2005

- It is an Act to provide for setting out the practical regime of right to information for citizens to secure access to information under the control of public authorities, in order to promote transparency and accountability in the working of every public authority, the constitution of a Central Information Commission and State Information Commissions and for matters connected therewith or incidental thereto.

The Indian Contract Act, 1872

- It prescribes the law relating to contracts in India and is the key act regulating Indian contract law.
- The objective of the Contract Act is to ensure that the rights and obligations arising out of a contract are honored and that legal remedies are made available to an aggrieved party against the party failing to honour his part of the agreement.

Sale of Goods Act 1930

- It was introduced with the objective of balancing the rights, duties, claims, and expectations arising in the process of transferring property from one person to another i.e of buyers and sellers.

63(C). The Competition Act, 2002 was enacted by the Parliament of India and governs Indian competition law.

It replaced the archaic The Monopolies and Restrictive Trade Practices Act, 1969. Under this legislation, the Competition Commission of India was established to prevent the activities that have an adverse effect on competition in India. This act extends to whole of India.

64(B). Section 2(36) of Companies Act is related to p rospectus.

Section 2(36) in The Companies Act, 1956 , prospectus means any document described or issued as a prospectus and includes any notice, circular, advertisement or other document inviting deposits from the public or inviting offers from the public for the subscription or purchase of any shares in, or debentures of, a body corporate.

65(A). Mr. Shushant is the owner of a house, the details of which are given below the gross annual value would be 36,000 Municipal value Rs. 36,000 Actual rent Rs 32,000 Fair Rent Rs. 36,000 Standard Rent Rs. 40,000.

A) Fair Value = Rs. 36,000
B) Municipal Value = Rs. 36,000
C) Higher Of A and B = Rs. 36,000
D) Standard Rent = Rs. 40,000
E) Expected Rent (Lower Of C and D) = Rs. 36,000
F) Actual Rent = Rs. 32,000
GROSS ANNUAL VALUE (Higher Of E and F) = Rs. 36,000

66(B). Income Tax and Corporate Tax are direct taxes.

A direct tax is paid directly by an individual or organization to the imposing entity. A taxpayer pays direct taxes to the government for different purposes, including real property tax, personal property tax, income tax. A corporate tax is a direct tax imposed by a jurisdiction on the income or capital of corporations. Excise duty is a form of tax imposed on goods for their production, licensing, and sale. It is an indirect tax. Customs Duty is levied when goods are transported across borders between countries. It is an indirect tax.

67(C). In the balance of payment account, the transfer payments are included in current account.

The balance of payments of a country is the difference between all money flowing into the country in a particular period of time (e.g., a quarter or a year) and the outflow of money to the rest of the world. These financial transactions are made by individuals, firms, and government bodies to compare receipts and payments arising out of the trade of goods and services.

68(B). IFC encourage the growth and development of Public Sector Enterprises in member countries statements is false.

The International Finance Corporation (IFC) is an international financial institution that offers investment, advisory, and asset management services to encourage private-sector development in less developed countries. The IFC is a member of the World Bank Group and is headquartered in Washington, D.C. in the United States.

69(B). The central bank is an apex bank that controls the entire banking system of a country. It is the sole agency of note-issuing and controls the supply of money in the economy.

It performs the following functions as per the Reserve Bank of India Act, 1934:

1. Banking functions:

- The Reserve Bank acts as the Banker, Agent, and Adviser to the Government of India and states. It performs all the banking functions of the State and Central Government and it also tenders useful advice to the government on matters related to economic and monetary policy. It also manages the public debt of the government.
- It performs the same functions for the other commercial banks as the other banks ordinarily

perform for their customers. RBI lends money to all the commercial banks of the country.

2. Supervisory functions:
- It supervises other banks and governments into various economic conditions and guides them at the time of inflation or deflation in the economy.

3. Promotional functions:
- The central bank also performs promotional functions which include integrating with world economies and maintaining foreign reserves. They represent the country's economy internationally.

70(B). 'Chi square test' measures goodness of fit.
A chi-square test, also written as $\chi 2$ test, is a statistical hypothesis test that is valid to perform when the test statistic is chi-square distributed under the null hypothesis, specifically Pearson's chi-square test and variants thereof. Pearson's chi-square test is used to determine whether there is a statistically significant difference between the expected frequencies and the observed frequencies in one or more categories of a contingency table.

71(B). The error committed by rejecting an applicant who would have been successful on the job is called f alse negative error. A false negative error is a test result that wrongly indicates a condition does not hold.
For example, when a person is guilty of a crime or when an applicant who can be successful on the job is rejected, these are false negatives.
The condition "a person is guilty", or "an applicant can be successful" holds, but the test (the trial in the court of law or the interview) fails to realize this condition, and wrongly decides that the person is not guilty or the applicant is not fit for the job.

72(B). The industry refers to a group of firms/companies that does related primary activities for their business.
When the number of firms in an area increases then those firms enjoy some of the benefits like availability of raw materials, transport, and communication, research and invention, etc. and they also receive financial assistance from banking and non-banking institutions. Here we can conclude that the concentration of all firms in the industry leads to economies of concentration.

73(C). Surcharge is levied when the total income 1 Crore exceeds for domestic corporation.
A surcharge is an additional charge or tax to the tax being already levied. A surcharge of 10% on a tax rate of 30% effectively increases the combined tax rate to 33% . Marginal reliefs are also provided to individuals as sometimes an increase in tax liability after factoring surcharge becomes more than the increase in income above Rs 1 crore.

74(C). External Assistance is not the part of net invisibles of Balance of Payments Current Account.
The current account net Invisibles record the receipts and payments with respect to
- Services
- Transfers
- Remittance

Services: Export and import of services is recorded under net invisible. It includes travel, transportation, insurance, Government Not Included Elsewhere(GNIE) and miscellaneous services.
Transfers: It includes grants gifts etc which do not need to be compensated or reciprocated. Once it is received it need not be repaid.
Remittance: These are the transfers sent to native countries which are directly earned by labour or workers in foreign countries.
External Assistance is the part of Capital Account.

75(D). Assertion (A): Primary and secondary capital markets are integrated after LPG reform in India.
- Most of the capital market reforms were introduced during 1996- 97, including primary and secondary markets, equity and debt, and foreign institutional investment.
- Primary market reforms aimed at imparting greater flexibility in the issue process and strengthening the criteria for accessing the securities market.
- Reforms in the secondary market aimed at improving market transparency, integrity and trading infrastructure.

Reason (R): Globalization integrates the domestic economy with the world economy
- Globalization is the process of interaction and integration among people, companies, and governments worldwide.
- The goal of globalization is to boost economies around the world by making markets more efficient.
- It is believed that global trade will lead to more competition, which will spread wealth more equally.

76(D). There are various forms of relationship between the banker and the customer depending upon the services availed by the customer from the bank.
Debtor-Creditor, Agent-Principal, Licensor-Licensee, Bailor-Bailee, Pledger-Pledgee, etc. are various kinds of relationships between the banker and the customer.
Licensor-Licensee:
- When a banker provides the locker facility to a customer, the relationship between them is that of licensor and licensee or lessor and lessee.
- A bank is a licensor and the customer who hires the bank is the licensee.

Debentures:
- Section 71 of the Companies Act, 2013 permits a company to issue debentures with an option to convert debentures into shares either wholly or partially at the time of redemption.
- Provided that this conversion of the debenture to shares shall be approved by a special resolution passed at a general meeting.
- The Companies Act 1956, Section 2(12) defines debentures as, "Debenture includes debenture stock, bonds and any other securities of a company whether constituting a charge on the Company's assets or not. Debenture means a document, which either creates a debt or acknowledges it, and any document which fulfills either of these two conditions is a debenture."
- Thus, debentures are governed by company law.

77(B). Assertion (A): High-powered money is the source of all other forms of money that impact the money supply.
- There are two theories of the determination of the money supply.
- According to the first view, the money supply is determined exogenously by the central bank.

- The second view holds that the money supply is determined endogenously by changes in the economic activity which affects people's desire to hold currency relative to deposits, the rate of interest, etc.

Reason (R): Credit is credited by commercial banks

- Credit creation is the most significant function of commercial banks. This is done when commercial banks accept deposits and lend loans and advances.
- In this process, they create two types of deposits, namely primary deposits and derivative or active deposits.
- Primary deposits refer to the cash deposited by a customer in a bank or deposit a cheque with the bank for collection.
- The derivative or active deposits refer to the deposits which are created out of the percentage of loans and advances granted by the banks.

78(A). Tarapore Committee was constituted by the Reserve Bank of India for suggesting a roadmap on full convertibility of Rupee on Capital Account. The committee submitted its report in May 1997.

The committee observed that there is no clear definition of CAC. The CAC as per the standards refers to the freedom to convert the local financial assets into foreign financial assets or vice versa at the market-determined rates of exchange. The Tarapore committee observed that the Capital controls can be useful in insulating the economy of the country from the volatile capital flows during the transitional periods and also in providing time to the authorities so that they can pursue discretionary domestic policies to strengthen the initial conditions.

79(C). Auditor: An auditor is an authorized person who verifies and reviews the financial records and financial statements of a company and ensures that they are prepared in accordance with the norms. He also checks whether any tampering or manipulation has been done with the financial data with the aim of hiding any fraud or malpractice within the company.

Audit Programme: An audit programme is a plan or blueprint of what procedures would be followed by an auditor to validate a company's financial records. It states policies, regulations and guidelines according to which the auditing activities would be performed. An audit programme is also called an audit plan.

80(D). Audit: Audit is an unbiased examination and evaluation of an organization's financial statements is performed to ensure that the financial records are a fair and accurate picture of the transactions they claim to represent.

Auditing is mainly performed to avoid any errors and frauds in the books of accounts so that true financial records are reflected to the public.

Mock Test 10

1. Ensuring the safety, health and welfare of the employee is the primary purpose of which of the following acts?
   (a) The Factories Act, 1948
   (b) The Payment of Wages Act, 1936
   (c) The Equal Remuneration Act, 1976
   (d) The Industrial Disputes Act, 1947

2. Match the items of List - I with the items of List - II.

List - I	List - II
(a) Pension scheme	i. Health care for family
(b) Personal security	ii. Severance pay
(c) Financial assistance	iii. Provident fund
(d) Allowance	iv. Transport allowance

   (a) (a) - i, (b) - ii, (c) - iii, (d) - iv
   (b) (a) - iii, (b) - i, (c) - ii, (d) - iv
   (c) (a) - iii, (b) - ii, (c) - i, (d) - iv
   (d) (a) - i, (b) - iv, (c) - ii, (d) - iii

3. Market control process consists:
   (a) Formation of Performance standards
   (b) Performance Appraisal
   (c) Correcting Deviations
   (d) All of the above

4. Match the items of List - I with the items of List - II.

List - I	List - II
(a) Perfect competition	(i) No control
(b) Monopolistic competi tion	(ii) Some Control
(c) Oligopoly	(iii) Practically Some Con trol
(d) Monopoly	(iv) Usual control

   (a) (a) - (i), (b) - (ii), (c) - (iii), (d) - (iv)
   (b) (a) - (ii), (b) - (iii), (c) - (iv), (d) - (i)
   (c) (a) - (iii), (b) - (ii), (c) - (iv), (d) - (i)
   (d) (a) - (iv), (b) - (iii), (c) - (ii), (d) - (i)

5. "A marketing policy is a statement of a course of action which will be followed under a given set of circumstances." Who said it?
   (a) William J. Stanton (b) McCarthy
   (c) Manson and Rath (d) None of these

6. Cash flow arising from interest paid in the case of financial enterprise is a cash flow from:
   (a) Operating activities
   (b) Financing activities
   (c) Operating activities and financing activities
   (d) Investing activities

7. Which of the following is not a property of indifference curve?
   (a) Indifference curve slopes negatively.
   (b) Indifference curve is convex to the point of origin.
   (c) Indifference curve necessarily has to be parallel.
   (d) Two indifference curves do not intersect each other.

8. Find the correct matching between items of List - I and the items of List - II.

List - I	List - II
(a) Increase in d emand	(i) Leftward movement along the d emand curve
(b) Contraction of demand	(ii) Rightward shift of the demand c urve.
(c) Cross deman d	(iii) Demand of more than one com modity to satisfy one specific want
(d) Joint deman d	(iv) Demand of one commodity wit h changes in the prices of another r elated commodity

   (a) (a) - (ii), (b) - (i), (c) - (iv), (c) - (iii)
   (b) (a) - (i), (b) - (ii), (c) - (iii), (d) - (iv)
   (c) (a) - (ii), (b) - (iv), (c) - (iii), (d) - (i)
   (d) (a) - (i), (b) - (ii), (d) - (iii), (c) - (iv)

9. Match the items in List I with the items in List II.

List I	List II
a - Unity of command theory	1 - F. W. Taylo r
b - Bureaucratic theory of managem ent	2 - Max Webe r
c - Scientific management theory	3 - Henry Fay ol

   (a) a - 1, b - 2, c - 3 (b) a - 2, b - 1, c - 3
   (c) a - 3, b - 2, c - 1 (d) a - 2, b - 3, c - 1

10. Match the items in List I with the items in List II.

List I	List II
a - Autocratic Leade r	1 - Makes and announces de cisions
b - Participative Lea der	2 - Seeks ideas before makin g decisions
c - Democratic Lead er	3 - Decides with the group o n one on one basis

   (a) a - 1, b - 2, c - 3 (b) a - 1, b - 3, c - 2
   (c) a - 3, b - 2, c - 1 (d) a - 2, b - 3, c - 1

11. In vertical communication, the communication flows:
   (a) Upwards only
   (b) Downwards only
   (c) Upward as well as downwards
   (d) None of the above

12. Which of the following factors lead to group cohesiveness?
   (a) Agreement on group goals
   (b) High intra-group competition
   (c) Frequent interaction of members
   (d) Personal attractiveness
   Codes:
   1. (a) and (b)
   2. (a), (b) and (c)
   3. (a), (c) and (d)
   4. (a), (b) and (d)
   (a) 1 (b) 2
   (c) 3 (d) 4

13. The most appropriate concept to be adopted for physical distribution of goods is:

(a) Marketing concept (b) Total cost concept
(c) Selling concept (d) System concept

14. Which of the following is the best example of an Agreement between Oligopolists?
(a) GATT (b) OPEC
(c) WTO (d) UNIDO

15. In the line and staff form, the function of the marketing manager is to:
(a) Obey the line (b) Serve the line
(c) Inform the line (d) Advise the line

16. The estimated requirement of total funds for working capital met from long-run sources is known as:
(a) Matching approach
(b) Aggressive approach
(c) Conservative approach
(d) None of the above

17. In 'job evaluation', the key jobs are designated as ones:
(a) Which are more in number in the organization
(b) Which are most important for the survival of the organization
(c) Which are most secure
(d) Which represent different levels of each of the compensable factors

18. **Direction** : Study the given statements carefully and choose the correct answer.
I. Employee development is more future oriented and more concerned with education than employee training.
II. Apprenticeship programme is one of most widely used off-the-job training methods.
(a) Both are correct
(b) Both are incorrect
(c) I is correct and II is incorrect
(d) I is incorrect and II is correct

19. Match the items in List I with the items in List II.

List - I	List - II
a. Brain stor ming	1. A freewheeling group discussion
b. Business g ame	2. A development activity in which o ne's action is guided by others
c. Role playin g	3. A technique in which one assumes different identities

(a) a - 1, b - 2, c - 3 (b) a - 2, b - 1, c - 3
(c) a - 1, b - 3, c - 2 (d) a - 2, b - 3, c - 1

20. Which of the following is the correct formula for net cash inflow of a project?
(a) Sales - Operating expenses - Interest - Tax
(b) Sales - Operating expenses
(c) Net profit after tax + Depreciation
(d) Gross profit + Depreciation

21. Which of the following may be an ethics code?
(a) We push the customer from the shop.
(b) Our first responsibility is to our customers.
(c) Do and die.
(d) Let's go money!

22. Which of the following is not a mode of 'direct distribution system'?
(a) Trading mediators (b) Vending machines
(c) Own sales depot (d) Franchise shops

23. Which one of the following is a DataBase Management System?
(a) MS Access (b) MS Excel
(c) MS Outlook (d) None of the above

24. A product line strategy is where a company adds a higher priced product to a line in order to attract a broader market, which helps the sale of its existing lower priced products. This strategy is called:
(a) Trading up
(b) Trading down
(c) Life-cycle extension
(d) Product line extension

25. Match the items of List - I with List - II according to 'The Harvard Framework' developed for HRM.

List - I	List - II
(a) Stakeholders interest	(i) Work systems
(b) Situational factor	(ii) Cost effectiveness
(c) HRM policy choice	(iii) Individual well bein g
(d) HR outcome	(iv) Government
(e) Long term consequenc e	(v) Business strategy

(a) (a) - (iv), (b) - (i), (c) - (ii), (d) - (iii), (e) - (v)
(b) (a) - (v), (b) - (iv), (c) - (ii), (d) - (i), (e) - (iii)
(c) (a) - (iv), (b) - (v), (c) - (i), (d) - (ii), (e) - (iii)
(d) (a) - (i), (b) - (v), (c) - (ii), (d) - (iii), (e) - (iv)

26. Which of these is/are considered in designing capital structure of a corporate?
(a) Trading on equity (b) Cost of capital
(c) Profitability (d) All of the above

27. An interview conducted at the time of an employee leaving the organisation is called:
(a) Exit interview
(b) Feedback interview
(c) Convincing interview
(d) Directed interview

28. Which of the following training methods exposes the newly recruited employee to the various business functions, divisions and departments?
(a) Orientation (b) Vestibule training
(c) Off-the-job training (d) Role playing

29. Which of the following plays a crucial role in determining international trade?
(a) Elasticity of demand
(b) Price elasticity of demand
(c) Income elasticity of demand
(d) Cross elasticity of demand

30. SDR's are popularly known as
(a) Currency Notes (b) Paper Gold
(c) Silver Coin (d) Gold Coin

31. Which of the following is not a form of economic integration in the context of intra-regional trade?
(a) Customs Union (b) European Union

(c) Economic Union (d) African Union

32. The chief audit executive establishes a method for prioritizing all of the following except:
(a) Business units with low-risk levels
(b) Branch or field office with low-risk levels
(c) Outstanding risk areas
(d) Low inherent risk areas

33. Which of the following modes of payments is used for international money transfer?
(a) RTGS (b) NEFT
(c) SWIFT (d) None of the above

34. DFEC stands for:
(a) Direct Foreign Exchange Control
(b) Direct Finance Exchange Control
(c) Duty Free Export Credit
(d) Duty Free Exchange Credit

35. In rounding of the income under Section 288 A of the Income Tax Act, the rounding off is done:
(a) To the nearest of Rs. 10 or its multiple
(b) To the nearest of Rs. 100 or its multiple
(c) To the nearest of Rs. 1
(d) None of these

36. Which of the following is the highest in the hierarchy of income tax authorities?
(a) ITO
(b) CBDT
(c) Commissioner of Income Tax
(d) Director General of Income Tax

37. Which of the following tools would best give a graphical representation of a sequence of activities and decisions?
(a) Flowchart (b) Control chart
(c) Histogram (d) Run chart

38. **Direction** : Read the given statements carefully and choose the correct option accordingly.
Assertion (A): When there is evidence of a linear relationship between two variables, it may not always mean an independent dependent relationship between the two variables.
Reason (R): The causal relationship between the two variables may not imply a reasonable theoretical relationship between the two.
Choose the right answer from the following codes.
(a) Both (A) and (R) are true and (R) is the correct explanation.
(b) Both (A) and (R) are true, but (R) is not the correct explanation.
(c) (A) is true, but (R) is false.
(d) (A) is false, but (R) is true.

39. Kyoto Protocol relates to:
(a) Competition
(b) Consumer protection
(c) Environment protection
(d) Atomic energy generation

40. Which of the following should be achieved by a business firm at the earliest?
(a) Budgeted sales
(b) Break-even point
(c) Return on Investments
(d) Market share

41. Match the items given in the lists.

List I	List II
(a) Economic liberalizatio n	(i) IT-enabled services
(b) Outsourcing	(ii) SFIO
(c) Corporate frauds	(iii) Microeconomic sta bility
(d) Second generation ref orms	(iv) Increased competiti on

Indicate the correct combination.
(a) a - (i), b - (ii), c - (iii), d - (iv)
(b) a - (i), b - (iii), c - (ii), d - (iv)
(c) a - (ii), b - (iii), c - (iv), d - (i)
(d) a - (iv), b - (i), c - (ii), d - (iii)

42. What does lower debtor-turnover ratio indicate?
(a) Quick recovery (b) Delay in recovery
(c) High debtors (d) None of the above

43. Which of the following methods of inventory valuation results in lower valuation of inventory and low income when inflation is on the rise?
(a) LIFO
(b) FIFO
(c) Simple average method
(d) Weighted average method

44. Which of the following pairs is incorrectly matched?
(a) Capital expenditure : Transportation costs of a machine
(b) Fund flow statement : Working capital
(c) Reduction of share capital : Reconstruction
(d) Contribution : Sales - Cost

45. Match the following lists.

List - I	List - II
(a) Matching princi ple	(i) Ignores future profit estimat ions
(b) Materiality pri nciple	(ii) Normal basis for valuing as sets
(c) Conservatism p rinciple	(iii) Revenues and expenses of a particular period
(d) Cost principle	(iv) Relates to relative size or i mportance of item or event

(a) a - (i), b - (iv), c - (ii), d - (iii)
(b) a - (ii), b - (iii), c - (iv), d - (i)
(c) a - (iii), b - (iv), c - (i), d - (ii)
(d) a - (iv), b - (iii), c - (ii), d - (i)

46. Which of the following statements is correct?
(a) Monopolist charges the maximum possible price.
(b) Monopolist always makes (economic) profit.
(c) Monopolist operates on an inelastic demand curve.
(d) None of the above

47. Price discrimination policy helps in increasing profits in case of:

(a) Perfect competition
(b) Monopolistic competition
(c) Monopoly
(d) Oligopoly

48. The nature of cross-price elasticity of demand in case of complementary products will be:
(a) Positive (b) Negative
(c) (A) and (B) both (d) Zero

49. Directions: Match the following.

Group - I (Products)	Group - II (Market structure)
(a) Food grain	(i) Monopoly
(b) Airlines	(ii) Pure competition
(c) Railway	(iii) Monopolistic
(d) Cars	(iv) Oligopoly

(a) a - (i), b - (ii), c - (iii), d - (iv)
(b) a - (ii), b - (iv), c - (i), d - (iii)
(c) a - (iii), b - (i), c - (iv), d - (ii)
(d) a - (iv), b - (ii), c - (iii), d - (i)

50. Which of the following tests do we normally apply for qualitative data?
(a) Z-test (b) T-tests
(c) (X^2) Chi-square test (d) ANOVA

51. Match the following.

List - I	List - II
(a) Capital market	(i) IRDA
(b) Monetary policy	(ii) SEBI
(c) Telecom services	(iii) RBI
(d) Insurance	(iv) TRAI

(a) (a) - (ii), (b) - (iii), (c) - (i), (d) - (iv)
(b) (a) - (ii), (b) - (iii), (c) - (iv), (d) - (i)
(c) (a) - (ii), (b) - (iv), (c) - (iii), (d) - (i)
(d) (a) - (ii), (b) - (i), (c) - (iv), (d) - (iii)

52. Which of the following modes indicates a strategic alliance in international business?
(a) Franchising (b) Leasing
(c) Turnkey project (d) Joint venture

53. **Direction** : Complete the statement with the correct option out of the alternatives given below.
Acting in accordance with a request or command, and rules or instructions by which an organization ensures statutory laws and regulations as applicable to it is called:
(a) Discipline (b) Compliance
(c) Code of conduct (d) Business ethics

54. Reinforcing the Code of Conduct and ethical behaviour standards for all internal auditors can protect which of the following?
(a) Business risk (b) Audit failures
(c) Audit assurance false (d) Audit reputation risk

55. In independent India, the first major foreign exchange crisis occurred in the year:
(a) 1955 (b) 1956
(c) 1969 (d) 1991

56. The closing stock was overstated by Rs 9,000 being a casting error in the schedule of inventory. If this error located after the preparation of the final account then which of the following rectification entry is correct?
(a) Stock A/c Dr. 9,000 To Suspense A/c 9,000
(b) Suspense A/c Dr. 9,000 To Stock A/c 9,000
(c) Suspense A/c Dr. 9,000 To Profit and loss A/c 9,000
(d) Profit and loss A/c Dr. 9,000 To Stock A/c 9,000

57. When one party grants the right to use the asset to the other party, in return for a periodic payment, it is known as ________.
(a) Lease financing (b) Factoring
(c) Public deposits (d) Debts

58. Budgetary control helps in the implementation of:
(a) Stantdard Cost (b) Marginal Cost
(c) Ratio Analysis (d) Technical Analysis

59. Which convention gave birth to the International Monetary Fund (IMF)?
(a) Uruguay Round Conference
(b) Round Table Conference
(c) Bretton Woods Conference
(d) Shimla Conference

60. Under the lease agreement, the lessee gets the right to ________.
(a) Share profits earned by the lessor
(b) Participate in the management of the organisation
(c) Use the asset for a specified period
(d) Sell the assets

61. Which of the following is not a disadvantage of using mean?
(a) It is affected by extreme values
(b) It cannot be computed in grouped data with open-ended class intervals
(c) It does not possess the desired algebraic property
(d) None of the above

62. The best measure of dispersion to compare between two colleges/university's result:
(a) Coefficient of variation
(b) Quartile deviation
(c) Mean Deviation
(d) Standard Deviation

63. Which of the following relationships is NOT true in a model distribution?
(a) Mean - Mode = 3 (Mean - Median)
(b) Mode = 3 Median - 2 Mean
(c) 3 Median = 2 Mean + Mode
(d) 2 Median - 3 Quartile Deviation = 2 Mean

64. Tele - Marketing is a part of:
(a) Viral Marketing
(b) Social Marketing
(c) Direct Marketing
(d) Relationship Marketing

65. The budgets are classified on the basis of:

(a) Capacity (b) Time
(c) Functions (d) All of the above

66. Identify the indirect taxes from the given option.
(a) GST, corporate tax
(b) Custom duty, corporate tax
(c) Income tax, GST
(d) GST, custom duty

67. __________ terminology are not related to income tax.
(a) Tax Deduction and Collection Account Number (TAN)
(b) Leave Travel Allowance (LTA)
(c) Dearness Allowance (DA)
(d) Taxpayer Identification Number (TIN)

68. The form 'ITR-1' is a form for using?
(a) Income Tax Return (b) Income Tax Challan
(c) VAT (d) Excise Duty

69. X, an employee of the private company, gets Rs. 30,000 p.m. basic salary and entitled to Rs. 1,500 p.m. as entertainment allowance. What are the deductions u/s 16 (ii) from gross salary in respect of entertainment allowance?
(a) 5,000 rs (b) 18,000 rs
(c) 72,000 rs (d) Nil

70. Which of the following does NOT come under the purview of 'paper taxes'?
(a) Gift tax (b) Estate duty
(c) Excise tax (d) Wealth tax

71. Which of the following is correct with respect to GST in India?
I. GST The Act was passed by the Parliament in 2016.
II. GST The law came into force from July 2016.
(a) Only II (b) Only I
(c) Neither I nor II (d) Both I and II

72. Legal relationship between the middleman and the businessperson is governed by:
(a) Law of business (b) Law of Surety
(c) Law of agency (d) None of the above

Ques (73-76): Direction: Read the following passage carefully and answer the question.

Life insurance in its modern form came to India from England in the year 1818. The Oriental Life Insurance Company started by Europeans in Calcutta was the first life insurance company on Indian soil. All the insurance companies established during that period were brought up with the purpose of looking after the needs of the European community and Indian natives were not being insured by these companies. However, later with the efforts of eminent people like Babu Muttylal Seal, foreign insurance companies started insuring Indian lives too. But Indian lives were being treated as sub-standard lives and heavy extra premiums were being charged upon them. The Bombay Mutual Life Assurance Society heralded the birth of the first Indian life insurance company in the year 1870 and covered Indian lives at normal rates. Starting as an Indian enterprise with highly patriotic motives, insurance companies came into existence to carry the message of insurance and social security through insurance to various sectors of society. In 1907, the Hindustan Co-operative Insurance Company took birth in one of the rooms of 'The Jorsanko', house of the great poet Rabindranath Tagore in Calcutta. The Indian Mercantile, General Assurance and Swadeshi Life (later Bombay Life) were some of the companies established during the same period. Prior to 1912, India had no legislation to regulate the insurance business. In the year 1912, Life Insurance Companies Act and Provident Fund Act were passed. The Life Insurance Companies Act, 1912 made it necessary that the premium rate tables and periodical valuations of companies should be certified by an actuary. But the Act discriminated between foreign and Indian companies on many accounts, putting Indian companies at a disadvantage.

73. The paragraph is about which of the following?
(a) Genesis of insurance in India
(b) Struggle of insurance business
(c) Conflict of insurance business
(d) Complications of insurance business

74. Identify the correct statement from the following.
(a) Initially, insurance companies used to discriminate Indian and European clients.
(b) There was no discrimination in Indian and European clients by the insurance companies initially.
(c) Indian clients were charged lower premium by the insurance companies in the beginning.
(d) Indian insurance companies charged higher premium to Europeans at a later stage.

75. Which one among the following grew along with insurance business in India?
(a) Pension Fund (b) Provident Fund
(c) Gratuity (d) Arbitrage

76. The insurance business in India was started first by which one of the following?
(a) Americans (b) Indian merchants
(c) Europeans (d) Afro-Indians

Ques (77-80): Read the following passage carefully and answer the question that follows.

The mutual fund is a special type of investment institution which acts as an investment conduit. It pools the savings of relatively small investors in a well-diversified portfolio of sound investment. Mutual funds issue securities (known as units) to the investors (known as unit-holders) in accordance with the quantum of money invested by them. The profits (or losses) are shared by the investors in proportion to their investments. A mutual fund is set up in the form of a trust which has (i) a sponsor, (ii) trustee, (iii) Asset Management Company (AMC) and (iv) custodian. The trust is established by the sponsor who is like promoter of a company. The trustees of the mutual fund hold its property for the benefit of unit-holders. The trustees are vested with the general power of superintendence and direction over AMC. They monitor the performance and compliance of the SEBI regulations by the mutual fund. The AMC manages the funds by making investment in various types of securities. The custodian holds the securities of the various schemes of the mutual fund in its safe custody. As an investment intermediary, mutual funds offer a variety of services/advantages to the relatively small investors who, on their own, cannot successfully construct and manage an investment portfolio mainly due to the small size of their funds, lack of expertise/experience and so on. These inter-alia include convenience in terms of lower denomination of investment and liquidity, lower risk through diversification, export management and reduced transaction cost due to economies of scale.

77. Who monitors the compliance of SEBI regulations by the mutual fund?
(a) Sponsor (b) Trustee
(c) AMC (d) Custodian

78. The sponsor of a mutual fund is similar to which of the following?
(a) Sole proprietor of a firm
(b) Partner of a partnership firm
(c) Promoter of a company
(d) Director of a company

79. The AMC manages the fund by investing in which of the following?
(a) Stock market securities only
(b) Credit instruments only
(c) Government bonds only
(d) Various types of securities

80. Which among the following is/are not a part of mutual fund trust?
(a) Sponsor (b) Custodian
(c) Depository (d) Trustees

// Smart Answer Sheet //

Correct Percentage of students who answered correctly.
Skipped Percentage of students who skipped.

Q.	Ans.	Correct / Skipped	Q.	Ans.	Correct / Skipped	Q.	Ans.	Correct / Skipped
1	A	63.11% / 36.76%	2	B	51.16% / 47.91%	3	D	87.87% / 10.98%
4	A	46.67% / 46.19%	5	A	24.47% / 68.01%	6	A	43.89% / 38.22%
7	C	53.15% / 35.69%	8	A	17.15% / 78.49%	9	C	22.21% / 70.49%
10	B	46.16% / 46.28%	11	C	89.2% / 10.0%	12	C	52.12% / 37.32%
13	D	23.18% / 70.0%	14	B	32.67% / 67.26%	15	D	64.66% / 31.22%
16	C	67.25% / 32.06%	17	B	87.88% / 10.29%	18	C	10.57% / 78.94%
19	A	46.43% / 46.74%	20	C	23.6% / 69.08%	21	B	81.41% / 14.39%
22	A	86.69% / 10.68%	23	A	84.83% / 10.35%	24	A	47.1% / 52.5%
25	C	40.1% / 45.87%	26	D	60.68% / 33.12%	27	A	77.6% / 22.38%
28	A	89.37% / 10.43%	29	B	14.34% / 79.54%	30	B	78.1% / 19.84%
31	D	41.29% / 34.93%	32	D	16.08% / 79.49%	33	C	76.95% / 15.79%
34	C	65.79% / 33.04%	35	A	48.49% / 49.99%	36	B	83.57% / 11.7%
37	D	61.3% / 38.49%	38	A	31.32% / 67.98%	39	C	76.28% / 22.32%
40	B	82.13% / 16.67%	41	D	51.97% / 33.35%	42	B	79.01% / 14.67%
43	A	55.41% / 31.11%	44	B	76.78% / 19.1%	45	C	24.03% / 74.15%
46	A	78.21% / 21.4%	47	C	62.45% / 34.63%	48	B	43.77% / 40.76%
49	B	78.58% / 11.05%	50	C	17.27% / 70.03%	51	B	77.17% / 18.15%
52	D	55.42% / 44.44%	53	B	62.74% / 33.05%	54	D	52.61% / 42.78%
55	D	89.34% / 10.55%	56	D	53.04% / 32.96%	57	A	89.77% / 10.18%
58	A	52.92% / 40.58%	59	C	49.48% / 50.0%	60	C	88.08% / 11.08%
61	C	64.47% / 32.59%	62	A	51.24% / 36.56%	63	D	20.93% / 69.36%
64	C	54.08% / 39.91%	65	D	79.41% / 15.48%	66	D	55.91% / 35.65%
67	D	47.52% / 40.41%	68	A	51.12% / 42.1%	69	D	41.52% / 51.26%
70	C	68.79% / 30.33%	71	C	45.85% / 30.75%	72	C	66.91% / 31.98%
73	A	63.99% / 32.5%	74	A	68.8% / 30.83%	75	B	58.9% / 40.75%
76	C	52.82% / 33.56%	77	B	48.08% / 30.78%	78	C	62.71% / 36.78%
79	D	83.19% / 12.25%	80	C	26.78% / 67.14%			

// Hints and Solutions //

1(A). Ensuring the safety, health and welfare of the employee is the primary purpose of The Factories Act, 1948.
The Factories Act, 1948 is a social legislation which has been enacted for occupational safety, health and welfare of workers at work places. The objective of the Act is to regulate the conditions of work in manufacturing establishments coming within the definition of the term 'factory' as used in the Act.

2(B). The correct code is: (a) - iii, (b) - i, (c) - ii, (d) - iv
A Provident Fund is a government-sponsored retirement scheme. Both the employer and the employee are required to contribute to the provident fund account with an aim to create a retirement corpus for the employee.
Personal safety and security is a major concern for families living away from home. Luckily for most of our families, they feel as safe and secure in their new homes. For some this was not the case at all as they now endured a range of new threats to the safety and security of their families.
Severance pay amounts to a week or two of pay for every year that the employee was with the company. Executives may receive a month's pay for each year of service and senior executives generally receive severance pay as outlined in the employment contract.
While transport allowance is an allowance given to meet commuting expenses between place of residence and office or to meet personal expenditure of employee of transport business, conveyance allowance is an allowance granted to meet the expenditure on conveyance in performance of office duty.

3(D). The market control process consists of the Formation of Performance standards, Performance Appraisal and Correcting Deviations.
Marketing Control can be defined as "the process of measuring and evaluating the results of marketing strategies and plans, and taking corrective action to ensure that marketing objectives are achieved."

4(A). Correct match:

List - I	List - II
(a) Perfect competition	(i) No control
(b) Monopolistic compe tition	(ii) Some Control
(c) Oligopoly	(iii) Practically Some Co ntrol
(d) Monopoly	(iv) Usual control

Firms in the perfect competition have no control over prices. Firms in the monopolistic competition have some control over prices. Firms in oligopolies practically have some control. Firms in a monopoly have usual control over prices.

5(A). William J. Stanton said, "A marketing policy is a statement of a course of action which will be followed under a given set of circumstances."

6(A). Cash flow arising from interest paid in the case of financial enterprise is a cash flow from operating activities.
Cash flows from interest and dividends received and paid should each be disclosed separately. Cash flows arising from interest paid and interest and dividends received in case of a financial enterprise should be classified as cash flows arising from operating activities. In the case of other enterprises, cash flows arising from interest paid should be classified as cash flows from financing activities while interest and dividends received should be classified as cash flows from investing activities.

7(C). Indifference Curves are not necessarily parallel to each other. Although, they are falling and negatively inclined to the right. Yet the rate of the fall will not be the same for all Indifference Curves.
Indifference curve slopes negatively, indifference curve is convex to the point of origin, two indifference curves do not intersect each other all these are property of indifference curve.

8(A). Correct match:

List - I	List - II
(a) Increase in demand	(ii) Rightward shift of the deman d curve.
(b) Contractio n of demand	(i) Leftward movement along the demand curve
(c) Cross dema nd	(iv) Demand of one commodity w ith changes in the prices of anoth er related commodit.
(d) Joint dema nd	(iii) Demand of more than one co mmodity to satisfy one specific w ant

9(C). Unity of Command means getting orders/ command from only one supervisor. Fayol has stated "As soon as two superiors impose their authority over the same person or department, uneasiness makes itself felt. Dual command is a perpetual source of conflict."
The German sociologist Max Weber argued that bureaucracy constitutes the most efficient and rational way in which human activity can be organized and that systematic processes and organized hierarchies are necessary to maintain order, maximize efficiency, and eliminate favouritism.
Taylor's philosophy focused on the belief that making people work as hard as they could was not as efficient as optimizing the way the work was done. In 1909, Taylor published "The Principles of Scientific Management." In this, he proposed that by optimizing and simplifying jobs, productivity would increase.

10(B). Correct match:

List I	List II
a - Autocratic Leade r	1 - Makes and announces d ecisions
b - Participative Lea der	3 - Decides with the group on one on one basis
c - Democratic Lead er	2 - Seeks ideas before maki ng decisions

Authoritarian or autocratic - the leader tells his or her employees what to do and how to do it, without getting their advice. the leader allows the employees to make the decisions, however, the leader is still responsible for the decisions that are made.
The democratic/participative leadership style places significant responsibility on leaders and their staff. This is true for all organizations — from private enterprises and government agencies to educational institutions and nonprofit entities.
Democratic leadership, also known as participative leadership or shared leadership, is a type of leadership style in which members of the group take a more participative role in the decision-making process.

11(C). Vertical communication, in other words, means upward and downward communication. In this channel of communication, messages do not jump directly from the top to the bottom or vice versa, but they come through a correct channel.

12(C). Agreement on group goals, Frequent interaction of members and Personal attractiveness are the factors lead to group cohesiveness.

13(D). Physical distribution is managed with a systems approach and considers key interrelated functions to provide efficient movement of products. The functions are interrelated because any time a decision is made in one area it has an effect on the others.

14(B). OPEC is the best example of agreement between oligopolists.
The Organization of the Petroleum Exporting Countries is an intergovernmental organization of 13 countries. Founded on 14 September 1960 in Baghdad by the first five members (Iran, Iraq, Kuwait, Saudi Arabia, and Venezuela), it has since 1965 been headquartered in Vienna, Austria, although Austria is not an OPEC member state.

15(D). In the line and staff form, the function of the marketing manager is to advise the line.
Marketing manager will be responsible for carrying out marketing activities and personnel manager will be responsible for looking after the personnel matters in all the departments of the organization.

16(C). The estimated requirement of total funds for working capital met from long-run sources is known as the conservative approach.
The conservative approach is a risk-free strategy of working capital financing. A company adopting this strategy maintains a higher level of current assets and therefore higher working capital also.

17(B). In 'job evaluation', the key jobs are designated as ones that are most important for the survival of the organization.
A job evaluation is a systematic way of determining the value/worth of a job in relation to other jobs in an organization. It tries to make a systematic comparison between jobs to assess their relative worth for the purpose of establishing a rational pay structure.

18(C). I is correct and II is incorrect
Employee development is more future-oriented and more concerned with education than employee training is a true statement.
The apprenticeship programme is one of the most widely used off-the-job training methods is a false statement

19(A). Brainstorming combines a relaxed, informal approach to problem-solving with lateral thinking. It encourages people to come up with thoughts and ideas that can, at first, seem a bit crazy. Some of these ideas can be crafted into original, creative solutions to a problem, while others can spark even more ideas.
A business game is an interactive structured training activity with specially created conditions, which aim to reproduce those of a working situation in a successful business.
Role-playing the acting out of the part of a particular person or character, for example as a technique in training or psychotherapy.

20(C). Net cash inflow= Net profit after tax + Depreciation
Net cash flow refers to the difference between a company's cash inflows and outflows in a given period. In the strictest sense, net cash flow refers to the change in a company's cash balance as detailed on its cash flow statement.

21(B). Our first responsibility is to our customers are the ethics code.
For any kind of business their intent clearly in the opening line: "our first responsibility is to our customers". Our customer services team not only embodies this culture but, more specifically, takes responsibility for line six of the credo: "your orders will be serviced promptly and accurately". To ensure we are meeting these commitments, a number of measures have been put in place.

22(A). Trading mediators is not a mode of 'direct distribution system'.
Direct Distribution system is a mode of distribution where the manufacturer directly sells its product to the consumer without the involvement of middlemen and intermediaries. Trading mediators can be referred as wholesaler, retailer, distributors and agents. With the presence of trade mediators in the distribution channel, there is no direct contact between the company and the customer.

23(A). Microsoft Access is a database management system (DBMS) from Microsoft that combines the relational Microsoft Jet Database Engine with a graphical user interface and software-development tools.

24(A). Trading up is a type of selling in which the customer is persuaded to buy a more expensive item, or a larger quantity of the same item than originally intended in exchange for an attractive discount or some other incentive.

25(C). The correct combination is (a) - (iv), (b) - (v), (c) - (i), (d) - (ii), (e) - (iii).
The model starts, on the left, with stakeholder interest. These stakeholders include shareholders, management, employee groups, government, and more. These interests define HRM policies.
At the same time, situational factors influence these interests. Situational factors include workforce characteristics, unions, and all the other factors that were also listed in the 8-box model.
Situational factors and stakeholder interest influence HRM policies. These include the core HR activities, like recruitment, training, and reward systems.
When done well, HRM policies lead to positive HRM outcomes. These include the previously mentioned retention, cost-effectiveness, commitment, and competence.
These positive HRM outcomes lead to long-term consequences. These can be individual, organizational, and societal.

26(D). All of the above are considered in designing capital structure of a corporate.
Capital structure refers to an arrangement of the different components of business funds, i.e. shareholder's funds and borrowed funds in proper proportion. A business organization utilizes the funds for meeting the everyday expenses and also for budgeting high-end future projects. Computation of capital structure involves a lot of analytical thinking and strategical approach. The calculation consists of different ratios and formulae like the cost of capital, the weighted average cost of capital, debt to equity ratio, cost of equity, etc.

27(A). An interview conducted at the time of an employee leaving the organisation is called exit interview.
An exit interview is a wrap-up meeting between management representatives and someone who is leaving an organization, either voluntarily or through termination. Exit interviews are common in business, education and government environments.

28(A). Orientation exposes the newly recruited employee to the various business functions, divisions and departments.
Orientation means providing new employees with basic information about the employer. Training programs are used to ensure that the new employee has the basic knowledge required to perform the job satisfactorily. Orientation and training programs are important components in the processes of developing a committed and flexible high-potential workforce and socializing new employees.

29(B). Price elasticity of demand plays a crucial role in determining international trade.
Price elasticity of demand (Epd), or elasticity, is the degree to which the effective desire for something changes as its price changes. In general, people desire things less as those things become more expensive.

30(B). SDR's are popularly known as Paper Gold.
Special drawing rights (SDRs) are supplementary foreign exchange reserve assets defined and maintained by the International Monetary Fund (IMF). SDRs are units of account for the IMF, and not a currency per se.

31(D). African Union is not a form of economic integration in the context of intra-regional trade
The African Union (AU) is a continental union consisting of 55 member states located on the continent of Africa. The AU was announced in the Sirte Declaration in Sirte, Libya, on 9 September 1999.

32(D). The chief audit executive establishes a method for prioritizing all of the following except Low inherent risk areas.
Audits of lower risk level business units, branch types, or field office types need to be periodically included in the internal audit activity's plan to give them coverage and confirm that their risks have not changed. Also, the internal audit activity establishes a method for prioritizing outstanding risks not yet subject to an internal audit. High inherent risk areas, not low inherent risk areas, are prioritized.

33(C). SWIFT payments, also called international wires, are a type of international transfer sent via the SWIFT international payment network. The SWIFT international payment network is one of the largest financial messaging systems in the world.

34(C). DFEC stands for Duty Free Export Credit, which enables duty free import of inputs for production of certain specific goods.

35(A). As per section 288A of the Income Tax Act, the total income computed as per various sections of this act, shall be rounded off to the nearest Rs 10. For the purpose of rounding off, firstly any part of rupee consisting of paise should be ignored.

36(B). The Chairperson, Central Board of Direct Taxes (CBDT) is the senior-most IRS civil servant in the Government of India. The Chairperson of CBDT is the ex officio Special Secretary to the Government of India and also cadre controlling authority of the Indian Revenue Service.

37(D). According to its definition, a flowchart is a graphical representation of a sequence of activities and decisions.

38(A). Both (A) and (R) are true and (R) is the correct explanation.
When there is evidence of a linear relationship between two variables, it may not always mean an independent dependent relationship between the two variables is true.
The causal relationship between the two variables may not imply a reasonable theoretical relationship between the two is also true and correctly explains the assertion.

39(C). Kyoto Protocol relates to environment protection.
The Kyoto Protocol is an international treaty that extends the 1992 United Nations Framework Convention on Climate Change (UNFCCC) that commits state parties to reduce greenhouse gas emissions, based on the scientific consensus that (part one) global warming is occurring and (part two) it is extremely likely that human-made CO2 emissions have predominantly caused it. The Kyoto Protocol was adopted in Kyoto, Japan, on 11 December 1997 and entered into force on 16 February 2005. There are currently 192 parties (Canada withdrew from the protocol, effective December 2012) to the Protocol.

40(B). Break-even point should be achieved by a business firm at the earliest.
The break-even point (BEP) in economics, business and specifically cost accounting is the point at which total cost and total revenue are equal, i.e. "even". There is no net loss or gain, though opportunity costs have been paid and capital has received the expected return.

41(D). Correct combination is a - (iv), b - (i), c - (ii), d - (iii).
Liberalization leads to increased competition. This competition can be related to product and service cost and price, target market, technological adaptation, quick response, quick production by companies etc. When a company produces with less cost and sells cheaper, it is able to increase its market share.
IT-enabled service, also called Business Process Outsourcing, include functions like call centres, accounting, payroll, employee benefits, tax preparation, radiology analysis, films and cartoons production, and even research and development. Outsourcing location can be onshore, nearshore, offshore or far shore.
The SFIO is mandated to conduct Multi-disciplinary investigations of major corporate frauds. It is a multi-disciplinary organization having experts from the financial sector, capital market, accountancy, forensic audit, taxation, law, information technology, company law, customs and investigation.
Macro-economic stabilization reforms (along with structural economic reforms) were launched in June 1991.So to increase the GDP growth rate, agriculture GDP, industrial production, service sector GDP, saving rate, gross domestic investment and to decrease the fiscal deficit a "Second generation reform" Is needed.

42(B). A low debtor-turnover ratio might be due to a company having a poor collection process, bad credit policies, or customers that are not financially viable or creditworthy. Typically, a low turnover ratio implies that the company should reassess its credit policies to ensure the timely collection of its receivables.

43(A). LIFO method of inventory valuation results in lower valuation of inventory and low income when inflation is on the rise
LIFO is a method used to account for inventory. Under LIFO, the cost of the most recent products purchased (or produced) are the first to be expensed. LIFO is used only in the United States and governed by the generally accepted accounting principles (GAAP).

44(B). Incorrectly matched pair is Fund flow statement : Working capital.
Fund flow statement: A fund flow statement is a statement prepared to analyze the reasons for changes in the financial position of a company between two balance sheets. It portrays the inflow and outflow of funds i.e. sources of funds and applications of funds for a particular period.
Working capital: the capital of a business which is used in its day-to-day trading operations, calculated as the current assets minus the current liabilities.

45(C). The correct combination is a - (iii), b - (iv), c - (i), d - (ii).
Matching principle is the accounting principle that requires that the expenses incurred during a period be recorded in the same period in which the related revenues are earned. This principle recognizes that businesses must incur expenses to earn revenues.
Materiality is a concept in accounting which states that firm can ignore small information which does not have any significant impact on the business.

This also means that a business must include all other information in its financial statements which is material/significant enough.
The principle of conservatism in accounting gives guidance when recording cases of uncertainty or estimates. In other words, you should always lean towards the most conservative side of any transaction.
The cost principle is an accounting principle that requires assets, liabilities, and equity investments to be recorded on financial records at their original cost.

46(A). Monopolist charges the maximum possible price.
Monopolies will produce at quantity where marginal revenue equals marginal cost. Then they will charge the maximum price that market demand will respond to at that quantity.

47(C). Price discrimination policy helps in increasing profits in case of monopoly.
A monopolistic market is a theoretical construct that describes a market where only one company may offer products and services to the public. A monopolistic market is the opposite of a perfectly competitive market, in which an infinite number of firms operate. In a purely monopolistic model, the monopoly firm can restrict output, raise prices, and enjoy super-normal profits in the long run.

48(B). In the case of complementary goods, cross-price elasticity is negative. A proportionate increase in the price of one commodity leads to a proportionate fall in the demand of another commodity because both are demanded jointly.

49(B). The correct combination is a - (ii), b - (iv), c - (i), d - (iii).
Perfect Competition is a type of market structure where many firms sell similar products - and profits are virtually non-existent due to fierce competition. With that said, it is important to realize that perfect competition is an abstract term used to compare against real-life markets.
One could argue that the U.S. airline industry is an oligopoly, controlled by the four main domestic carriers: American Airlines, Delta Airlines, Southwest Airlines, and United Airlines.
The Railways is a monopoly that has underinvested in capacity and created a systemic shortage. To squeeze the monopoly-induced artificial shortage to jack up fares is unfair.

50(C). A chi-square (X^2) statistic is a test that measures how expectations compare to actual observed data (or model results). The data used in calculating a chi-square statistic must be random, raw, mutually exclusive, drawn from independent variables, and drawn from a large enough sample.

51(B). The correct combination is (a) - (ii), (b) - (iii), (c) - (iv), (d) - (i)
All statutory powers for regulating Indian capital market are vested with SEBI itself. To safeguard the interests of investors and to regulate the capital market with suitable measures. To regulate the business of stock exchanges and other securities market.
Monetary policy is the macroeconomic policy laid down by the Reserve Bank of India. It involves the management of money supply and interest rates. The central bank tweaks interest rates to achieve macroeconomic objectives such as liquidity, consumption and inflation.
Accordingly, Telecom Regulatory Authority of India (TRAI) was established in the year 1997 in pursuance of TRAI (Ordinance) 1997, which was later replaced by an Act of Parliament, to regulate the telecommunication services.
The Insurance Regulatory and Development Authority of India (IRDAI) is an autonomous, statutory body tasked with regulating and promoting the insurance and re-insurance industries in India.

52(D). Joint ventures involves strategic alliances. The reasons for these alliances may be complementary capabilities and resources such as distribution channels, technology or finance.

53(B). Acting in accordance with a request or command, and rules or instructions by which an organization ensures statutory laws and regulations as applicable to it is called compliance.

54(D). Reinforcing the Code of Conduct and ethical behaviour standards for all internal auditors can protect Audit reputation risk.
A leading practice to protect the reputation of internal audit's "brand" name is to reinforce the Code of Conduct and ethical behavior standards for all internal auditors.

55(D). In independent India, the first major foreign exchange crisis occurred in the year 1991.
In 1991, there was significant downward pressure on the value of the rupee from the international market and India was faced with depleting foreign reserves that necessitated devaluation.

56(D). As the closing stock was overstated that means the profit of the company is also overstated this is because, when closing stock has overstated the cost of goods sold reduced thereby increasing profit (SALES - COGS). Hence, to rectify the mistake, the rectifying entry will be:-
Profit and loss Adj A/c Dr. 9,000
To Stock A/c 9,000

57(A). When one party grants the right to use the asset to the other party, in return for a periodic payment, it is known as Lease financing.
A lease is a contractual agreement whereby one party, the owner of an asset, grants the other party the right to use the asset in return for a periodic payment. The lessee pays a fixed periodic amount called 'lease rental' to the lessor (owner) for the use of the asset.

58(A). A standard costing system involves estimating the required costs of a production process. Standard costs are estimates of the actual costs in a company's production process because actual costs cannot be known in advance. This helps a business to plan a budget.

59(C). IMF an international financial institution, headquartered in Washington, D.C., consisting of 190 countries working to foster global monetary cooperation, secure financial stability, facilitate international trade, promote high employment and sustainable economic growth, and reduce poverty around the world while periodically depending on the World Bank for its resources.

60(C). A lease refers to a contractual agreement whereby the owner of the asset grants the lessee the right to use the asset for a specified period of time in return of a periodic payment. It can be simplified as an agreement between a landlord and a tenant.

61(C). The average of the information set is the mean. Summing all the numbers and dividing through the range of items withinside the series yields the mean (now and then referred to as the "average").
The mode is the maximum not unusual place range in an information series. The mode is the most usually going on range withinside the information.
The median is the fee that falls withinside the center of a fixed of numbers. The median is calculated by sorting the information from lowest to maximum and locating the precise midpoint. The median is simply the center range.

62(A). Coefficient of variation commonly used to compare the data dispersion between several series of data. A standard deviation's size in proportion to its mean is shown by the coefficient of variation (CV), a relative measure of variability. It is a standardised, unitless measurement that enables comparisons of variability among various groups and traits.

63(D). Mean is the average of the data set which is calculated by adding all the data values together and dividing it by the total number of data sets.
Median is the middle value among the observed set of values and is calculated by arranging the values in ascending order or in descending order and then choosing the middle value.
The mode is the number from a data set that has the highest frequency and is calculated by counting the number of times each data value occurs.
In the case of a moderately skewed distribution, i.e. in general, the difference between mean and mode is equal to three times the difference between the mean and median. Thus, the empirical relationship as Mean – Mode = 3 (Mean – Median).
If solved further, Mode = 3 Median - 2 Mean and 3 Median = 2 Mean + Mode
Hence 2 Median - 3 Quartile Deviation = 2 Mean is NOT true in a model distribution.

64(C). **Direct marketing:**
- Direct marketing gives the opportunity of promoting goods and services directly to the customers who need them the most.
- Direct marketing helps in building relationships with new customers.
- All promotional information is relayed without intermediaries and any third parties.
- Emails, newspapers, outdoor advertising, SMS marketing, Tele-marketing, websites, catalog distribution, etc. are various types of direct marketing strategies.
- Therefore, Tele-marketing is a part of Direct marketing.

65(D). Budgeting is the process of forecasting revenues and expenses of the company for a specific period and examples of which include the sales budget prepared to make a projection of the company's sales and the production budget prepared to project the production of the company etc.
Budgets may be classified on the basis of:
(A) Functions
(B) Conditions
(C) Periods (time)
(D) Activity levels (flexibility)

66(D). Indirect taxes are basically taxes that can be passed on to another entity or individual. They are usually imposed on a manufacturer or supplier who then passes on the tax to the consumer. The most common example of an indirect tax is the excise tax on cigarettes and alcohol.
GST is an indirect tax levied on the supply of goods and services. GST is majorly divided into four types: Central Goods and Service Tax (CGST), State Goods and Service Tax (SGST), Integrated Goods and Services Tax (IGST) and Union Territory Goods and Services Tax (UGST).
Customs Duty is a type of Indirect Tax which is levied on goods which are imported into India. In some cases, it is also levied when the goods are exported from India.

67(D). Taxpayer Identification Number is a number issued to individuals and organizations to track tax obligations and payments they make to the Internal Revenue Service (IRS). TIN is issued by the federal government.

68(A). The Central Board of Direct Taxes (CBDT) has proposed a single income tax return (ITR) form for all taxpayers.
There are seven kinds of income tax return (ITR) forms, which are used by different categories of taxpayers.
They are as follows:
- ITR Form 1, called 'Sahaj', is for small and medium taxpayers.
- Sahaj forms can be filed by individuals who have an income up to Rs 50 lakh, with earnings from salary, one house property/ other sources (interest etc).
- ITR-2 is filed by people with income from residential property.
- ITR-3 is intended for people who have income as profits from business/ profession.
- ITR-4 (Sugam) is, like ITR-1 (Sahaj), a simple form, and can be filed by individuals, Hindu Undivided Families (HUFs) and firms with total income up to Rs 50 lakh from businesses and professions.
- ITR-5 and 6 are for limited liability partnerships (LLPs) and businesses respectively.
- ITR-7 is filed by trusts and non-profit organisations.

69(D). Entertainment Allowance Under Section 16:
Entertainment Allowance for a Government Employee:
- For employees of the central government and state government, the deduction available is the least of the following:
- 20% of basic salary
- Rs 5000
- Amount granted as entertainment allowance in the financial year

To determine the allowance, a taxpayer must ensure the following particulars are met:a
- Any other allowance, benefit from the employer, or perquisite received must be deducted from the salary. Essentially, the wage must be the gross amount earned before any extra benefits are taken into account.
- Never consider the actual amount spent out of the entertainment allowance received from the employer.

Entertainment Allowance for a Non Government Employee:

- Non-government employees are not eligible for the entertainment allowance deduction.
- The deduction is only available to employees of the federal or state governments. Furthermore, the deduction is not available to employees of municipal governments or statutory corporations.

70(C). tax which carry their significance only on paper and have no significance in terms of revenue yield are called paper taxes.
Taxes like Gift tax, Estate duty, Wealth tax are paper taxes:
Excise duty is a form of tax imposed on goods for their production, licensing, and sale. It is an indirect tax.
Wealth tax:

- Levied on accumulated wealth or property of every individual.
- The tax was abolished in the 2016 budget.

Estate duty:

- It was imposed on the estate of a person which was inherited by him.
- The rate ranged from 4 to 40% of the value of the estate.
- It was imposed and collected by the central government but proceeds were passed on to states.
- It was abolished in March 1985 as the yield was too low.

Gift tax:

- Imposed in April 1958.
- Charged and collected every financial year on gifts received during the previous year.
- Again abolished in 1998 due to low yield.

71(C). Goods and Services Tax (GST) is an indirect tax (or consumption tax) used in India on the supply of goods and services. It is a comprehensive, multistage, destination-based tax: comprehensive because it has subsumed almost all the indirect taxes except a few state taxes.

72(C). Legal relationship between the middleman and the businessperson is governed by the law of agency. The agency is the agreement in which one party entrusts another party to conduct business on their behalf. The agency agreement comes in the following forms: Express agreement (both oral and written) Implication.

73(A). The paragraph is about genesis of insurance in India. The passage talks about origin, creation and development of insurance in India. Insurance in India has evolved over time heavily drawing from other countries, England in particular.

74(A). Life insurance in its modern form came to India from England in the year 1818. Oriental Life Insurance Company started by Europeans in Calcutta was the first life insurance company on Indian soil. Initially, insurance companies used to discriminate Indian and European clients. Indian lives were being treated as sub-standard lives and heavy extra premiums were being charged upon them.

75(B). Provident Fund sector grew along with insurance business in India. In the year 1912, Life Insurance Companies Act and Provident Fund Act were passed. In 1956, 245 Indian and foreign insurers and provident societies were taken over by the central government and nationalised. Provident Fund is a welfare scheme for the benefits of the employees. Under this scheme, both the employee and employer contribute their part, but whole of the amount is deposited by the employer.

76(C). Insurance in this current form has its history dating back to 1818, when Oriental Life Insurance Company was started by Anita Bhavsar in Kolkata to cater to the needs of European community. The pre-independence era in India saw discrimination between the lives of foreigners (English) and Indians with higher premiums being charged for the latter. In 1870, Bombay Mutual Life Assurance Society became the first Indian insurer.

77(B). A mutual fund is set up in the form of a trust, which has sponsor, trustees, Asset Management Company (AMC) and custodian. The trustees are vested with the general power of superintendence and direction over AMC. They monitor the performance and compliance of SEBI Regulations by the mutual fund.

78(C). The sponsor of a mutual fund is similar to promoter of a company. The sponsor brings in capital and creates a mutual fund trust, and sets up the AMC. The sponsor makes an application for registration of the mutual fund and contributes at least 40% of the net worth of the AMC.

79(D). Asset Management Companies (AMCs) are firms pooling investments from various individual and institutional investors. An AMC manages the investment by investing in capital assets such as stocks, real estate, bonds, and so on.

80(C). A mutual fund is set up in the form of a trust, which has sponsor, trustees, Asset Management Company (AMC) and custodian. The trust is established by a sponsor or more than one sponsor who is like promoter of a company. The trustees of the mutual fund hold its property for the benefit of the unit-holders. AMC approved by SEBI manages the funds by making investments in various types of securities. Custodian, who is required to be registered with SEBI, holds the securities of various schemes of the fund in its custody. The trustees are vested with the general power of superintendence and direction over AMC. They monitor the performance and compliance of SEBI Regulations by the mutual fund.

www.ingramcontent.com/pod-product-compliance
Ingram Content Group UK Ltd.
Pitfield, Milton Keynes, MK11 3LW, UK
UKHW061704190726
13853UKWH00008B/2392